Sacred Landscape

The publisher and the author gratefully acknowledge the generous contributions to this book provided by the General Endowment Fund of the Associates of the University of California Press and by the United States Institute of Peace.

Sacred Landscape

THE BURIED HISTORY OF THE HOLY LAND SINCE 1948

Meron Benvenisti

Translated by Maxine Kaufman-Lacusta

UNIVERSITY OF CALIFORNIA PRESS

BERKELEY LOS ANGELES LONDON

University of California Press
Berkeley and Los Angeles, California

University of California Press, Ltd.
London, England

Library of Congress Cataloging-in-Publication Data

Benvenisti, Meron, 1934–
Sacred landscape : the buried history of the Holy Land since 1948
/ Meron Benvenisti ; translated by Maxine Kaufman-Lacusta.
p. cm.
Includes bibliographical references and index.
ISBN 0-520-21154-5 (alk. paper)
1. Israel-Arab War, 1948–1949—Refugees 2. Israel—Historical
geography. 3. Names, Geographical—Israel—History. 4. Arab
-Israeli conflict—Social aspects. 5. Israel—Ethnic relations.
6. Villages—Israel—History. 7. Palestinian Arabs—Israel—
History—20th century. I. Title.
DS126.954B46 2000
956.04'2—dc21 99-37874
CIP

Manufactured in the United States of America

08 07 06 05 04 03 02 01 00 99
10 9 8 7 6 5 4 3 2 1

The paper used in this publication meets the
minimum requirements of ANSI/NISO Z39.48-1992
(R 1997) (*Permanence of Paper*). ∞

For Dorith

Table of Contents

Illustrations

MAPS

PLATES (following page 192)

Map 1. Administrative Map of Mandatory Palestine

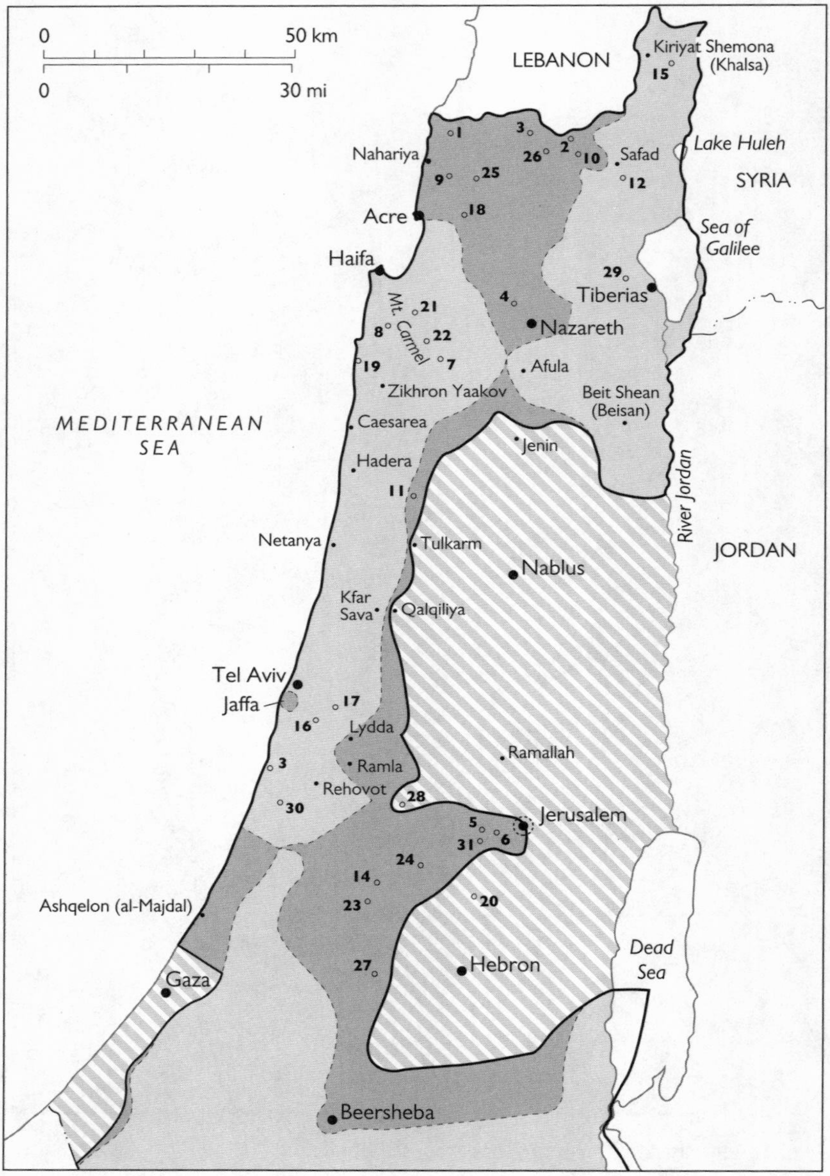

Map 2. Eretz Israel / Palestine (1947–49)

Jewish state according to 1947 UN Partition Plan

Arab state according to 1947 UN Partition Plan (taken by Israel 1948–49)

The West Bank and Gaza Strip

Boundaries of Arab state (1947)

Boundaries of Israel (1949)

Jerusalem (internationalized)

1 Bassa (Shlomi)
2 Kafr Birim (Baram)
3 Iqrit
4 Saffuriyya (Zippori)
5 Qastal
6 Deir Yasin
7 Mishmar Haemeq
8 Ein Hawd
9 Ghabisiyya
10 Safsaf (Sifsofa)
11 Kh. Jalama
12 Akbara
13 Nabi Rubin
14 Zakariyya (Zecharia)
15 Khisas
16 Yazur (Azor)
17 Yahudiyya (Yahud)
18 Birwa (Ahihud)
19 Tantura (Dor)
20 Etzion Block
21 Balad al-Sheikh (Nesher)
22 Abu Zureik
23 Ajjur (Agur)
24 Beit Atab
25 Yehiam (Jidin)
26 Sasa (Sasa)
27 Dawaima (Amazia)
28 Latroun
29 Hittin
30 Yibne (Yavne)
31 Sataf

Introduction

This book is about my troubled internal landscape as much as it is about the tortured landscape of my homeland. "Landscape is the work of the mind," writes Simon Schama.[1] "Its scenery is built up as much from strata of memory as from layers of rock." As long as I remember myself, I have moved within two strata of consciousness, wandering in a landscape that, instead of having three spatial dimensions, had six: a three-dimensional Jewish space underlain by an equally three-dimensional Arab space. My late father, a geographer and mapmaker, was responsible, unwittingly, for this dual image and split consciousness. From a very early age I was taken along on his expeditions and on his visits to Arab friends. So the Arab landscape was never alien or threatening to me; on the contrary, it gave rise to images, smells, and a sense of human warmth so powerful that their mark has not been erased after half a century.

The Jewish space—Rehavia, our Jewish neighborhood in Jerusalem, and Pardess Hannah, the Jewish colony near the coast where I spent months of carefree childhood vacation time—existed on a different planet, totally separated from the Arab landscape. Only those who have experienced the dichotomous environments of Sarajevo, Beirut, or Belfast can truly comprehend the phenomenon of the "white patches" on the mental maps carried around in the heads of the Jews and Arabs of Eretz Israel/Palestine, which cover the habitat of "the other," a theme I try to develop in this work.

My father's expeditions, his friendly contact with Arabs notwithstanding, were not innocent scientific excursions. He had a clear agenda: to draw a Hebrew map of the land, a renewed title deed. In his naive or self-serving way, he genuinely believed that he was doing so peaceably, that there was enough room in the country for everybody. And he was convinced beyond any shadow of a doubt that it was his absolute right to reclaim his ancestral patrimony. The map he drew and the textbook he wrote were meant to transform symbolic possession of the land into actual possession by inculcating his children and countless other young Israelis with the Zionist ethos of *moledet* (homeland): knowledge of its glorious Jewish past, intimate communion with its nature, and personal commitment to pioneering in collective agricultural settlements.

The Arabs did not take him seriously at first, and when they realized the danger, it was too late. His map triumphed, and I, his dutiful son, was left with the heavy burden of the fruits of victory. The victory was so overwhelming that it utterly destroyed my childhood landscape, and my sense of loss was mixed with pride in my people's triumph. I often reflected on the irony of the fact that my father, by taking me on his trips and hoping to instill in me a love for our Hebrew homeland, had imprinted in my memory the very landscape he wished to replace.

This troubled internal landscape did not surface immediately. I was totally immersed in the saga of Israel's creation. Too young to actively participate in the 1948 War, I witnessed only its local effects: the sudden disappearance of our neighbors on Gaza Road, a Bosnian Muslim family; the ugly spectacle of the survivors of Deir Yasin being paraded through the main streets of Jewish Jerusalem by their captors; playing basketball with thirty-five young men who later perished in battle on their way to defend the besieged Etzion Block; the siege of Jerusalem and the joy of welcoming the convoys bearing food after the battle of Qastal; the looting of Arab homes in Qatamon, the neighborhood bordering ours; the mass funerals. And then—the first postwar summer camp, traveling through the detritus of war, the abandoned Arab villages, helping kibbutzniks harvest the ripe barley left by the Arab farmers of Hittin in the Lower Galilee; working with our youth leaders to establish their kibbutz in the abandoned Arab village of Sarʿa. As a member of a pioneering youth movement, I myself "made the desert bloom" by uprooting the ancient olive trees of al-Bassa to clear the ground for a banana grove, as required by the "planned farming" principles of my kibbutz, Rosh Haniqra.

I recall the first time I felt the tragedy of the Palestinians penetrate my Zionist shield. Five years after the war, while working in the South, measuring underground water levels, I went to inspect the village well of Rana, near Beit Jibrin. I remembered the place from a trip with my father, and the desolation—the empty houses still standing, the ghost of a village once bustling with life—stunned me. I sat with my back against an old water trough and wondered where the villagers were and what they were feeling.

It took me almost fifteen years to find out. The 1967 war reestablished contact with them. I went to a refugee camp near Jerusalem to study and report on the needs of the refugees. I asked the people I met where they were from before the 1948 War. One told me he came from Deir al-Sheikh, one from Ajjur, and another from Rana. Suddenly I saw before my eyes the geography of my childhood, and I had the feeling that the men talking to me were my brothers—a feeling of sharing, of affinity. I could not share their sense of loss, but I could and did share deep nostalgia mixed with pain for the lost landscape and a nagging feeling of guilt, for my triumph had been their catastrophe.

They were indeed my brothers but also my mortal enemies: I knew that had they won they would have destroyed our landscape. That was the nature of our "shepherds' war," and all our self-serving beliefs that there was enough room for everybody were false. The Arabs viewed us as foreign intruders who had invaded their land, and from their point of view they were right. There was no way they could have accepted Zionism as a just cause, and therefore the 1948 War was inevitable. The sword had decided, and both sides must share the responsibility for the outcome. I couldn't interfere in their attempts to draw lessons from what came to pass and expect them to assume even partial responsibility for their catastrophe. But what were my lessons? Do we not have a special responsibility, if only because we turned out to be the victors? What have we done to the vanquished enemy? Have we transformed a struggle for survival into an ethnic cleansing operation, sending people to exile because we wanted to plunder their land?

War is indeed devoid of human values, despite attempts to establish norms of "civilized warfare"—and ethnic conflict is especially cruel—but have we not actually prolonged the state of war so that we might suspend human values indefinitely? I met Palestinian refugees twenty years after their expulsion; in those twenty years many dreadful deeds had been done—and more have since—deeds impossible to blame on the "overriding necessities" imposed by a war for survival. How much of this was a result of evading confrontation with the moral dilemmas of the 1948 War? Is there not something we must do now to assuage the burning sense of injustice, however one-sided, of the uprooted? Finally, how much compassion and guilt can I allow myself to express in order to pacify my troubled conscience, thereby exposing myself to accusations of betrayal on one side and of hypocrisy on the other?

This book is essentially an attempt to provide answers for myself; to lay to rest a subject that has haunted me for so long. The answers I seek do not necessarily fit the questions asked by others because my concerns might be different from theirs. It is clear to me that despite all my attempts to abide by the rules of scientific research, some readers will perceive my writing as biased or incomplete. After all, these are the most contentious issues in the most controversy-ridden conflict of the second half of this century. Even a short bibliography of the refugee problem encompasses some 3,000 items. I do not pretend to have studied them all, nor have I unearthed any previously unknown buried archives. The primary source for this book is myself. In this context, at the risk of appearing presumptuous, I wish to quote what S. Yizhar (Y. Smilanski), perhaps the greatest Hebrew fiction writer of my generation, wrote about himself: "I am but one seeing man, and what he sees makes his heart ache. Here is a place that has left its place and is no more. No enemies here, no non-enemies. Just a story of what happened told in the past tense. Human lives, with a moral for anyone who seeks it."

Soon, those of us for whom the "place that has left its place" is cause for heartache will also vanish, and the old landscape will be totally erased from the collective memory of those who already have succeeded in transforming it almost beyond recognition. One need only read Israeli textbooks or see the albums with "before and after" photos—the Land before 1948 and today—to realize how close we are to the point when the vanished Arab landscape will be considered just a piece of Arab propaganda, a fabrication aimed at the destruction of Israel through incitement of "The Return."

This much I can do for my brothers-enemies: erect signposts of memory. Not that they need me to do this, and some of them might claim that I have robbed them not only of their land but also of their memories. But I claim a share in their vanished landscape, for it is part of me. More important, it is an ineradicable epoch in the history of our shared land, and its destruction is a wound that cannot be healed by ignoring it. Perhaps my genuine affinity and shared nostalgia, my willingness to assume responsibility by openly expressing a sense of guilt for wrongdoings and compassion for suffering will help rekindle hope for a better, more equitable coexistence in our common homeland.

Palestinian critics will undoubtedly say that my work falls in the category of "history written by the victors." They will not like my conclusions regarding their responsibility in what came to pass. For them the conflict began when "the newly formed Palestinian national movement [fought a] desperate losing struggle against the greatest imperial power of the age, Great Britain, and its protégé, the Zionist movement"; the 1948 War was "a series of overwhelming military defeats of the disorganized Palestinians by the military forces of the Zionist movement," culminating in a catastrophe (*al nakba*) that "ended any hope that the Arab state called for [by the United Nations resolution of November 1947,] which provided for the partition of Palestine—would ever come into being."[2] The need to depict the Palestinians as defenseless and peace-loving people who fell victim to evil forces is so compelling that they even blame the Zionists for "ending any hope" that an Arab state will be established. There is no need to prove here that the 1948 War started because the Palestinians refused to accept the United Nations Partition Plan (and "accepted" it forty years too late, in 1988). It is difficult to assume responsibility for one's own calamitous decisions, but I refuse to take more than my share of this responsibility and certainly cannot accept the contention that my birth in this land was an imperialist sin. No attempt to manipulate my sense of guilt will succeed in shaking my belief in my birthright to this Land.

One cannot escape the fact of the politicization of what has conveniently been defined as "the refugee problem." It has been a political football for decades, and this book will undoubtedly be perceived in this context, too. In this narrative, however, the hero is the landscape and its transformation, not the refugees. Indeed, one should not differentiate between physical and human landscapes, because human beings create their environment and design the physical space to suit their needs and their particular civilization. Once the human landscape disappears, the physical space is inevitably transformed. The destruction of the physical landscape of Eretz Israel/Palestine (the name used, intentionally, throughout this book) was not a direct result of the hostilities but the inevitable outcome of the eradication of the human landscape. The combatants did not have at their disposal the means for mass destruction, such as planes capable of carpet bombing or heavy artillery. When the Palestinian community was uprooted from its space and other people settled there, they transformed the landscape to conform to their needs and their tastes. I have therefore tried to focus on the physical space, perhaps neglecting the cultural, sociological, and political aspects of the society that inhabited it.

Another possible distortion caused by focusing on the physical landscape is the tendency to depict its transformation as a benign, linear change from the "backward and primitive" past to the "modern and fully developed" present. One has only to juxtapose a photograph of an Arab village taken in the thirties with one taken in the nineties, showing a lovely suburb built on the same site, or an aerial photo showing the empty, dusty landscape of those days with one showing the vast fields of golden grain and green orchards now planted on it, and everybody is convinced that great "progress" has been achieved.

But, as S. Yizhar says, "The land, in its depth, does not forget" that this is not a linear, unbroken progression, "even when it has already been plowed and has already brought forth fair, new crops." This progress is not a continuation of the past but is built on the ruins of another civilization, violently destroyed. Who has the right to pass judgment on its "backwardness"? It is an elementary ploy to freeze the past of others while claiming dynamic progress for oneself. The Palestinian landscape, for all its "lack of modernity," was a whole world for those who lived in it and were comfortable there—sometimes more comfortable than those who live in the modern world that replaced it. This "primitive" landscape, too, gave rise to a profusion of achievements and had the potential for change and modernization in the image of its inhabitants. It deserves our respect and appreciation, not our derision.

But my focus on the landscape meant that I ignored one very important segment of the story: the Arab urban centers. Before the 1948 War, more than a third of the Arab population lived in sixteen cities and towns. Some of the urban centers were homogeneously Jewish or Arab, and some were mixed. The Arab urban middle class was affluent, certainly more modern than rural society. More important, being the agent of modernization, it was the element capable of revolutionizing the whole of Palestinian society. The initiative, material achievements, modern lifestyle, and sophistication of the members of this class are still visible in the elegant neighborhoods and lovely homes they left behind, which were taken over by Israelis who were less "modern" then their original occupants.

The uprooting of almost 90 percent of the urban Arab population had delayed the process of change and modernization of Palestinian-

Israeli society. But the most grievous outcome of the destruction of Arab urban life was that even fifty years later no Arab urban society worthy of the name has been created in Israel. There are, indeed, Arab towns in Israel, but they are merely dormitory communities, devoid of real city life. Despite the extreme importance of the urban element in the physical and human landscape, this book will treat it only in passing, because it represents only a small fraction of the physical space that has undergone transformation. The total area occupied by Arab neighborhoods in the cities and towns does not exceed 50,000 *dunams* (12,500 acres), as compared to millions of *dunams* of the countryside. This book focuses on the countryside, and therefore our main concern is the Arab villages. The question of how many villages were destroyed is apparently extremely important to researchers of the Palestinian disaster: It is a way to quantify it. Walid Khalidi states that "efforts to quantify the destroyed villages range from 290 to 472."[3] The problem of resolving what type of human habitation qualifies as a "village" is complicated and controversial, and it should not detain us here. I attach less importance to the numbers than do my Palestinian counterparts, although I respect their intentions in publishing lists of names and statistics for each one of them as a kind of memorial.

The demolition of Arab villages was, of course, a major component of the destruction of the old landscape, but the destruction of Arab agriculture—orchards, citrus and olive groves, terraces—had an even more devastating effect. Arab citrus groves, olive trees, and other fruit orchards covered an area of almost 1 million *dunams* (250,000 acres). Most of the abandoned trees were neglected or destroyed outright as the Israelis destroyed whatever the Arabs had left that could not be integrated into their framework. Most citrus groves were uprooted to make room for housing developments, ancient olive trees were left uncared for or destroyed to make room for field crops. This does not fit Israel's self-image as a people that "makes the desert bloom," but it gives added credence to the conclusion that it is not the hostilities that directly caused the devastation but the disappearance of the human community that had shaped the landscape in accordance with its needs and preferences. And who is to say that uprooting olive trees to create fields of cattle fodder represents progress?

The demolition of village sites has attracted the most attention, but I prefer to emphasize other aspects of the landscape as well, particularly religious historical and cultural sites. Ghazi Falah has compiled a useful map and list of such sites, and Shukri ʿArraf has written a two-volume book on Muslim holy sites. I attempt to place these sites in their proper historical context as "signposts of memory," lest their identity and original meaning be forgotten or denied.

The insight that "landscape is the work of the mind" prompted me to explore Israeli and Palestinian literary expressions concerning the dramatic changes that took place during and in the aftermath of the 1948 War and the transformation of their perceptions in the last fifty years. I am neither an expert in literary text analysis nor an anthropologist. But I read enough to follow Israelis and Palestinians in their long march toward a blank wall. The Israelis traveled from the quest to impose on the landscape their Zionist identity to its converse—its privatization, at the price of turning the landscape into a desert of concrete and asphalt. The Palestinians came from the opposite direction, from the intimate communion with the land to perceptions of the homeland in abstract, "nation-building" terms. This journey brought them to the blank wall of Oslo, which confronted them with the need to adjust their collective longings to the political realities.

Exploring a vanished landscape is difficult and frustrating. At first I traveled the land on foot, later driving an all-terrain vehicle, either alone or accompanied by displaced Palestinians—not a tourist making a brief visit, but time and time again in the course of several decades. In many places all that remains are pitiful relics: a few layers of weathered stone, a half-buried arch, a broken millstone. In some places a few structures still remain—neglected mosques, school buildings, imposing houses renovated by Israelis—and seven villages completely escaped destruction because Israelis found them picturesque enough to preserve. Most of these are described or at least mentioned in the book. One needs a powerful imagination to mentally reconstruct the landscape of bygone times, even with the assistance of uprooted villagers. One often gets the same disappointing reaction as when inspecting an archaeological site and trying to see scattered stones as the setting of a momentous event that took place right there.

I couldn't have done anything without the marvelous detailed maps (scale 1:20,000) compiled by the Mandatory authorities and updated just before the 1948 War. I would spread the relevant map on the ground, and suddenly the old landscape arose like an apparition: village houses, mosques, school buildings, paths, stone hedges marking plot boundaries, limekilns, threshing floors, holy tombs, sacred oak trees, springs and cisterns, caves, fruit trees, patches of cultivation. And each plot and every prominent feature had its Arabic name marked on the map, so poetic and so apt (chapter 1) that my heart ached. Only the human landscape was missing. And where the human landscape was, the physical landscape was missing.

It wasn't my human landscape, nor was it the physical space that my people created; they were its destroyers. But the pain and the sorrow were deep and genuine, and with them arose a compelling need to commemorate the vanished landscape, both because it was a human creation and because it is my homeland, a land that never forgets any of her sons and daughters. I cannot envisage my homeland without Arabs, and perhaps my late father, who taught me to read maps and study history, was right in his naive belief that there is enough space, physical and historical, for Jews and Arabs in their shared homeland.

1

The Hebrew Map

On 18 July 1949 a group made up of nine scholars, well known in their respective fields of cartography, archaeology, geography, and history, gathered at the prime minister's office in Tel Aviv. They were all longtime colleagues who had previously collaborated in the plotting of maps and in joint research projects, and all were associated with the Israel Exploration Society (IES). Bringing together the most respected experts in fields of scholarship related to Eretz Israel (Hebrew for the Land of Israel), the IES initiated research projects and published their findings, and organized conferences that attracted hundreds of enthusiastic participants.

Although similar to geographical research bodies active in many other countries, the IES was held in unique regard by the Jewish public, among whom its prestige and influence were reminiscent of the respect accorded the Royal Geographical Society during the Victorian era, in the heyday of British imperialism. The IES numbered high-ranking political leaders among its members, and its activities transcended the narrow confines of its fields of research, acquiring an almost official status. Just as the British Royal Geographical Society, through its research and its expeditions into the interior of Africa and the heart of Canada, expressed the British desire to learn about the world in order to annex it to the empire, so did the IES articulate the Jewish ambition to lay claim to the ancestral homeland. Its declared objective was "to develop and to advance the study of the Land, its history, and pre-history, accentuating the settlement aspect and the sociohistorical connection between the People of Israel and Eretz Israel." The IES researchers sought to provide "concrete documentation of the continuity of a historical thread that remained unbroken from the time of Joshua Bin Nun until the days of the conquerors of the Negev in our generation."[1]

PLANTING THE FLAG

Imbued with this sense of mission, the nine scholars willingly responded to the summons from the Israeli cabinet secretary, who, at the behest of Prime Minister David Ben-Gurion, constituted them as the Committee for the Designation of Place-Names in the Negev Region (hereafter the Negev Names Committee, or NNC). Just four months previously, the Israeli army had consolidated its control over the vast expanses of the Negev and Arava—more than half the area of the newly founded state—planting the flag of Israel on the shore of the Gulf of Eilat ('Aqaba) on 10 March of that year. The new committee's task was "to assign Hebrew names to all the places—mountains, valleys, springs, roads, and so on—in the Negev region."[2]

The nine did not wonder what moved the prime minister—beset as he was by the momentous problems of a state that had only recently emerged from the cycle of war and death and had absorbed unprecedented waves of immigration—to concern himself with the names of obscure geographical and cartographic features. They understood the importance of the task laid upon their shoulders by Ben-Gurion, in whose heart beat a vision of the development of the Negev—which he viewed as the supreme challenge facing the new state. Nor did they require any explanation of the significance of the creation of an official Hebrew map of the Negev and Arava. Mapmaking and the assignment of place-names were their fields of endeavor, and they knew that this particular job was neither simply a technical exercise nor merely a work of research—it was an act of establishing proprietorship: they had been asked to draft a deed of Jewish ownership for more than half of Israel's territory.

The members of the NNC did not commence this work only in 1949. As far back as 1920, two of them had been appointed advisers to the British Mandatory government on all matters relating to the assignment of Hebrew names and had fought hard to persuade the authorities to restore biblical Hebrew place-names to the map of the country in place of the Arabic ones currently in use. When the Geographical Committee for Names, which operated under the aegis of the Royal Geographical Society (the only body authorized to assign names throughout the British Empire), decided to call the Mandatory geopolitical entity "Palestine" and the city whose biblical name was Shechem, "Nablus," these Jewish advisers saw this as an act of anti-Jewish discrimination and a searing defeat for Zionism. Suffused with the sense that "it is impossible for a present-day Hebrew map not to identify by name the places of Hebrew settlement mentioned in the Bible and in post-biblical Hebrew literature," they set about identifying these sites and putting them on "Hebrew maps," which they placed opposite the official Mandatory maps.

These scholars regarded their active involvement in the survey departments of the Mandatory government and the British army as a Zionist act that afforded them influence while providing them with military data of use to the Jewish underground militia, the Haganah. In clandestine cartographic offices, the data from British maps were copied and Hebrew maps were produced for use in Haganah operations. When the British captured the Haganah archives in 1946, and these maps were seized as well, the director of the Mandatory Mapping Division asked an Israeli cartographer, with a wink, "Why did the Haganah need to draw its own maps?"[3] This was a rhetorical question. "Mapmaking," write Harley and Woodward in *History of Cartography,* "was one of the specialized intellectual weapons by which power could be gained, administered, given legitimacy and codified."[4] Cartographic knowledge is power: that is why this profession has such close links with the military and war. Accurate topographical maps are often considered highly confidential and are emblazoned with the warning: "This is a classified intelligence document. Its presence in enemy hands will endanger our forces."

Mapmaking is not, however, solely an instrument of war; it is an activity of supreme political significance—a means of providing a basis for the mapmaker's claims and for his social and symbolic values, while cloaking them in a guise of "scientific objectivity." Maps are generally judged in terms of their "accuracy," that is, the degree to which they succeed in reflecting and depicting the morphological landscape and its "man-made" covering. But maps portray a fictitious reality that differs from other sorts of printed matter only in form. Borders plotted on a map, the detailed presentation of certain features and the omission of others, the choice of agreed-upon icons (map symbols), the depiction of the relative size of places of habitation, and especially the choosing of names for features of the landscape and for human settlements—these are in fact the vocabulary with which the "literature" of maps (or their fiction) is written. Benedict Anderson quotes a Thai scholar who wrote:

"A map [is perceived as] a scientific abstraction of reality. A map merely represents something which already exists objectively 'there.' In the history I have described, this relationship is reversed. A map anticipated spatial reality, not vice versa. In other words a map was a model for, rather than a model of, what it purported to represent—it had become a real instrument to concretize projections on the earth's surface."[5]

The members of the NNC needed no lessons regarding the significance of maps. Their decades-long work in designing the Hebrew map of the Land of Israel was proof that their cartographic and historical labors had always been motivated by the desire to concretize the military, political, and symbolic possession of the patrimony of the Jewish people. By virtue of the November 1947 United Nations resolution on the partition of Mandatory Palestine, the Jews were entitled to the Negev and Arava. They realized their claim by conquering the entire area in a brilliant military operation. Now it was necessary to establish "facts on the ground," and the creation of a Hebrew map was an extremely powerful means of doing so, no less important than the building of roads or the founding of settlements. It was, of course, also easier, quicker, and cheaper. In the space of a few months (the committee's work went on for ten months in all), it was possible to compile the entire map and present it to the public, who in any case were unable to visit this inaccessible region, but whom the map infused with the sense that a new—Jewish—reality had indeed been created in the desolate expanses of the Negev. And were the NNC members in need of any further incentive, this was provided by a letter from the prime minister to the chair of the committee, in which he wrote: "We are obliged to remove the Arabic names for reasons of state. Just as we do not recognize the Arabs' political proprietorship of the land, so also do we not recognize their spiritual proprietorship and their names."[6]

MAPPING OF EMPIRE

Ironically, the NNC only was able to successfully accomplish the task of the Hebraization of the map of the Negev thanks to the fact that the very regime and civilization it had come to uproot and expunge from memory had furnished it with all the necessary tools and means. The entire area had been mapped, plotted, and drawn, and names had been collected—by emissaries of the British Empire. As is well known, the British had made mapping the cornerstone of their dominion throughout the empire. The first official maps they prepared were of Ireland, in 1653, when they wished to confiscate the landholdings of the rebellious Irish and to bestow them on English soldiers and settlers. Ever since then, the surveyor has walked beside the British officer, and sometimes has gone before him.

British officers serving with the Royal Engineers engaged in surveying and mapmaking everywhere in the world: maps of borders, geological maps, administrative maps, explorers' maps, railway maps—large and small scale—replacing the white areas (denoting "terra incognita") on the map of the world with splotches of pink, the color denoting territory that had become a part of the empire, beyond which lay "the other side of the moon," in the words of Lord Salisbury.

The mapping of the empire was, to the people of that day, a task akin to the mapping of outer space in ours. James Morris recounts: "Napoleon, surveying the Great Pyramids of Giza, is supposed to have cried to his veterans: 'Soldiers, forty centuries look down upon you.' The British, almost as soon as they arrived in Egypt, lugged a theodolite to the pyramid's summit and made it a triangulation point."[7]

It is no coincidence that the 1:125,000 scale map that served as the basis for the work of the Israeli NNC had been prepared by two of the most famous figures in the annals of the British Empire, Herbert Horatio Kitchener and T. E. Lawrence (Lawrence of Arabia). The map itself was named for the director of the survey expedition, Captain Stewart Francis Newcombe of the Royal Engineers, who had begun mapping this region in the latter half of 1913 and had completed the job at the end of May 1914, a few months before the outbreak of the First World War. Britain's imperial interests in the Middle East were, of course, related to the Suez Canal and its defense. The British, however, concealed the military objectives of the surveys and of the maps that were based on them, representing them instead as part of a research study whose purpose was to investigate the history of the land of the Bible and to trace the wanderings of the Children of Israel in the desert. Even the body under whose auspices they were working was a civilian one, the Palestine Exploration Fund (PEF), which shall be discussed further elsewhere.

Nonetheless, evidence of the close ties between the British military and cartography, archaeology, and politics can be found in the fact that, over the years, Kitchener the surveyor became by turns a general, a field marshal, and British minister of war during the First World War; Lawrence the archaeologist became an intelligence officer and the moving force behind the Arab Rebellion, whose crowning achievement was the capture of ʿAqaba from the Turks in 1917; whereas Captain (later Colonel) Newcombe subsequently filled political posts in the Middle East and was responsible for the delineation of the borders of Mandatory Palestine.

Captain Newcombe was not the first to survey the Negev and Arava. He had been preceded by expeditions mounted by the PEF, notably one led by geologist Edward Hull, which surveyed the area in 1883. Kitchener joined Hull's expedition and set up the triangulation network between ʿAqaba and the Dead Sea. The importance of this work was confirmed in 1914, when the Turkish authorities prevented Newcombe from gaining access to the ʿAqaba region and he had to rely on Kitchener's survey. He could not, however, place full confidence in the Arabic names assigned to topographical features in this survey. As Kitchener himself wrote in his report: "Owing to the rapid passage of the party through the country, and the impossibility of getting guides with local knowledge, the names are not, in my opinion, in every case reliable, although I took every opportunity to check them by local information, as much as possible."[8] Collecting names and recording them on the map were, in Newcombe's estimation, vital activities. He, like all British surveyors, ascribed critical importance to toponymy (the doctrine of geographical naming), and not out of geographical-cartographic considerations only. Local names are the essence of the cultural heritage of a place; they commemorate historical events and open the way to an understanding of the local population's worldview. In Palestine, especially, place-names were of crucial importance, since it had been proven that the Arabs had preserved many ancient names that could serve as means for the identification of archaeological sites. This connection between toponymy and archaeology motivated Newcombe to invite two young archaeologists, T. E. Lawrence and Charles Woolley, to survey the ancient sites and to gather names. "Much trouble is being taken to get their names, but there is even more difficulty than usual, owing to the very suspicious nature of the local Bedouins, and though guides with general knowledge of the country are easy to find, those who know the smaller place-names in each locality are not."[9]

On his map, therefore, Newcombe was forced to record place-names gathered by other travelers, especially those collected by the Czech surveyor Alois Musil, who reconnoitered the area between 1895 and 1902. Musil's map was imprecise and had been severely criticized, but this fact did not deter Newcombe, who copied many names from it. From all of these sources he succeeded in compiling a list of some 600 names, which appear on a 1:125,000 scale map, in the sector destined to be included in Mandatory Palestine. Newcombe's map was printed in 1915 and classified as secret. It was used by the British army during the First World War, after which it was published in many editions and was later redrawn by the Survey Division of the British Mandatory government. This map served as the basis for the more detailed ones carried by the Israeli army during its conquest of the area, and the names that appeared on it were the ones the NNC would later turn into Hebrew ones.

"NAMES STRANGE TO OUR EARS"

The members of the NNC—all experts in their professions—were well aware that the place-names were largely inaccurate and that their transliteration from Arabic into English had resulted in further distortion. They had no choice but to rely on them, however, if only because all of the Bedouin inhabitants of the region had been expelled by the Israeli army during 1949 and 1950, and there simply wasn't anyone to ask. They did indeed try to transliterate the Arabic names scientifically, but they did not attach much importance to correcting them. After all, their whole objective was to replace them. "The names that we found," states the NNC's summary, "not only sound strange to our ears, they are themselves inaccurate. Their meanings are unclear and many of them are nothing but random names of individuals or epithets of a derogatory or insulting nature. Many of the names are offensive in their gloomy and morose meanings, which reflect the powerlessness of the nomads and their self-denigration in the face of the harshness of nature."[10]

This contemptuous dismissal of the Arabic names was refuted, to all intents and purposes, by the fact that all the work of the committee was based on these names. All of the new names it chose (except for an insignificant minority) were determined in direct reference to the old names, and no fewer than 333 of the 533 new names were either translations of Arabic names or Hebrew names that had been decided upon on the basis of their similarity in sound to Arabic names. Moreover, the very principle of eradicating the Arabic names was itself not accepted by some of the members of the NNC, and was only approved in the wake of political pressure and the influence of the patriotic arguments put forth by some members.

The serious scientists among the members of the committee were quite cognizant of the devastating consequences attendant upon the eradication of the Arabic names: "The erasure of everything written on the map," said S. Yeivin, "is a scientific disaster." With a clap of the hand they were wiping out an entire cultural heritage that must certainly conceal within it elements of the Israeli-Jewish heritage as well. The researchers did indeed endeavor to identify all those names that had links to ancient Hebrew ones in an attempt "to redeem, as far as possible, names from days of yore." But they could only rely on what was known then, when the historical-geographical knowledge of the area was scanty, and in many cases the identities of the places were hotly disputed. "In my opinion," stated Y. Breslavski, "there is no argument regarding the necessity for Hebraization itself. However, the Arabic names must not be wiped off the map. Otherwise we shall thwart scientific research. It would also be worth our while to leave an opening for the future emendation of our conclusions. Erasure of the Arabic names would be detrimental to both science and the map." And Breslavski argued further, "We must not disregard the Arab population of the country or dismiss its need for familiar Arabic names."[11]

This attitude encountered stiff opposition from another member: "In my opinion there is no point in keeping them (the Arabic names). The claim that this is necessary on democratic grounds is baseless: for the benefit of a minority made up of 10% of the population we cannot compel the 90% who constitute the majority to use the Arabic names: . . . After all, the very source of our information from the Arab community is sealed: the Arabs are no longer there." The committee's chair, Zalman Lifshitz, declared: "Just as the Bedouin of the Negev did not sink roots in that place, so also are the names not rooted there." And in any case, "The Hebraization of the names has a political intent, and that is the direction in which our deliberations must be channeled. The task that has been laid upon us is fundamentally political. In truth, the whole question of Arabic place-names in the Negev has become irrelevant since there are almost no Bedouin there."[12]

Echoes of this debate apparently came to the attention of the prime minister, who intervened by sending a directive "to remove the names for reasons of state." In a compromise, so as to mitigate the "scientific disaster" of "the erasure of everything written on the map," the committee published a gazetteer containing the new names alongside the old ones. This was the last time the Arabic names were published. Indeed, on the series of maps drawn by the Israeli Survey Department around that time, there was already no reference to the old names. For a time, veteran desert hikers continued to refer to the wadis and wells by their Arabic names, in a sort of ostentatious allusion to their being "old-timers." But even this custom did not last long, and the Hebrew map soon became fait accompli: the concretization of the projection of the Hebrew map onto the rocks of the Negev and the canyons of the Arava was complete.

An entire world, as portrayed in what one member of the NNC called "the primitive names given by the Bedouin," vanished, along with the human beings "who hadn't sunk roots there"—insofar as they had followed a nomadic way of life and eventually were expelled by force. There was no longer anyone to call the geographical features of the land by their "distorted and inaccurate" names, in place of which names "necessitated by the enormous changes that have taken place in the Negev," in the words of one committee member, took root. The maps, the signs directing travelers on the roads and at junctions, names of communities, mailing addresses, and usage in newspapers, guidebooks, and geography texts saw to that. One Arab-Israeli geographer went to great lengths in an attempt to preserve the Arabic names and publish them in books, but no Jewish-Israeli read them. Generations of Israelis became familiar with the names of the historical sites and geographical features of the Negev without it ever occurring to them that these were nothing but distortions of Arabic names. The name of the Ramon Crater, for example, perhaps the most dramatic geological formation in the Negev, "is derived from the Hebrew adjective 'ram' (meaning elevated)," states an Israeli guidebook. The fact that its name in Arabic was Wadi Rumman (Pomegranate Arroyo), and that Timna (the name of the site of ancient copper mines) is a distortion of the Arabic name, Muneiye', and Nahal Roded was Wadi Radadi—was not considered worthy of mention.

"After all," stated the committee, "it is likely that Hebrew names became garbled and acquired an alien form, and these are now being 'redeemed.'" That is to say, it wasn't the Israelis who distorted the Arabic names, but the other way around. This arrogant attitude extends even to Arabic names immortalizing Bedouin tribal leaders or other prominent figures: Abu Jarwal became Goral ("fate" in Hebrew); Abu Rutha changed not only his nationality but also his sex—and became Ruth. Places whose names "possessed a negative meaning" acquired new ones "expressing rebirth and the beauties of the location": instead of Bir

Khandis (Well of the Shadow of Death) they chose the name Be'er Orah (Well of Light), and instead of Ein Weiba (Spring of the Plague) they chose a name with a biblical ring to it—Ein Yahav.

NEW, BIBLICAL WORLD

The effort to find biblical-sounding names that would therefore be regarded as ancient was conspicuous in all the work of the NNC. No Israeli would imagine that the name of Kibbutz Grofit comes from Umm Jurfinat, that Be'er Ada was Bir Abu 'Auda, and that the name of Yerukham (a town near Beer Sheva) replaced the Arabic name, Rakhma. This pseudobiblical ring was necessitated by the dearth of Hebrew names in the ancient sources. Only a small number of place-names are to be found in early Jewish sources, and the NNC consented to make use of Greek and Roman names only if "there was a clear possibility of reconstructing them in Hebrew." Not only were Arabic names unwanted, it seems, but even Greco-Latin names from the fourth century of the common era.

In addition there were (and still are) fierce differences of opinion among scholars regarding the identification of names of ancient places with specific sites. But the committee members could not resist the temptation, and they bestowed names like Yotvata (Yotbatha—Num. 33:33–34), Evrona (Ebronah—Num. 33:34–35), and Mount Hor (Num. 33:37), despite unresolved controversy over the identification of their exact locations. In order to avert criticism, they appended the following disclaimer: "This list (which contained 65 names) is not intended to determine the [scientific] identity of the locations. It includes historical names whose sites have not been identified, but which were chosen to serve as a basis for names of geographical locations."[13] Except that, of course, this disclaimer appears in a forgotten document published in 1951. A traveler parking a car in Yotvata, on the road to Eilat, is convinced that he or she is actually stopping at the site of one of the encampments of the Children of Israel during their wanderings in the desert.

On one notorious occasion the NNC was unable to hide behind the disclaimer that the names were not "intended to designate identity." It had specified the location of Mount Hor, the burial place of Aaron the High Priest (Num. 20:26) as a certain mountain not far from the phosphate mines in the central Negev. This site was designated despite the fact that the location that had been accepted since the first century C.E.

was near Petra in Edom (now Jordan), where the grave of Aaron—venerated by Muslims and Jews alike—is actually to be found. Some twenty years after the name of the place was assigned, it became clear that it was impossible to persist in identifying this mountain as Mt. Hor (which had been a dubious exercise from the start), and it was renamed Mt. Zin. But in order to maintain the honor of the committee, the name Mount Hor was left in parentheses.

The committee members found another "partial solution to the problem of the Judaization of the place-names" when they intensified the pseudobiblical connection via the assignment of no fewer than fifty names of personages from the Bible—"names of our forefathers and our kings"—who had no real connection to those particular sites.

The "primitive names" given by the Bedouin turned out to be well suited not only to distortion "according to similarity of sound" but also to word-for-word translation. Committee members were unable to ignore the extraordinary descriptive aptitude, the beauty of expression, and the sense of rootedness of the Bedouin "who had not sunk roots in the desert"—qualities that were revealed in the Arabic names describing natural phenomena, morphological formations, plants, and living creatures. They therefore translated no fewer than 175 of these names, nevertheless retaining for themselves the right to determine which of them were "accurate," which were "not properly defined," and which were "epithets unworthy of translation."

The nomadic desert dwellers did not invent names while seated around a table in scholarly deliberation. The names they used evolved organically, in the course of a lengthy process—gradual and mysterious—that culminated in the spontaneous assignment of the name best describing the qualities of each place or most aptly identifying its inhabitants (while being both readily assimilable and easy to remember). The Bedouin made no conscious "nationalistic political" effort to cover the lands of their wanderings with a network of "strongholds and settlements" secured via the assignment of names. And only someone viewing the expanses of the Negev from a bird's-eye perspective, on a piece of paper purporting to depict them on a convenient "scale," could possibly perceive this haphazard collection of names as constituting an assertion of "spiritual proprietorship" that must be countered by the immediate launching of a bureaucratic process of "colonization"—of "renaming the mountains and hills, the canyons, the water sources, etc." Qaʿat el Qireiq, Ras al-Zuwwayra, Naqb al-Amaʿz, Ein Murra, Wadi Hiyyani, and Ein Ghidiyan had not received their names in the same way as did their Hebrew replacements: HaMeishar, Rosh Zohar, Ma'ale Amiaz, Ein Mor, Hiyon, and Yotvata; that is, following a short discussion at a meeting. They were simply there—until certain people came and erased them in the name of "political exigencies."

This excerpt from the minutes of the eighth meeting of the NNC, 20 October 1949, gives us a glimpse of the process of assigning place-names:

Kurnub:

Y. Ben Zvi: I suggest Cerubim. This term has two meanings: a kind of vegetable (cabbage) and angels (cherubim).

S. Yeivin: I propose restoring the historical name of Kurnub, Mampsis.

M. Avi Yona: Impossible to leave the name Mampsis because it's a foreign name [Byzantine-Greek, appearing on the map of Madaba and in the writings of the fathers of the Christian church].

B. Ts. Eshel: The present-day Kurnub is on a hill above the ruins of Mampsis. The name Mampsis can be used for the ruins, and for Kurnub a new Hebrew name should be found that is suitable for a place that is slated to become a population and transportation center.

A. Y. Brewer: I suggest Karnov.

S. Yeivin: I'm opposed to Cerubim and to Karnov. If we're not going to retain the Greek name Mampsis, it would be best to assign a new Hebrew name.

Y. Press: I suggest City of the Negev.

S. Yeivin: When people say City of the Negev they mean Beersheba.[14]

The discussion continued at the next meeting, and in the end the committee members decided to call the ruins of Mampsis (the remnants of a large Christian settlement containing the ruins of two churches) Mamshit. In the opinion of the committee, this was the original Hebrew name, which had been distorted by the Greeks. The place "slated to become a population and transportation center" did indeed become a town, and its name is Dimona. "The name is biblical (Joshua 15:22). The sound of this name had been preserved in the Arabic name Harabat Umm Dumna," stated the committee.

Herbert Horatio Kitchener, were he to rise from the dead, would surely be saddened by the loss of the old names that he endured such hardships to collect. But the legendary empire builder—son of an English colonist in Ireland—would have understood the logic of the Israeli bureaucratic campaign. After all, that is precisely how the British had behaved in every region they chose to colonize—from Ireland in the seventeenth century to the plateaus of Kenya in the early years of the twentieth; in Canada, Australia, and Rhodesia. In every one of these British colonies, topographical maps were plotted, and upon them were printed official names: a mixture of English names (personalities and places in the old country), names chosen by colonists and soldiers, and local "native" names, altered so as "to be pronounceable in a civilized tongue." The natives, who had been "resettled," adapted themselves to the new map, to the point where they themselves often forgot the original names.

Similarly, few among those of the Bedouin who were not banished beyond Israel's borders—but were instead "concentrated" in the northern Negev—remember the Arabic names. And no wonder. The bureaucracy wields tremendous power in its imposition of the new map: road signs, postal cancellations, office correspondence, and journalistic reports all reinforce the effort. The bureaucracy is even mighty enough to have compelled the Bedouin to accept the names it chose for the new communities where they are being "concentrated." One Bedouin town near Beersheba, for example, is called Rahat, a euphonious Hebrew name.

The NNC completed its work on 20 March 1950. According to its official report, the committee held twenty-four plenary sessions and numerous subcommittee meetings, and made an aerial tour of the Negev. It discussed approximately 2,500 proposals and from them chose 533 names, which the report enumerated as follows:

Seventy historical names, which were also given to an additional 50 nearby geographical features	120
Names of biblical figures	50
Translations (from Arabic)	175
Names chosen for their similarity in sound to the Arabic	150
Names that were modernized	30
Names that were left unchanged	8

In addition, the names of 27 existing Jewish communities in the Negev were recorded, bringing the total number of names listed on the 1:250:000 scale map of the southern part of Israel, published in 1951, to 560.[15]

JUDAIZATION OF HILLS AND VALLEYS

The introduction to the gazetteer of geographical names published by the NNC stated: "In the process of Jewish settlement we [the Zionist organizations, see below] have always given Hebrew names to all of our communities, striving as far as possible to redeem names from ancient times. But we did not initially carry our activities beyond the domain of the settlements, to the mountains and hills, the wadis and valleys." In having done so in the Negev, the NNC had completed the task for which it had been founded. The committee remained in existence, however, because its members wished to "continue their activities" in other areas of Israel as well. They regarded the "Judaization of the geographical names in our country as a vital issue," and the experience they had amassed in the Hebraization of the map of the Negev made it possible, in their estimation, for them to successfully carry out such a mission.

The committee operated for some time without a new mandate until, in March 1951, the government resolved: "To appoint a governmental naming committee whose decisions shall be binding on state institutions." If in its previous role the NNC had created "something from nothing," in its new incarnation it was entering a realm already occupied by a seasoned committee that had devoted decades to determining names for Jewish settlements throughout Eretz Israel. This committee had been set up in 1925 on the initiative of the Jewish National Fund (JNF) and had been in operation ever since. The solution decided upon was to merge the two committees, especially since several members already served on both. However, even though many of the people involved, the level of professional expertise, and the sense of mission were identical for the two committees, there was an essential difference between them. Whereas the NNC had operated under an official mandate from a sovereign state, the JNF committee had functioned as a voluntary body whose authority was solely moral. It was a relic of the prestate period, and its decisions were binding on the Jewish community alone.

During that period, the authority to draw official maps and to assign names to topographical features had been the exclusive province of the British Mandatory regime. The JNF committee could give names only to communities established on land the JNF owned, but it could not venture "beyond the domain of the settlements, to the mountains and hills, the wadis and valleys." The British jealously guarded their exclusive authority in the assigning of official place-names in Palestine. Evidence of this sentiment is apparent in the fact that they compiled, updated, and published gazetteers of official names encompassing thousands of names of communities, ruins, and geographical features; and these names only, in precise spelling (in English), appeared on the maps. The first gazetteer, issued in 1931, was revised in 1940, in 1945, and, for the last time, in 1948, literally on the eve of the British withdrawal from Palestine. Not more than 5 percent of the names included therein were Hebrew, the remainder being Arabic. The efforts made by representatives of the Zionist community to persuade the Mandatory authorities "to redeem the ancient Hebrew names" had not been successful. The British were, of course, aware of the Hebrew origins of many of the Arabic names, but they were reluctant to open an additional front in the Jewish-Arab conflict and therefore scrupulously preserved the toponymic status quo: the only names they authorized the Jewish bodies to add to the map and the gazetteer were those of the communities that these bodies had founded.

Of course the Zionist organizations were angered by the Mandatory government's position and regarded it as a reflection of a hostile attitude. "Throughout all the years of foreign occupation of Eretz Israel," one member of the committee summarized retrospectively, "the original Hebrew names were erased or garbled, and sometimes took on an alien form." One may therefore understand the sense of the righting of a historical injustice with which the members of the JNF committee hailed the announcement by Avraham Biran, the chair of the new amalgamated committee: "The committee shall have official status. The names assigned by it to the new settlements continually being established and to geographical sites throughout the land shall be published in the official government gazette—*Reshumot*—and their utilization by the state and local authorities and national and public institutions shall be obligatory."[16] Most important, only the names assigned by the committee would be recorded on maps of the State of Israel. To the men who had dedicated their lives to the creation of a Hebrew map, this was the fullest possible expression of Israel's independence and of its national sovereignty in the homeland.

The members of the JNF Naming Committee brought with them an impressive record of achievements: In the course of its twenty-six years of operation this committee had assigned approximately 400 names to Jewish communities. Despite its having been a voluntary body whose authority derived "from the Zionist Congress" (according to the official description of the committee) and the fact that its decisions were binding on the Jewish community only, it nevertheless had official status. The Mandatory government had recognized it as the body authorized to provide it with the names of Jewish communities (in Hebrew and in English transliteration) for inclusion in official publications, in the gazetteer of names, and on official maps.

A community whose name was not listed in official gazettes was not "recognized" as far as the Mandatory authorities were concerned, and was thus unable to conduct its affairs with the authorities. A letter sent to the JNF by the Committee of the Bloc of Jewish Settlements in the Western Galilee in May 1941 endeavors repeatedly to convey the urgency "of the great need for the recognition of the 'points' Shavei Zion, Evron (Ein Sarah), and Mishmar Hayam as 'settlements' by the committee, in the gazette; and that having been done, the mukhtars [Arabic term for settlement headmen] will be able to receive their wages [from the Mandatory government]."[17] Settlement representatives were not the only ones who tried to rush the JNF Naming Committee. The chief secretary, head of the British Mandatory administration, did as well. In June 1928, the chief secretary approached the JNF, requesting the names of the new settlements in order to publish them in the gazette. The naming committee was in no hurry to oblige. In its reply, the JNF informed the chief secretary that committee chair Menachem Ussishkin "has gone abroad and will return in a few months, and it will be possible to convene the committee only after his return."

It was no coincidence that Menachem Ussishkin (1863–1941), chair of the JNF directorate, who ran this key Zionist institution with almost imperial centralization, also headed the naming committee. This man, who for decades had directed the JNF—the Zionist body that acquired land in Palestine and thereby made possible the establishment of rural and urban Jewish settlements—was not occupied with land acquisition alone. The entire course of Ussishkin's life embodied the dedication, the ability to mobilize people and resources and to translate lofty ideals into the language of everyday action, the allegiance to a goal that would brook no scruples or delay, the aggressivity, and the tribalism that carried the Zionist saga to the pinnacles of its achievements.

As one who had participated in the establishment of the Union of Hebrew Teachers in Eretz Israel, Ussishkin well understood the strong bond between the spiritual and material worlds. He was the moving force behind the establishment of the Hebrew University in Jerusalem, which he regarded as a "new national Temple, Mt. Zion's palace of wisdom and science." But he stated openly: "Not for the sake of a spiritual center did I make my call, but for the political strengthening of our position in this land. A spiritual center without a political center is a head without a body."[18] Ussishkin did not take part in geographical and toponymic research for its own sake; he was concerned with the establishment of settlements, but he reserved the right to call them by names that "redeem the name of the place from the oblivion of the ages, restore it to life, and establish the historical Hebrew name on the rightful patrimony of the Jewish people."

It was Menachem Ussishkin who laid out the basic principles for determining the names of settlements:

> First of all, we must examine them from a Hebrew-historical point of view. The historical Hebrew names of places in Eretz Israel are the most reliable testimony that these places have been our patrimony from time immemorial and that our rightful claims to these places and to this land are historical and ancient. Therefore, if the JNF Naming Committee is convinced that a new settlement is located near a place—especially a place where there was a Jewish settlement during one of the periods when the nation of Israel dwelt in Eretz Israel, but whose name was forgotten in the course of generations or was preserved in a different form by various conquerors, reaching us in its present form, embodied as an Arab village, the remains of a "ruin," or an archaeological "tel," or such like—the committee shall assign to the new or restored settlement the historical Hebrew name of the place in its original form. If the committee is not convinced that the new or restored settlement is located in the vicinity of a place where there was a Jewish settlement during a prior period in the history of Israel in its land—the committee shall assign it a name memorializing a personality or a symbolic name.[19]

Of course, the need to provide justification for "rightful claims to these places and to this land" through the revival of ancient Hebrew names made the biblical experts and the scholars specializing in the antiquities of Eretz Israel the most important members of the committee. These experts were equipped with vast stores of knowledge, acquired from primary sources and from the study of the scholarship of generations of researchers in biblical topography, both Jewish and non-Jewish. The problem was that the identification of ancient sites is not an exact science, and thus controversies among the scholars proliferated without there being any concrete evidence to indicate who was right.

ESOTERIC AND SCIENTIFIC MAPS

The desire to reproduce the map of the ancient Land of Israel via the identification of places mentioned in the Bible goes back many years. At first it was motivated not by the need to find a basis for claims of ownership but by religious objectives and the pursuit of historical scholarship. Pilgrims, travelers, and scholars all tried their hand at identifying these sites, relying on ancient traditions and the groundless speculations offered by their local tour guides. In the Middle Ages, for example, the

Philistine city of Ekron was identified with Acre because of the similarity in the sound of their names in European languages; the ancient lighthouse of Acre came to be called "the Tower of Flies," since a temple of Beelzebub (Lord of the Flies) was located in Ekron. Travelers and ecclesiastics sometimes fabricated identities for convenience' sake. When it was dangerous to visit a given site, they would transfer the name of the holy place to a location on a main road. Thus was created a synthetic and esoteric geography that today arouses one's sense of the ridiculous.

It is widely accepted that the American scholar Edward Robinson introduced order to the ancient geography of Palestine; however, Jewish travelers and others who preceded him had already begun the work of identifying biblical sites, based on logical scientific principles. In his book *Biblical Researches in Palestine,* Robinson warns against "all ecclesiastical tradition respecting the ancient places in and around Jerusalem and throughout Palestine."[20] He recommends (with particular emphasis, in the body of his book) that attention be paid to "the preservation of the ancient names of places among the common people." "The Hebrew names of places," states Robinson,

> continued current in their Aramaean form long after the times of the New Testament. . . . After the Muhammadan conquest, when the Aramaean language gradually gave place to the kindred Arabic, the proper names of places found their ready entrance: and have thus lived on upon the lips of the Arabs, whether Christian or Muslim, townsmen or Bedouin even unto our own day, almost in the same form in which they have also been transmitted to us in the Hebrew scriptures.[21]

Robinson proved his thesis to be correct, identifying many dozens of ancient sites in the course of his travels and essentially laying the foundation for the study of the biblical geography of Palestine. Many have followed in his footsteps, collecting names and identifying the sites to which they belong. However, the most thorough survey was not made until the 1870s—by the British PEF, whose activities in the Negev and Arava have already been mentioned. Between 1872 and 1878, the PEF's expeditions, under the command of officers from the Royal Engineers, mapped all of Palestine "from Dan to Beersheba" and published a series of twenty-six maps on a scale of one inch to the mile, the accepted scale in Britain at the time. Their topographical mapping was quite accurate, and, after being updated, these maps served the British army well during the First World War.

The principal contribution of the PEF survey was in the recording of ancient remains and the collection of some 9,000 place-names and names of geographical features. The commanders of the survey expeditions, following in Robinson's footsteps, were of the opinion that the study of Arabic place-names was the key to identifying ancient sites, and they boasted of their achievements in that area. Claude Conder recounts: "The work [in the Shephelah region] had extended over 180 square miles in the three weeks, and 424 names, only 50 of which were previously known, had been collected including more than 200 ruins."[22] Herbert Kitchener reports that in the year of his term as commander of the expeditions (1878–77), he "described 816 ruins and collected 3,850 names." Conder tells of "new difficulties" that arose as a result of the effect of the scientific identification of a place on the Arabic name by which it was known among its inhabitants:

> The peasantry were convinced that the Franks [Europeans] knew the old names better than they did themselves. . . . at Adullam one man refused to tell me the name of the place, saying that the Franks knew it best. . . . I protest against the immorality of corrupting the native traditions, by relating to the peasantry the theories of modern writers, as authentic facts, for it destroys the last undoubted source of information as to ancient topography.[23]

The more the literature of place identification flourished, the more there developed a "scientific ancient topography" that was no less esoteric and fantastic than the "sacred topography" of the pilgrims, a fact that would have serious implications for "the establishment of the Hebrew name on its Jewish patrimony" and the distortions that it produced in the map of the country. Of the 9,000 Arabic names collected, only a tenth were ancient; the rest were descriptive. The experts working for the PEF went to the trouble of translating all these names into English—not an easy job, since the collection of names was not always an exact process. Many were gathered orally by members of the British expedition, who would give them to a local scribe, who, in turn, would write them down, sometimes on the basis of conjecture. Thus the meaning was often twisted or lost, and the translation erroneous and lacking in credibility. Nonetheless, the volume entitled *Arabic and English Name Lists,* edited by E. H. Palmer in 1881, constitutes a veritable treasure trove for the scholar of the cultural heritage of the Arab population. Sadly, though, scholarly interest has focused on the tenth of the names whose origins are ancient—this was, after all, the motivation behind their collection in the first place—and thus the study of those Arabic names whose origin is not Aramaic-Hebrew has been neglected.

The British Mandatory authorities carried on in the time-honored tradition of their compatriots: the topographical maps that they plotted served the needs of the Mandatory administration and its security forces. Also, the long-standing interest in remnants from the past and in gathering and recording place-names did not dissipate. Frederick John Salmon, who initiated and executed the series of 1:100,000 scale maps (the standard map of Palestine), recognized the great importance of these ancient remains and ruins, and incorporated them in his maps. Dov Gavish, a scholar of the cartography of Mandatory Palestine, quotes Salmon: "The face of Palestine is covered, not only with existing settlements, but also with a plentitude of visible ruins and sites from periods of the past. . . . Sites like these interest not only archeologists, geographers, and historians, they . . . possess names that must under no circumstances be omitted from the maps."[24] Hence, the maps of Mandatory Palestine were crammed with the names of settlements, ruins, and caves. And all these names were, naturally, Arabic. But the toponymic wealth of the land was greater still. While drawing maps for assessment and taxation purposes (cadastral maps), the surveyors collected thousands of names of plots of land, and these too they recorded on large-scale maps.

The "Arab character" of the land, which became all too clear in the wake of the maps' being filled with Arabic names, upset the Jewish community. On 22 April 1941 the Emeq Z'vulun Settlements Committee wrote to the head office of the JNF:

> The 1:5,000 scale site plan has come into our possession. . . . In this plan such names as the following are displayed in all their glory: Karbassa, al-Sheikh Shamali, Abu Sursuq, Bustan al-Shamali—all of them names that the JNF has no interest in immortalizing in the Z'vulun Valley. . . . We recommend to you that you send a circular letter to all of the settlements located on JNF land in the Z'vulun Valley and its immediate vicinity and warn them against continuing the above-mentioned practice [i.e., the use of] old maps that, from various points of view, are dangerous to use.[25]

WITHOUT "EXCESSIVE FASTIDIOUSNESS"

Although the JNF Naming Committee under Menachem Ussishkin had clearly defined goals, its efforts to effect "redemption" of the names of places and restoration of the ancient Hebrew names encountered difficulties within its own ranks when committee members and experts carried their disputes over biblical geography all the way to the offices of the JNF. On 18 March 1928, committee member A. Y. Brawer requested that the decision of a group of pioneers from Yugoslavia to call their moshav (or smallholder collective) Beit She'arim be reconsidered. In his opinion, "There is not complete certainty that the city of Beit Sheʿarim indeed stood on the land of the Arab village of Jeda," and he therefore suggested that a different name be given to the place "in order to avoid the possibility of scientific misrepresentation."

Joseph Klausner replied: "If we follow this route, we will never restore a historical name to a new place of settlement, because there is hardly a settlement in Eretz Israel about which there is no controversy regarding whether it stands on the historical site whose name it was given. But we have a national duty to redeem historical names (in accordance with) the opinion of the majority of the experts. And we must not defer it out of excessive fastidiousness."[26]

The chairman had no patience with the academic debate that developed among the committee members, peppered with allusions and quotations in Aramaic and Greek, and he put the question to the vote. Four members supported the name Beit Sheʿarim, and even its opponents were content to abstain. A short while after the name, which remains to this day, was assigned, it was proven beyond a doubt that the historical site of Beit Sheʿarim was located eight kilometers away from the moshav.

The assignment of ancient Hebrew names to modern settlements on the basis of mistaken identity was repeated on a number of occasions. Sometimes names were conferred upon places other than their original locations when the latter were occupied by Arab villages. In 1941 the name Yavne was given to a religious kibbutz, "Purposely 'Yavne' and not 'Yavne Village,' in order to clearly articulate the fact that we are the heirs of ancient Yavne"[27] (the town where rabbinical scholarship was carried on after the destruction of the Second Temple by the Romans). At the time, the site of ancient Yavne was occupied by a large Arab village called Yibna, and no one dreamed that a problem would arise. But early in April 1949, the Arab village, which had been abandoned during the 1948 War, was repopulated, and its new Jewish residents began using the ancient name. The members of Kibbutz Yavne were angered by the abandoned village's new inhabitants' use of "a title that wasn't theirs." They appealed to the committee, requesting that it find a suitable name for the "new site"—Bnayahu, for example.

Sometimes an erroneous name was assigned in response to pressure from settlers, who succeeded in besting the committee's resistance. Early in 1949 a kibbutz was established in the northern Galilee, choosing for itself the ancient biblical name of Yiron. The naming committee rejected the name because the historical site of Yiron was in Yaroun, Lebanon, "regrettably located," wrote the committee, "outside the boundaries of the State of Israel." The kibbutz members did not give up, and they refused to accept the symbolic name they were offered, Shefer. In spite of "forceful requests" by the committee, the incorrect name remained on the map.

HISTORICAL CONNECTION AND BLOOD TIES

In one case, it was precisely adherence to a biblical name—in its proper place—that aroused anger toward the committee. On 21 September 1939, it received an angry letter from the chief rabbinate in Tel Aviv requesting the "removal of the shameful presence of the names Sodom Colony and Sodom Workers Camp from the map of our land and from among our communities." Sodom, stated the chief rabbis, "which is, in the Bible, the symbol of evil, corruption of human qualities, and social injustice; Sodom, which even in foreign literature is synonymous with impurity (the word 'sodomite' in European languages means a man who burns with desire for homosexual union [*sic*]), cannot serve as a name for a town of Jews in the Land of Israel, and this ugly name must be erased immediately from our maps and our childrens' lips."[28]

On several occasions the committee was forced to choose between two competing supreme national values: revival of a biblical name versus the memorialization of soldiers who had fallen in battle. In March 1949 a heated dispute broke out between the naming committee and the council of the village of Yazur near Tel Aviv. Situated on the road to Jerusalem, Yazur had been the site of an Arab village, and in January 1948 seven Jewish soldiers escorting a convoy were killed there. The village was captured in May of that year, and its Arab inhabitants abandoned it. That October the site was settled by Jewish immigrants, who chose the name Mishmar ha-Shivʿah, in memory of the seven fallen soldiers (*shivʿah*—seven): "Out of an inner desire to recompense, in some measure, the heroes to whom we are indebted for the opportunity given us to live in this wonderful place, to settle here, and to build our lives in the homeland."[29]

To the immigrants' amazement, the committee refused to permit their use of that name and instead assigned the settlement the name Azor, which was the ancient name of the place and had been preserved in its Arabic name. Azor, wrote the committee, "was in the territory bequeathed to the tribe of Dan in the time of Joshua Bin Nun. It was known by this name during the First and Second Temple periods. . . . Today, when the People of Israel is reestablishing the State of Israel on the basis of its rightful historical claims, it is our obligation to renew its ancient glory by restoring the names of the historical places of our land, which are the most reliable testament to the fact that these places are the heritage of the nation of Israel from the very earliest periods of our political existence. We understand and feel the emotional considerations that are motivating you to set up a memorial there to the seven soldiers who fell in this place. However, setting up memorials to our dear martyrs cannot be allowed to take precedence over the historical names of places . . . because the historical connection is what brought the Jewish community in this country and volunteers from abroad to this war and to all that it entailed."[30]

The priority accorded the historical connection over blood ties aroused the wrath of the seven bereaved families whose sons had fallen in the village. In a letter of reply to the committee they wrote:

> Your desire to cancel the new Hebrew name . . . shocked us and badly hurt our sorrowing feelings. . . . The village deserved to receive your encouragement and blessings for this initiative. Instead, what came from you was rigid determination to continue chasing after archeological allusions instead of faithfulness to the claims of our new life and present-day reality. . . . Without getting into a major argument and evaluating every idea associated with assumptions regarding distant past history and ancient names that were never mentioned in Jewish literature, we are opposed to the dropping or changing of the name Mishmar Hashivʿah. [We] believe that you will give priority to the sacred emotions of the present over a sense of obligation to archeology—which hardly expresses what is taking shape at this time in our land and our state.[31]

The naming committee did not retreat from its stance, and in spite of all the pressure, the village was given its historical name, Azor. Even so, a compromise was ultimately achieved between "the sacred emotions of the present" and the "sense of obligation to archeology": a new settlement established on the land of the Arab village of Yazur received the name Mishmar Hashivʿah.

A BLANK SLATE

Such a compromise was certainly possible only because, in the aftermath of the 1948 War and the mass exodus of the Arabs from their towns and villages, the country had become a blank slate upon which the committee could inscribe names as it wished, without being restricted to the very limited areas under Jewish ownership. Now it could restore the names of historical places to their exact sites—most of which had become abandoned villages—perpetuate the memory of war heroes, or give some other symbolic expression to nationalist yearnings. And the committee did indeed behave like one suddenly released from all restraint: in the three years following the establishment of the state, from May 1948 until March 1951, when it was absorbed into the Governmental Naming Committee (GNC), the JNF Naming Committee assigned 200 new names—the same number that it had assigned in the entire twenty-two years of its operation during the British Mandate. The committee's accelerated pace of activity of course reflected the speed at which new Jewish settlements were being established throughout the country during the early years of the state (which will be dealt with elsewhere). Every one of the new settlements required a name, and the committee endeavored to provide one promptly. Gone were the days of lengthy academic deliberations concerning the faithfulness of a particular name to the ancient sources. In fact, the rate of settlement and the pressure from the settlers were so great that the committee was forced to place the onus for providing historical data upon the settlers themselves, and in many cases the corresponding secretary of the committee responded to requests from new settlements with a reply worded something like the following: "In order for us to be able to assign you a name, please send us a list of the hills, valleys, stream beds (wadis), and archaeological tels with distinctive names in Arabic."

Choosing a name for one of the Jewish settlements that were springing up in or beside abandoned Arab villages was generally quite uncomplicated: the committee simply restored the ancient Hebrew name that had been preserved, almost unchanged, in the Arabic one. Thus Faradiyya became Parod; Dallata became Dalton; Kasla—Ksalon; Beit Dajan—Beit Dagon; Yibna—Yavne; and Zirʿin—Yizraʿel. Biblical names or Hebrew names that appeared in the Mishna or Talmud received distinct priority. When such could not be found, places were named for biblical characters—who did not necessarily have any connection to that particular location—or were given names based on lyrical phrases from the Bible. Over the years, the distinction between names based upon the actual identity of an ancient site, like Yoqneam, and names of biblical characters like Aviel or biblical expressions like Te'ashur—that had been chosen quite randomly—became blurred, and all of these together came to be perceived as "biblical or ancient names."

A classification undertaken by Nurit Kliot determined that "of 770 names of places of Jewish settlements within the pre-June '67 borders of Israel, 350 are names of 'biblical or ancient' places," that is, 45 percent.

The mixing of authentic ancient names with synthetic, pseudobiblical names was done, of course, to provide a basis for "our rightful historical claims," and in retrospect, they were all perceived as being authentically "biblical and ancient."[32]

A special place is occupied by modern Hebrew names that are translations or interpretations of Arabic names, "on the assumption that the Arabic name was based on an earlier Hebrew name." The settlement of Alona was called that because it is situated beside the Arab village of Sindiyanna, which means Oak (Alon): "The name is ancient and one may assume that its source is Hebrew," the committee stated.

On occasion the designation of a Hebrew name bordered on outright falsification. The name of the abandoned Arab village of Deir al-Qasi, which was settled by Jews, was changed to Elkosh. "There are those who are convinced that this was the birthplace of Nahum the Elkoshite," wrote the committee, with full knowledge that most scholars do not agree that this is the true identity of the spot and assert that the prophet's place of birth was in Syria, Lebanon, or near Beit Govrin in the Shephelah (Judean foothills). To salve its conscience, the committee added that Elkosh was so named to commemorate "the prophet's vision of peace: Behold upon the mountain the feet of him . . . that publisheth peace" (Nahum 1:15). That is to say, this name does not necessarily imply the identification of the ancient site. But who takes the trouble to check the committee minutes?

Regarding the Arabic names of ancient villages such as Suhmata and Tarbikha, the committee noted that "there is no historical identification," meaning that they have no Jewish historical connection, or at least that no such connection is known to the committee. For this reason they chose to assign symbolic names in such instances: Hosen (Strength), or Shomera (from shmirah, guarding). Some 70 Jewish communities have symbolic-abstract names of this sort. The names of another 170 were derived from agriculture and nature: Avivim (from *aviv* [springtime]), Goren (Threshing Floor), Shoshanat Haʿamakim (Lily of the Valley), Gefen (Vine), Kfar Zeitim (Olive Village), and the like.

No fewer than 20 percent of the names on the Hebrew map belong to the founders of Zion, public figures of our day, Israeli leaders, and people who have made a significant contribution to the state. Nonetheless, when choosing these names the committee scrupulously "implemented the principle of not employing names in foreign tongues." In most cases, therefore, it used the Hebrew given names of these public figures, most of whom had "foreign" family names, or made use of their titles, as in the case of Eshel Hanassi—the President's Tamarisk, in honor of Haim Weitzman, the first president of Israel, or Ein Hashofet (Spring of the Judge), named after the famous Jewish U.S. Supreme Court justice, Louis Brandeis. Thus they upheld the principle of the purely Hebrew map, though at the cost of blurring the identity of the very names they sought to immortalize. For how is one to know that behind some forgettable Hebrew given name is hidden a famous personage who is generally known by his or her foreign family name? Another eighty or so place-names commemorate events in the history of the Jewish people, the Holocaust, Israel's wars and their heroes. And a total of about one-third of the names of Jewish communities are based on various aspects of Zionist-nationalist ideology and history. In any case, the balance between "obligations to archeology" and "the sacred emotions of the present" has been scrupulously maintained.

In spite of all its efforts, the JNF Naming Committee did not succeed in erasing all the Arabic names from the map, or even from all Jewish towns (the names of Arab towns and villages will be dealt with elsewhere). Some Jewish communities bear Arabic names that have never been changed: Hadera, Ramla, Hamadiya, Metullah, Hulda. Others carry names that were given a Hebrew form on the basis of similarity to the sound of the Arabic name—Zecharia from Zakariyya, Manot from Manawat, Kamon from Kamana, Gillon from Jalun—without their necessarily being meaningful in Hebrew. But even this fact has become obscured: Who's to know that the biblical-sounding name Tefen, for example, is actually the Arabic name al-Tufaniyya?

The GNC found new territory in which to carry on Zionist activities after the Six-Day War. The settlements being established in the Occupied Territories also required Hebrew names, and the committee applied its tried-and-true principles there as well. Settlements were given place-names from the Bible (Bethel, Shiloh), biblical proper names (Otniel), names of scriptural passages (Alfei Menashe), agricultural names (Katif/Fruit Harvest), symbolic names (Alon Shevut/Oak of Return), names of Zionist personalities (Givʿat Zeʾev, after Zeʾev Vladimir Jabotinski), and names commemorating heroic deeds from Israel's wars.

When the committee began assigning names to Jewish settlements in the Occupied Territories, its task within the boundaries of the State of Israel had already been essentially completed. Not only had Hebrew names been bestowed upon nearly all of the Jewish settlements (with the exceptions noted previously), but all of the geographical features of the map—streams, springs, mountains, and wadis—as well as ruins and tels, had acquired Hebrew names as well. The discussion will now turn to this tremendous undertaking: the Hebraization of the landscape.

A CLOSED CIRCLE

In embarking on the task of giving Hebrew names to features of the landscape, the Naming Committee followed the well-worn path blazed by the NNC at the time of the assignment of names in the Negev and Arava. It is, however, one thing to assign names in uninhabited expanses of desert and quite another to do so in areas that have long been heavily populated and where many historical sites and places of sensitive symbolic significance are located. First and foremost the committee sought to restore ancient Hebrew names. The difficulties encountered in so doing are recorded in a report it issued in September 1958: "In the Bible are recorded a total of thirty-two names of streams and rivers, of which only eighteen are west of the Jordan River; another five names have reached us from the Mishna and Apocrypha and from Greek and Roman sources—twelve more. This comes to approximately fifty names that we have inherited from the ancients, including duplicate names for one river and names whose location has not yet been identified." Nevertheless, "the committee has given biblical names and names from post-biblical sources to 135 streams, and has given another 85 streams names of personalities from the Bible." In fact, most of the streams were named after plants, birds, or animals, "or according to the translation of the Arabic names or by similarity of sounds."[33] Altogether the mapping of the hydrographic network involved the naming of 780 streams and 520 springs.

The determination of the names of ancient sites, tels, and ruins was apparently particularly difficult for the committee: out of 720 ancient sites, only 170 were identified and assigned their biblical names or presumably authentic names from nonbiblical or postbiblical sources of comparable antiquity. "The remaining sites, and they are the overwhelming majority," stated the committee report, "have still not been identified, and their Hebrew names have been determined in accordance with the meaning of the Arabic name or its similarity in sound, or derived from the surrounding landscape or nearby geographical features." Little by little, then, a "closed circle" evolved: first a mountain, stream, or ruin was assigned a name, and then everything else in the vicinity—

"gullies, plains, caves, hills, and crossroads"—was given a name derived from the first, which often enough had itself been invented "in accordance with similarity of sound."

"Nine years ago the map of our country was poor in names," continues the 1958 report. The compiler of the report knew that this was an incorrect statement, so he hastened to explain what he was referring to: "and particularly Hebrew names." That is to say that if a map was not Hebrew, it was, to all intents and purposes, "empty." The committee summarized, with satisfaction, its nine years of work: "It has proposed some 3,000 names" and is "pressing forward on its mission" to continue the work of getting names onto a detailed map on a 1:20,000 scale. Indeed, the naming committee did continue its activities until the Hebrew map of the Land of Israel, including the Occupied Territories, was completed.

A random selection of the names assigned by the committee and the reasons given for choosing them will demonstrate its method of operation. The following is taken from the minutes of the twenty-ninth session of the Historical Subcommittee (15-11-57):

Misr'fot Yam/ in Arabic: Minat al-Mushairifa. The name: after the biblical name.

Horbat Ein Kovshim/ in Arabic: Khirbat Ein al-Beida. The name: after the spring (whose name "Conquerors' Spring" commemorates the settlers who established Kibbutz Hanita).

Horbat Bannai/ in Arabic: Khirbat Banna. The name: by similarity of sound (to the Arabic).

Horbat Abbas/ in Arabic: Khirbat ʿAbbasiyya.

Horbat Tabour/ in Arabic: Khirbat Tibiriya. The name: by similarity of sound.

Horbat Nemal Akhziv/ in Arabic: Minat al-Zib. The name: by translation of the term "mina" (anchorage/"namal"=port) and after the biblical name Akhziv.

From the 121st report of the Geographical Subcommittee (17-5-59):

Nahal Hur: Flows into Nahal Kalil, Wadi Hur in Arabic. By similarity of sound.

Ein Guni: Ein Abu Zeina. After one of the sons of Naphtali (Genesis 46:24).

Nahal Selav: After a common fowl (quail).

Ein Dolev: In Arabic Ein al-Dilba. By similarity of sound and meaning (Plane Tree).

Similarly, Jabal Kharuf (Sheep's Mountain) became Har Harif (Spicy Mountain); Jabal Mushaqqah (Split or Forked Mountain) became Har Sulam Tsor (Mt. Ladder of Tyre); Jabal Jarmaq, the highest mountain in Palestine, became Mt. Meron, named for the settlement at its foot. Wadi Hamam (Wadi of the Doves) became Nahal Arbel (named after an ancient Jewish city); Wadi Difla (Oleander Wadi) became Nahal Dahlia (after a Jewish settlement that had adopted part of the Arabic name Daliyat al-Ruha); Tel Abu Hurayra (named for one of the prophet Muhammad's companions) became Tel Haror (by similarity of sound, with no meaning in Hebrew); Khirbat Umm al-Basal (Mother-of-the-onions' Ruin) became Horbat Batsal (Onion Ruin); Khirbat ʿAris (. . . Bridegroom) became Horbat Arissa (. . . cradle); Ein al-Tina (. . . fig) became Ein Uzi (a Hebrew proper name); Bir al-Haramis (Thieves' Well) became Be'er Hermesh (Scythe Well); Khirbat al-Sneineh (. . . the Little Tooth) became Horbat Snunit (. . . Martin or Swallow); Wadi al-Kana (Wadi of Reeds) became Nahal Elkana (a Hebrew proper name). And so it went, on and on and on: thousands of names changed meaning, erasing an entire universe and replacing it with "similar sounds."

HISTORICAL, CURRENT, AND HEBREW

Reading the minutes of subcommittees of the naming committee, one gets the impression that its members were eager to complete their work quickly, and that had they not been in such haste, they would have been able to do justice to the old names, rather than exempting themselves from responsibility via "similar sounds." This haste was not simply the outcome of a strong desire to be rid of the Arabic names and to have them forgotten in a hurry; it also was a response to objective necessity: The names that they assigned became reality only once they were printed on maps. And in order for them to appear on maps, the committee would have to complete all its work, since it was impossible to print maps containing partial corrections and to update them as the work progressed. The committee held an exhaustive evaluation session with the director general of the Government Survey Department at their meeting of 7 February 1960 (meeting number 133). The meeting was opened by committee chair, Professor Avraham Biran: "Our committee has assigned many names; however, they have not yet appeared on 1:100,000 scale maps, and thus the names that we have assigned remain unknown to the public and have not become a part of life. When we request that people use the names we have chosen, we receive a request in return: 'Give us maps with the new names.'"

The director of the Survey Department, Yosef Elster, replied:

> This year we shall issue a new series of twenty-six 1:100,000 scale maps, grouped according to a new system of classification. We have ascertained that the replacement of Arabic names with Hebrew ones is not yet complete. The committee must quickly fill in what is missing, especially the names of ruins. The Historical Subcommittee is requested to do this at a rate that will allow these names to be printed on the new maps; . . . I am giving you a draft of the new series, with all of the features that still lack a Hebrew name marked. Be so kind as to increase the pace of the assignment of names so that these will appear as Hebrew maps without defect.[34]

One may suppose that this prodding did, in fact, increase the pace of name assignment; it surely influenced the quality of the work. At that same meeting Elster stated: "We are taking strict care not to strike any features from the map, because every feature has great value for purposes of orientation. A ruin of which no visible trace remains will not be listed, since our intention is not to produce a historical map, but a current one." His words were extremely significant, since at the time he uttered them, maps had already been printed with the abandoned Arab villages erased despite the presence of many remnants usable "for purposes of orientation." But even those who used the map for guidance and orientation were destined to pay the price imposed by the Hebraization of the map, as even the state Survey Department addressed itself to concretizing the projection of national interests on the earth's surface.

The committee's hesitation to choose between a "historical map," the "current map," and the "flawless Hebrew map" was obvious in those issued by the Israeli Survey Department during the first decade of its existence. The most dramatic expression of this was a map for civilian use, which was published in two editions, in 1956 (D/2005) and 1958 (D/P 350). These were essentially the Mandatory maps from 1946, printed in English on a scale of 1:100,000, upon which—in a striking shade of violet—was overprinted an "Update of Roads and Settlements." The update designated Jewish settlements that had been established, and new roads that had been built, since 1947. The hundreds of new Jewish settlements were indicated schematically by circles of uniform size (for security reasons). Beside each circle appeared, of course, the settlement's new Hebrew name. All features of the landscape that were in existence on the eve of the 1948 War (cities, towns, villages, ancient ruins, holy places, and areas of cultivation) were left as they had been on the Mandatory map. The update for most of the Arab localities was expressed by a single Hebrew word, in parentheses, printed beside the Arabic name: *harus* (destroyed). This was a "current map." But the violet Hebrew overprint on the black of the English made it perforce a "historical map," immortalizing the cataclysm of 1948, when the old world disappeared and a new world was founded on its ruins. No wonder that the Israeli Survey Department's "updated" maps are cited in every Palestinian book about "The Catastrophe," often constituting the principal illustrations in the volume: no graphic artist could have created a more apt plastic expression of this event.

The Israeli cartographers certainly had no intention of commemorating the Palestinian catastrophe. The publication of the updated maps was the outcome of time constraints that obliged them to temporarily continue using Mandatory maps. But they wasted no time in their efforts to produce the "flawless Hebrew map," which would erase in print what had already been eradicated in actuality—or that "should have been." At the time of publication of the Updated Maps, a map for exclusive military use had already been issued (1958, number D/2007), in which the update was incorporated into the body of the Mandatory map in such a manner that the changes were swallowed up by the text of the original as if they had been there forever. The Israeli mapmakers used the same type of lettering in the same color print and the same conventional symbols as had their English predecessors to denote the new Jewish settlements (whose names were written in English transliteration). The ruins of the Arab communities, by contrast, were erased as if they had never existed.

Not every detail of the old landscape disappeared, however; ancient ruins, caves, springs, and graves of Muslim holy men were marked as before, only the names of some of them had been replaced by Hebrew names (in English transliteration). Arab villages that had been razed completely disappeared from the map, but the access roads that had led to them, and the areas of greenery surrounding them, remained. Other villages, of which visible ruins survived, were given symbols denoting "ancient ruins," and beside them was written a new geographical term, coined by the committee: *iyim* (heaps). Thus large villages—like Beit Jibrin, Ajjur, and al-Faluja—that had been totally destroyed were completely and utterly erased, whereas others, of which something remained, were denoted by their new Hebrew name, with "Iye" tacked on: Iye Qeratya for the village of Karatiya, Iye Sidim for ʿIraq Suwaydan, and so on.

The speed at which the names were changed on the map was determined by the rate at which the committee worked, so that new Hebrew names (recently changed) appeared side by side with the Arabic names of other places (whose names had yet to be "updated")—both in English transliteration. The process of consolidation of the "current map" with the "Hebrew map" went on as long as the eradication of all signs of habitation in the abandoned Arab villages (which will be dealt with elsewhere) continued; thus were the "ruins of which no visible traces remained" wiped from the map—along with their names. At the committee meeting of 16 August 1959, the chairman, Avraham Biran stated: "We have ascertained that no traces are left of the abandoned villages. Since the locations to which the committee gave the name of 'heaps' no longer exist 'on the ground,' their names are hereby abolished." Accordingly a list was drawn up of dozens of "heaps" that had been "canceled" (and removed from the map). It was no coincidence that Yosef Weitz, the initiator and moving force behind the destruction of the abandoned Arab villages (with which we will deal at greater length later), was one of the most active members of the committee.

By the early sixties a new Hebrew map of the whole country had been published, in a graphic style entirely different from that of its British predecessor. And of course this new map depicted the new reality: settlements, cities, villages, roads, nature reserves and scenic spots, ancient sites and waterworks, canals and pumping stations, all with new Hebrew names: "the flawless Hebrew map." And what of the abandoned villages? One need only quote Yizhar Smilanski ("S. Yizhar"), perhaps the greatest Hebrew writer of this generation:

> Old tales, so well-known we're sick of them. Abandoned villages? And where aren't there? What was the name of this place? A few years ago there was a place and it had a name. The place was lost and the name was lost. What was left? At first, a name stripped of a place. Soon enough, that too was erased. No place and no name. May G-d have mercy. And it was turned on its face, plowed it was, and become a field. Here it is, furrowed and yielding before you, among the stones, young carob trees. What happened to the place happened to its name: for a time the name tarried, hanging there, lingering in the air until it vanished. Names without places hover for a while like bubbles, stay for a while, then burst. Here it is, a leveled hill; they leveled it well. Humble and lacking any sign of life; they have returned it to before it was.[35]

But names are borne in the mouths of human beings and cherished in their hearts; and so long as their tradition is preserved and their memory endures, the names are not truly erased. No "flawless Hebrew map" could ever wipe out the names that the villagers carried with them into exile. They gave streets and neighborhoods in the refugee camps the names of the destroyed villages. They recorded them on their gravestones and immortalized them on maps.

PALESTINIAN SACRED GEOGRAPHY

Palestinian mapmaking has been the reply to Israeli maps. On the Palestinian maps, reality is frozen at 1946. Hundreds of villages and towns, ruins, and hallowed graves that no longer exist fill the map of Palestine, whereas the Jewish settlements appear under the classification of "Jewish Colonies, divided according to the stages of the Zionist conquest, from 1882 to the present." Everything created in Palestine by the Jews was considered an aberration. The Palestinians created their own "sacred geography." They had no interest in the "current map," only in the "historical map" that, in their opinion, proved "the flawless Hebrew map" to be a fabrication and evidence of the plundering of their land, its history, and its civilization. The symbolic act of taking possession, expressed through the assignment of names, was answered by the converse symbolic act, whose purpose was to deny the right to take possession. And the maps became a battleground: I'll destroy your map just as you destroyed mine.

A comparison of the Hebrew and Arabic maps is instructive. The Arabic maps were prepared on a small scale (1:250,000) and are sparsely detailed: their entire purpose was to perpetuate the names of the Arab villages that had been destroyed. However, they portray but a minute fraction of the riches of Arabic toponymy. Even a detailed list compiled and published by the Arab-Israeli geographer Shukri ʿArraf contains only a few of the eradicated names. Palestinian scholar Mustafa al-Dabbagh, whose monumental eleven-volume opus *Biladuna Filastin* (Our Homeland Palestine) is the most comprehensive study of the historical geography of Arab Palestine, proposes many interpretations of the Arabic names, which are notable for his efforts to blur their Hebrew, biblical, or postbiblical roots. The name of the village of Abil al-Qamh, derived from the biblical name Abel Beth Maʿacha (2 Sam. 20:14), is explained thus: "In Arabic the word Abil, in this specific context, means a hill, and therefore the meaning of the name is Hill of Flour—because of the quality of the flour that was produced in this village." The name of the Arab village of Birʿim, which preserved its ancient Hebrew appellation exactly, is explained as "derived from the Canaanite word 'peryam,' meaning a place where there is much fruit." There is, however, no connection between "Biram" and "Peryam," and if we follow al-Dabbagh's lead, we find that the "Canaanite" word is in origin the Hebrew word *piryam* (their fruits). But the Palestinian scholar is striving to erase any Hebrew connection. Thus all of the ancient Hebrew-Aramaic names are labeled Canaanite, Syriac, or Phoenician, or, of course, Arabic—"according to similarity of sound."

There is no comparison between the level of Palestinian cartography and toponymic scholarship and that achieved by the Israelis. Here as in other realms, the power wielded by Israel—a country that has invested tremendous resources in cartography and related sciences—is considerable. As quoted earlier: "Map making is one of the specialized intellectual weapons by which power could be gained, administered, given legitimacy and codified." Israel has always been aware of this fact. How an official, sovereign entity goes about "gaining legitimacy" for its choice of names is succinctly articulated in an article by Naftali Kadmon, an Israeli expert in toponymistics (the assigning of geographical names) and Israel's representative to a number of international bodies. He explains the steps involved in the standardization of place-names (i.e., getting them approved by the GNC for use on maps and listed in the official gazette): "The first is geographical: the birth of the name. It may be a 'natural birth.' On the other hand, in the event that a name is given by order of an official body, it will be a 'test-tube baby.' For example: In Israel we can regard the [biblical] names Gilgal, the Dead Sea, Jordan, and others as being of the first type; and names like Halamish, Nahal El Al, or Har-El as being of the second type—given by a kind of administrative order from the Governmental Naming Committee."

All of these names are Hebrew, of course—Arabic names were not even "naturally born," let alone "test-tube babies" authorized by an administrative order. According to Kadmon, the reason for the dearth of Arabic names on the map is that "a geographic name has a defined legal status; for that reason existing names require the approval of a responsible authority. Since the committee established by government decision in 1951 was at first concerned with Hebrew names, these were the only ones among the names already in existence to be granted official approval retroactively." Others (most of them Arabic) were local "endonyms" (local unstandardized names); and since prior to the founding of the state no governmental authority responsible for names had ever been set up in this country, these [Arabic] names were not even "standardized endonyms."[36]

The writer might simply have pointed out that the sovereign Israeli authorities chose to grant "legal status" only to Hebrew names, and hence erased every Arabic name that had not gained the "approval of the responsible authority." But then he would have been putting Israel in the same category as totalitarian, colonialist states that assigned names by fiat—only to see the territories so named, upon gaining their freedom and independence, drop the imposed names and return to their former ones: "All changes of name mandated by the state appear to be acts of administrative toponymy," states Kadmon. "Sri Lanka rather than Ceylon, Burkina Faso rather than Upper Volta, Myanmar rather than Burma." One might add the replacement Leopoldville by Kinshasa, Salisbury by Harrare, and hundreds of other such changes.

As far as Kadmon is concerned, Israel does not belong to this group, and in order to prove this manifestly groundless contention, he resorts to half-truths. Supposedly the Israeli GNC dealt "only with Hebrew names in the beginning," from which one might deduce that it intended to deal "afterward" with Arabic names, and not as it actually operated, purposely erasing almost all Arabic names except those of towns and villages populated by Arabs. "Only the Hebrew names gained approval retroactively," as if they had existed from time immemorial and had not been invented "by an act of administrative toponymy." The Arabic names supposedly never gained approval and were therefore never standardized, because "a governmental naming authority had never been set up in the country." The British Mandatory governmental authority, which had scrupulously attended to the standardization of names—perhaps even with excessive zeal—never "existed," in the opinion of this Israeli scholar, since it was a colonial authority rather than a Jewish-Israeli one. In any case, the names it assigned had never had any legal validity, according to Kadmon, and Israel was entitled to expunge them. Thus does this scholarly piece of professional research affirm the legitimacy and legality of the Hebrew map—the very device by means of which "power could be gained and administered."

However, there remained a need to add to the narrative told by the map itself another narrative explaining how the map had been drawn—in terms of historical rights—and justifying it in legal terms. This need was not a manifestation of remorse. The hand of the draftsman of the

Hebrew map did not tremble, and the work was accomplished without either guilt or hesitation. Brimming with a burning faith in the right of the Jewish People to return to its homeland, the Zionists strove to anchor this right in the landscapes of the Bible. They established a connection with the ancient landscapes, and this connection could be made concrete only by the use of the ancient names—since the actual physical landscape they found was alien, threatening, and populated with alien, threatening people. The resurrection of the ancient Hebrew names domesticated this alien landscape and served as a powerful means for turning the spiritual homeland into a real, earthly homeland.

BRIDGING THE ABYSS OF EXILE

Like every immigrant society, the Zionists endeavored to erase foreign names from the map of the country and tried to domesticate the new landscape by naming its features in their own tongue, giving them names that were meaningful to them, exactly as the English had named New England, New Zealand, New York. But the comparison becomes strained because, unlike other immigrants, the Zionists were able to renew their connection with landscapes from which their ancestors had been exiled 2,000 years before—a connection that had been severed physically but not spiritually. The Jews had not forgotten the names, and for 2,000 years they had borne with them the Hebrew map—containing not only the memory of the places but also the intimate recollection of the changes in the seasons, of the varieties of plant life, of seed time and harvest. They had repeated the names of communities that had been eradicated from the face of the earth and had vowed to return to Zion and rebuild them. Generations of Jews in the Diaspora lovingly compiled all the geographical names that appeared in the Holy Scriptures and published them in books written in Hebrew. They did not know a thing about those vanished communities, but they knew the names by heart. It is no wonder, then, that when the first Zionist immigrants "returned," they strove to affix these ancient names to concrete locations and thereby to bridge the abyss of a 2,000-year exile.

The irony was that the Jews were returning to their ancient homeland, but were able to identify the places there only because the people who had inhabited them during the Jews' long absence had preserved their names. Had the Arabs not adhered closely to the ancient Hebrew-Aramaic names, the Zionists would not have been capable of reproducing a Hebrew map. In turn, however, they rewarded the Arabs by erasing the Arabic names from the map: not only were names of biblical origin Hebraized, so was virtually every Arabic name, even if no ancient Hebrew name had preceded it. This was an act of sheer ingratitude; the destruction and eradication of all record of the 2,000 years of their absence from the land and of the civilization that had existed there in their stead, only because of their desire to make direct contact with their own ancient heritage.

Perhaps this ingratitude was inevitable. After all, naming is a declaration of exclusive proprietorship, and making such a claim over one's homeland is the essence of nationalism. Or perhaps this immense effort to eradicate the non-Hebrew heritage arose from a sense of the rootedness and power of the Arabic names, which, if not extirpated, were liable to imperil the new map. This was not a show of contempt for the Arabic heritage. On the contrary, it was a declaration of war on it. The effort the Zionists invested in this project is proof of their recognition that the Arabic shadow-map—that rests alongside the Hebrew map—had not vanished but in fact would remain very much in existence as long as there were people living in this land who took care to preserve it.

And indeed, Israelis whose business is the historical and cultural geography of Eretz Israel/Palestine are fully aware of the wealth and magnificence of the geographical tradition they have been endeavoring to erase. Some even harbor feelings of remorse for the reckless and unforgivable acts that were committed in the nationalist fervor of the first decade of Israel's existence. To this geographical heritage, buried beneath the "stratum" of the Hebrew map, we shall now turn our attention.

ARAB GEOGRAPHICAL HERITAGE

The Arabic map of Palestine was not created by administrative fiat, nor was it drawn for the purpose of providing the basis for a claim to proprietorship: it took shape through an evolutionary process, layer upon layer and generation after generation. The Arab conquerors who colonized the land following the conquest of 638 C.E. settled among its Jewish, Samaritan, and Christian natives. They easily assimilated the Hebrew-Aramaic geographical and topographical names, and, their language being closely related to the Semitic languages spoken there, they made only slight changes in spelling and pronunciation. They had no difficulty finding Arabic forms for names such as Ashkelon—which they transformed into Asqalan—Beit Horon to Beit Ghur, Beersheba to Bir Saba'a, and Eilat to Aila. Aramaic names were easily adapted (Matsuba became Khirbat Maʿasub), and Greek and Roman names were assimilated as well, Qarantana and Neapolis becoming Qarantal and Nablus. New communities, and geographical features that had no ancient names (or at least not ones that were known to the Arabs), were given authentic Arabic names.

All these names appear in the writings of Arab and Muslim geographers, who produced numerous descriptions and chronicles of Palestine, beginning in the ninth century C.E. In addition, others are to be found in documents from the Crusader and Mamluk periods and in the writings of Christian and Jewish travelers. To the approximately 1,200 names of places known to have existed during the period preceding the Ottoman conquest of 1517, thousands more were added in succeeding centuries. In the late nineteenth century the British PEF gathered and published some 9,000 Arabic names, about a tenth of which were of Hebrew-Aramaic origin, the remainder dating from the 1,400 years since the Arab conquest.

It is difficult to categorize these names according to distinguishing characteristics and even harder to investigate their origins, since they evolved by an ongoing, spontaneous process. The question of how and why various names were chosen is addressed in an Arab legend told to Alon Galili.[37] Galili recounts that the old people of the Bilad al-Ruha district, south of the Carmel ridge, tell the following story: A father whose time to die was drawing near decided to divide up his property among his sons. To do so, he went with them on a tour of his landholdings, and so that they would not mistake one place for another and quarrel over them, in the course of their tour he gave each place a name. Beside the first spring that they found, they saw a drunk old man. "Remember, my sons," said the father, "this spring will be called Ein al-Sakran (Spring of the Drunkard)." When they ascended a hill, they beheld a ridge from which flowed eight wadis, and so they called the mountain Ras al-Matmuniya (the Octagonal Head). On their way they came to a village and "they were greeted by the mukhtar, who had just awakened from his night's sleep and was still bareheaded, his hair blowing in the wind." They therefore called the village Abu Shusha (Father of the Forelock). From there they walked in the valley, where they encountered camels loaded with sacks of salt, and they named the valley Wadi Milh (Salt Wadi); they met some pretty young women and called their village Umm al-Zinat (Mother of the Pretty Women). They came to a high hill from which a breathtaking view could be observed, and so they called it Umm al-Shuf (which means Mother of the Sights); they encountered some people who annoyed them, and called their village Kafr ʿAra (the Damn Village). Finally, as they approached their home, the girls of the village came out and danced before them and beat on drums, so they named the place Umm al-Dufuf (Mother of the Drumming Women). The whole region was called Bilad al-Ruha (Land of the Winds) because of the pleasant sea breezes that blow there.

The legend provides an explanation for names whose origins are in forgotten events, shrouded in the mists of folklore, or are simply impossible to place in rigid categories. According to a study conducted by Nurit Kliot of names of Arab communities in Israel and the Occupied Territories (excluding those that were destroyed and their names eradicated), 57 percent of the names are of unknown origin. That is, "the various lexicons could not provide an explanation for the origin of the name or were divided in their opinions regarding it."[38] Approximately one-quarter of the 584 Arab villages that were standing in the 1980s had names whose origins were ancient—biblical, Hellenistic, or Aramaic. Ten percent had symbolic names (like House of the Dawn, Place of Rest, the Green Village, or the Seven). The names of about 5 percent of the villages were taken from nature, agriculture, and the geographical surroundings, and another 5 percent were named after their founders or Muslim saints. This classification suffers from a deficiency, however, in that it does not include the nearly 400 permanent villages that were destroyed between 1948 and 1950, but more especially, because over 8,000 Arabic names of geographical features other than villages are neither mentioned nor classified.

A POETIC QUALITY

The wealth of Arabic toponymy is astounding in its beauty, its sensitivity to the landscape, its delicacy of observation and choice of images. Its metaphors have a poetic quality; its humor is sometimes refined, sometimes sarcastic. The knowledge of the climate, the familiarity with nature and inanimate objects is absolute. The people who chose these names had no need to articulate their love for their land in vast lyrical creations or to sing songs of longing from a distant Diaspora. They expressed it by naming a piece of land the Setting of the Moon; a spring of pure water, the Blue Spring; and a picturesque village, the Charming Village. "One who lives with his heart's beloved does not feel the need to express his feelings for her in poetry, since she is tangible to him," claimed a Palestinian in response to a Jew who had mocked him, saying that he had not found expressions of feeling for the homeland in Arabic literature like those to be found in Hebrew writings, both ancient and modern. "Only one who has lost his beloved or is far from her needs to give poetic expression to his longing for her. We are connected to the stone fence that our father built and the fig tree that our great-grandfather planted. One doesn't write poems about such connection."

And perhaps because of this intimate, unmediated relationship with the land and its names, Arab scholars did not engage in the systematic collection and analysis of the names. But the tragedy of their uprooting caused them, too, very quickly to begin writing songs of yearning for the lost homeland; and the old names, the former expression of their connection with the land, were largely forgotten. Arab writers living in Israel proper began using the new Hebrew names for their own landscape—since these were the only ones to appear on the maps—not knowing that many were nothing but Arabic names that had been Hebraized "in accordance to similarity of sound," distorted, their lyrical meanings lost.

Perusal of a list of the lost names allows one a glimpse at the world and the culture of the Arab inhabitants of the land. These names, too, can be divided into a number of categories. In one we have names describing the topographical and physical characteristics of the sites (shape, color, conspicuous features): Jabal Muntar (Lookout Mountain); Jabal Tawil (Long Mountain); Tel al-Safi (Bright or White Tel); Wadi Zarqa (the Blue Stream); Tel al-Asmar (the Black Tel); Khirbat Ruseis (Ruin of the Pebble); Ein al-Beida (White Spring); Umm al-Shuf (Mother of the Sights); al-Mushairifa (the High Place or Altar); Bat al-Jabal (the Mountain's Armpit); al-Bassa (the Marsh); Abu Hushiya (Father of the Parched); Ein al-Shuqaq (Canyon Spring); Tantura (the Peak); Wadi al-Qarn (Stream of the Horn); Qasr al-Sename (the Camel's Hump Fort); Ein al-Maiytah (Dead Spring); Qubayba (Little Dome); Khirbat Umm al-ʿAmud (Ruin of the Mother of the Columns); Khirbat al-Jubbain (Ruin of the Two Pits); al-Farsh (the Carpet, i.e., level ground).

The names in the second category describe properties attributed to the place or some activity connected with it: Ein Weiba (Spring of the Plague); Jabal Kafkafa (the Delaying Mountain); Tarbikha (the Prosperous); Jabal ʿArus (Bridegroom's Mountain); Wadi Haramiyya (Robbers' Valley); Ein al-ʿAjla (Spring of Haste); Ein Sakran (Drunkard's Spring). A third category, animal names, encompasses hundreds, many of which are repeated in several different locations throughout the country. The animals in these names include lion, panther, bear, water buffalo, wolf, fox, hyena, jackal, gazelle, buzzard, raven/crow, dove, and other kinds of birds, dog, donkey, pig, camel, cow, sheep, kid—as well as snake, bee, scorpion, lizard, mouse, fly, and others. It is hard to know how one ruin acquired the name Khirbat al-Asad (Lion's Ruin) and another came to be called Khirbat al-Namus (Mosquitoes' Ruin)—or when it was that bears last waded in the Bears' Stream.

A place of honor is occupied by names associated with historical or legendary figures: prophets, saints, heroes, famous women. We shall consider the names of sacred sites in another context, but there are also places that have been given the names of common people whose qualities excited the imagination of the villagers. Anton Shammas, in his book *Arabesque,* relates the story of the origin of the name of a piece of land near his village, Fassuta:

> At the turn of the century, Zeinab was the most beautiful woman in the Galilee. Folk poets spent many long nights rhyming songs in her praise. . . . But the men of her village did not look kindly upon the beautiful woman, and they began to spin the web of her death. First they spread rumors about the fiery lust between her legs and said that there was no man alive who could satisfy her appetite. . . . Thus the elders gathered one night to consider how to put an end to the scandal. At dawn several young men of the village burst into Zeinab's house, dragged her from the bed of her husband and brought her to the outskirts of the village. There they bound her hands and her feet, lifted the hem of her dress and poured gunpowder into her underpants, inserted a wick in her private part, lit it and ran for their lives. And to this day the place is called Khallat Zeinab (Zeinab's Plot).[39]

And in what category might we fit names such as Father of the Nipple, Father of the Hats, Stream of the Father of the Beard, Barefoot's Spring, Beggar's Ruin, Stream of the Forelock, the Crazy Stream, Repose, Dungheap Stream, Hindrance, One-Eyed Man Stream, Mother of the Brides, Cave of the Skulls, Valley of the Righteous, Wadi of the Lance, Spring of the Mother of the Flame, and Treasure Spring?

Several of the Israeli students of the Land of Israel who participated in the naming committee in its various incarnations were renowned experts in the field of Arabic toponymy, and they loved its richness and rootedness. One of these, Yeshayahu Press, included in his Hebrew *Topographical-Historical Encyclopedia of the Land of Israel*[40] thousands of Arabic names—in Arabic script—and also interpreted them. However, his profound knowledge of these names was not a hindrance when, as a member of the committee, he was called upon to uproot them from the map one by one. On the other hand, another eminent scholar, Yosef Breslavski, requested of the committee "not to be in a hurry to write new names, . . . and to leave all the Arabic names on the map." He recommended "preserving the Arabic names alongside the Hebrew ones," and he himself designed a bilingual map, with the Hebrew and Arabic names appearing together. But the committee had no interest in such bilingual or bisocietal proposals, since the very essence of its purpose was to secure the absolute and exclusive dominion of the Hebrew names.

Had the committee not been so locked in to its rigid conception of Hebraization at any price and of dissociating the new names from the Arabic social-folk tradition, it might have found a golden mean, allowing both Hebraization and preservation of the Arabic past. After all, there was no reason to change the Arabic name Khirbat Ngeass, whose meaning was Ruin of the Pear (Horvat Agas in Hebrew) to Horvat Nagos, which has no meaning, or the name Khirbat Ruseis (. . . pebbles) to Horvat Rotsets, again meaningless; or the name of the "Salt Wadi" to Yoqneam Stream—a Hebrew name that no one uses, because everyone calls it by its Arabic name, Wadi Milh. They could have translated most of the Arabic toponymy, and not hidden it and distorted it through the "assignment of names in accordance with similarity of sound." How the map would have been enriched, since many of the landscape's qualities, whose picturesque Arabic names these sites had been given, had not changed. But there was a compulsive need to give a black tel—whose Arabic name was exactly that: Tel al-Asmar—a meaningless Hebrew name, Tel Ashmar, simply because the former name was Arabic and it was a national duty to change it.

BILINGUAL NAMES AND COEXISTENCE

There are many countries in the world where double, bilingual, names are commonly in use. Any place where a person encounters road signs that display two different names for the same place or different names on a postal cancellation, he or she knows is a country where socioethnic coexistence prevails. In Israel, on the other hand, although many signs appear in the scripts of the two languages, the Arabic is simply a transliteration of the Hebrew name. Most ironically, Neve Shalom/Wahat al-Salaam, a community of Jews and Arabs living together in Israel, has two official names, but the official road sign shows only Neve Shalom—the Hebrew name—in two scripts.

The erasure of topographical names that are not the ones generally used by members of the ruling majority and the prohibition of the use of such names are typical symptoms of ethnic oppression and efforts to blur the identity of minorities. The erasure of names, which is widespread in countries where ethnic conflict reigns, is sometimes carried out in conjunction with the prohibition of the teaching of the minority language in the schools and of the use of family names that identify their bearers as belonging to a specific ethnic minority. "Ethnic cleansing" of maps has been carried out in a large number of countries at different periods of history, such as in South Tyrol (Alto Adige) in the Italian Alps; in the Kurdish regions of northern Syria; in the Balkans and other countries of Eastern Europe. In biethnic or multiethnic countries like Belgium, South Africa, and Canada, legislation guarantees equal status to bilingual and/or bisocietal variants of place-names. For example, an agreement between the Nisgaʾa nation, Canada, and the Province of British Columbia (1997) stipulates that Nisga'a names and background historical information for geographical features will be recorded in the official Names Database and also that Nisga'a names will replace English names on maps.

International charters for ethnic minorities and international treaties (such as that between Italy and Austria regarding the German-speaking region of South Tyrol) recognize the rights of ethnic and linguistic minorities to "equal status . . . in all fields of toponymy." This is defined as a "fundamental right," encompassing not only the prerogative of ongoing use of such names but also the stipulation that "[names of] places shall . . . where necessary, be re-established to their original form."[41] Thus, names that were given by the dominant majority or an occupying force can be superseded by the original name of the place.

In most cases Israel is careful to use Arabic names for Arab communities and to provide road signs in the two official languages (as well as English), with the exceptions mentioned above. However, the Arabic toponymy of all geographical features that are not existing Arab settlements has been erased—with the legal argument (that does not stand up to critical examination) that the Arabic names had never been officially approved, even during the Mandatory period, and therefore have not been standardized.

There are few examples elsewhere in the world of such radical alteration of the map. In other places where population exchange has taken place in the wake of war, such as Silesia, Sudetenland, and Asia Minor, there was also a wholesale change of place-names, but the new names were always ones that had been continuously utilized by a population belonging to the neighboring socioethnic group, which became official when this group came to power. Thus Danzig became Gdansk, Breslau became Wroclaw, Fraustadt was replaced by Wschowa, Karlsbad by Karlovy Vary, Eger by Chev, Smyrna by Izmir, and Meander by Menderes. But in the overwhelming majority of cases, these names had existed for countless generations in all of the languages of the region: German, Polish, Czech, or Greek and Turkish, as the case may be, each ethnolinguistic group having its own version. It seems that only in Israel was a new toponymy imposed by an official naming committee, which invented most of it. Hundreds of ancient Hebrew names were, indeed, revived in a way not essentially different from that used in other places, but these were in the minority. The drawing of the Hebrew map mirrors the ferocity of the Israeli-Palestinian conflict and its vengeful nature: "I'll destroy your map just as you destroyed mine."

But the map is only a symbolic expression of the aspiration to Hebraize the landscape. The makers of maps and assignors of names were following in the footsteps of the builders of cities and villages, planters of trees, pavers of roads, and destroyers of Arab communities—and sometimes went before them. As S. Yizhar writes: "They even gave new names to them all. More civilized of course, and from the Bible, too. They covered over and inherited from those who were on their way into exile. And may there be peace over Israel."[42] But there was no peace over Israel; and as long as maps serve as an article of faith and a battle cry, and not as a means for geographical orientation, there is no chance that it ever will come.

2

White Patches

> From the hilltop the village looks out over the land, its land, its patrimony, the worker's legacy spread out at its feet, parched by the glowing days of the year. . . . The village looks out over its little-blessed land—like the breasts of a shriveled and wizened woman, who sustains it and all its burdens meagerly and in haste, shamefacedly and with the mercy of heaven. . . . The village looks out—looks afar and scatters abroad scents and smells, echoes and reverberations: a scorched odor and the smoke of *taboon*-ovens fed on straw and manure. . . . The village looks afar and scatters odors of settlement and habitation, voices and commotion that warm the heart of the passerby, the stranger and newcomer who has chanced upon the place—auguring lodging.[1]

This description is taken from the opening sentences of a book aimed at a youthful audience, published in 1946 by the Federation of Jewish Workers (the Histadrut), which at that time was of a socialist-Zionist ideological and political bent. In the introduction to his book, Moshe Stavsky writes that his description was based on

> places where I worked and labored in the fields for most of my days and on the *fallah* (Arab peasant-farmer) with whom it was my privilege to come in contact and to develop connections of fellowship and friendship. The thrust of the book is to give a comprehensive description of village life in this country (similar, as it is, to that of our ancestors in ancient times), a life whose form is rapidly changing, in response to the progress, technology, and plenty that Jewish settlement has brought with it. It is doubly important for us—a nation returning to its homeland—to acquaint ourselves with the land and

> its inhabitants. This knowledge may aid somewhat in promoting normal relations between our two peoples, who live as close neighbors . . . and a person endowed with a sense of discrimination, who knows what to cultivate and what to keep at a distance, will learn something from the villagers. . . . If someone were to accuse me of an excess of affection for that which I depict and an overabundance of color in my description, I would accept this verdict.[2]

The fact that the book was published in 1946 and its being tailored to suit the adolescent reader are worthy of comment, as are its introduction and content. Just two years later, the young people who read it would find themselves embroiled in a terrible war in the course of which the Arab village, described so picturesquely in the book, was laid waste. For most of its readers the book conjured up visions of a reality with which they were not acquainted: few young Jews had ever visited an Arab village, and even those who had done so did not speak Arabic and so could not communicate with the villagers, in any case. In fact, they had no reason to make such a visit, since all their contacts were with members of their own people who lived in Jewish communities and in the Jewish neighborhoods of mixed cities like Jerusalem and Haifa. Even the insignificant minority who showed an interest in their Arab neighbors hesitated to actually venture into those alien communities, for fear of being harmed. On the mental map carried by the Jewish young person and his or her parents, the Arab communities were white patches—terra incognita.

THROUGH A GLASS WALL

The Jews were, of course, aware of the Arab communities, but these towns, villages, and neighborhoods had no place in the Jews' perception of the homeland's landscape. They were just a formless, random collection of three-dimensional entities, totally isolated from the Jewish landscape and viewed as if through an impenetrable glass wall. There—in that other landscape—were houses, orchards, and people who had meaning for the Jews only as the objects of their perceptions and political concerns, but not as subjects in their own right. The attitude of the Jewish population toward the Arab landscape—physical and human alike—was a strange mixture of disregard, anxiety, affection, superiority, humanitarianism, anthropological curiosity, romanticism, and, above all, European ethnocentricity.

Stavsky felt the need to apologize for the publication of his book and "accepted the verdict" that he was guilty of relating to the Arab village with "an excess of affection"—for really, how could the primitive, dirty, foreign, and threatening village be an object of affection for a Jew? Stavsky relied on the "person endowed with a sense of discrimination" knowing "what to cultivate and what to keep at a distance." He also hinted at "what to cultivate": village life was "very similar to the life of our ancestors in ancient times" and had benefited from "the plenty that Jewish settlement has brought with it." He had no need to point out "what to keep at a distance," nor was there any chance of his infecting his readers with affection for the Arab peasant-farmer. These Jewish young people were the products of an educational system that had thoroughly imbued them with a disregard for the Arab landscape and a sense of its foreignness. Moreover, it had taught them to erase it from their mental map.

Earlier in the same year that Stavsky's book came out, a textbook entitled *Our Land,* written by my late father, David Benvenisti, had been published.[3] This was one of the most popular texts for the teaching of the subject called *yediat ha'aretz* (Knowing the Land), an important component in the education of every young Jew in Eretz Israel. This subject encompassed geography, geology, history, ethnology, botany, and zoology, but it was not simply a course of studies: it was a mechanism of indoctrination by means of which Zionist ideology was implanted in the heart of the Jewish child. It is no wonder, then, that *Our Land* praises "our pioneers, our laboring brothers who till the soil surrounding their flourishing settlements. . . . They have turned areas most of which were desolate into a valley of plenty for the people and the country."[4] Nor is it any wonder that in this three-volume work, scarcely two or three pages are devoted to the Arab communities. Describing the Coastal Plain region (along the Mediterranean coastline, south of Tel Aviv) David Benvenisti writes:

> In the days of the Second Temple . . . the Jews ruled over the Judean Plain. Along the coast they built great cities, whose impressive remains amaze us even today. . . . When the Temple was destroyed, the remnant of Israel migrated en masse from the hills to the Judean Plain, where a well-developed Jewish community lived, rooted in the land and possessing great houses of learning. . . . Following the Bar Kochba Rebellion, the community on the Judean Plain was destroyed. . . . Once again there was nothing to stop the shifting sands, which inexorably covered the fertile fields. Wandering tribes from the South and from Egypt moved about the area grazing their herds in the river valleys. A few of them worked plots of land, and poor villages arose. . . . The people of the villages did not succeed in improving on the conditions of nature. They knew not the riches concealed in the fertile land nor

> the wealth of water hidden there. . . . Such was the state of the Judean Plain for many years, until our brothers came and conquered its desolation and transformed it into a fertile land, rich in citrus groves and vegetable gardens, with scores of flourishing settlements. And the blessing they brought was upon the Arab villages in their vicinity as well.[5]

"There are two categories of Arab villages," writes Benvenisti,

> villages most of whose land belongs to rich men (in Arabic they call them effendis, from the Turkish for "lords") who live mainly in the cities, and villages where most of the land belongs to the peasant-farmers themselves. The parcels of land owned by the rich men are worked by tenant-farmers and planted with citrus groves. Some of these villages have well-developed economies thanks to the influence of neighboring Jewish agricultural settlements, and some do not. The villages are poor-looking, barren of trees. The houses are quite crowded together. Each house has a courtyard surrounded with windowless rooms built adjacent to one another, as well as a chicken coop, grain store-rooms, etc.

Not a word is said about the inhabitants of the villages, their lives, or their culture. No wonder Stavsky's 400-page book opened up a whole new universe for Jewish youth, at least for those who bothered to read it.

NOBLE SAVAGES AND LAZY PEASANTS

It is worth noting that in 1946, the year both of these books were published, hundreds of thousands of Arab villagers lived on the Coastal Plain (the region described in both books), inhabiting more than a hundred villages, and most of the region's citrus groves belonged to them. The way in which Jewish authors dealt with these facts was to categorize the Arab inhabitants of the country according to subethnic or religious groupings, thereby fragmenting the Arab majority into segments whose small size would obscure the numerical inferiority of the Jewish minority. David Benvenisti describes the Arab residents of the Galilee as follows:

> In the Galilee, more than in any other region of our land, one finds peasant-farmers of a variety of ethnic and geographical origins. Besides the Muslim Arabs, whose religion is that of the majority of peasant-farmers (*fallahin*) in our country, the following are also to be found: The Druze—a courageous people, hardworking and freedom-loving; they value order and cleanliness. The Mutawallis [obsolete name for Shiʿites] . . . ; they are not easy to get to know, but if one approaches them cautiously and with a positive attitude it is possible to develop ties of friendship with them. The Circassians . . . excel

> at maintaining the health of their bodies . . . and are considered to be industrious workers. Their villages differ from those of the other *fallahin,* in that their houses are well-built and clean. . . . [There are also] Christian *fallahin* . . . [whose situation] is better than that of their [Muslim] comrades, whom they surpass educationally and economically.

Here we have not only a convenient fragmentation of the Arab population but also a ranking system according to which the Muslims—who constitute the overwhelming majority—are on the bottom rung. This patronizing attitude, based on a sense of European superiority, reflects Zionist pretensions regarding the "progress" that the Jews would bring to the "backward" East, and especially to the Muslim peasant-farmer—lazy, dirty, ignorant, and disease-ridden.

Much as this variation on the theme of the "white man's burden" appears insupportable from the perspective of half a century, it at least relates to the Arab peasant without blatantly racist connotations. On the other hand, a Knowing the Land textbook by J. Paporish, also published in 1946, classifies the Arabs according to overtly racial criteria: "The racial mixture of the country's inhabitants is obvious from the color of their skin, their facial features, their build, etc. Among both *fallahin* and city-dwellers different shades of skin-color can be found, ranging from Negro [*sic*] to the very light skin color of the people of the northern countries."[6] The Arab peasant-farmer earned a low rating according to these racial criteria: his origins "are not purely Arab [i.e., Arabian] from a racial [*sic*] point of view," whereas the Bedouin is highly praised: "The Bedouin are the purest Arabs, because they haven't mixed with foreigners; they therefore embody the type closest to that of the ancient Semitic population." Their likeness to the ancient Semites makes them descendants of the same stock to which the ancient Hebrews belonged, and thus blood relations of the Jews.

Their purported racial similarity to the Jews is just one factor contributing to the closeness and affection toward the Bedouin nurtured by Zionist writings. The Bedouin was the "noble savage" in the literature of Knowing the Land: strong of spirit, freedom-loving, satisfied with little, preserving the ways of the ancient Hebrews and the biblical lifestyle, loyal to leader and tribe—in short, a worthy role model for the early Zionist pioneers, who did indeed copy his dress, weaponry, and manner of riding Arabian horses. But there was an additional aspect to this admiration for the noble son of the desert: by endowing the Bedouin—the "pure Arab"—with positive traits, the Zionists also reinforced the image of all Arabs as sons of the desert. Some—the *fallahin,* who weren't "pure Arabs" in any case—had become slightly domesticated when they abandoned the nomadic lifestyle, but their real character would eventually show itself, and then the true contrast between the desert savage and the civilized Jew, who made the desert bloom, would be revealed.

The classical Zionist narrative—the war of the barbarous desert against progress and development—was able to accommodate the Bedouin, who wandered the desolate expanses with his herds. But of course only until the Zionists began "to make the desert bloom"; then they would banish him to the barren wilderness, where he would continue to be an object of their affection, though as an exotic, external element. The identification of the Bedouin with the desert—the absolute antithesis of settled land—ignored the fact that tens of thousands of Bedouin had always lived in the heart of the fertile regions of the country and had nothing to do with the nomadic life of the desert. In fact, the differentiation between the Bedouin and the *fallah* was altogether unclear, and the distinctions were altered to suit changing Zionist ideological and political requirements.

The Arab was "not only the son of the desert but also the father of the desert," in the famous words of Major C. S. Jarvis—the British governor of Sinai—which were adopted by the Zionists. And thus the *fallahin*—tillers of the soil for generation upon generation—could easily be transformed into "bloodthirsty desert savages," who not only sought to annihilate the Jewish community but also were guilty of turning Eretz Israel—flowing with milk and honey—into desolate desert. In the textbooks for courses in Knowing the Land, the Arabs are portrayed as being responsible for the ecological ruin of the entire country: they destroyed the ancient farming terraces, thereby causing soil erosion and exposing bare mountain rock; because of them the streams were blocked and the coastal valley became a land of malarial swamps; their goats ravaged the ancient forests that had covered the Land; with their violent feuds and their murderous hostility toward all agents of progress, they turned the Land into a perpetual battlefield.

Hence the Zionists did not rob the country's inhabitants of their land; they redeemed it from desolation. The Jewish pioneer battled not the Arab *fallah* but the forces of nature. The Zionists had no quarrel with the *fallah,* and no one wanted to dispossess him; after all—so the narrative goes—there's room in the land for everyone. And anyway, the Arabs are part of the natural fauna, and their villages and culture are just background, part of the picturesque landscape. Their way of life is worthy of preservation as a part of the environment, like an exotic ornament of anthropological interest, as well as living testimony to the way of life of our ancient forebears. But should the savage desert urge reawaken in the *fallahin,* causing them to violently attack the peace-loving Jewish community, then the battle between the desert and civilization will be renewed in all its force, and the "sons of light" will prevail.

Some scholars discern differing emphases in the attitudes of Zionists of various periods toward the Arab landscape—physical and human. In the early days of Zionist colonization, European presumptions of superiority and disdain for the "natives" predominated. When socialist Zionism became the predominant influence in the Jewish community and its educational system, a humanitarian-paternalistic approach was stressed, which on the one hand depicted the impoverishment of the Arabs sympathetically and on the other stressed how the Zionist project would benefit the local population, "and the blessing would be upon them also." When the Arab Revolt broke out in 1936, emphasis was placed on the murderous nature of the sons of the wilderness, and complaints proliferated concerning the ungratefulness of the Arabs—who instead of thanking the Zionists for the development they had brought to the Land, were paying them back with the destruction of what they had built and the uprooting of what they had planted.

"JUST LIKE OUR FOREBEARS"

These shifts in emphasis, however, reflected not only changing political and security conditions but also differences in factional coloration within the Zionist political and educational systems, and all were expressed to some extent in all periods. For example, the romanticization of the Arab never totally disappeared—the perception of the *fallah* as a son of the land, rooted in its landscape and tried by its hardships, and, as such, an example to the Jewish immigrants who sought to become "natives" in their new homeland, and to their native-born offspring. And because an excessively close identification with the Arabs was problematic, a legitimate pretext was found for learning about the way of life of the *fallah*. David Benvenisti and Pinhas Cohen comment: "He preserves ancient practices such as customs regarding home and family, food and drink, the ethic of hospitality, ways of working, linguistic expressions, etc. These can be considered as authoritative sources in the reconstruction of the life of our ancient forebears and have the power to shed light on obscure biblical and linguistic topics."[7]

Observing the *fallah*'s way of life and drawing comparisons between it and life in biblical times became tremendously popular with European scholars and travelers alike, especially the clergy among them, and many books described the strong connections between the lifeways of the *fallah* and biblical traditions. A typical book was *Village Life in Palestine,* penned in 1907 by Rev. G. Robinson Lees, the vicar of Saint Andrew's Church in Lambeth (a borough of London), which went into a second edition.[8] Lees describes several aspects in the life of the fallah, and beside each description appears the appropriate biblical reference. Many of these references are intended to confirm writings from the New Testament. For example, Lees describes the Arab village guard who stands on the roof of the tallest house and peers into the distance, exactly as written in the Gospel of Matthew: "Let him which is on the housetop not come down to take anything out of his house" (24:17). The Arab infant is swaddled in diapers, so tightly that he cannot move, just like Jesus in the manger: "Ye shall find the babe wrapped in swaddling clothes, lying in a manger" (Luke 2:12).

Of course, modern Hebrew writers did not make use of passages such as these, nor did they place an emphasis on "confirmation of the truth of the Bible [as] supplied by the life of the people in the land of the Bible," the aim of the Anglican priest's book. For Jewish scholars, the biblical contexts served as a means for reinforcing claims to ownership of the ancient homeland: the preservation of the way of life of the ancient Jews confirmed, in their opinion, that the connection between the Jewish people and its land had never been severed. This interpretation also implied that the Arabs were the descendants of Jews who did not go into exile, but instead changed their religion. Yitzhak Ben-Zvi—an ethnographer and Ben-Gurion's partner in the leadership of the Jewish workers' movement (the Histadrut) and the Yishuv (the pre-state Jewish community), an active member of the Governmental Naming Committee, and eventually president of the State of Israel—displayed a particular interest in any local customs that hinted at the possibility of the fallahin's having Jewish ancestry. Ben-Zvi tells of numerous families from the villages in the Hebron Hills and the mountainous area around Jerusalem where traditions of Jewish origin were preserved. He even recounts how a member of one of these families, Sheikh Abu ʿAyash (a sheikh is a Muslim religious leader), was hanged in the Gaza city square in 1948, having been accused of "being of Jewish descent, and therefore, 'of course,' spying for the Israelis."[9] With this story, Ben-Zvi sought to establish that the idea of the Jewish origin of the fallahin was not a Jewish invention.

Ben-Zvi gathered every available scrap of information that suggested the existence of Jewish fallahin living in mixed Jewiṣh-Arab villages throughout the recorded history of Eretz Israel and came to the following conclusion: "There was not a single moment in our history when the ties binding the whole nation to its homeland, by virtue of its presence there, were severed; the delicate strands of the remnant of the ancient Jewish community were a tangible, living expression of this bond."[10] The ties to the Land, and especially to the soil and agriculture, were of utmost significance to the Zionist faction with which Ben-Zvi was affiliated: This was "the connection between the laboring Jewish nation and its land"—the indissoluble bond nurtured by the Zionist pioneers, who had forsaken the Diaspora and the city and had dedicated their lives to making a land that had lain desolate for generations bloom by means of backbreaking agricultural labor in collective settlements. The Jewish youth who had been educated in the love of his homeland through grueling treks in the desert, the planting of forests, and training in agriculture would be taken by his teachers to the village of Peqiʿin (Buqeah in Arabic) in the Upper Galilee, where he would meet members of the Jewish Zenati family. This family "had never deserted this remote Druze-Christian-Muslim village" (according to "tradition," as propagated principally by Ben-Zvi himself) and therefore were living proof of the "connection that had never been severed," whose preservation necessitated the loosing of others' ties. Thus the mental map became firmly established not only in physical space but also in time, and the white patches covering the Arab communities and their inhabitants infiltrated the stratum of history as well.

A VIRGIN LANDSCAPE

One way of dealing with this disturbing human presence, and with the conflicts it created, was to relate to the landscape as if it had not been disturbed by any man-made covering at all, Jewish or Arab. The obsession with the pristine, virgin landscape made it possible to express endless love for the hills and plains of the homeland without the object of this love being able to react, since it was mute, inert matter. S. Yizhar, whose literary works describe the complexities and contradictions of the native Israeli soul, from the beginnings of its formation to the present, writes:

> And all the weight of the ancient earth is hidden by a hazy dust, a void, nebulous but real and one, full and dark blue, that comes to an end right at this line above which lies all the emptiness of the heavens, the fullness of their totally empty, mighty dome. . . . And suddenly there awakens in it, in the palm of the hand, the desire to move it lightly and touch it slowly, slowly until totally infatuated. It caresses the back of this roundness slowly and with desire, up and down, as if it were the back of a young foal or the body of a young girl. . . . In this total nakedness, all of her completely flattened, supine, naked—with nothing on, to the edge of the low horizon that is not yet clothed; nothing growing, no evergreen-cones or houses or anything on it, and only the line of backs running there, exposed, and one part . . . only rising agilely and bending nimbly, like the back of a horse, like the body of a young girl, like infinity.

The narrator strokes the landscape with an erotic caress, and the landscape surrenders itself to him. But the narrator also puts words into the mouth of the landscape:

> As if an understanding takes hold of you suddenly—which may [simply] be nothing but a fundamental error—that perhaps this land does not want us at all, not really. . . . And that the expanses of the plain back there, too, need to remain big and empty and without anything on them and even almost no dust—just alone, gigantic, open, and empty, without anything on them, no tree and no shade and no road, and only perhaps a few abandoned herds of sheep here or goats there, that one doesn't notice and which are swallowed up in the perfect infiniteness; and perhaps also a humble Arab village that doesn't change anything and doesn't compel it to make any change; and time passes and does not leave any signs on it.[11]

These words, published in 1992, describe the landscape of Israel in the author's distant youth. By the time they were written, not one bit of this virgin landscape remained; his yearning for the empty horizon, unspoiled and unsullied by human hands, conveys much nostalgia but also the desire to escape from a cruel history, which has memorialized human conflicts on the face of the landscape. Yizhar would also be the writer to describe, with a sharp pen and great empathy, the tragedy of "the humble Arab village," as we shall see below.

In 1988 Meir Shalev's book *Roman Rusi* (A Russian Novel) was published by Am Oved in Tel Aviv.[12] This young author—a third-generation descendent of the pioneers of the Jezreel Valley, who drained the malarial swamps and in their place founded a flourishing *moshav ovdim* (workers cooperative settlement)—is obsessed with the moist and verdant landscape of north-central Israel. He reveals an astonishing mastery of "the scent stations of the deer and the sticky nets of the orb weaver in the rockrose, . . . all kinds of tractors and species of fruit, wild flowers, and the colors of orchids."[13] Shalev faithfully describes the mythical world and way of life of the first Zionist pioneers in the valley, and perhaps for this reason he hardly touches on the existence of Arabs.

Almost the only point of contact between the book's narrator, Baruch Shenhar, and Arabs is the murder of his parents "by Arab raiders [who] threw a bomb into their house." " 'In the diaspora too, the Jewish people spills its blood,' . . . the village newsletter . . . [said in reference to the murder of Baruch's] parents. 'Yet there Jewish blood is as pointless in death as in life. Here there is meaning to both our lives and our deaths, because our Homeland and our Freedom call to us.' " The settlers consoled themselves, and "the village got over the tragedy."[14] This tragic event was but a fleeting episode in the lives of both the village and the narrator.

A JEWISH BUBBLE

The lives of the settlers in the Jezreel Valley were conducted inside a Jewish "bubble," and their only contacts with the outside world were with neighboring Jewish communities, with Jews living in the city, and with the English. Shalev, the third-generation pioneer, is not enslaved to the Zionist myths, and he puts disparaging words about them in the mouths of several of his elderly characters: "We may have drained the swamps," says old Pinness, "but the mud we discovered beneath them was far worse. Man's bond with the earth, man's union with Nature—is there anything more regressive and bestial? We raised a new generation of Jews who were no longer alienated and downtrodden, a generation of farmers linked to the land, a society of the grossest, most quarrelsome, most narrow-minded, most thick-skinned and thick-headed peasants!"[15]

Pinness's claim to fame lay in his discovery of a cave, containing prehistoric human skeletons, on the land of his village. After finding the remains of "our ancient forbears," he hastened to leave the cave: "He sat in the entrance looking down on the broad, obeisant, fertile Valley at his feet. The humble cabins of the village . . . suddenly seemed to float on the fallow, long-historied earth, bobbing on its countless strata." "Canaanites, Turkmens, white wagtails, Jews, Romans, wild goats, Arabs, swamp cats, German children, Damascene cows, and English soldiers had vied to leave their prints in the crumbling and amnesiac soil." Pinness "felt the futility of all things" and envied his comrade Meshulam, "who, caring nothing for the long pinions of Time, chose to follow its winged flight only from the day the founding fathers first alit in the Valley. . . . Meshulam is convinced that it was the founders of the village who drove away the cavemen and the swamp flora. . . . He thinks the earth just sat here waiting for them, trembling like a bashful bride." Pinness mocks the Zionist perception that the land had been waiting for the return of the Jewish people: "'And for whom? For whom? Waiting for whom?' (from an Israeli children's song) chanted the old teacher in a thin, mocking voice. . . . 'Why it's nothing but a tissue of poor fictions anyway, the earth! . . . The earth cheated on us,' he informed me with a salacious smile. 'She wasn't the virgin we thought she was.'"[16] But "the flight of time," according to Pinness, the skeptic and cynic, passes over his Arab neighbors (who, in his opinion, are simply a transient episode in the historical continuum, somewhere between "swamp cats" and "Damascene cows"), and he doesn't describe just what the earth had been doing "in the meantime"—she who "wasn't a virgin" and hadn't waited, but had been worked by downtrodden Arab tenant farmers and Bedouin shepherds, and had been sold to the Jews by her owners, rich Arab merchants from Beirut, in whose eyes she was nothing but a worthless commodity. Meir Shalev describes old Pinness's envy of prehistoric man, "who had wandered to this guileless land . . . to find it unpossessed and unscarred by the petty footprints of human loyalty and love." No wonder that when Pinness put an end to his life, he returned to the cave of prehistoric man and "fell headlong, tumbling among the slivers as dozens of tons of earth from distant glacial epochs buried him with the antediluvian bones of his ancestors."[17]

Shalev's mockery of the Zionist myths and of the yearning for "the guileless land . . . unscarred by the petty footprints of human loyalty and love"—Jewish or Arab—is apparent to only the small minority of Israelis who know how to read between the lines. For most of his readers, and especially for those who read the book in translation, the life of the Zionist village might just as well have been transplanted to Australia, New England, or South Africa, with, of course, the changes necessitated by the different physical landscape and cultural background of the settlers. His magic realism places them floating over the surface of "the fallow, long-historied earth," thereby enabling the Hebrew reader to weave them into his or her pattern of disregard for the Arab landscape.

Sociologist Oz Almog, in his study of the sabra (native-born Israeli), sums up:

> The verbal erasure [of the Arab villages] is reflected in compositions by sabras of all ages writing about hikes and trips. . . . The Arab villages and their inhabitants are hardly mentioned at all. The Arab village appears mainly as a lifeless landmark, or a place to stop to get food and water, or a dangerous place that one must beware of. Sometimes the landscape is described as virgin land, upon which no one lived until the arrival of the Jews.[18]

"SCIENTIFIC" ERASURE

The white patches that covered the Arab communities have received exact, "objective and scientific" mapping in research papers and academic textbooks prepared by Israeli geographers and teachers. In 1996 the Open University published a self-study text for a course leading to a B.A. degree, entitled *Spatial Experiments: Settlement Geography of Eretz Israel.* "In the course before us," states the introduction, "we shall focus on the study of various phenomena associated with places of habitation of human groups. The territorial unit that will serve as a case study is Eretz Israel, and the period of time we shall concern ourselves with is from the mid–nineteenth century onward." The exact significance of the general designations "human groups," "territorial unit," and "period of time" becomes increasingly clear as the course unfolds. The first part deals with the development of the "patterns of settlements" of the Jewish population and, to a lesser degree, with the development of "patterns of settlement" in general in the face of the "increasing influence of the European presence." The designers of the course describe in great detail every "spatial experiment" undertaken by the Jewish "human group," and explain the development and consolidation of the landscape into blocks of Zionist settlement communities. The other "patterns of settlement," that is, the Arab communities, which encompassed six times as much territory as the blocks of Jewish settlement scattered among them, don't even rate the designation "human group." The description of the Arab communities is restricted to a discussion of mixed cities and their development "in the face of the European presence." The entire configuration of Arab rural settlement, with its hundreds of villages, remained anonymous, perhaps because no intentional "spatial experiments" took place there, just normal evolutionary development. These white patches supposedly belonged neither to the "territorial unit" of Eretz Israel nor to "the period of time" discussed in the course.

The student learns not one bit about this unidentified "settlement configuration," nor even about the points of contact between the Arab and Zionist landscapes, as if the Jewish enclaves were floating in the air. But the designers of the course were obliged to make some reference to the Arab "configuration": After all, the Zionist "spatial experiments" were carried out in reaction to challenges set by the Arabs by their very presence and by the assortment of means they employed with the intent of thwarting the "Zionist experiment." The course treated the Arab configuration like an object worthy of attention only in relation to its influence on the Zionist project, but not as a subject in and of itself deserving of examination—even though without at least a minimal knowledge of it, an understanding of the processes taking place in the Jewish sector was impossible: "Among the considerations leading to the preference for the Lower Galilee [for Jewish settlement], which was not densely populated by Arabs—among whom demand for land there was slight, due to a hostile natural environment—were low prices and the fact that the land was owned by city-dwelling families in Beirut." The student learns that the success of the Zionist spatial experiment owed much to the backwardness of the Arab sector. Everything pertaining to the acquisition of available land was examined subject to a cost-benefit analysis:

> The valleys and plains had an obvious advantage [for the Jews]: both in the valleys and on the plains, large tracts of land were in the hands of a small number of owners. In large part these were absentee landlords, whose land was worked by tenants who had no interest in improving the soil. This circumstance lowered the value of these properties and made them a burden to their owners, who had to invest in their drainage and improvement. However, for the potential buyers [the Zionists], they became attractive for this very reason. . . . On the Coastal Plain things were different . . . [there], small strips of land were divided among numerous owners, most of them *fallahin* who lived on their land.[19]

These geographical, economic, and demographic data on the Arab sector are supposed to be sufficient for the students taking the course. The economic and social processes that took place within this sector are defined as "external constraints that left their mark on the Zionist settlement effort" and obliged its initiators "to search for new ways" of spatial experimentation—but these constraints are not elaborated on.

The building of the Zionist "pattern of settlement" is described in terms of economic and geographical planning, whereas the Arab configuration is portrayed in political and military terms:

> Extreme anxiety regarding British support for the activity of the Zionist movement . . . exacerbated the anti-Zionist tendencies of the country's Arab leadership. In the beginning this trend expressed itself in petitions and speeches, but very soon it also took on a violent aspect, [which at first] was local in character [and afterward developed into] guerrilla warfare by the Arabs against the British regime and the Jewish settler community.[20]

The student still has received no data on the Arab community, but at this stage there is no longer any point in describing this "territorial unit," which is now perceived as lying behind enemy lines.

The situation in Palestine from 1936 onward is defined by the course's designers as one of "quasi-war": "Political changes and cultural and economic differences create quasi-war conflicts. . . . These conflicts have spatial consequences, especially on the regional or local level, such as the evacuation of border areas . . . and the limited destruction of urban and rural districts and infrastructure." From the moment "quasi-war" was declared, it was possible to cease defining Zionist settlement activity as "the conquest of the desert," and the spatial experiments were transformed into "a central means for gaining control of new territory": "The use of this means for the attainment of territorial and strategic objectives typifies quasi-belligerent situations. With no possibility of employing a regular military force possessing heavy firepower, a method that is nonmilitary in character, such as settlement, serves as a means for attaining these objectives." The first part of the text for the geography course concludes, at any rate, with a description of the Zionist settlement plan prepared by the general staff of the Haganah (the Jewish underground militia), the objective of which was to prepare for the eventuality when the "quasi-war" would turn into an actual war, the War of 1948.

The diligent student thus reached 1948, when the white patches had become embedded in his consciousness and their boundaries were transformed into the front lines of the war. It would not be difficult for him to adapt to the situation created in the wake of that war, when the white patches on his mental map became empirical fact with the eradication of the Arab community from the real landscape. And perhaps this was the reason that the designers of the geography course (the textbook for which was published in 1996) did not deal with the Arab settlement configuration: in any case it no longer existed, so why occupy students with something that had vanished, especially since mentioning it and analyzing the causes of its disappearance were liable to be thought of as espousal of a political position? And so the destroyed Arab communities are placed outside the definitions of "human group," "territorial unit," or "period of time"—retroactively, as if they had never existed. The "Israelization of Palestinian geography" would eventually become the subject of heated controversy between Palestinian and Israeli geographers, as will be described later.

MILITARY INTELLIGENCE

But what is permissible for academics often is forbidden for military men. On army maps, enemy territory must not remain terra incognita. And indeed, the information concerning the Arab settlement configuration, which accumulated in the hands of Jewish intelligence personnel, was comprehensive, verifiable, and reliable. Perusal of this information is interesting not only in and of itself but also because it shows us what the Jews were interested in knowing about the Arab communities and what sort of picture emerged from the knowledge they had amassed, selective as it necessarily was.

Relatively few studies were published based on information that had been gathered regarding the Arab communities. During all the years of the British Mandate, fewer than ten books on the subject were written in the Hebrew language. These included works by "Arabists," who presented a positive picture of rural life, and others in which the backwardness and miserable conditions of the village were stressed. Particular interest in the Arab villages was displayed by experts in matters of land acquisition and agriculture employed by the Zionist organizations. They studied the Palestinian land tenure system, farming methods, and economy so as to identify opportunities for acquisition of land by the Jewish National Fund (JNF) and to be able to respond to accusations regarding the dispossession of the *fallahin* as a consequence of Zionist settlement activity. Considerable material was also gathered by the British Mandatory government, both for administrative purposes and for the preparation of reports for various commissions of inquiry. Part of the official information was made public only on the eve of the termination of the Mandate.

The Yishuv's intelligence experts regarded the available material as dangerously inadequate. Those responsible for security proclaimed "a need to commence the systematic in-depth study of the Arab community of Eretz Israel/Palestine in all aspects of its life and livelihood."[21] In 1940 the preparation of "village dossiers" was begun; more than 100 had been compiled by 1945, when it was decided to revamp "the Arab Village Intelligence Operation." By the outbreak of the 1948 War, over 600 village dossiers had been completed.

"In May of 1944," recounts a patrol member of the Palmach, an elite Haganah formation,

> three crews of us went out . . . to prepare "dossiers." For "cover" we took with us botany books in Hebrew, German, and French, and divided them up among us: "We were botanists." . . . When we arrived at one of the villages, a crowd of villagers would gather and would not leave us alone until we left. And so we would prepare our sketches: at some interesting place, for example beside the mukhtar's house, I would gather the people, bend down and pick some plant, hold it up and show it to them: "Will you look at this plant?" . . . Then our people would go into the house, ask for water, and until the owner returned, would take note of the details of the house. . . . At the end of the trip we would sit down to relax and while resting—we would write the summary of what we'd seen on the way or corrections of our notes.

In the case of many of the reports it can be surmised that the information gathered originated with Arab informers and was later translated into Hebrew. "We have had the opportunity to penetrate the depths of the Arab village and to obtain the smallest details of its way of living such that we have acquired quite a full picture of village life," boasts Ezra Danin, one of those who headed the village dossier project. Examples from these reports will prove the correctness of his words.

The General Survey of the Villages of the Acre Subdistrict of April 1943 is given here in its entirety, followed by an example of one village dossier, both quoted verbatim (with minor typographical corrections).

> GENERAL SURVEY OF THE VILLAGES IN THE ACRE SUBDISTRICT, 10 APRIL 1943
>
> *Antiquities* Most of the villages in the Acre subdistrict are ancient and are built on ruins so old that the inhabitants themselves do not know anything about the history of their villages. In most of the villages that are built on ruins, the inhabitants have found antiquities while digging wells or constructing buildings and have hidden everything that they discovered or have sold it secretly to antique dealers. What has been discovered up to now: ancient crosses, jewelry, and gems, which they sold cheaply. They don't dare reveal these antiquities to the [Mandatory] government for fear of being held liable [for their removal]. They believe that in most of these villages there are valu-

able antiquities that are still concealed within the earth. And when you ask someone about his land—whether it is on the site of a ruin—he will answer that he has a valuable treasure [there]. At various times Jews have come to the villagers and asked them to show them the locations of some ruins in exchange for monetary payment, and the villagers have refused to show them.

Water sources As to the supply of water in the villages, it is still as nature has provided since ancient times, and only in a very few vicinities have they improved it. Thus, most of the villagers have depended on rain water and have dug cisterns for this purpose. They do not know the amount of water they have, but they know that a given cistern provides for their needs. A man who requires more water digs a second and a third cistern, until he satisfies his own needs and those of his family and his herds.

Roads The roads inside the villages are generally unpaved, unless the village has a local council that sees to their paving. Even if they have, the dirt and lack of care is conspicuous. Were it not for the government's tending to the paving of major thoroughfares, the situation of the villages would be extremely bad.

Construction in the villages The buildings in the villages are generally ancient. Building materials are usually stone and mud brick and ceilings are of wood, some with ancient arches. Lately, in the past ten years or slightly more, some wealthy villagers have started building stone structures with reinforced concrete ceilings. But these are few in relation to the total number of houses.

Agriculture The principal agricultural pursuits in this subdistrict are the cultivation of unirrigated field crops, olives and tobacco, sheepherding, and raising citrus fruit on land through which water passes or where there are springs of plentiful flowing water. As to chickens; these are scarce these days in all the villages because of an epidemic that has hit them for the past two years. There are no special pens for the raising of livestock, yet each family has a few sheep of its own and ten to twenty chickens on which they subsist.

Landless villagers Many of the villagers have a house but no land. They work for the families that have large landholdings for a yearly wage or by leasing land in exchange for a third or half [of the harvest]. In this manner such families eke out their livelihood by raising a few sheep and some other livestock.

Improvements No fundamental improvement has been made in agriculture or in the raising of sheep in these villages as a whole, because of the poverty of the Arab peasant farmer and because he has not learned the fundamentals of technology.

Interfamilial relations Most village families are not understanding of one another, and although there are no important disputes between them, such as incidents of murder or violations of honor or quarrels over land, there is jealousy in matters of honor, leadership, and wealth. . . . The poor man envies the rich man his wealth, waiting for the opportunity to rise up to steal it or to get even with him: Some poor men [in a village] know that so-and-so is a respected member of the community and has money, and two or three of them come to an agreement among themselves, attack him, and rob him of whatever they can get their hands on. This is almost a daily occurrence in the villages of the Acre subdistrict.

Political leanings of the villagers The inhabitants of the villages in the Acre subdistrict are mostly extreme in their politics: they revere Haj Amin al-Husseini and exploit every opportunity to make their feelings obvious. And anyone who was injured bodily or whose property was damaged [during the disturbances of 1936–39] awaits the return of Haj Amin, who will compensate them for what they lost or sacrificed for the sake of the rebellion.

Regarding the stance taken by the *Christians,* I can say that half their number lean toward the policies of Haj Amin and the other half despise him. The *Druze* follow the man of the hour. During the disturbances, they would go with the rebels and hand them whatever they needed and relate to them affectionately. They even produced a few rebels, contrary to the wishes of their leaders and clergy. But when the government forces appeared in the Druze villages during the disturbances, they would go along with them and their policies. So they emerged from the disturbances having pleased both sides. In any case, Druze policy is to follow the stronger side.

Schools Most of the schools in the villages are at the elementary level and are very backward in their teaching methods.

Trades Most of the shop owners in the villages earn a living, aside from their commercial enterprises, from some land that belongs to them and from dealing in sheep.

Madafehs (guest houses) In these villages it is still the custom that the larger families have private guest houses. In villages that do not have *madafehs* of this sort, the *mukhtar* will maintain a *madafeh* for extending hospitality to strangers.

Contacts with Jews Some villagers used to have connections with Jews to whom they lent assistance in land speculation. When the disturbances broke out, there began a period of revenge against those who had aided the Jews; the help ceased, and many of those who had assisted Jews fled their villages. But now helping the Jews has returned in a big way, out of a lust for material gain. I believe that every Arab in these villages, of whatever sort (i.e., religious or class background) or viewpoint, can be bought.

Relations with the authorities The villagers' relations with the government and police are currently good, because money and graft fill an important role these days. All traces of several important court cases were erased, and they were settled to the satisfaction of whoever had paid bribes.

Debt Instances of debt and lending at interest are few in the villages, because the financial situation of the *fallah* is now good, and he feels that interest would weigh upon him, and so keeps his distance from loans—except for fools who have no trade but have fields or goats and lend at interest to satisfy their greed.

Weapons Regarding the smuggling of arms: There was not a hint of it left at the conclusion of the disturbances [of 1936–39], due to fear of the government. But today the practice has returned to a large extent. Most of those involved in smuggling are Syrians or Lebanese who operate via agreements with inhabitants of border villages. No one among the villagers can state what quantities of weapons there are, but everyone believes that there is no house without arms and ammunition.

ABU ZUREIK (HAIFA SUBDISTRICT), 7 JANUARY 1943

General information The name of the village of Abu Zureik (zureik=magpie) commemorates a local saint who is buried there. His grave is inside the village, with a simple structure over it. It was there before the village was built. Abu Zureik is located a third of the way between Kibbutz Hazoreʿa and Kibbutz Mishmar Haʿemeq, on the slopes of the hills south of the road. The fields are in the valley on the other side of the road. The village is built in a scattered fashion, and the houses are constructed from local stone. According to the 1922 census, 301 members of the Tawhashe hamula of the Arab Turkmen (Turkmen nomadic) tribe live in Abu Zureik, 142 males and 159 females; today about 500 souls, in 80 families.

Historical information Today Abu Zureik is the home of the al-Tawhashe hamula, one of seven Turkmen hamulas. All of them are Sunni Muslims. According to the traveler Volney (1775), Turkmens could be found in all of the lands surrounding the Caspian Sea, in Armenia, Asia Minor, Syria, and the Palestine. Their language is Turkic. They live like Arab Bedouin, organized in tribes. Their estimated number in Syria and Palestine at that time was 30,000. They are all Muslim, but apathetic in religious matters. In 1878 Claude Conder wrote in the PEF quarterly that "The Turkmens are of a distinct race, resembling most closely the Kurds. However, few of them still speak their original language; most of them are Arabic speaking."

Today the people of Abu Zureik think of themselves as Arabs, without being able to explain the meaning of the name Turkmen. According to a legend current among the villagers, one of their families is of Jewish origin. Another family, according to them, is made up of descendants of the saint, Abu Zureik al-ʿAttili, who was originally from the village of ʿAttil (which is between Nablus and Hadera). They have no recollection of the fact that they once spoke a language other than Arabic. Perhaps this is influenced, consciously or unconsciously, by the desire to eradicate all memory of their non-Arab origins.

There are four black families in the village, who may have come with the armies of the Egyptian Ibrahim Pasha in the previous century. Or they may be the descendants of purchased slaves of Bedouins. Two brothers from one of these families (Abu ʿOthman and Abu Jumʿaa) work as laborers with the Public Works Department on the road between Wadi Qasab and Yoqneam.

On PEF maps and records from 1878, Abu Zureik appears, not as a place of habitation, but simply as a spring. On the other hand there are accounts of Turkmens living in the caves of Qira. According to what people from the village say, until the previous [i.e., First] world war they were nomads, who since then have settled and built the village. The first house, that of Samur al-ʿIsa, was built a short time before the war. The second was the home of ʿAbd al-Karem ʿAbd al-Shitawi, built during the war.

According to an unclear bit of village tradition, the tribe has relatives in Transjordan. They also talk about kinship with the tribe of Bani Sakhr. The basis in fact to this contention is that they certainly were under the rule of the Sakhrites in the days when the latter ruled over all the valley.

Economy and farming The area of the village land is some 4,000 dunams. Officially, all of the land is mushʿa (communally owned). It remained mushʿa even after the last [Mandatory] "Land Settlement" in 1941. In actuality everyone works the same plot on a permanent basis and thinks of himself as its owner. The reason for this arrangement (as stated by the villagers themselves): In this way they enjoy the advantages of both *mulk* [private ownership] and *mushʿa* [communal ownership] at the same time. Each one has a permanent plot of land, but no one has a title deed, and there's no chance that someone will sell any village land to the Jews or to Arab land-dealers.

There are landless families in the village. The other families each have between half a feddan and four feddan (One feddan=about 200 dunams), an average of perhaps three feddan. Diab al-ʿIsa has four feddan; Fahd al-Tay, two feddan; ʿAbd Shitawi, 40 kil or 1.5 feddan; Sahanus has a little less; ʿAbd al-Halaq Shabbash, half a feddan.

Water There is a spring over which a well was constructed by the government. Its water irrigates vegetable gardens. In 1942 a plan was initiated to exploit the well on a larger scale by installing an electric pump and laying pipes. The plan is in the process of being implemented. The [size of] the area under irrigation is not known to me.

They raise winter and summer crops, as is usual among the *fallahin* of the valley. There is also tobacco and a few olive, apple, plum, etc. orchards. In recent years they have also attempted to grow potatoes; however, without success. They sell their surplus produce mainly at the Haifa market. In the village there are several horse-powered harvesters, which also do outside work, in other villages. This work is an important source of income. They don't fertilize their fields. Their planting schedule is as customary among the *fallahin* of the valley.

There are not many herds in the village. Some of the tribe's members still live in tents like Bedouin, and these have flocks of sheep. They have few cattle, generally just two or three cows providing milk for the needs of the household. There are also a few chickens for household use. There are no artisans in the village. The houses are built primarily by Druze from Daliyat al-Carmel. Abu Suleiman, a coppersmith from Damascus, lives in the village, but not all the time. There are two or three small shops. There are no motorized vehicles in the village. In general, the people of this village excel in terms of agricultural economy. They are diligent and skillful and their name as good workers precedes them. The village has a healthy socioeconomic base: There are neither extremely rich nor extremely poor people. Most have land and live from working their own plots. The land of this village is some of the best in the country.

Health and medical care The people of the village are generally healthy and robust. They have no medical services. In cases of illness they visit doctors in Haifa, and in recent years, more and more frequently the medical facilities of Mishmar Haʿemeq and especially Hazoreʿa (neighboring kibbutzim).

Culture Many in the village know how to read and write. In the younger generation the percentage of illiterates is not high. But children go to school for only two, three, or four years. Then the parents take them to work. There are no women in the village who know how to read and write and no girls studying. Not one of the villagers has studied or is studying at an urban school.

In 1935 or 1936 a school was built for the two villages of Abu Zureik and Abu Shusha on Abu Zureik land, near the Abu Shusha border. The building materials were donated by the people of the village, and labor by the government, as was usual. In 1940 there were about fifty pupils. In 1941 about the same number, in four classes. In 1942 (when this report was compiled) there are just three classes. Only the children of Abu Zureik attend this government school; the children of Abu Shusha go to Muhammad al-Tay's *kutab* [religious elementary school], which was in Abu Shusha until 1940 and is now in Qira. The teacher [at the government school] until September 1940 was Rahman Daʿas, who was then transferred to Yaffa (near Nazareth) and in his place came ʿAbd al-Rauf ʿAbushi from Jenin. The first teacher was a follower of the mufti; the new one does not express a political position, but seeks the company of Jews. He passed an additional government teachers' examination and studies a lot on his own, but his educational background is fairly poor, especially his secular education. He is pretty well liked by the children and successful in his work, as far as is possible in the existing circumstances. He has ties in Balad al-Sheikh, where he lived during the winter of 1939–40, and even now he visits there frequently. His wife lives there as well. He is about thirty-two years old and has no children. He studied in Jerusalem.

In 1938 a small mosque without dome or minaret was built. The first imam was Sheikh Asʿad from Umm al-Zinat. Now the imam is Sheikh ʿAmr, a man of Egyptian origin from Haifa; he studied at the school run by the French monks and afterward at a Muslim school in Haifa. He was born in 1905. His level of learning is poor and his horizons narrow. There is no Waqf property in the village.

There are no radios and they do not usually read newspapers.

Public and social matters In this village there are no practices that are out of the ordinary. In general one wife per man. Samur has two wives because the first bore him only daughters. Khalil al-Jalil has two wives because he "likes to get married." The villagers are not excessively aware politically. During the disturbances of 1936–39 its people were peaceful. On the whole they opposed the armed bands, but not actively. At the end of the disturbances there were some searches by the [British] army for weapons there, but they didn't turn up much. They haven't many weapons. People who opposed the armed bands: Diab, Daʿas, Hamad al-Hamad, the Abd al-Shitawi family, Dahnus, Fahd al-Tay. Those who supported them: the teacher Abd al-Rahim, the imam Sheikh Asʿad, Salah Hussein al-ʿAli, Moustafa al-ʿAwdi. The last-named handed over a French rifle and a pistol to the authorities at the end of the disturbances.

Hatred for the English is not as pronounced or as strong in this village as in others. ʿAbd al-Karem Shitawi speaks of them sympathetically. Of the Germans he speaks with hatred because of bad experiences with the settlers of Waldheim and Bethlehem-of-the-Galilee (neighboring Templar-German settlements). Up until about 1937 the *mukhtar* was Dahnus. He is a somewhat difficult man, but respected. After him ʿAbd al-Halaq al-Shabash was appointed. He is not one of the village "notables" and he hasn't much property. He leans toward sympathy with the armed bands and thinks that the Jews intend to expel the Arabs. He hasn't much influence in the village. In 1942 the village council was reelected with the same makeup as before: ʿAbd al-Faris Shitawi, Khalil Halayil, Fahd al-Tay, and one other. They are respected and peace-loving men. The richest people in the village are the brothers Diab and Samir al-ʿIsa. Respected but not liked—egoistic. Another respected man is Muhammad al-Hamed, in whose home numerous visitors gather. ʿAbd al-Karem's family includes six sons (of whom the eldest, Abdullah, and two others are married) and three daughters who are noteworthy for their diligent work and their good relations with everyone.

Contact with the Jewish community Most of their contact is with (Kibbutz) Hazoreʿa. Generally, good relations prevail between the two settlements. There are hardly any disputes between them. Economic relations: before the war they often had their work tools and household implements mended in the kibbutz machine and carpentry shops. As time went on, the kibbutz was forced to reduce the scope of this work due to a shortage of labor and materials. More than once the villagers asked kibbutz members for advice on agricultural matters as well as, for example, the purchase of a pump or the setting up of a grid of irrigation pipes. The people of the village also often enjoyed the benefit of medical assistance from the kibbutz for a small payment.

Social relations: mutual visitation; distribution of Haqiqat al-Amr [an Arabic-language newspaper of the Jewish Workers Federation—the Histadrut]; visits to the village school—one member of the kibbutz has begun studying Arabic with the village schoolteacher.

One cannot but insert here what befell this flourishing village in the 1948 War. Abu Zureik was utterly razed by the Israeli army, assisted by the village's kibbutz neighbors, with whom it had maintained such friendly relations. Benny Morris quotes a member of Kibbutz Hazoreʿa:

> When the village was occupied, its inhabitants fled and tried to save themselves by hiding in the fields. . . . there was an exchange of fire during which several Arabs were killed . . . and they were not members of the [armed] gangs . . . but defenseless *fallahin;* defeated. . . . Also, several men who were

hiding in the village were caught and killed, hours after the battle had ended. . . . Later they blew up all the village houses and the well.[22]

PALESTINIAN IGNORANCE

That the Arabs had little information in their hands from sources of their own was quite evident. When most of the Palestinian villages were destroyed during and following the 1948 War, and the Palestinians began to collect fragments of information on their vanished civilization (see chapter 6), they had no choice but to rely on data from the research done by the British and the Jews. Material from their own sources was extremely limited, and the alienation and lack of connectedness between the educated urban Arab population and the *fallahin* was so great that no serious attempt had been made to learn about the latter's way of life. Not only to the Jews but also to many urban Arabs—especially the intellectual and political leadership—the Arab village was something of a "white patch" and its inhabitants objects of disdainful mockery. This attitude of arrogant disregard toward the "primitive" and "ignorant" villagers was a decisive factor in the defeat of the Palestinians in 1948. After the defeat, many sought to atone for this attitude, and began publishing books and studies about the villages that had been obliterated. The Arab *fallah* has become the symbol of Palestinian nationalism. His tenacious holding on to the land, his dress, way of life, and folklore were extolled by urban intellectuals who found it handy to mobilize the Palestinian villager as the answer to the Zionist cult of "Knowing the Land." But in spite of all their efforts at gathering information from the refugees and from secondary sources, they were unable to hide the meagerness of their firsthand knowledge regarding the Palestinian rural landscape they wished to immortalize in their works. Emile Habibi, the greatest writer of the Palestinian community in the State of Israel, once wrote in his characteristically sarcastic manner: "We of Haifa used to know more about the villages of Scotland than we did about those of Galilee."[23] The paucity of research using Palestinian sources had disturbed Arab intellectuals and scholars, who acknowledge the fact that "there has been a dearth of sound historical scholarship by Palestinians."[24] Rashid Khalidi explains this deficiency in terms of historical circumstance, especially the fact that the Palestinians—lacking sovereignty—were vanquished in every war: all their archival materials were seized by the Jews or destroyed, and their research institutes were unable to function in exile or under Israeli rule. Data collection and research was, therefore, conducted by Israelis and Europeans who lacked "intimate familiarity" with the subject of their scholarship and who displayed biases and a lack of objectivity in their work. But the arrogance of Palestinian scholars who claim that the principal focus of research—"what happened on the village level"—was purposely obscured, and that "sources reflecting local reality disregarded" is expressed in the words of Rashid Khalidi himself: "The population of the countryside was poor, illiterate, and largely inaccessible for much of the modern era, and as such left few records of its own."[25]

This rural population was "inaccessible" to the city-dwelling Palestinian intellectuals but not to Jewish observers and Mandatory officials. And fifty years later, Palestinians are asserting that they are not allowed to tell their story, and Palestinian scholars are denouncing the Jews and the British, who took the trouble to gather and publish the data, as "biased." In 1991 the Institute of Palestine Studies published a facsimile edition of *A Survey of Palestine,* which was submitted to the Anglo-American Committee of Inquiry in 1946 and to the UN Special Commission on Palestine in 1947. This survey serves as an extremely important source for those seeking a summary of the period of the British Mandate. The objective of those who brought it out again in 1991 was to immortalize the Palestinian community as it was before its destruction in 1948. But how ironic it is that, at the time, the Palestinians boycotted the UN Special Commission and regarded the survey, when it was submitted, as part of a conspiracy against them. Now, fifty years afterward, they view this document as a "dispassionate source." Two generations late, the Palestinians have begun to attempt to make up for their backwardness, and even now they are compelled to depend on hostile sources, including Jewish intelligence operatives, from the pre-1948 years.

PALESTINIAN VILLAGES BEFORE 1948

Taken together, the data from the village dossiers and from numerous other sources, including Palestinian ones, lead us to an inescapable conclusion: with a few exceptions, the Palestinian landscape, the way of life of the rural population, the level of development of the rural economy, and the cultural life of the villages were not substantially different on the eve of the 1948 War from how they had been at the beginning of the British Mandate. The old descriptions of the traditional Arab village—with everything crammed together and congested, with its dead-end alleys lined with windowless houses constructed from local building materials, its inner courtyards where man and beast lived side by side, the few public buildings, and the poorly maintained access roads—was still relevant in the forties, as pointed out in a Mandatory government report from 1944: "To the approaching visitor the most noticeable feature of the typical Arab village is the concentration of the houses in a thick cluster on the high ground of the village lands." This depiction of the village is not unlike that which appeared in G. Robinson Lees's book:

> [The villages] are built at the top or side of a hill, and seem at first glance in the sunlight of a bright summer day to be part of its rocky site. When the rain has washed the white dust from their walls, or when surrounded by trees and gardens, they are more distinct and often picturesque. The position on or near the summit of a hill commands a view of the surrounding country. . . . To add to this desirable situation the houses are built like little forts and close together.[26]

When the inhabitants of these picturesque villages eventually went into exile, the clusters of abandoned buildings would attract Jews with a sense of the aesthetic, who would transform them into artists' villages or luxury dwellings—after, of course, installing all the modern plumbing and wiring that had not existed in the days when they were inhabited by their Arab residents.

The number of Arab villages extant on the eve of the 1948 War is a subject of controversy because of different definitions of what should be counted as a village: independent villages, hamlets dependent on a mother village, semipermanent Bedouin encampments, ruins inhabited during the agricultural season only, or isolated farms. According to a variety of calculations, all based on Mandatory government data, there were approximately 850 to 900 permanent villages (in addition to cities and towns) in Mandatory Palestine, of which some 400 to 450 were in areas that became part of the sovereign territory of Israel. In the villages that were on land occupied by Israel in the course of the 1948 War, on the eve of the war there lived approximately half a million souls (and over a quarter million more in the cities and towns). The following description of the Palestinian landscape, both physical and human, is organized according to the order in which the surveys for the village dossiers were carried out.

ANTIQUITIES, HISTORY, AND DEMOGRAPHY

According to Ottoman census records from the late sixteenth century, at that time there were 516 permanent villages in the territory that later became Mandatory Palestine. By the end of the nineteenth century, their number had reached approximately 700 (in addition to 18 cities and towns). At any rate, it is clear that the number of permanent settlements swelled considerably between the sixteenth century and 1948, but that does not mean that the new settlements were founded on virgin ground. The overwhelming majority were built on the ruins of ancient settlements that had been destroyed or abandoned in earlier periods. This phenomenon—of abandonment followed by reestablishment of settlements on the same site—is known to have occurred frequently in the long history of the Holy Land. It is an outcome of the fact that physical requirements and living conditions did not change significantly until the middle of the twentieth century. The topographical placement of the village site at the top of a gently sloping hill, or along a mountain ridge overlooking a fertile valley, gave it certain advantages in terms of security (particularly vantage point) and microclimate. Proximity to water sources (a few springs as well as cisterns hewn from the rock) and convenient access to rich soil (scarce in the rocky hill areas), closeness to roads leading to the cities (but not too close—for security reasons), and the presence of the remains of ancient structures that could be exploited for the purpose of new construction—all of these factors led to the practice of building the additional Arab villages founded in recent centuries by and large either on or very near to ancient sites.

What is amazing is how the villagers who settled the ancient ruins knew the biblical names of these sites and thus, as we have seen, maintained both the physical continuity of the places and their toponymic-cultural continuity. What this means is that the Arab villages internalized the traditions of their places of settlement and the names of geographical features in their vicinity, even when a place had not been continuously inhabited, and even when an ancient site had stood alone in desolation for many centuries, having been repopulated only some 200 years before. Their utilization of the ancient names created the erroneous impression that all of the Arab villages with ancient names were settlements where there had been a continual human presence.

Indeed, some of the settlements that arose the course of the last hundred years were the product of a natural, spontaneous process whereby families moved from the villages to nearby ruins close to the land they had under cultivation, and restored them. Other villages were abandoned because of vulnerability to invasion or natural disasters, and when conditions improved, their inhabitants returned to them. Many, however, were populated by immigrants who had made incursions into the country over the past few centuries.

The question of the degree of antiquity of Arab rural settlements in Palestine and the makeup of their populace are sensitive subjects, at the center of a heated political debate. This debate was recently rekindled by the publication of Joan Peters's sensationalistic book, *From Time Immemorial*,[27] in which she attempts to prove that the majority of the Arab population that inhabited the territory of Mandatory Palestine—and especially those areas settled by Jews—were of nonlocal origin. According to Peters and others, these migrants came from outside the region, and their numbers increased with the growth of Jewish immigration and the economic prosperity that accompanied it. These contentions were brought forward as a counterweight to Arab propaganda that represented the Jewish community in Palestine as being made up of immigrants who had taken control of a land that was not theirs. The debate, in which Israeli, Palestinian, and other scholars participated, quickly degenerated to the level of polemics bearing little or no resemblance to scientific inquiry. According to Charles Kamen, the total number of non-Jewish immigrants to Palestine during the entire Mandatory period was 58,000, or 7 percent of the *increase* of the non-Jewish population.[28]

Geographer David Grossman studied the geographical and demographic aspects of the development of the Arab villages during the Ottoman period, before Jewish settlement activity had commenced and when it was just beginning; his findings give us a proper sense of proportion regarding this debate. Grossman concludes that there was indeed an "incursion" by migrants from "outside," but he points out that "there is not necessarily a significant difference between 'international' and 'internal' migration, at least as long as we are dealing with population movement taking place within the confines of the Ottoman Empire." In his opinion there is no difference, for example, between population movement between the Hebron Highlands and Samaria (both of which would later be inside Mandatory Palestine) and between Mount Lebanon and Mount Carmel, only one of which would be included in Mandatory Palestine but both of which were within the Ottoman Empire.[29] A far more meaningful distinction is that between "incursion and migration whose end is permanent settlement" (with no differentiation between movement from outside the country and from one region to another within it) and "cyclical movements that are seasonal in origin (i.e., in response to the requirements of agricultural cultivation and animal husbandry) as well as movement taking place in the context of intervillage connections."[30] Grossman concluded that the cyclical processes were more significant than were those involving settlement from outside the region ("incursion") in all regions where there was permanent rural habitation—that is, in the valleys of the Lower Galilee, in Samaria, in the Jerusalem region, the Coastal Plain, and the valley of Lydda. By contrast, "incursion" was of greater import in areas with scanty rural communities, which, not coincidentally, were the areas of Jewish settlement. Participating in these incursions were Bedouin who made seasonal migrations within the permanently inhabited regions (unlike the desert nomads), villagers who had detached themselves from their mother village and sought territory where they could support themselves in the distant valleys, emigrants from Egypt and the Hauran region of Syria, and Druze from Mount Lebanon, as well as migrants from the far reaches of the Ottoman Empire, who had come with the encouragement of the Ottoman authorities: Turkmens, Circassians, Bosnians. This settlement activity was accompanied by the takeover of extensive pieces of territory by urban notables (effendis) through the exercise of their political and financial powers. On these tracts of land they set up agricultural plantations cultivated by tenant farmers.

The processes of rural settlement and the establishment of permanent villages accelerated from the mid–nineteenth century onward, in the wake of the intensive urban growth of Acre-Haifa, Jaffa, Ramla, and Lydda, and thanks to the development of export trade in agricultural produce, especially oranges. According to Grossman, at the close of that century noncyclical "intruders," who settled in ancient ruins and on vacant land, constituted about a quarter of the approximately 400,000 inhabitants of the area that was to become Mandatory Palestine. These demographic data are liable to be seen as suggesting that there were cultural differences or even tensions between the "intruders" from outside the country and the "local" population, but such an impression is erroneous, if not tendentious. The immigrants, most of them Muslims, were quickly assimilated into the local culture, learning the Arabic language (if they came from non-Arabic-speaking countries) and becoming an integral part of the Palestinian population. Differences in material culture were, indeed, preserved, finding expression in the layout of the villages and the agricultural methods employed by the communities whose origins were outside the Middle East. Similarly, traditions regarding an immigrant family's having originated in Syria, Iraq, or especially Egypt or Transjordan, were maintained, both within the families themselves and among their neighbors.

Palestinian scholars grumble that the Zionists take all the credit for the great improvement in the state of the economy, the acceleration in the rate of population growth, and the development of Arab cities and villages that have taken place since the First World War. This question has been dealt with by many scholars and is beyond the scope of the present discussion, but there is no doubt that massive Jewish investment in the development of Palestine contributed considerably to the improvements experienced by the Arab sector. Even so, the vital contribution of the Mandatory regime—in the initiation and implementation of a number of large development projects (the Port of Haifa, the road system, etc.), and especially in the introduction of a modern system of governance and the imposition of security conditions—must be emphasized. Arab entrepreneurs were wise enough to exploit the new conditions, and they developed expertise in several sectors where they surpassed their Jewish counterparts (e.g., citrus groves). The accelerated pace of development in the Coastal Plain attracted large numbers of villagers from the hills, who settled in the coastal cities of Haifa, Acre, and Jaffa and in the Arab villages on the periphery of the Jewish community. Nevertheless, no dramatic changes occurred in the overall demographic balance between Arab town-dwellers and the rural population. In 1922, 34.3 percent of the Arabs lived in towns, and in 1944 the percentage of town-dwellers had only increased to 36 percent. Although many villagers moved to the towns, the high rate of natural increase of those who stayed behind ensured that the relative size of the fraction of the population classified as rural changed only modestly.

The rate of natural increase in the Arab villages increased precipitously during the Mandate years, reaching 40 per 1,000 in 1944. This was primarily the result of a decline in the mortality of children aged five and under—which fell from approximately 400 per 1,000 in 1922 to 250 in 1944. In the same period average life expectancy rose from thirty-seven to forty-nine years, a change attributable to improved sanitation and nutrition. These conditions, however, remained inferior to those prevalent among the Jewish population. The numbers of doctors, nurses, and paramedical professions were very low, sanitary conditions were shocking, and malnutrition of children was widespread. The Arab rural population (Christian and Muslim) increased by 25 percent between 1922 and 1931, and by another 42 percent between 1931 and 1944, reaching approximately 770,000 in 1947 (in all Palestine), compared with about 160,000 Jews living in rural settlements (figures taken from *A Survey of Palestine*). Population size differed among villages;

about a quarter of villages had more than 1,000 inhabitants and a quarter less than 500. The average population was 700 to 800. Arab villages were built in clusters, and the relationships between them were organic and hierarchical. The hamlets that were scattered over the land of larger villages were linked to the "mother villages" from which their inhabitants had come. The clusters of villages "were attached to townships where they purchased goods and sold their agricultural produce. These townships functioned as intermediaries between the village farmers and the big city."[31] There was no spatial economic or cultural interaction between Jewish settlements and Arab villages, because Jewish settlements had direct connections with Jewish centers of economic, social, and cultural activity in big cities.

Geographical separation was only one dimension of the deep-seated segregation between the two communities. This self-evident fact, however, was overemphasized by both sides for political ends, thus eclipsing the considerable economic interaction between Arabs and Jews in the agricultural sector. For example, Jews and Arabs cooperated in the growing and exporting of citrus fruit; Jews consumed Arab agricultural produce; and a small but not insignificant number of Arabs were employed in the Jewish agricultural sector. Most important, as Kamen sums up, "Arabs and Jews were joint participants in a single economic system. What distinguished Arabs and Jews economically was their different positions in the national economy, but it is clear . . . that mutual influences of Arab and Jewish economic activity were great."[32] But this was from the macroeconomic point of view. On the microeconomic plane the contacts between adjacent Jewish and Arab settlements were indeed superficial or even nonexistent.

The Arab villages were an organic part not only of the physical landscape but also of the dimension of time. Their history, however, has by and large been viewed as relevant and noteworthy only in the context of European history. Even Palestinian scholars attempting to stress "the continued existence of human settlement at these sites since time immemorial" state that many of the villages have been "bypassed by history," while others saw "major battles, the passage of great armies, or the visit and largesse of Caliph or Sultan."[33]

In their detailed descriptions, the purpose of which is to immortalize the demolished villages, Palestinian scholars return again and again to the same historical periods—the classical era, the Middle Ages, and the Crusader, Mamluk, Ottoman, and British periods—but they do not depict the organic, local history of these villages from the viewpoint of their inhabitants. From the villagers' point of view, all these foreign occupiers were alike: all of them robbed the *fallah,* harassed him, slaughtered him, and incited him against his neighbor. Differentiating between rulers—be they Christian or Bedouin, effendis from Hebron or Nablus, Albanian, Turkish, or Egyptian, Arab or foreign—had no importance to the *fallahin.* Of the Crusader rulers it was said, in accounts of Muslim travelers, that the Arab villagers preferred their rule over that of the Muslim rulers in the neighboring countries, since the Crusaders treated them more justly. Time after time the villagers had thrown their support behind Ottoman governors against local sheikhs and rulers from among their own people, who robbed and murdered them.

But perhaps the historical portrayal of the villages from the inhabitants' point of view is discomfiting to modern Palestinian scholars, since such a description would not draw an altogether positive picture of "a civilization that had enriched the human heritage,"[34] but rather would be replete with images of blood feuds, despoliation and destruction, intrafamilial conflict, and incessant, unabated violence. The violent history of the Arab villages in Palestine had its beginnings in the seventh century, during the period of settlement by Muslim conquerors. With them from Arabia the conquerors brought the wars between the Quays and Yaman tribes, which continued into the early twentieth century. This state of violent factionalization spawned alliances among *fallahin* and Bedouin, Muslim and Christian alike, who rallied around the white Yaman banner and similar intergroup alliances under the red banner of the Quays faction for purposes of self-defense and launching attacks against each other. It was essentially an ongoing civil war in the course of which villagers from one side would attack those from the other (sometimes living within the same community), murdering, sowing destruction, and killing livestock. The Ottoman authorities, for their part, fostered conflict between the two camps, employing the tried-and-true methods of divide and rule. There are numerous detailed descriptions of the cruel destruction wrought by the Quays-Yaman Wars, and they left a lasting imprint on the rural landscape: entire regions were reduced to rubble, orchards were uprooted, and many people lost their lives. The common perception that the impoverishment of the rural community during the four centuries of Ottoman rule was the outcome of Turkish cruelty and rapacity was only partially correct. In large part, responsibility for the destruction could be laid at the door of the villagers themselves, and it is no wonder that this long chapter of schism and destruction has not received suitable attention by Palestinian scholars out to glorify the national heritage of the rural population and their contribution to the landscape—and to denounce the devastation of this landscape at the hands of foreign occupiers.

Even after the dispute between the Quays and Yaman factions had died down considerably (although not entirely), the villagers' hardships were not over. They continued to be exploited by their "brothers," members of well-connected city-dwelling Arab families with ties to the regime. These city-dwellers, longtime champions of Palestinian nationalism, gained control of the landholdings of *fallahin* who were unable to pay the high taxes imposed on them, and by means of some questionable legal conniving dispossessed their fellow Palestinians and sold their land to Zionists and other Europeans.

A more detailed account of local history and its heroes and villains would be outside the scope of the present work, but these events and personalities are immortalized in the landscape of the countryside. One can still see the towers of the walls of the Old City of Tiberias, built by the Druze emir Fakhr al-Din, of the early seventeenth-century Maʿan Dynasty; the castles of Deir Hannah, Jidin (Yehiam), Shafaʿamr (Shefarʿam), erected by the Bedouin sheikh Dahr al-Omar, from the Zaidan family, perhaps the greatest leader to arise among the Arabs of Palestine in the Ottoman era; Suba, the ruins of the fortress of Sheikh Abu Ghosh, the leader of the Yaman camp in the Jerusalem Hills; and the ruins of the fortress of his mortal enemy, the leader of the Quays camp, Sheikh al-Lahaam, in the village of Beit ʿAtab. Many of these sites have already been destroyed, and there is a real danger that by the time someone awakens to the necessity of preserving what remains, nothing will be left. The memory of leaders, revered personages, holy people, and miracle workers who lived and were active during many centuries is preserved in hundreds of shrines and sacred tombs scattered over the landscape—which we shall deal with separately (in chapter 7).

WATER

Assurance of a reliable supply of water was a cardinal preoccupation for the Arab villager, and the accessibility of water sources was the primary condition for his survival. Villages were therefore established near or around springs. Because of the paucity of springs and the great number of years when drought halted the flow of their waters, the villagers bored deep wells to tap directly into the underground water. Where underground water sources were not to be found, they made do with rainwater cisterns; hence the choice of village sites where the ground was of soft rock, where cisterns could easily be dug. The water source was the center of village life, both literally and figuratively. "The well is public property," writes Stavsky, "drilled by the villagers and providing water to everyone in the village—its men and its women, its children and its infants, its sheep and its cattle; to the wanderer, the sojourner, and the stranger." Pumps powered by men or animals (see plate 4) drew the water from the depths of the well to a pool from which the women would fill large clay jugs, which they then carried home on their heads. Water drawn from springs outside the village was carried on the backs of donkeys—or even by people—even though these springs were sometimes located at a distance of several kilometers from the village.

The flow in most of the springs (according to the PEF survey, which was conducted in the 1880s, there were approximately 800 springs in Palestine) was quite meager. Only the few that created streams or rivulets had sufficient water to irrigate vegetable gardens and orchards. A network of irrigation ditches led to various plots, in accordance with their owners' water rights; water use was measured by hours of irrigation or the water level in the reservoir pool. Of course, under these conditions the areas planted in crops requiring irrigation were very small. The exploitation of water resources expanded dramatically during the first quarter of the twentieth century as deeper wells were bored and internal combustion engine-powered pumps came into use. The greatest increase in water use took place on the Coastal Plain, in conjunction with the widespread planting of citrus groves. In other regions as well, motorized pumps were put in, spring water was collected, and pipes laid to carry it to the villages, but only rarely into villagers' homes. Despite these developments, at the end of the Mandate less than 5 percent of the total cultivated area in the Arab sector was under irrigation (mainly citrus groves), and the use of water for domestic purposes remained at a primitive level.

ROADS AND COMMUNICATION

Location of a village close to roads had both advantages and disadvantages. Convenient access to urban commercial centers was vital for the marketing of fresh agricultural produce; on the other hand, being too close to roads exposed the village to security risks—from robbers or from undisciplined military units that roamed there. When the security situation improved, the tendency to build houses within walking distance of the roads, or even right along them, increased. The roads themselves improved beyond recognition during the period of the British Mandate; paved roads connected all the urban population centers, and secondary roads branched off to the villages. Remote villages, too, enjoyed improved transportation conditions, especially during the Arab Revolt of 1936–39, when the British army built roads through the hilly regions, thus opening up remote areas that had previously been inaccessible by motor vehicle. Despite this relatively fast development, most village access roads remained unpaved and were impassable in the winter in rainy weather.

In the villages practically no one owned a private vehicle, and bus service was on a primitive level, although large villages usually had a bus or two, and the smaller villages nearby also benefited from this service. There was virtually no postal or telephone service. In 1946 there were post offices in only twenty villages, and telephone service existed only in the cities and larger Arab towns. There were practically no radios in the villages. Permits for the operation of only 9,500 radio receivers were issued, nearly all of them in the cities, as opposed to 44,000 in the Jewish sector.

VILLAGE STRUCTURE

It was not until the early thirties that the Arab village began to deviate from its traditional structure—a closely packed cluster of houses with narrow dead-end alleys between them, divided into neighborhoods according to clan affiliation. The house and courtyard constituted a single unit, where man and beast dwelled together. A low, narrow passageway led into the courtyard, which was surrounded by a row of rooms constructed on different levels, each one serving a specific purpose: a storeroom for tools and heating-fuel, a granary for storage of grain and straw, a dairy barn, a sheep pen, a chicken run, and the room that housed the family. The villager's residence served all the members of his family, and there they ate, slept, raised children, and extended hospitality to guests. "This room, where the *fallah* first saw the light of day, absorbed into itself the spirit of many generations," writes Moshe Stavsky. "It was witness to the events and twists and turns of numerous lives, and between its walls the *fallah* would give over his soul to the will of Allah, when his time came."[35]

It is difficult to exaggerate the supreme significance to the Arab villager (even to those who had pulled up stakes and moved to the cities) of the house, in comparison to which all other possessions were temporary and lacking in importance. The house and the piece of land surrounding it were evidence that a man in whose consciousness the nomadic way of life was so deeply ingrained had made a permanent home in a settled part of the country. His marriage, the birth of his first son, and the construction of his house are the central events in the life of the villager because they symbolize continuity in the dimension of time as well as on the physical plane. For that reason the completion of the roofing of the house is a festive occasion, celebrated with a feast to which relatives, friends, and neighbors are invited. The relatives and the neighbors who participated in the construction work—especially in the completion of the roof—share in the meat of a sheep slaughtered on the threshold of the new house, a sacrifice meant to placate the evil spirits. In response to the fear that evil spirits and demons will bring misfortune to the house and its inhabitants, the villager hangs blue glass beads, garlic, a worn-out child's shoe, and an iron horseshoe—to keep away the evil eye. "Allah yeʿamer beitak" (May Allah build your house) is one of the most important benedictions with which a person blesses his fellow, and the converse, "Allah yakhreb beitak" (May Allah destroy your house), is an extremely passionate curse.

The supreme importance that the *fallah* attached to his house was known to the British Mandatory authorities, and for that reason they blew up houses as an extreme form of punishment during the Arab Revolt. The Defense (emergency) Regulations stated that a military commander was authorized to demolish a house whenever he had cause to suspect that shots had been fired or bombs thrown from it, or that its inhabitants had participated in acts of violence; after seizing it, the commander was empowered to demolish it along with all its contents (Article (1)119). The British army demolished hundreds of homes, including extensive sections of the city of Jaffa, during the 1936–39 disturbances.

The blowing up of houses and the destruction of entire villages were, as we shall see, means of punishment also employed in many places by the Jewish forces (and subsequently by the sovereign State of Israel as well) in the course of the 1948 War. It is easy to imagine the terrible significance of the demolition of a man's house and his eviction from it: along with the house, his whole world was destroyed.

The population density in the villages was high: half the rural population lived more than four to a room. Even by 1945 standards these were regarded as "severely overcrowded conditions."[36] The villager spent relatively little time inside his cramped, dark house. Most of his time was spent out of doors: in his garden, in the olive grove or the pasture, at the mosque, or in the village guest house (*madafeh*). "The village spatiality was more externalized contextually," writes Ghazi Falah, "the peasant home was extended, its boundaries amplified."[37] The village and its inhabitants were planted firmly in the landscape; its houses, its land, its terraces, the plants and other objects of the landscape constituted a single, unified whole. The villagers' powerful connection to their surroundings found expression in the rich toponymy they created in order to identify the elements of the landscape in which they lived (as we have seen in chapter 1). Their ability to blend in with the landscape was also reflected in the placement of the village, which accented the contours of the hills on whose tops it stood, as well as in the construction materials of its houses. The villagers used local materials: stone in rocky areas and adobe in the coastal regions. In the midthirties the emergence from the traditional nucleated village format became more pronounced. New houses built from modern building materials—that is, reinforced concrete—began to be constructed here and there on the slopes of the hills and along the access roads leading to the village. As Moshe Brawer observes, "While some villages, especially those in the vicinity of the main urban centers, on or near holy sites, or well placed on a main artery of communication, had lost their original layout and become largely dispersed by the end of the British Mandate period, others, particularly in parts of the highlands still inaccessible in the 1940's to modern transportation, were experiencing only the initial stage of departure from extreme nucleation."[38]

According to Brawer, by the end of the Mandatory period, the proportion of the rural population living in houses built outside the old village nucleus had reached 10 to 18 percent in the hilly regions and as much as 30 percent in the large villages adjacent to the cities of the Coastal Plain. The expansion of the built-up area and the concomitant dispersal of the population were themselves consequences of societal transformations, and they, in turn, perhaps played a part in accelerating the relaxation of the rigid *hamula* (clan) system that prevailed in the villages. The British authorities took a few steps toward improving rural living conditions, but these were primarily in the nature of building codes designed to assure adequate space between houses or the allocation of land for public buildings and roads. Governmental investment in infrastructure remained minimal.

LAND AND AGRICULTURE

In the mapping done for taxation purposes by the Mandatory government, Palestine was divided into 936 villages (Jewish and Arab), for each of which a map of the boundaries of "village land" was drawn. This was an administrative division, designed to facilitate registration of landownership in the Registry of Deeds and determination of agricultural property taxes. The map of the 13-million-*dunam* settled portion of the country (i.e., excluding the Negev and the Arava) was divided into "village lands" whose borders were contiguous and whose area ranged from over 300,000 *dunams* in Tubas, the village with the largest amount of land, to less than 1,000 *dunams* in the smallest villages. The average extent of a village's landholdings was between 1,200 and 9,000 *dunams*. Each of about twenty villages had holdings that covered more than 70,000 *dunams*. The apportioning of land in this manner did not denote its ownership by the village but was intended to provide a basis for the registration of individual ownership classified under the name of the village and subdistrict where it was located and for the subdivision of village land into blocks and parcels.

The British created this administrative cadastral division because of their perception that "the village was accepted as an administrative unit that must be preserved."[39] Cadastral maps were also prepared for forty cities and towns (Jewish and Arab). This administrative division is cited by Palestinian scholars as proof that the entire area designated as "village land" was owned by the villagers. In fact these administrative boundaries also encompassed land owned by the state and tracts owned by Arabs who were not residents of the village, as well as Jewish-owned land. Parcels of land belonging to Jewish settlements established after the borders of "village land" were fixed in 1935 were recorded in the Registry of Deeds under the name of the Arab village within whose territory they were located. Hence Palestinian scholars today can claim that Jewish settlements that were established during the Mandatory period, on land that had been legally purchased, were "stolen by force." Of course most of the "village land" was indeed owned by inhabitants of the villages. According to Mandatory government figures from 1945, Arab villagers owned 6,039 square kilometers of arable land.

"Village land" was divided into four main categories: the built-up "nucleus" of the village; adjacent to that was a compact belt of vegetable gardens and fenced orchards; beyond them was land that was seasonally cultivated with various degrees of intensiveness. The remainder of the land, up to the border of the village's holdings, was worked communally or leased on a temporary basis. The first three categories generally consisted of designated areas, called *mafrouz* areas, that were permanently under private possession. Land transferred to villagers for temporary use or worked communally, including pasture, was called *mushʿa* land.

It is not possible, in the present context, to fully describe the system of land tenure in force in Palestine and the legal complexities of the landownership system at that time. However, *mushʿa,* the collective ownership arrangement, deserves a brief description. Prior to the agricultural season, the village's elders would distribute its communally held land for cultivation. The villagers would gather in the square or the *madafeh,* where they would determine the allocation by the drawing of lots or some other means. A villager would work the specific plots he had acquired for one, two, or even five years. The *mushʿa* system required close cooperation among members of the community and has therefore been presented as evidence of the social cohesiveness of the inhabitants of the village, as Ghazi Falah states: "The village population was a 'family of families.'" This system, however, gave rise to tensions and to conflicts in which the strongest and most influential villagers generally prevailed, receiving the best plots of land. Thus the economic disparities among the village's inhabitants were exacerbated and differences among families increased. Ultimately, the *mushʿa* system had a destructive effect: Because their land tenure was temporary, the villagers had no incentive to improve the quality of the soil or to invest in long-term development. The British Mandatory authorities strove to abolish this system, and indeed, the proportion of village land classified as mushʿa decreased from 56 percent in 1923 to approximately one-quarter by the end of the Mandate.

The reason the British did not abolish the *mushʿa* system outright was political: the Arabs regarded it as a means of preventing the sale of land to Jews, since the agreement of the entire village was required for the sale of such land. Neither this nor a variety of efforts undertaken by the Palestinian leadership to prevent the sale of village land to Jews succeeded, however. The Palestinian leaders, including members of the Arab High Committee—which had decreed the death sentence for those selling land to Jews—themselves sold large parcels of land clandestinely to the Jews. Even the efforts of the British government, which had prohibited the sale of land in many parts of the country to Jews, did not prevent the Zionist bodies from obtaining land. The Palestinians have published itemized lists of land sold by Arabs and have listed all the names of the Lebanese, Syrian, and "other" families involved in sales. But they do not furnish data on the sale of hundreds of thousands of *dunams* that were sold by well-known Palestinians, including the al-Husseini, ʿAbd-al-Hadi, al-ʿAlami, and Canaan families. Jews owned land in more than 400 "village lands," but most of these parcels were small, and Jewish holdings were confined to nine of the sixteen Mandatory subdistricts.

The acquisition of land by the Zionist organizations is presented by Palestinian scholars as a major factor in the dispossession of the Arab villagers and their transformation into landless peasants. Studies conducted in recent years,[40] however, reveal that the number of Arab villagers who were actually evicted from land that had been purchased by Jews did not exceed 30,000—or 6,000 households—out of approximately 180,000 households whose principal occupation was agriculture, that is, roughly 3 percent. Although twice that number lived on land that was sold to Jews, some did not own the land, some sold only a small portion of their land, some had not engaged in agriculture at all, and some remained on the land as tenants entitled to the protection of the British authorities. In fact, more than a quarter of all villagers owned no land but instead were hired laborers or tenant farmers (in addition to another 10 percent who were nonagricultural laborers). This was not, however, because they had been dispossessed in the wake of the acquisition of their land by Jews, but was the inevitable outcome of the inequitable system of land tenure. According to various estimates, landowners with title to over 500 *dunams* (ten times the size of the average family parcel) owned roughly a quarter of the land. In many cases these were absentee landlords who lived in the cities and leased their land to villagers, and a few of them had holdings that extended over thousands of *dunams*. This unequal distribution was less extreme than that found in many other countries, where owners of gigantic estates often control the bulk of the land. But the inequality was sufficiently great to impoverish the landless tenant farmers and to prompt their migration to the shantytowns that were springing up on the outskirts of the coastal cities, where they subsisted as day laborers.

The overwhelming majority of villagers, of course, made their living from agriculture, and most of the cultivated area (over 4 million *dunams*) was sown with grain (wheat, barley, and sorghum). Methods of cultivation were nonintensive, and crops were meager, but during the forties the use of tractors and modern plows increased, and improved strains of wheat and barley were developed. The image of the Arab village and its fields as sun-parched wasteland "with neither tree nor shade"—in contrast to the verdant Jewish settlement with its abundant greenery—does not concur with the statistics. According to data gathered at the end of the British Mandate, 600,000 *dunams* were planted with olive trees and 350,000 with fruit orchards, and the Arabs' citrus groves covered a greater area than did those of the Jews. Of the total agricultural output of Mandatory Palestine, the Arabs produced 99 percent of the olives, 99 percent of the dates, 73 percent of the grapes, 77 percent of the fresh vegetables, 95 percent of the watermelons and other melons, 76 percent of the plums and apricots, 57 percent of the apples and pears, and 53 percent of the bananas. Arab livestock farming was, however, backward compared with that of the Jews, and it has been written that the milk yield of a cow in an Arab village was "similar to that of a nanny goat on a Jewish farm." Despite this, Arab farms produced approximately 57 percent of the country's total milk output: in 1944 there were 220,000 cows and 550,000 sheep and goats in the Arab agricultural sector, as well as 100,000 donkeys. Signs of modernization in Arab villages during the forties included the establishment of credit unions in some 125 communities—with whose help the villagers were able to liberate themselves from the world of usurious moneylenders—and the setting up of agricultural marketing and investment associations.

The principal problem confronting the Arab village in the forties was the ever-increasing pressure on its land resources from a population that was growing faster than its agricultural output. Inheritance laws, which guaranteed a share of the father's property to each of his sons, resulted in the fragmentation of landholdings, rendering their cultivation unprofitable in many cases, especially for field crops. The lack of investment by the Mandatory government (except for seasonal public works projects of limited scope), the scarcity of industrial job opportunities (caused mainly by Jewish industries' policy of not employing Arab workers), minimal public investment in education and health services, the absence of a system for marketing fresh agricultural produce in the cities, resistance to technological innovations, and a traditional social structure resulted in economic backwardness, a low standard of living, and rampant unemployment. During the Second World War the war effort led to a heightened demand for agricultural produce. But once the war had ended—on the eve of the 1948 War—the economic crisis in the villages made itself felt with renewed force.

Zionist scholars have enumerated the economic factors behind the backwardness of Arab villages as follows: the predominance of subsistence farming with primitive technology, feudal land-tenure practices, lack of funds for the intensification of agriculture or for the utilization of scientific knowledge to increase productivity, and poor marketing arrangements. To these they added another: the "mentality" of the *fallah* and the backwardness of the structure of Arab society.

Kamen quotes an Arab scholar who seeks to defend the honor of the *fallah* and to rebuff claims regarding "his fatalism and laziness":

> One should not be hasty in passing judgment. The *fallah*'s holding seldom exceeds the lot viable (a holding sufficient for the subsistence of a farmer and his family) while on the average it is smaller. . . . [H]is fatalism is observed only in adversity, when circumstances beyond his control deprive him of his meager means of livelihood. . . . [I]n reference to anyone but a *fallah* such an attitude would compel admiration as fortitude in adversity, but where a *fallah* is concerned it is downright fatalism.[41]

In its 1946 survey the Mandatory government presented three detailed theoretical models of typical Arab rural properties that, in its estimation, an Arab family made up of two adults and three children could cultivate without hired labor, assuming that the family was composed of persons with "reasonable intelligence who make the maximum use of their abilities while employing modern and improved methods of husbandry."[42] One such property was situated in the hills of Jerusalem or Ramallah. Its hypothetical area was ninety-five *dunams* (as compared with the actual average of less than fifty *dunams* per family). It was divided into fifteen *dunams* of rocky, nonarable land; five *dunams* for the family's home, farm buildings, and rocky land where shrubs suitable for use as fuel grew; thirty *dunams* of orchards and vineyards (ten of olives, ten of figs, five of table grapes, three of apricots, and two of almonds); and forty-five *dunams* of field crops (of which fifteen were planted with wheat and barley and ten with lentils and peas). On this farm two cows and a calf, two goats, twenty chickens, one mule, and ten hives of bees were kept. Its operation brought in an *annual* income of approximately 100 Palestinian pounds, out of which the farmer had to meet his family's food and clothing and other expenses, pay his taxes, and make payments on debts. If we keep in mind that the size of this hypothetical piece of property was twice that of the average Arab farm, that its means of production were greater than average, and that a significant portion of even this farmer's income went to cover repayment of debts, we shall have some idea of the extremely low standard of living of the average rural Arab family. By comparison, the salary of a middle-level government clerk was about thirty-three pounds *per month,* whereas that of an unskilled Arab laborer (working in the Arab sector) was ten pounds *per month* (1946).

PUBLIC INSTITUTIONS

Every village dossier, like other Jewish sources, placed particular emphasis on the presence of a guest house—called the *madafeh* (or *diwan*)—apparently because it was there that the Jews met with the village headmen. This was where members of a given *hamula* or other inhabitants of the village met in the evenings to discuss village business and politics, and it was where they hosted visitors from outside the village and met with representatives of the authorities. The *madafeh* was located in the home of the head of the *hamula,* of the local sheikh, or the mukhtar, and the cost of its maintenance was paid by the host or by the heads of the families in turn. "The village never lacked for idlers and gossips," writes Moshe Stavsky. "One would leave and another would enter; adding some twigs and a cake of dried manure to the fire and, so that the coffee in the pot would not run out, they would add more coffee and more water, stir, mix and bring to the boil, and pour out, filling each cup a quarter or a third full; serving everyone who entered, exchanging greetings with those present, and grabbing a place to sit." This meeting place was the focal point of the social life of the village, along with the well, of course, where those who did not come to the *madafeh*—young people and women—gathered.

There was also a gathering place for purposes of public prayer—a mosque—in many villages, but not in all. Where there was no permanent building for religious use, worshipers would gather in the *madafeh* or in a room in the home of some religious personage. Even when there was a special building to house the mosque, it was not always a spacious structure with a tall minaret towering over it. Often it was a modest room. On occasion prayers were held adjacent to a sacred site (*maqam*—a subject that will be dealt with in chapter 7) that was itself an important meeting place, sometimes for the inhabitants of the entire region. The coffeehouses that sprang up in villages located on major thoroughfares filled the role of *madafeh* to a certain extent.

Village schools were established only toward the end of the Ottoman period, replacing the old method of teaching, where a nonprofessional—sometimes itinerant—teacher would teach a bit of reading and writing to children of various ages. In the twenties there were altogether 24 village schools partially funded by the government; by 1927 their number had doubled. The British Mandatory government assessed the villagers the cost of erecting the school buildings, and according to its reports, the villagers had a positive attitude toward education. Ten years later the number of village schools had reached 257, and by the end of the Mandate there were 426; that is, there were schools in only half of the villages, and 63 percent of the boys and only 7.5 percent of the girls were enrolled. The curriculum in the villages was different from that of Arab schools in towns. The British heads of the Government Education Department believed that if one educates peasants beyond literacy they will abandon the land and move to the towns, where they will join the ranks of the semieducated unemployed, prone to nationalistic propaganda and subversive activities. The colonial officials refused to open secondary schools in the countryside and insisted that vocational training in agriculture was important, but "lack of funds" did not allow them to build such schools, except one, which operated only several years and then closed down. Schools in the smaller villages went up to grade four, and in the larger ones, to grade seven. The dropout rate was high, and the incidence of illiteracy was over two-thirds; very few women knew how to read and write.

LEADERSHIP

The layout of the Arab village was determined by *hamula* affiliation. The smaller villages were populated by the members of one *hamula* exclusively, but in most villages there were two or three *hamulas,* each of which lived in its own quarter. If one *hamula* was richer or more respected than the others, the authorities appointed its head as *mukhtar* (headman) of the village and its representative in dealings with the government. In villages where there were conflicts among strong *hamulas,* the authorities would appoint several mukhtars but would take care to preserve the hierarchical relationship among them. The traditional role of the *mukhtar* was to maintain peace in the village, to publicize announcements from the authorities, to prepare a registry of births and deaths, and to keep a record of the boundaries of the plots of land assigned for temporary cultivation and of the identity of those holding them. The mukhtar received his salary from the government but also collected payment from the villagers for a variety of services.

The British authorities were dissatisfied with the performance of the *mukhtars* and sought to replace them with village councils, but their efforts failed because of the absence of any indigenous tradition of self-rule and because they encountered opposition on the part of the villagers, who were concerned that this would entail the imposition of taxes to cover public expenditures. In many villages where councils were installed, the end result was either friction among rival *hamulas* or domination by undesirable elements. At the close of the Mandatory period there were only forty Arab village councils in existence, of which a large proportion were nonfunctioning.

The village leadership was engrossed in matters affecting their own villages and the areas surrounding them and—with the exception of those in communities close to urban population centers—not involved in Palestinian nationalist activity on a countrywide level. That was the domain of members of the well-connected, prosperous families living in the big cities, who took advantage of their position as landowners to influence the villagers, many of whom were their tenants.

Palestinian villagers made a significant contribution to the Arab Revolt of 1936–39. According to a survey by Yehoshua Porat, the revolt was carried primarily on the shoulders of Muslim villagers from the lowest social strata, and most of the guerrilla leaders also came from that background. In fact, there was only one mukhtar among them, although a significant number of mukhtars were slain by the rebels. The rebel forces imposed a reign of terror on the villages and did not hesitate to murder dozens of villagers, whenever the latter dared refuse them assistance. The British army instituted harsh punishments, hanging scores of villagers, demolishing houses, and destroying orchards. The villagers thus found themselves caught between a rock and a hard place.

Toward the end of the revolt a brutal civil war broke out between rival Palestinian factions, intensifying the bloodshed and the destruction of the agricultural sector. Relations between the Jewish and Arab settlements reached a low point in the wake of murderous attacks on Jews by Arab villagers, the burning of Jewish fields, and even shooting attacks on Jewish villages. By the end of the revolt and subsequent internal strife, the inhabitants of the Arab villages were exhausted, and in spite of their economic recovery during the Second World War, they were still in a weakened state with the arrival of the real moment of truth—the 1948 War.

Arab village life has been depicted in many books of folklore written by Arabs, Jews, and Europeans (see also chapter 6). All of these present the reader with thrilling descriptions of customs related to marriage and mourning, revenge and peacemaking, with the complexities of etiquette, picturesque blessings and curses, superstitious beliefs, and juicy epigrams. These descriptions reveal an exciting and colorful world, which existed alongside of—and perhaps because of—the harsh routine of village life. The most conspicuous traits of the villager—those cited most frequently by observers—are his patience, self-restraint, composure, shrewdness, conservatism, mistrustfulness, and thrift, his deferential attitude toward the venerable elderly members of the community, his manipulative behavior and sycophancy in the face of those stronger than he, his ability to be deceitful without hesitation, his vengefulness, and his exclusive loyalty to family.

However, perhaps the most eloquent encapsulation of what has been briefly described here is, again, what Israeli author S. Yizhar has to say about the Arab village:

> Have I said that this village was some sort of dwelling-place of the virtuous, who received not the reward they deserve? I did not say that, not at all; they were not at all virtuous. Albeit I know nothing about them. Perhaps they were—and naturally there were all kinds—like all of us, . . . [and] this unmediated innocence, this unsophisticated "being" of theirs, back then, which knew not how it was supposed to look so as to appear nice and correct and easily acceptable; their resignation before forces that today are almost possible to restrain, and their acquiescence in the helplessness and humbleness that is apparently another side of limitation, and their acknowledgment of the laws of what is above one . . . the resignation that is perhaps the beginning of greatness; this humbleness, if you recall; the penury above which the highest of heavens are opened. Which contain silences. Which contain swallowed tears as well. But which also contain a kind of murmuring decency—even to the extent of meeting a fleeting glance from G-d. If He is looking. If He is. If.[43]

3

Exodus

The opening shots of the 1948 War were fired on 30 November 1947 at 8:12 A.M. at a Jewish bus on its way to Jerusalem.[1] In the attack, which took place on the main road between the Jewish town of Petah Tikva and the Arab city of Lydda (later renamed Lod by the Israelis), five Jewish civilians were killed—two men and three women—the first casualties in a war that was to deprive tens of thousands of their lives. Those responsible for the shooting were members of a gang of Arab criminals based in Jaffa, who had already committed dozens of robberies and murders that year, of both Arabs and Jews. Even though the timing was such that this incident (and others carried out on that day and in the days that followed, with increasing frequency) took place immediately after the ratification of the United Nations resolution on the partition of Palestine (29 November), it was not then perceived as marking the beginning of an all-out war that would go on for fifteen months. Jewish intelligence agencies chose to label it a criminal incident "disguised as a reaction to the U.N. resolution." The leadership of the Jewish community viewed this attack and the others that followed it as "disturbances," like those of 1936–39, rather than defining them as the opening shots in a war. Only in retrospect, with the wisdom of hindsight, was the shooting on the Lod/Lydda road immortalized as "the first shot" of the 1948 War, and even then, only in Israeli history books. The Arabs chose a different event, which took place on 3 December, to regard as the start of the 1948 War: this was of course an incident where Jews opened fire on Arabs.

Identifying the "opening shots" in a war is always an arbitrary decision and one not uncontaminated by the differing positions and perceptions held by the sides involved in mortal conflict. The definition of an event as marking the start of a war is undertaken in a limited historical context, separate from the continuous stream of events, but it is more than simply an arbitrary factual statement. The objective is to determine which side committed the first acts of violence and is therefore responsible for the consequences. Every deed has its context, causes, and consequences, but context is a matter of ethnic affiliation, and the linkage of cause and effect is not an objective-logical syllogism, but rather is based on the perceptions of one side or the other. Historical continuity and the chain of violence are nourished by contradictory definitions of the relationship between challenge and response. What appears to one side to be a cause is seen by the other as an effect, and all efforts to present an objective chain of cause and effect contradict the partisan narratives of the two sides and are therefore perceived by both as one-sided or even hostile.

FIRST BLAST

Chronicling the 1948 War is of concern here only in the context of the war's effect on the physical and human landscape. Thus we too must begin with a depiction of the "first blast"—the event that launched the process of the destruction of the landscape—and here too the choice is decidedly arbitrary.

Apparently the first Arab house was blown up on the night of 7 December 1947—in the village of Abu Kabir, on the outskirts of Jaffa—in the course of a reprisal raid carried out by the Haganah after people from the village had shot and killed Jews in an adjacent neighborhood. On 13 December the Haganah staged a raid deep into Arab territory, in revenge for the murder of a veteran Haganah commander shot in an attack on a bus passing by the village of Deir Ayyub, near Latroun. During the incursion several houses were demolished and a number of villagers killed. However, the single event that is worthy of serving as the point of departure in our description of the destruction wrought by the 1948 War is the attack on the Arab village of al-Khisas, situated in the northern end of the Huleh Valley, not far from the Lebanese border. This attack was carried out on the night of 18 December 1947; the chain of events that followed, their causes, and their consequences are vital components of the story of the first phase in the tragedy of the destruction of the Arab landscape.

On the morning of 18 December a horse-cart from an adjacent kibbutz was fired upon while traveling past al-Khisas, and one of the passengers was killed. The local Palmach commanders decided to launch a retaliatory raid against the village from which they (erroneously) assumed the shots had come. They argued that if there were no reaction to the murder, the Arabs would interpret this as a sign of weakness and an invitation to further attacks. Several "Arabists" who were residents of the area opposed the action for fear that an attack on al-Khisas would cause problems for the Jews with the villagers' powerful leader, Emir Faour, whose manor stood just outside al-Khisas and was one of the targets of the planned attack (the emir himself was in Syria at the time). Their reservations were brushed aside, and the Haganah High Command approved the action on condition that the attack be directed against "men only, and they should burn [only] a few houses." The action was carried out that same night, and, according to the report of the commander in charge, twelve persons were killed—seven men, one woman, and four children—and several houses were demolished. The attack was widely publicized; even the *New York Times* reported on it. According to reports in the Arab papers, an Arab reprisal was being planned; and indeed, three weeks later members of Emir Faour's tribe attacked Kibbutz Kfar Szold, situated not far from al-Khisas. The Arab forces, which had come from across the Syrian border, were repulsed after suffering heavy losses, but escalation was unavoidable, and the violence soon spread throughout the Upper Galilee.

The retaliatory raid on al-Khisas was sharply criticized by the Jewish leadership on both moral and practical grounds: "The murder of women and children violates the principle of 'purity of arms'" (i.e., using force only for defense, and not harming civilians), stated one prominent figure, while another cautioned that "every response must have a clear objective, in terms of both place and time, [and the Khisas action] was the complete opposite of our set policy [regarding avoidance] of provocations in an area where we are interested in maintaining peace and quiet."

PRINCIPLES OF RETALIATION

That raid and similar reprisals served as the backdrop for two continuous days of crucial deliberations held on 1–2 January 1948 in Tel Aviv, which revolved principally around the Jewish forces' policy regarding retaliation. These talks took place in the wake of the worsening of the security situation and the launching of attacks on Jewish border settlements by the Arab forces. On 3 December an urban kibbutz in the Petah Tikva region was raided; on 27 December 600 Arabs attacked the isolated settlement of Kfar Yavetz (following Jewish provocation), and were it not for the resourcefulness of its defenders, there is no doubt that the fate of this Jewish village would have been more bitter than that of al-Khisas; on 29 December Kibbutz Amiad (near Rosh Pina in the Galilee) was attacked—its attackers, from the town of Safad, were repulsed.

At the deliberations—whose participants included all the leaders of the Jewish community and the Haganah High Command—guidelines for the execution of reprisal raids were formulated:

> Active self-defense by means of strong counter-attacks everywhere we are attacked, at the time and place of the attack on us, except for holy places, schools, and other objectives of this sort. . . . Not to take the initiative in disturbances, riots, or provocations . . . in regions where we have not yet been attacked and which have not yet come under fire; to make an effort to harm [only] the guilty ones and, knowing the impossibility of being meticulous about targeting the right individuals, to be careful to target the right settlement, village, or region.[2]

The conclusions of the 1–2 January deliberations were later criticized on the grounds that the political and military leadership of the Jewish community did not understand that they were involved in an all-out war and still believed that it was possible to contain the hostilities. They had therefore set down directives restricting the use of force and had instructed that it be employed only in reaction to Arab attacks, thus giving the enemy the initiative. This decision no doubt stemmed primarily from the leadership's perception of the weakness of the Jewish forces, which were just getting organized and suffered from a severe shortage of arms (particularly artillery), and only to a minimal degree from the influence of those who sought to curtail hostilities in hopes that it might still be possible to build Jewish-Arab coexistence. Nevertheless, the Principles for the Execution of Reprisal Actions are an indication that in the early stages of the 1948 War there was no policy of "ethnic cleansing"—premeditated destruction of villages and the expulsion of their inhabitants—as claimed by Palestinian scholars. There were, indeed, instances where villages were evacuated and even where houses were demolished, but these were local initiatives, several of which were severely criticized by the national military command and leaders of the community.

An indication that Arab military observers have acknowledged Jewish attempts to limit the scope of military confrontation is provided by General Ismail Safawat, commander of the Arab League Military Committee, who wrote the following summary in his report on the military situation (23 March 1948):

> Despite the fact that skirmishes and battles have begun, the Jews at this stage are trying to contain the fighting to as narrow a sphere as possible in the hope that partition will be implemented and a Jewish government formed; they hope that if the fighting remains limited, the Arabs will acquiesce in the fait accompli. This can be seen from the fact that the Jews have not so far attacked Arab villages unless the inhabitants of those attacked them or provoked them first.[3]

The Palestinian editor who published a translation of this report in 1998 had annotated the text with the following footnote: "This is inaccurate, as is clear in Safawat's own report." But the attempt to find inconsistencies is not convincing. Palestinian historiography insists on representing the destruction of the Palestinian landscape as a single, continuous process, planned from the start by the Zionist leadership. This assertion is not supported by the facts, but that does not mean that destruction did not take place.

During the winter months of 1948 (January–March) the hostilities were already having a noticeable effect on the landscape. According to Israeli historian Benny Morris, the first Arab village to be largely abandoned was Khirbat ʿAzzun, north of the Jewish town of Raʿanana, on 21 December 1947. After that, Bedouin tribes who were living in the area of the Sharon Plain that was heavily populated by Jews fled. In the months of February and March 1948, several villages located near the large Jewish settlements of the Coastal Plain were abandoned, and Arab communities in the Upper Galilee, in the vicinity of the Sea of Galilee, and at the foot of the Carmel Range were vacated as well. The areas where these demographic transformations and changes in the landscape took place were, in any case, limited to where the friction between the Arab and Jewish populations had reached the level of violent confrontation. At that time the number of villagers who had left their homes was still small. By the end of March, the total number of refugees from towns and villages reached some 50,000 (3.5% of the total Arab population). Most of those who pulled up stakes moved to other Arab population centers within the country and viewed their dislocation as temporary. The inhabitants of the big cities, particularly members of the more prosperous classes, displayed little staying power, abandoning their homes and neighborhoods on a massive scale. Nonetheless, had the 1948 War ended in March of that year, the damage it left behind would have been relatively light. One could even say that the warring sides were making efforts to minimize destruction to the environment, at least as far as agricultural crops were concerned. In areas distant from the foci of violence, residents of Jewish agricultural settlements and Arab villages refrained from opening fire on each other, out of their desire that agricultural areas not be harmed and that the grain harvest, in particular, not be disrupted. A shared interest in the preservation of the citrus industry resulted in the signing of a nonaggression pact by the mayors of Tel Aviv and Jaffa on 9 December 1947. According to this agreement, the two sides were obligated not to harm citrus groves or packing plants, and to allow the transportation and export of produce via the port of Jaffa. The citrus groves, which extended in a broad semicircle bordering Jaffa and Tel Aviv, were owned to an approximately equal extent by Jews and Arabs. There was close cooperation between Jewish and Arab growers in all stages of production and marketing, and the export of citrus fruit was of great economic importance to the two sides. In 1947 the British government bought the season's entire citrus harvest—12 million crates, from both Jewish and Arab growers—and the earnings from this transaction ensured the livelihood of thousands in the two communities.

The pact was more or less honored, despite the fact that both Mufti Haj Amin al-Husseini and several Haganah commanders, including Moshe Dayan, opposed it. David Ben-Gurion, however, was of the opinion that, although it was necessary to lay siege to Jaffa, the citrus industry must not be harmed. As a result of this compromise, the growers were able to continue exporting their fruit. With the conclusion of the season, however, the nonaggression pact, too, came to an end, and the Arab-owned citrus groves were occupied by the Haganah, along with the city of Jaffa and all the surrounding villages. Ironically, the Arab citrus groves, whose preservation had been so great a concern during the war, were allowed to dry up and were destroyed in its immediate aftermath, as we shall see later.

ACCELERATED VIOLENCE

This seemingly peaceful picture is misleading, however, and does not fully portray the ferocity of the intercommunal violence that was running riot during the winter and spring of 1948, increasingly assuming the character of an all-out war with the participation of large-scale forces on both sides. Early in January of that year, the Palestinian leadership came to the realization that the urban guerrilla war they were waging was going against them, and that many Arabs were abandoning the mixed cities. Therefore, the commanders of the local Arab forces decided, at a meeting held in Nablus and chaired by ʿAbd al-Qadir al-Husseini, to shift the focus of hostilities to the villages and to employ large forces to attack Jewish settlements. In the space of six days (9–14 January), attacks were launched against Kibbutz Kfar Szold in the Upper Galilee, Kfar Uriah in the Shephelah, and the Etzion Block in the Hebron Highlands. The hundreds of irregulars who carried them out were joined by thousands of villagers. All the attacks were repelled, with heavy losses to the perpetrators. At the same time, the Arab Liberation Army (ALA), organized by the Arab League and made up of several thousand fighters from the Arab world, who had volunteered to come to the aid of the Palestinians, arrived in the country. An ALA force attacked Kibbutz Yehiam in the Western Galilee on 1 January, and it too was repulsed.

The Jewish leadership, however, sensed that the initiative was being lost to the other side, and after thirty-five Jewish fighters were killed on their way to the besieged Etzion Block, decided to carry out a large-scale operation with the objective of striking deep into enemy territory, disrupting supply routes and undermining morale. On 14 February a Palmach unit raided the village of Sʿasʿa, which was far from any Jewish settlement, killing sixty people and demolishing sixteen homes. Concurrently, the Haganah destroyed seven bridges in various parts of the country and blew up houses in three villages. Two days after the raid on Sʿasʿa, the ALA attacked Kibbutz Tirat Zvi in the Beit Shean Valley and was pushed back after sustaining heavy losses. The failure of the offensive against the Jewish settlements led the Palestinian military leadership to implement a new strategy: the besieging of Jewish settlement blocks via the obstruction of major roads, most of which passed by Arab villages and towns.

"The war of the roads" had actually commenced immediately upon the outbreak of hostilities, but the fighting ability of the Arab irregulars and their military commanders was now greatly improved, and they succeeded in inflicting several defeats on the Jewish forces: four large convoys were obliterated by Arab forces—the number of dead exceeded 100—and most of the armored vehicles belonging to the Haganah fell into Arab hands.

The greatest danger of all was to be faced by the Jewish inhabitants of Jerusalem, whose lifeline, the highway to Tel Aviv, was coming under constant attack. The increasing success of the Palestinian irregulars, the presence of the ALA in the country, and the imminent threat of the involvement of the armies of the Arab states in the conflict upon termination of the Mandate gave rise to the need for a military strategy to guide the Jewish forces through the critical stage that the Jewish community was going through. On 10 March 1948 the Haganah High Command approved "a plan for gaining control of the territory of the Jewish State and for the defense of its borders." (The name of the state was as yet undetermined, and its territory was perceived as that of the 1947 partition plan.) This was called Plan D (Dalet), because it was the fourth in a series of strategic plans that the Haganah had compiled since 1941.

PLAN D

This plan was of crucial importance to the matter that concerns us here, since it had far-reaching implications for the Arab rural landscape. The enemy was defined as consisting of the irregular troops of the Arab League's ALA, the regular military forces that would soon be invading from across the borders, and "gangs" operating from bases inside the country. These three forces would combine their efforts to cut areas of Jewish settlement off from one another and from supply centers and the like, to gain control of territory in the heart of the future state, and to isolate the three largest cities, Jerusalem, Tel Aviv, and Haifa. The task of the Jewish forces was defined as self-defense by means of a static defense system from within the perimeters of Jewish settlements, attacks on bases deep within enemy territory, and protection of vital traffic arteries via the capture of population centers inside enemy territory.[4] According to the plan:

> Actions [would be launched] against enemy settlements located within or near our defended areas, with the aim of preventing their being used as bases for an active armed force. [These actions will include] the destruction of such villages, the carrying out of searches and, in the event of resistance, the elimination of the armed force and the expulsion of the [village] population to [territory] outside the borders of the State, [and in cases where there is no resistance] an army unit will be garrisoned in the village.

Detailed instructions were given to the brigades responsible for specific regions, in which explicit goals were set out: the occupation of police stations, the occupation of dozens of villages (whose names were given), and preventing the transformation of other villages into enemy bases. The commanders were instructed to destroy villages "over which it was impossible to gain permanent control," and the decision regarding which would be destroyed and which would be spared was left in their hands. Plan D was scheduled to be set in motion on the final day of the Mandate (15 May 1948) or a few days before that. The critical situation that prevailed in March, however, obliged the Haganah to begin the plan's execution almost immediately after it was approved.

This plan, and especially highly charged key phrases such as "destruction of villages" and "expulsion of the [village] population to [territory] outside the borders of the State," are employed by Palestinian and pro-Palestinian historians as proof that Plan D was a program of premeditated ethnic cleansing. As they perceive it, this was not a plan for achieving military objectives, but "thirteen military operations aimed at driving Palestinians from their villages. . . . Jewish forces initiated a war of demographic and territorial expansion, which took on the dimension of space purification—expulsion and prevention of the return of the expellees." For purposes of demonstrating that Plan D was indeed as they saw it, the Palestinians state: "At least until May 15, 1948, there was no regular army pitched [*sic*] against [the] Jewish forces. Their enemy was essentially the indigenous civilian Palestinian population."[5]

The emphasis on the absence of "a regular army" is included, of course, to stress the "essentially civilian" character of the Palestinian population against whom the regular "Jewish forces" were operating, and to hint that these attacks had not been provoked by the villagers—and constituted deliberate acts of "ethnic cleansing." On the one hand, the Jewish forces are portrayed by Palestinian historians as being "relatively weak," lacking the manpower needed for all-out war and therefore compelled to resort to deeds of intimidation, terrorism, destruction, and rape that would panic the local population and destroy their morale. On the other hand, the Jewish forces are depicted by these same historians as being stronger than all the Arab regular and irregular forces put together and therefore unable to hide behind the claim that the total war they had launched, and its consequences, were precipitated by their desperate situation. The Palestinian historians' attitude toward the military weakness of the Arabs is also presented in two ways: First, they express scorn for the semiregular forces that fought inside Palestine before the end of the Mandate (especially those recruited by the Arab League) and declare their low estimation of the endeavors of the regular armies of the Arab states after May 15. Of greater importance, however, in bolstering Palestinian assertions regarding the war against the rural civilian population, is their attempt to ignore—or at least not to emphasize in the context of the destruction of villages—the role of indigenous Palestinian irregular forces in the war. This is not only a distortion of history but also a desecration of the memory of Palestinian fighters who struggled for the achievement of national objectives as they understood them. Even though they failed and paid with their lives, it is unfair to ignore the part they played—out of a desire to lend credence to the myth of innocent civilians killed by cruel "Jewish military forces."

Plan D was set in motion almost two months before the designated date precisely because the local Palestinian forces had presented such a great threat to the Jewish community that the Haganah was compelled to launch the operation on short notice. It was no coincidence that the first areas in which the policy of permanent occupation and destruction of villages was implemented were those where Arab attacks had imperiled the lifelines of the Jewish community: the road to Jerusalem and the area around Mishmar Haʿemeq.

QASTAL

Late in March 1948 the Jewish population of Jerusalem was in dire straits. The approximately 100,000 Jewish residents were suffering from a severe shortage of foodstuffs, since the Palestinian forces commanded by ʿAbd al-Qadir al-Husseini had essentially succeeded in blocking the road from Tel Aviv. The Palestinian commander had skillfully and efficiently deployed his troops—in companies or even larger formations, aided by villagers—along the full length of the mountainous highway. The Jewish forces who were assigned to defend the convoys bearing food and supplies to siege-bound Jerusalem were plagued by a divided command, disputes over authority, and shortages of manpower and arms. As a result, in the last ten days of March, only forty-one supply trucks reached Jerusalem, whereas thirty-nine fell into Arab hands, twenty-six were destroyed, and thirty returned to Tel Aviv.

The military crisis precipitated a political crisis: in the international arena, doubts regarding the Jews' ability to establish a state were beginning to be voiced, and the suggestion of replacing the Mandatory regime with a United Nations trusteeship had been proposed. This military-political crisis forced the Jewish leadership and the commanders of the Haganah to undertake a new strategy, the essence of which was the setting up of a large military formation that would operate as one organic unit and, what is of particular interest here, the permanent occupation and domination of continuous stretches of territory vital to control of the route to Jerusalem. The key point in the eastern section of the route was the small village of al-Qastal, which was situated on a hill dominating the western approaches to the city. The village was taken on the night of 2–3 April and found to be deserted, its inhabitants having left the previous day. The Palmach force that stormed Qastal easily overcame the few guards who had been left there. Other Jewish troops had been positioned in the vicinity of the village to defend two small Jewish settlements situated on the slopes of the hill and a large quarry located not far from it. The soldiers who dug in at Qastal laid fourteen charges with the intention of blowing up houses to create a clear field of vision for firing, but the charges were not detonated at the time.

Large numbers of Arab troops that had gathered in the nearby villages of Ein Karem, Suba, Qalunya, and Saris attacked the Jewish positions on the fifth and sixth of April. They succeeded in dislodging the Jewish soldiers from two of them and getting as far as the neighboring Jewish settlement of Upper Motza. The following day the Arabs captured the nearby quarry and continued their advance toward the village of Qastal. On the night between the sixth and seventh they reached the building housing the Jewish forces' headquarters in Qastal. The commander of the Arab forces, ʿAbd al-Qadir al-Husseini, stood at the head of the forward squad and was killed by a bullet fired by Sergeant Major Meir Karmiol, who was himself killed several hours later. The Arab attack was repulsed, and the identity of the dead al-Husseini did not become known to the Jewish soldiers until the afternoon of the eighth. The Arabs, however, upon learning of the fall of their revered commander, quickly mustered a force numbering more than a thousand machine gun–equipped fighters, retook Qastal on the afternoon of 8 April, and retrieved the body of their leader. In that battle thirty-nine Jewish soldiers were killed and thirty-five wounded; the Arabs suffered ninety casualties.

Once again the Arabs were in control of the Jerusalem–Tel Aviv Highway, but the death of their commander had demoralized them, and Jewish troops recaptured the village the night of 8–9 April. This time most of the houses were blown up, and the hill became a permanent command post. Two days later the village of Qalunya, beside the road to Jerusalem, on the slope of Mount Qastal, was captured and its houses, too, were demolished. On the night between 15 and 16 April, the village of Saris, situated to the west of Qastal, was occupied and destroyed. The Palmach commander explained his decision to destroy Saris thus: "Because I didn't want to leave a unit stationed in Saris . . . I decided to demolish the houses thereby prevent their becoming a base for Arab fighters. . . . I preferred occupying the village and expelling its inhabitants to [later] wiping out a gang of fighters."

Thus was the Haganah's Plan D implemented for the first time, and the village of al-Qastal is mentioned in the official history of the Haganah as "the first Arab village that was occupied with the intention of holding it permanently. . . . In place of sorties and raids against enemy bases, efforts were begun to take control of them."[6] There is no doubt that the considerations at the time of the occupation and destruction of the villages were purely military, and the decision to occupy specific villages was itself determined by operational requirements. Additional evidence for this can be found in the fact that nearby villages such as Suba and Ein Karem were not attacked, because they were not as close to the Tel Aviv road, and despite the fact that they served as bases for the activity of irregular Arab forces, they were not occupied at that time, even though it was well within the ability of the Haganah to overrun them in April 1948.

The Israeli designation of Qastal as the first village captured with the intent of "permanent conquest and occupation" does not seem accurate to Palestinian historians, who do not differentiate between villages that were vacated by their inhabitants before April of 1948 and subsequently taken over by Jewish forces as a local initiative and those that were conquered and occupied in accordance with Plan D. They see the distinction between the Principles for the Execution of Reprisal Actions of January 1948 and Plan D (from March of that year) as artificial and self-serving, and they regard the process of Jewish domination of the Arab landscape as having been continuous and premeditated. Palestinian scholars therefore stress that Plan D was "a Zionist program whose principle points were already determined before the 1948 War, its final version having only been adapted to suit the new reality created by the war."[7]

It is, of course, impossible to force this distinction on those who evaluate a process on the basis of its results. Why should the villagers of al-Qastal, who were uprooted by Plan D, feel that they are different from the villagers of the Sharon Plain, who fled from their homes as a result of attacks, executed according to the Principles for the Execution of Reprisal Actions? This way of looking at things is, however, based on a perception of the Arabs as powerless victims who had no influence on the actions of the all-powerful Zionist forces. To buttress this point of view, Palestinian historians divorce the conquest of the villages from the broader military context and do not deal at all with the "war of the roads," the Arab victory which obliged the Jews to adopt the strategy of conquest and occupation of vital areas. As mentioned earlier, everything is determined by context—but the context itself is determined by ethnic affiliation, and each side will choose what to define as cause and what as effect.

Indeed, the inhabitants of al-Qastal, Qalunya, and Saris had no interest in defining cause and effect, nor had they any consolation. Blame for their active participation in the war could in no way justify to them their uprooting and the destruction of their homes. On the eve of the 1948 War, approximately 150 souls were living in al-Qastal (according to the Haganah village dossier); they were affiliated with two *hamulas*, the Adwan and Matar clans. They inhabited about twenty-five stone houses and cultivated some 100 *dunams* of fruit trees, fifty *dunams* of olive groves, a few score *dunams* of vegetables, and additional plots of field crops. There was no school in the village. Its single shop and coffeehouse sat beside the main road to Jerusalem and were the property of an Armenian named Abu George. Most of the younger villagers had taken an active part in the Arab Revolt of 1936–39 under the command of ʿAbd al-Qadir al-Husseini and remained loyal to him in the 1948 War as well. Saris, located to the west of Qastal, was one of the largest villages along the Jerusalem road. "Village land" extended over more than 10,000 *dunams* and the number of inhabitants was roughly 600. The built-up area covered about ten *dunams*, and the houses were built of stone. There was a school and a mosque in the village. The inhabitants raised field crops on some 3,500 *dunams* and had orchards on 300. They participated in the harassment of Jewish convoys on the way to Jerusalem, and the village also served as a base for ʿAbd al-Qadir al-Husseini's force.

QALUNYA

The largest and most prosperous village along that section of the road to Jerusalem was Qalunya, which was situated in an area with plentiful water and abundant greenery. In the village, whose population was about 1,500 (2,500 according to the village dossier), were the summer homes of a number of well-connected Jerusalem families, both Muslim and Christian: Husseini, Nusseibeh, Maroum, and Niqula. Mufti Haj Amin al-Husseini maintained a large house and vineyard there. The villagers raised olive and fruit trees, as well as vegetables. A roadside restaurant, coffeehouses, and shops made this a pleasant stopping place for travelers on the main road to Jerusalem. According to the village dossier, "Qalunya as a whole is thought of as being the Husseinis' village, because of the property they have there. All of the inhabitants of the village are totally under their influence." It was perhaps for this reason that relations were tense between Qalunya and the neighboring Jewish village of Motza.

In 1929 villagers from Qalunya had attacked Motza, burning homes and killing several Jews; during the Arab Revolt, there were many gun battles between these Jewish and Arab settlements, and the British police station in the village was raided by the Arabs. The British authorities imprisoned many of the villagers and also imposed a collective fine on the village. On 5 April 1948 an Arab unit that set out from Qalunya attacked Upper Motza, from which the women and children had been evacuated earlier. The Arabs approached to within fifteen meters of the community's houses and blew up a school. The settlement commander decided to abandon the village, stating, "I am responsible for the people's lives. One must not toy with honor." He requested permission from his superior officers, who answered that he should decide for himself. At the last moment, reinforcements arrived and the withdrawal was aborted. Forty-eight hours later, on the night between 10 and 11 April, two Palmach companies occupied the already empty village of Qalunya and blew up all the houses.

DEIR YASIN

The tragedies of Qastal and Qalunya, however, pale before what befell the neighboring village of Deir Yasin on 9 April 1948. The Deir Yasin Massacre has been described down to the smallest detail in the fifty years since it took place; indeed, no other event had such a grievous influence on the tragic uprooting of the Arabs of Palestine as the murder of the inhabitants of this village—men, and especially women and children—at the hands of Jewish fighters. There is no doubt that the Deir Yasin Massacre deserves to be characterized as ethnic cleansing of the cruelest and most brutal sort. This village, whose population on the eve of the war was approximately 700, was essentially a suburb of Jerusalem and lived peacefully with its neighbors, the Jewish suburbs on the west side of the city. Only a minority of its inhabitants made their living from agriculture. Many others worked in Jerusalem, but the village's main source of employment, as well as of its economic prosperity, was the quarrying, cutting, and hauling of stone. Deir Yasin sat on rich veins of a hard limestone called *mizi yahudi,* which was resistant to the rigors of the Jerusalem climate. The stone taken from the large quarry near the village—called *hajar yasini* (Yasin's stone) after the village—was of a yellowish hue and in great demand in Jerusalem. Prosperity was abundantly evident in the village's spacious stone houses, two elementary schools, two mosques, many shops, and the flour mill that operated there.

With the outbreak of hostilities, Deir Yasin and the adjacent Jewish neighborhood of Givʿat Shaul signed an agreement promising to be good neighbors, to hand over information regarding the movement of strangers on village territory, and to guarantee the safety of vehicles from the village traveling within the precincts of the Jewish neighborhoods. This agreement was approved by Haganah headquarters in Jerusalem. The inhabitants of Deir Yasin were fastidious in their fulfillment of the terms of the agreement, forcefully resisting incursions by Arab irregulars and rejecting the suggestion that they reinforce village defenses with fighters from outside. Five days before the attack, village dignitaries had refused to allow the entry of Arab forces that were preparing for raids in the Qastal area—emphasizing the peaceful relations that prevailed between them and their Jewish neighbors. These facts were known to IZL and LEHI (the "Irgun" and "Stern Group," Jewish extremist splinter groups), who planned the attack on the village and, after the massacre, falsely claimed that Deir Yasin was a village of troublemakers where Syrian and Iraqi troops were being harbored.[8]

The decision by the splinter groups to attack Deir Yasin—from which they would not budge despite their nominally being under the command of the Haganah—was not justified militarily. The attackers also did not operate as a military unit, instead behaving like uncontrolled rabble. In fact, the villagers succeeded in wounding forty of them, and only the intervention of a Palmach unit, summoned by the beleaguered Jewish forces, saved the remainder and led to the conquest of the village. During, and especially after, the initial attack, the raiders fired indiscriminately, blew up houses with their inhabitants still inside, executed men, women, and children—firing at close range—and looted whatever came to hand. Although the number of dead is not known for certain, the figure cited in both Jewish and Arab sources is 254 souls, or approximately one-third of the inhabitants, many of them women and children. New studies conducted by Sharif Kanaʿaneh reduce the estimated number of casualties to 120 killed. At the conclusion of the battle, the surviving villagers were loaded on trucks and paraded in a "victory march" through the main streets of Jerusalem, escorted by cheering fighters, weapons in hand. The writer of these lines, then a boy of fourteen, along with thousands of the city's Jewish residents, still remembers this disgusting spectacle.

The outrage, scorn, and shame felt by the majority of Jerusalem's Jewish residents found expression in the publication of statements condemning the massacre from all the official Zionist institutions, as well as the Haganah High Command. Those responsible expressed no regret, however: "Each enemy or criminal must be addressed in his own language. . . . The conquest of Deir Yasin instilled dread and fear in the Arabs of all the villages in the vicinity."[9] Long afterward, Menachem Begin boasted that the panic that descended on the Arabs caused them to flee from the cities of Tiberias and Haifa as well. And indeed, the consequences of this barbaric act of ethnic cleansing were far-reaching. The Deir Yasin Massacre, which was reported on over and over again in all the Arab media, inspired tremendous fear, which led many Arabs to abandon their homes as the Jewish forces drew near. There is no doubt that Deir Yasin was a turning point in the annals of the destruction of the Arab landscape.

The Jews, too, paid a heavy price in blood. Five days after the massacre, on 13 April 1948, Arabs attacked a convoy of supplies and civilian workers on its way to Hadassah Hospital and the Hebrew University, both situated on Mount Scopus in East Jerusalem, killing seventy-eight and wounding twenty-four. Dozens burned to death inside the buses, and the remains of twenty-three victims were never located. The British forces in the vicinity did not intervene, explaining that they were "letting the Arabs take revenge for Deir Yasin, so as to calm somewhat the rage of the Arab world."[10] Just one month later, the Arabs carried out a massacre no less cruel than that of Deir Yasin. On 13 May 1948 the Jewish settlement of Kfar Etzion (in the Hebron Highlands) surrendered. All of its defenders assembled near the school, waving white flags. After they were photographed with their hands in the air, the Arabs opened fire, killing many on the spot. The wounded were finished off with knives, while their murderers shouted "Deir Yasin." Fifty people, fled to a nearby cellar, went to their deaths when hand grenades were tossed into their hiding place. The building was then blown up, burying them all. Altogether, 129 of the 133 inhabitants of Kfar Etzion perished in this barbaric massacre, and the settlement was razed.

MISHMAR HAʿEMEQ

In contrast to the Arab leadership—whose propaganda regarding the atrocities of Deir Yasin made a decisive contribution to undermining the morale of the Arab public—the Jewish leaders held up the "courageous defense" mounted by the inhabitants of Kfar Etzion as an example of "holding their ground unto death," to be emulated by every Jewish settlement. According to guidelines laid down by the leadership of the Jewish community, "Settlements are not to be vacated: The decisiveness and willingness with which we are fighting for our existence . . . requires the defense of remote besieged communities. . . . which makes it possible to expand the territory of the state by occupying land that separates these communities from areas of contiguous Jewish habitation."[11]

"Occupying land that separates" obviously meant the takeover and premeditated destruction of Arab settlements lying between blocks of Jewish settlement; and the earliest application of Plan D to an extensive piece of "land that separates" occurred in the Mishmar Haʿemeq region, at the foot of the Carmel Ridge, facing the Jezreel Valley. On 4 April 1948 the Arab Liberation Army (ALA), a semiregular fighting force of several thousands with seven field cannons and armored vehicles at their disposal, under the command of Fauzi Qauqji, launched an offensive against Kibbutz Mishmar Haʿemeq. This kibbutz was chosen as a target because it was close to Qauqji's base near Jenin in the West Bank; it was on the main road to Haifa, surrounded by Arab villages. The attack was repulsed, and Jewish forces launched a counterattack (8–14 April), in the course of which they gained control of the Arab villages surrounding the kibbutz but were forced to vacate them during the day because of bombardment by the ALA. The villages—which had been emptied of most of their inhabitants—changed hands several times before finally being occupied and destroyed by the Jewish forces. The few remaining villagers, who had fled to the nearby fields and woods, were expelled across the front lines toward the Arab town of Jenin. Thus eight villages—with some 5,000 inhabitants and a total area of sixty square kilometers—met their end. One Palmach commander asked his friend, "What do you think about the fact that we are expelling Arabs?"

The latter replied, "We're not expelling them, they're running away. Maybe they should be expelled, but we're not taking people and expelling them."

"LIBERATED BLOCKS"

Most of the villagers did, indeed, abandon their homes in panic, and only a minority were forcibly expelled. Yet the far-reaching significance of the destruction of villages on such a wide scale was not lost on the policy makers. Even though Ben-Gurion had given orders to expel villagers and demolish their houses in the past, he was now, by his own account, being confronted for the first time with the difficult decision of whether to apply this policy to several villages at once. Benny Morris quotes Ben-Gurion: "[They came] and told me that we must expel the Arabs in the area and burn the villages. For me this matter was very difficult."[12] The biographer of Yitzhak Sadeh, commander of the Jewish forces in the battle of Mishmar Haʿemeq, describes the scene when the decision regarding that operation was made:

> Sadeh asked his senior officers, while sitting on his bed holding a topographical map, "So, what are we going to do?" The fellows suggested staggered attacks, to take one village at a time. Sadeh listened without taking issue with anyone. He held his glasses in one hand as a pointer and made a semicircular sweep [across the map], covering the whole area. . . . The other guys, who had [up to then] only studied or been involved in attacks on isolated targets, learned that here they were talking about the conquest and cleansing of large pieces of territory for the purpose of creating a liberated block.[13]

At the time, "the conquest and cleansing of large pieces of territory for the purpose of creating a liberated block," was understood in its military sense only, but the distinction between military conquest and occupation and the establishment of settlements was in itself alien to the classical Zionist worldview. The redemption of land for the establishment of an independent Jewish community in Eretz Israel was an integrated endeavor, comprising the consolidation of military power and the setting up of agricultural settlements. The fighting pioneer and the farmer defending his home and his homeland merged to form a unified force on the biblical model: " . . . [the man who] with one of his hands wrought in the work and with the other hand held a weapon. . . . [E]very one had his sword girded by his side and so builded" (Neh. 4:17–18). The paired values of "the plow and the rifle," "sheaves and a sword," and "defense and settlement" are the very essence of the Zionist ethos.

The establishment of pioneering settlements was a means for achieving both political and security objectives: the settlers provided the element of control required for safeguarding Jewish existence and domination in strategically and politically vital sections of the country. Economic and physical planning considerations, as well as the actual ability of the settlements to sustain themselves, were secondary. In the period preceding the 1948 War, almost all of the new settlements were established in response to decisions by the Jewish political leadership, based on plans drawn up by military experts. The role of the settlement agencies (the Jewish National Fund [JNF], the Jewish Agency, and the settlement movements) was reduced to determination of the exact locations for new settlements and allocation of resources.

The use of settlement as a means for taking control of territory was a by-product of the conditions in which the Jewish community was operating under British Mandatory rule. The Yishuv did not have at its disposal governmental means of enforcement, such as the ability to legally expropriate tracts of land, as was done, for example, for government-sponsored settlers in Algeria and Kenya. The Yishuv had to purchase every available piece of property at full market price; and, beginning in 1940, the area where Jews could freely purchase land was limited to 5 percent of the total territory of Palestine. In many instances the Jews could not even evict and resettle tenant farmers who lived on land they had purchased. Military force was, of course, out of the question, so the idea of "transfer" (the forcible removal of populations) to allow unrestricted Jewish settlement, with which several Jewish leaders were toying, was perhaps wishful thinking and a theoretical possibility, but it could not be put into practice as long as the country was under British rule.

Even after the outbreak of the 1948 War, these pre-state perceptions and practices did not change substantially. Committees actively engaged in settlement planning early in the war laid out a plan calling for the establishment of more than a hundred new settlements intended to absorb 1 million or 1.5 million new immigrants in the space of three years. These settlements were to be set up on land that was under Jewish ownership, on land whose Arab landlords were absent, and on state land that was to be inherited from the departing British Mandatory administration. Similarly, according to the plan, the Jews would acquire undeveloped village land, which the Arabs would hand over—under the terms of a proposed development law—in return for government investment in adapting the remainder of their land to intensive farming (see below, chapter 4).

Joseph Weitz, director of the JNF Land Department and a prominent member of the various settlement-planning committees, advocated the transfer of the Arabs to outside the territory of the future Jewish state, but his proposal was not even discussed. According to an unpublished doctoral dissertation by Arnon Golan, who based his conclusions on data from primary sources: "The agencies involved in planning, building, and developing the Jewish state made provision in their plans for the Arab population, which, it was assumed, would constitute approximately half its inhabitants." [14] During the early stages of the war, the use of military force as a means for gaining control of land for settlement purposes was not considered an option. It became realistic only after the launching of Plan D—despite the fact that the plan had been intended not for this purpose but for directing military operations.

This does not mean that the exceedingly strong connection between military conquest and the "redemption of land" had escaped the notice of the Yishuv leadership. As early as the beginning of February 1948, two months prior to the commencement of the takeover of Arab villages in accordance with Plan D, David Ben-Gurion told JNF leaders: "The war will give us the land. Concepts of 'ours' and 'not ours' are peacetime concepts only, and they lose their meaning during war." He made a similar statement on another occasion soon afterward: "In the Negev we shall not buy land. We shall conquer it. You forget that we are at war." Yet Ben-Gurion was neither consistent nor conclusive in his views. A while later, when some Arab villages had been captured, making it possible to turn "not ours" into "ours," Ben-Gurion was in no hurry to do so. When Joseph Weitz asked him, "[What about] ownership of the land?" he responded with a question of his own: "Shall we steal land?" He "had forgotten," comments Weitz in his diaries, "what he had said before, that he would capture the land in the war." [15]

THE WAR WILL GIVE US LAND

This was not the only time that David Ben-Gurion articulated contradictory positions regarding the fate of the Arab villages and their landholdings. For example, in February 1948 he ordered the military commander of Jerusalem to settle Jews in abandoned Arab homes, but when a detailed and comprehensive proposal for the repopulation of abandoned villages was presented to him, he did not give his approval. He authorized the destruction of a village and silently assented to the eradication of others but rejected a proposal for the systematic destruction of large numbers of villages, brought to him by Zionist activists. Anyone wishing to assign responsibility for the destruction of the Arab landscape to the leader of the Yishuv and supreme commander of the Jewish forces will be able to find much to support this view. But those who would like to see him absolved of such responsibility will likewise find evidence to support their views. Ben-Gurion, constantly aware of how history would judge his deeds, publicly expressed misgivings regarding the expulsion of Arabs, the destruction of villages, and the seizure of their land. He knew that these deeds would be perceived in the future—by people far removed from the atmosphere of the war—as acts of cruelty that morally stained their perpetrators. He therefore strove to distance himself from those directly responsible for carrying out such actions. Even those who, for one reason or another, justify the destruction of the Arab landscape in retrospect cannot ignore the fact that the then national leader not only did not boast of it but also took great care in his writings to obfuscate his vital contribution to its execution.

Ben-Gurion grasped, with a profound historical understanding, the inner logic of these events: the Jewish-Palestinian intercommunal conflict, which broke out in full force with the departure of the British regime, was by nature a total war. Such a war does not distinguish between combatants and noncombatants, and it is fought over every plot of land, every house, and every section of roadway. The struggle is not restricted to fighting between the military forces at the disposal of the two sides; its outcome is instead determined by the ability of the respective communities to mobilize themselves totally—militarily, economically, socially, and morally—and to endure a long, bitter campaign in which old people, women, and children are killed, homes are demolished, and people are uprooted. The Jewish community was accustomed to total mobilization and was united around its volunteer decision-making bodies. It generally displayed discipline and obedience to its elected leaders, and despite intense differences of opinion regarding interpretation, the entire community identified with Zionist ideology and loyally followed the strategies formulated in its name.

All-out communal warfare was at its peak in March and April 1948—coinciding with the withdrawal of the British regime, which had done its utmost to prevent generalized conflict throughout the years of its rule. Of course, as soon as the Jewish community perceived the struggle as a war for its very survival (all the historical assessments suggesting that the Jews were never in danger of annihilation are products of the wisdom of hindsight), the military component of the Zionist strategy overshadowed all other considerations. Once a piece of land was captured and the army command decided to hold on to it on military grounds, however, the other came into play, transforming it into "liberated territory" redeemed by the Jewish People, which could be retained only if settled by agricultural pioneers who embodied both "sheaves and the sword."

David Ben-Gurion did not have to give explicit orders. He knew he could depend on his military commanders to "cleanse" the area of enemies and on those in charge of land acquisition and the leaders of the settlement movements to press for the implementation of the doctrine of settlement, and to do so even without obtaining official permission. All he had to do was coordinate, oversee their activity, and subordinate it to the overriding military and political exigencies that were his exclusive province. Yet even Ben-Gurion could not anticipate the consequences of the total war for the Arab population. The scope of the Arab exodus from the cities and villages astounded him, as it did the rest of the Yishuv's leadership. There is a great deal of evidence on the extent of their surprise; it was so overwhelming that many believed that the mass flight had been planned in advance by the Arab leadership with the objective of making it easier for the Arab armies to exterminate the Jewish community without harming the Palestinian population. Joseph Weitz wrote, while touring the deserted streets of Jaffa: "Jaffa the great, clamorous with sounds of the Orient—silence reigns there [now], and the silence frightens me. . . . the deep and whispering silence. Yes it is whispering, and what horrors are concealed in the whispers? What will happen if, Heaven forbid, the tables are turned?"[16] And Moshe Shertok (Sharett) stated: "Who expected—who could have imagined—that when the calamity of war overtook [the Palestinian People], they would uproot themselves thus and move and wander away from their places of habitation?"[17]

The astonishment was quickly replaced by the feeling that a "miracle" had taken place—the "miracle of the flight." Not many days went by before intentional efforts began being made to speed up the flight by force of arms, to initiate widespread expulsions, and later to nationalize and repopulate the abandoned landscape. There is, however, a qualitative difference between "premeditated transfer" and "transfer ex post facto," labeled as such by the Israelis (*transfer bediavad* in Hebrew); and those who accuse the Zionists of starting the 1948 War in order to expel the Arabs of Palestine from their land cannot ignore the intra-

Palestinian factors that motivated the mass flight in its early stages and were exploited by the Jews.

Khalil Sakakini, a prominent Palestinian intellectual and educator, wrote in his diary: "By God, I don't know how we will stand up to the aggression of the Jews. . . . Has the time not come for us to understand that unity triumphs over division, organization triumphs over anarchy, preparedness triumphs over negligence?"[18] Whereas the Jewish community had prepared itself for all-out war, the Palestinian community was factionalized and divided, lacking in any tradition of national discipline, split up into groups vying with one another for control, and polarized between an upper class of wealthy, landholding urban families and the masses of poor villagers. This community had not recovered from the blow it had sustained when radical leaders launched a general revolt against the British Mandate and the Zionist movement in 1936–39. The revolt was forcibly suppressed, but most of the bloodshed occurred in the course of the brutal civil war that accompanied it, an outcome of the murderous antagonism between members of rival factions. Hence the Palestinians did not take advantage of the relatively calm period preceding 1947 to consolidate their community, and they entered the war—which they themselves had started in order to thwart the Partition Plan—without a chance of winning.

When hostilities broke out, the prosperous urban families were the first to abandon their homes. A telling comparison may be drawn between the military-age members of the Jewish and Arab elites. With rare exceptions, members of well-established Jewish families took their places in the Yishuv's military forces, and many of them gave their lives. By contrast, their Arab contemporaries (residents of the same cities) left town before the war or during its early months, and took refuge at universities in Beirut, Cairo, or overseas. The Palestinian masses, in both the cities and the villages, were left to their fate and were compelled to contend with the consolidated strength of the Jewish Yishuv—each village or neighborhood by itself.

During the first months of the war, the Palestinians posed a serious threat to the Yishuv by virtue of their numerical superiority and their command of the terrain. Eventually, however, organization triumphed over anarchy, and Jewish motivation prevailed over Arab fears, which grew even greater in the wake of the general collapse of Arab society. Palestinian historians desirous of placing total responsibility for the Palestinian exodus with the Israelis have attempted to refute the common Israeli assertion that the Palestinians left in response to orders from their own leaders. The debate over whether Arab leaders actually did encourage the exodus has generated numerous detailed studies intended to either shore up or confute this claim. But for the most part the preoccupation with this question does not really address the Palestinian communal leadership's contributing responsibility for the mass flight: they may not have ordered it, but neither did they do—nor was it in their power to do—anything to halt it. And perhaps the leadership's greatest failing—their having been incapable of giving any guidance, whether to stay or whether to leave—was more grievous than the accusation that they had called upon their compatriots to flee. They had left them like sheep without a shepherd, and that disgrace could not be eradicated by laying all the blame on others.

ETHNIC CLEANSING?

The second Palestinian contention, that the Israelis had pursued a premeditated policy of ethnic cleansing, produced in-depth analyses of the exact reasons for the abandonment of every community.[19] According to Benny Morris, these reasons can be categorized as follows: expulsion by Jewish forces; abandonment by order of Arab leaders; fear of Jewish attack or accidental involvement in hostilities; a military campaign against the community by Jewish armed forces; a rumor-mongering campaign (psychological warfare); and the influence of the fall of a neighboring community or of the exodus of its inhabitants. Palestinian scholars accept these categories but add to them mass murder and rape, thereby imbuing the exodus with the character of ethnic cleansing.[20]

The distinctions among these categories can be somewhat forced, since the abandonment of villages was generally the outcome of a combination of factors that are difficult to isolate, especially so many years later. And at the end of the day, from the point of view of a refugee who has abandoned his home, it makes no difference how his flight is categorized. Nevertheless, the question of whether the exodus of the approximately 380,000 refugees who left their homes during the first half of the war (December 1947 through May 1948) constitutes "ethnic cleansing," as that term is currently understood, is worthy of examination.

"Ethnic cleansing" has been defined as "the expulsion of an undesirable population from a given territory due to religious or ethnic discrimination, political, strategic or ideological considerations or a combination of these."[21] The very use of this term—which originated during the Bosnian civil war of 1992–95—to characterize events that took place two generations earlier is problematic. This sterile, clinical phrase cloaks a reign of terror directed at the Bosnian Muslims by the Serbs, the goal of which was to bring about the physical destruction of the Bosnian-Muslim entity. The "RAM Plan" was devised by the Serbs with the aim of destroying the Bosnian economy and ridding the country of the Muslim population by killing half of them, converting a few, and expelling the remainder to Turkey.[22] The strategy of ethnic cleansing was to undermine the morale of the Muslims by means of a systematic campaign directed against the most vulnerable elements in the Muslim "religious and social structure," that is, "women, especially young ones, and children." To that end a fighting force was assembled, consisting of 80 percent common criminals and 20 percent fanatical nationalists, who committed wholesale rape, killed children before their parents' eyes, annihilated a large portion of the male population, and wrought havoc on Muslim communities, with the aim of "thus causing first of all fear and then panic, leading to a probable retreat from the territories involved in war activities."[23]

Mark Danner makes it clear that the Bosnian version of ethnic cleansing is none other than genocide in its original sense, as it was defined by the person who first coined the term in 1944: "A coordinated plan of different actions aimed at the destruction of different foundations of the life of national groups, with the aim of annihilating the groups themselves."[24] And much of the international community regarded "ethnic cleansing," as employed in the case of Bosnia, as a euphemism for genocide as defined in the UN Convention on the Prevention and Punishment of the Crime of Genocide. The Palestinians would not dare go so far as to accuse the Jews of the crime whose principal victims they were. Designating the Arab exodus as "ethnic cleansing" seems more moderate to them, while at the same time it conjures up visions of the atrocities of the Bosnian civil war. They therefore make a point of emphasizing the isolated instances of rape and murder of women and children that took place during the last stages of the war, as we shall see later.

The rules of war prohibit the expulsion of civilians, the demolition of their homes, or damage to their property, not to mention injury to their persons. A distinction is made, however, between injury to civilians as a result of military actions in response to hostile activities, and ethnic cleansing carried out after hostilities have ceased and the area has been secured militarily. During civil wars or intercommunal conflicts, distinctions between civilians and soldiers become blurred, and acts of violence are perpetrated by armed militias that are not subject to control by any clear authority, and whose brutality is nourished by ancient hatreds and the frictions that arise daily from living in close quarters, as well as from mutual fear. All of the conditions leading to the Palestinian exodus (up to late May 1948) were typical of those that prevail during violent intercommunal conflicts, and they do not fit the definition of "ethnic cleansing"—unless it can be proven that they were the result of explicit orders whose objective was to promote a campaign of organized terror, rape, and systematic murder, with the aim of expelling civilians on other than military grounds and taking over their homes and landholdings and settling them with members of the other community.

The designation of the Arab exodus of the first half of the war as "ethnic cleansing" is, of course, controversial, and evidence supplied by even the most exacting researchers does not justify the use of that term. An order was indeed issued to take control of Arab villages and expel their inhabitants (Plan D), but there is no doubt that its objectives were military, it did not include a directive to target this territory for Jewish settlement, and generally the commanders were not required to forcibly expel the inhabitants, since they had fled prior to the capture of their villages. The commanders of the Jewish forces certainly did carry out some attacks whose objective was to terrorize the Arabs into leaving their homes, but on the other hand there is abundant evidence that the Jewish leadership was surprised at the scope of the exodus and even made efforts to persuade the Arabs to remain in their homes. Jews did take over abandoned Arab homes in the suburbs of Tel Aviv and Jerusalem as early as the winter of 1948, but they themselves were generally refugees who had been uprooted from Jewish border neighborhoods that had suffered Arab attacks.

It is certainly hard to isolate the military-oriented from the settlement-oriented aspects of the Jewish leaders' motivations, but the abandoned villages attracted those infused with the urge to "redeem the soil," and there is no doubt that the Jews' appetite was aroused by the "miraculous exodus," which spread before them possibilities they had not previously envisioned. It is of course true that the overwhelming majority of those who were uprooted were Arabs, yet thousands of Jews also abandoned their homes because of the hostilities, and several Jewish settlements were captured and destroyed. And there is no doubt that the Palestinians were the primary victims of the intercommunal warfare, but they cannot shrug off responsibility for the outbreak of hostilities. When all is said and done, the 1948 War erupted because of the Arabs' refusal to accept the UN Partition Plan. And even if this refusal arose from principled and legitimate motives, that does not reduce their responsibility for what took place as a result of the fatal error they made in choosing the military option. The astonishing helplessness exhibited by the Palestinian leadership contributed greatly to the flight of their people, and the contention that the Jews exploited the Palestinians' weakness in order to carry out unprovoked, premeditated ethnic cleansing does not stand up to close scrutiny.

But these unambiguous conclusions regarding "ethnic cleansing" apply only to the first part of the war. The violent situation, ideological perceptions, and demographic, economic, and political pressures, both internal and external—especially the proclamation of the State of Israel (14 May 1948) and the invasion by the armies of the Arab states—gave rise to changes that necessitate a different view of the Arab exodus during the second half of the war.

Before describing these changes (in the next chapter), however, it is fitting to chronicle in some detail the destruction of the Arab physical and human landscape up to that point. The following account is presented according to geographical region and not in chronological order.[25]

THE EASTERN GALILEE

In the Galilee Panhandle and the Upper and Eastern Galilee—the territory corresponding to the Mandatory subdistrict of Safad from Metullah in the north to the north shore of the Sea of Galilee and from Safad in the west to the Jordan River in the east—there were approximately sixty villages on the eve of the 1948 War. The exact number is in dispute because of the differing definitions of what constituted a village. Some of the "villages" of the Huleh Valley were Bedouin encampments whose inhabitants lived in huts made of reeds (see plate 2), in tents, and in mud structures. Of these sixty villages, fifty had been conquered by the end of May 1948, most of them in the Huleh Valley and on its western slopes and in the vicinity of the town of Safad. I estimate the number of villagers uprooted from their homes by the end of May as approximately 30,000 (excluding Safad, from which 10,000 fled) and the number of abandoned houses as 3,700. Most of the villages were small, with populations not exceeding 500. Only four had over 1,000 inhabitants, and the largest of them, al-Khalsa had approximately 2,000. Another sixteen villages in that area, with 10,000 inhabitants in all, were abandoned at a later date.

According to data from the Mandatory government, these villages contained about 200,000 *dunams* of arable land. The villagers of the water-rich Huleh Valley grew field crops and vegetables and had orchards of fruit trees. A branch of agriculture unique to this region was the raising of water buffalo. One of the commanders of the Jewish forces explained that convoys to the Jewish settlements in the area were planned taking into account the movement of the water buffalo to and from the swamps to avoid encountering these large animals on their way. Once a convoy was late leaving, and it ran into herds of water buffalo near the village of Khalsa. The commander gave an order to run down the animals, since he was afraid to halt his vehicles. As a result, "We got into a dispute with the owners of the herds, and relations with the Arabs deteriorated even more."

Raising water buffalo was a common practice among the Ghawarnah, that is, tribes that inhabited swampy areas (not necessarily only in the Huleh region but also the marshes of the Mediterranean Coastal Plain). The Ghawarnah were considered inferior not only by the permanently settled villagers but also by the seminomadic Bedouin. Their center was the large village of al-Khalsa, and their sheikh, Kamal Hussein, played an important role in the Jewish-Arab conflict. Sheikh Kamal was responsible for the incidents at Tel Hai in 1920: he led the raid on this isolated Jewish settlement, during which Joseph Trumpeldor and seven of his comrades were killed. This became one of the central myths of the Zionist movement, as expressed in the last words spoken (or not) by the one-armed Jewish commander: "It is good to die for our country." In the years preceding the 1948 War, Sheikh Kamal established close relations with the Jewish settlers, but the veterans of Tel Hai and older members of the neighboring settlement of Kfar Gilʿadi did not forget his part in the events of 1920 and had cultivated his sworn enemy, Emir Faour, leader of the al-Fadel tribe, whose members lived in the Golan Heights and the eastern part of the Huleh Valley. Emir Faour also acted as an agent in the sale of land to Jews, and during the forties either sold or negotiated the sale of plots of unallocated (*mushʿa*) land totaling some 12,000 *dunams*. In the Huleh also lived the descendants of Arab settlers who had come from Algeria in 1847 with their leader, ʿAbd al-Qadir, who had rebelled against the French regime in his homeland and fled to the Ottoman Empire. They were sent by the Turks to settle in this area and in other regions of Palestine and Syria.

The settlements in the rocky area between the Huleh and the Sea of

Galilee were inhabited by Bedouin, some of whom were of Turkmen descent. Hence the character of their settlements and ways of pursuing their livelihood were different from those of the inhabitants of the Huleh swamps and the streams that fed into them. The majority of the region's inhabitants were tenant farmers who cultivated the land of absentee owners, mainly Syrians and Lebanese. This fact made it possible for Jewish interests, both private and national, to purchase broad expanses of territory in the northern and central sections of the region. On the list of those who sold land to Jews appear the names of the emir Chehab, the emir Jazairi, the emirs Faour and Shaman, the Salam family, and many others. In 1934 the Jews received the concession to a large piece of swampy Huleh land (54,000 *dunams*) from the Mandatory government, on condition that they drain it. The JNF held rights to *mush'a* land in many areas, ranging from 14 to 70 percent of the rights in a given area. But the Jewish owners could not violate the rights of the tenants to remain on their land. A map of the region in 1947 shows that most of the area north and west of the Huleh was wholly or partially under Jewish ownership, and that there were only nineteen Arab villages where Jews did not have a foothold. On the eve of the 1948 War there were eighteen Jewish settlements in the northern and southern Huleh, the first of which had been established in 1882 and the last in 1945.

The Arab villages on the slopes of the Galilean hills and in the vicinity of the town of Safad were totally different in character from those in the Huleh Valley. They were typical hill villages, supporting themselves by raising field crops, olives, tobacco, and from fruit orchards and vineyards. The topography of the area—which included rocky hills separated by fertile valleys—meant that only a third to a half of the villages' land was arable. Most of the villages in this region that had been captured up to the last half of May 1948 were close to Safad and economically dependent on the town.

Most of the Huleh villages were abandoned in less than a month. The reasons were many and complex: some were vacated after being attacked, others were evacuated in response to orders from Syria or from commanders of the Arab irregulars (ALA), and some villagers fled as a result of the psychological warfare employed by the Jewish forces. Presumably, the relative ease with which most of the Arab inhabitants of the Galilee Panhandle left their villages stemmed from the fact that a significant proportion of them were seminomadic Bedouin and others were tenant farmers—and indeed, the first to abandon the area were the

Bedouin. The Jewish forces, whose strategic objective was to secure their rear in case of a Syrian attack from the east or a Lebanese incursion from the west, blew up the stone or concrete houses in the abandoned villages and burned the reed huts. A determining factor in the flight of the villagers of the Huleh and eastern Upper Galilee is known to have been the capture of Safad on 9–10 May. The fall of this important Arab center and administrative seat of the subdistrict resulted in large-scale flight, in the course of which some ten nearby villages—and in the Huleh Valley as well—were abandoned. Regarding the influence of the fall of Safad on the abandonment of the large village of al-Khalsa, Nafez Nazal states: "Upon the fall of Safad the villagers fled from their houses to the village of Hunin. About 100 men remained in the village (and one of them recounted): 'The morning Safad fell we met members of the Arab Liberation Army retreating towards the mountains. They suggested that we take our families across to Lebanon for a week or two. . . . They assured us that they were regrouping to recapture Safad.'"[26]

Several dozen militiamen remained in al-Khalsa; they could not, however, stand up to the Jewish attack and fled the village. One of them, who returned a few days later to retrieve money that he had buried in the courtyard of his house, found the village in ruins. The fate of Ein Zaytun, situated very close to Safad, was even more terrible. This village of 800 was attacked on 1 May 1948, as a prelude to the attack on the town itself. Following bombardment by mortars, Palmach units spread out through the village. Most of the men escaped, and the women, children, and old people were scared off by shots fired over their heads. A few score young men were captured and penned up as prisoners. Two days later they were taken down to a nearby wadi and were executed, with their hands bound, by order of the Palmach commander. All the houses in the village were systematically blown up so as to undermine the confidence of the Arab inhabitants of Safad, most of whom watched the destruction of Ein Zaytun from their homes on the other side of the valley. Safad was taken a few days later, and its more than 10,000 Arab occupants abandoned it. Arab inhabitants remained in only three villages in the Huleh Valley: Khisas, Qaytiyya, and Ja'una. In June 1949 they were expelled to 'Akbara, near Safad.[27]

All that remained in the Huleh Valley was one Bedouin settlement, now called Touba-Zanghariyya, whose inhabitants—members of the al-Haib Tribe—chose to associate themselves with the Jewish forces. By the end of May the surrounding Jewish settlements had already begun to harvest the Arab fields, where the winter crops had ripened. In the Huleh Valley alone, this land encompassed an area of 15,000 *dunams.*

THE SEA OF GALILEE RIFT VALLEY, BEISAN (BEIT SHEAN), AND THE EASTERN LOWER GALILEE

This region, which by and large corresponds to the Mandatory subdistricts of Tiberias and Beisan, is divided into several geographical units according to landscape type: the shore of the Sea of Galilee and its vicinity, the hills of the eastern Lower Galilee, the Yavniel Valley and the land bordering it, the Heights of Issachar, and the Beisan (Beit Shean) Valley. The Arab population of the area as a whole was sparse because the prevailing climatic and soil conditions were not conducive to rain-fed agriculture. As a result, Jewish organizations managed to acquire extensive landholdings on the western shore of the Sea of Galilee and in the Yavniel and Beit Shean Valleys, and to establish forty settlements there. The number of Arab villages in this region was forty-four, thirty-six of which (with a combined population of 20,000, plus approximately 4,000 Bedouin) had been captured and abandoned by the end of May 1948. These figures do not include the Arab inhabitants of the towns of Beisan and Tiberias, who numbered around 11,000. Another three villages were occupied at a later date (including the large villages of Lubia and Hittin), and their 4,000 inhabitants expelled. Most of these villages were small, with populations not exceeding 500. Only four villages had over 1,000 inhabitants. The town of Samakh, on the southern shore of the Sea of Galilee, had a population numbering approximately 3,600.

The flow of refugees from the region had commenced as early as February through March 1948, starting with Bedouin tribes. The villages in the Tiberias area were conquered and abandoned around the same time as the conquest of the Arab sections of the mixed town itself (on 18 April 1948), and the villages in the Beisan Valley were taken around the time of the fall of the Arab town of Beisan (12 May). Only a small minority of these villages were abandoned as a result of military raids, while in most cases the flight of the villagers was precipitated by their fear that the Jewish forces would harm women and children, as they had in the village of Nasr al-Din near Tiberias on 13 April—as well as by orders from the Arab leadership. By the end of May 1948, residents of the Jewish settlements had begun harvesting the abandoned Arab fields, and military units, aided by settlers, started demolishing buildings in those villages closest to the Jewish settlements.

The strategic importance of the occupation of the southern end of the Sea of Galilee and the Beit Shean Valley was confirmed when the Syrian and Iraqi armies invaded (south of the Sea of Galilee and the northern Beit Shean Valley, respectively). Heavy fighting ensued in both sectors, in the course of which the Arab armies retook several Arab villages (as well as two Jewish kibbutzim) but were ultimately defeated. The Beit Shean Valley was among the first areas where the raison d'être of Jewish control shifted from military necessity to settlement and "redemption of the land." Members of local Jewish settlements had been pressuring their leadership since late April 1948 to let them settle the Arab land that had been abandoned; indeed, by 10 June 1948 two Jewish settlements had been set up on the land of Arab villages. After the war, only five of the forty-four Arab villages in these areas remained.

THE JEZREEL VALLEY, RAMAT MENASHE, AND THE CARMEL RANGE

In the Eastern Jezreel Valley, a fertile agricultural region, there were twelve small Arab villages, the largest of which, with a population of 1,500, was Zirʿin. Seven of these villages, affiliated with the Zuʿabiyah *hamula,* made a pact with the Jews and were not harmed. However the villages of Qumya (440 souls) and Indur—the biblical Endor (620 souls)—which were not associated with this *hamula,* were captured and evacuated. Late in May 1948 three villages on the slopes of Mount Gilboa, facing the Jezreel Valley (Nuris, Mazar, and Zirʿin), were taken. Even though Zirʿin had a certain degree of military importance, one may assume that the objective in conquering the villages in the southern part of the valley was to obtain their land. The arable land of these five villages amounted to not less than 41,000 *dunams.* The Jews were particularly interested in the fields of the village of Qumya, which was entirely surrounded by JNF land, and those of Zirʿin (22,000 *dunams*) where Jews owned 7 percent of the *mushʿa* land. Altogether, approximately 3,500 souls abandoned this region.

On the western side of the valley, on the eastern and western slopes of Mount Carmel, within the borders of the Mandatory district of Haifa, were forty-four Arab villages, with a combined population of 56,000 (not counting the city of Haifa with its 79,000 Arabs, 7,000 of whom remained after the war). Some 30,000 souls had abandoned or been expelled from twenty-eight of these villages by the end of May, and another 13,000, in eight other villages, subsequently met the same fate. Eight villages (13,000 inhabitants) remained after the war. The villages that were abandoned can be grouped in several categories, which will now be described, beginning with the farthest north and proceeding southward.

The two largest villages in the immediate vicinity of Haifa (Balad al-Sheikh and Yajur) were captured and evacuated on 24–25 April, following the fall of Haifa. The Jewish forces thereby consolidated their control of the principal traffic artery serving Haifa from the south (the direct route to Haifa was under the control of the Arab villages of the western Carmel—see below), the southern portion of this road having been captured at the time of the battle of Mishmar Haʿemeq, described previously.

The eight villages to the north and south of Mishmar Haʿemeq had been destroyed immediately following the end of the battle, and their inhabitants fled or were expelled. According to the testimony of members of the neighboring kibbutzim (Hazoreʿa and Mishmar Haʿemeq), the conquering forces committed acts of brutality as well as widespread looting. They make particular note of the destruction of the village of Abu Zureik.[28] Joseph Weitz describes the devastated Arab villages immediately following the battle:

> In the meanwhile I visited the Arab villages that had been captured by our people, and I saw them in their ruined state. Not one person was left; the houses and mud huts were totally demolished. All that remained were the clay *taboon* ovens. From one of these rose the smell of burnt bread. Among the heaps of collapsed rubble echoed the cries of a deserted chicken, and a poor orphaned donkey wandered the paths of the village. This devastation brings in its wake many problems that we did not anticipate. These involve difficulties from a socioethical point of view and from the standpoint of the authorities.

The instinctive response of this man, whose life had been dedicated to "the redemption of the land," was what one might have expected; Jews must be settled on the abandoned sites, and the land must be cultivated: "settlement in the wake of military conquest."[29] Weitz put 1,000 Palestinian pounds (worth one pound sterling each) at the disposal of the army for the fortification of two positions, "on condition that they assist [the members of] Mishmar Haʿemeq to cultivate the land of Ghubayya al-Fawqa (an adjacent Arab village that had been destroyed), in order to strengthen our hold on it." He pressured the army "to evacuate Butaymat" (a village situated to the south of the village of Kafrayn), which had been occupied and destroyed. Butaymat's land was important to him because the JNF held 60 percent of the *mushʿa* rights in the village. Additional tracts of land were "put at [Weitz's] disposal" as a result of the occupation of five villages situated between the Mishmar Haʿemeq area and the large block of Jewish settlements in the Coastal Plain. The ones responsible for this action were the forces of the IZL (the "Irgun"), who had brutally expelled its 4,000 inhabitants.

Within the boundaries of the large block of Jewish settlements stretching from the town of Netanya in the south to the township Zichron Yaʿakov in the north were many small Arab villages as well as encampments of seminomadic Bedouin. By the middle of May 1948, these communities had been destroyed, and their inhabitants had abandoned them. It is worthy of note that neighborly relations had prevailed between these Arab communities and nearby Jewish settlements, and many of the Arabs had earned their livelihoods working in the Jewish communities. But the intensification of hostilities put an end to any local efforts to preserve peaceful relations, and even those Arabs who were prepared "to live under Jewish rule" did not escape expulsion.

According to Benny Morris, Caesarea, situated in the middle of the Jewish block (on the Mediterranean shore) was the first Arab village in the country "whose inhabitants were expelled in a pre-planned and organized manner in 1948."[30] On 20 February 1948 most of the houses of the village—surrounded by walls built by King Louis IX of France in 1251–54—were destroyed, and only six were saved "because of a shortage of explosives." The village's 960 inhabitants left, some as early as January of that year and some around the time of the blowing up of the houses. It is possible that their leaving was due to the fact that more than half the villagers were tenants of the Jewish land company known as the Palestine Jewish Colonization Association (PJCA), founded by Baron Edmond de Rothschild, and a large proportion of the land in Caesarea was its property. But the rest of the villagers, Muslims of Bosnian origin, lived in spacious homes with tiled roofs, and they left behind a thriving village.

Two Arab communities to the north of Caesarea were left in place, unharmed. The first was Jisr al-Zarqa, which had been built to accommodate the Bedouin of the marshes (the Ghawarnah). It was established in the twenties by the PJCA, which had drained the swamps and settled the tent- and hut-dwelling seminomads there. Some of the inhabitants, along with the villagers of the adjacent community of Furaydis, worked in the nearby Jewish towns of Binyamina and Zichron Yaʿakov, and this fact no doubt saved them from expulsion—which the Israeli army had proposed more than once. These two villages served as a haven for refugees from villages that had been destroyed, as well as a place to which the authorities sent people who had been ordered to leave their homes.

The fate of the village of Tantura, located on the seashore a little farther to the north, was very sad indeed. On the eve of the war the population of this village, one of the most highly developed in the area, numbered 1,650. Its homes, which stood on a low limestone hill overlooking the shoreline of two small bays, were built of stone with roofs of concrete and wood. They were supplied with running water pumped from a well in the eastern part of the village. A road built for the use of automobiles connected Tantura with the Haifa highway. The inhabitants made their living from field crops and vegetables, some fruit orchards, and large-scale fishing. Tantura had a school for boys and another for girls, eight shops, and a mosque. The four *hamula*s that lived there maintained good relations with one another, as well as with the Mandatory authorities. Fourteen villagers worked in government service as policemen, customs officials, and clerks in the Haifa Magistrate's Court, the Department of Antiquities, and the railway. Several had participated in violent activities during the Arab Revolt, and three of them were killed in a battle with the British army close to the village.

Sometime after the outbreak of hostilities, the wealthier families pulled up stakes and moved to Haifa, whereas the 1,200 who were left behind went on with their lives, while maintaining close ties with the villages to their north on the slopes of the Carmel, whose inhabitants were harassing Jewish traffic on the main road to Haifa. When Haifa was conquered, the villages on the Carmel slopes were isolated, and the Jewish forces decided to reduce the size of this Arab pocket by taking Tantura, whose port for fishing boats could have provided the villagers with a means for maintaining contact with the outside world. According to Jewish sources, the villagers refused a proposal that they surrender without a fight, and on the night between 22 and 23 May, Tantura fell, and all its inhabitants were expelled (or left voluntarily) and took refuge in the adjacent village of Furaydis. They were not allowed to take their belongings with them nor to work their fields, which bordered on those of Furaydis. As a result, the Tantura refugees' situation was desperate; ultimately, most of them were expelled to territory under Arab control. Only 171 of them, mostly women and children, remained in Furaydis.

THE SHARON, THE TEL AVIV AREA, AND THE SOUTHERN COASTAL PLAIN

About a dozen small Arab villages were scattered over the Sharon Plain. The largest were Qaqun (population 1,970) and Kafr Saba (population 1,270). The region was also inhabited by seminomadic Bedouin. Ten villages, with a combined population of 6,500, were abandoned, the last of their inhabitants having been expelled by the end of May 1948. Another two villages, situated on the western edge of the Sharon Plain—home to approximately 2,200 souls—were occupied in July, and their inhabitants expelled. On 5 May, Joseph Weitz was already able to drive through the region "in a little car, like in the good old days." "The Arabs have left; their huts have disappeared," he wrote in his diary. "I saw this great valley . . . and here it was, all ours and Jewish hands were working in it."[31] He was now finally able to get his hands on the land of Miska, Wadi Hawarith, and Khirbat Beit Lidd, which he had coveted for twenty years. The inhabitants of the surrounding Jewish communities had their eyes on the abandoned houses; they dismantled everything that could be taken apart and carried off everything they could manage: pumps, pipes, household accessories, cattle; and what they could not take, they destroyed. They harvested the crops.

The "cleansing" of the Arab areas bordering Tel Aviv–Jaffa was completed in late April. By the end of March all the villages north of Tel Aviv had been occupied and, following the mass exodus from the city of Jaffa, the large villages to its east were taken without a battle, in an operation dubbed "Hametz" (leavened bread—after the burning of leavened bread products before the holiday of Passover), 24–30 April. In the course of the first weeks of May, all the villages in the Rishon Lezion–Rehovot region were captured. By the end of May 1948, altogether forty-eight villages in this region, whose combined population exceeded 69,000, had been taken. These were mainly large villages in the process of becoming suburbs of neighboring towns and cities. Their inhabitants grew citrus fruit and bananas, but they also had set up modern industrial plants, and many were employed in the nearby Jewish cities and in Arab Jaffa. All of these villages had schools for both boys and girls, and most had running water and electricity.

The many lovely homes that had been built there during the prosperous period of the early forties attracted the attention of their Jewish neighbors; indeed, as early as December 1947, Jewish settlers broke into homes in the village of Jammasin, which bordered on Tel Aviv. In March 1948 the orderly takeover of the houses in the village of Sheikh Muwannis by Jewish residents of Tel Aviv began, and this process gathered momentum during the summer months. A few villages in the area had established good connections with neighboring Jewish communities and even expressed willingness to surrender and continue living under Jewish rule. In spite of this (and even after several villages did surrender and hand over their weapons), their inhabitants were expelled by force of arms and with the help of "psychological warfare." Serious atrocities were committed in the large village of Zarnuqa near Rehovot. The villagers, who had had good relations with their Jewish neighbors (and were therefore hated by inhabitants of the neighboring Arab villages), were expelled, and 2,500 souls were sent into exile.

In the southernmost section of the country, where the campaign against the invading Egyptian army was about to take place, the Jewish forces also commenced the "cleansing" of the area of its Arab population. This initiative was undoubtedly prompted by the need to secure the rear for the action of the Israeli army in the battle with the Egyptians. In the course of the campaign, twelve villages, with a total population of 14,000, were occupied. Thirty-three villages in this region, comprising some 47,000 souls, were captured during the summer of 1948, and their inhabitants either fled or were expelled.

Plan D, in accordance with which the actions involving the conquest and takeover of the villages were carried out, was "a plan for gaining control of the territory of the Jewish state and for the defense of its borders," as mentioned earlier. When this plan was drawn up, it was formulated with reference to the borders defined in the UN Partition Plan. Therefore, the territory that was captured and from which the Arab inhabitants fled was principally within the area that had been allocated to the Jewish state. Scrutiny of a map of the territory captured up to the middle of May 1948 reveals that the political and military leadership confined its targets to locations within the partition borders and dared not deviate from this guideline except in the face of compelling military constraints, such as the need to secure the road to Jerusalem or to gain control of the Western Galilee, where there were isolated Jewish settlements.

These restrictions on the scope of Israel's takeover of Arab territory stemmed, no doubt, from the paucity of resources at the disposal of the Jews, as well as from their assessment that the United Nations could be expected to work for the implementation of the Partition Plan, and it was not desirable to get into a confrontation with the international community in the sensitive context of the upcoming proclamation of the state and the necessity to obtain international recognition for it. Hence one may view Plan D as defensive, with an aim to take control of only those areas intended for the Jewish state. Nevertheless, the takeover of Arab territory and the expulsion of the village inhabitants can also be seen as a program of aggressive expansion resulting in the displacement of hundreds of thousands of human beings and the destruction of their world. One way or the other, the Jewish state was emptied of the overwhelming majority of its Arab inhabitants, who, according to the terms of the Partition Plan, were supposed to be full citizens of this state, with equal rights.

Most of the captured villages outside the designated boundaries of the Jewish state were located along the road to Jerusalem (seven villages with approximately 7,500 inhabitants) and in the Western Galilee (twelve villages, population about 10,000). The villages along the road to Jerusalem were situated in a narrow strip that ensured Jerusalem's contact with Tel Aviv, and there is no doubt that their capture was dictated by military considerations. The conquest of the villages of the Western Galilee was motivated by a combination of military needs and the desire for revenge. The villages that lined the coastal road linking the Jewish settlements of the Western Galilee with Haifa were captured on 13–14 May 1948 (Operation Ben-Ami, first phase), thereby connecting the block of Jewish communities that lay in an area designated as part of the Arab state with the body of the Jewish state.

One week later, the second phase of Operation Ben Ami was carried out—during which five villages situated to the east of the Jewish seaside town of Nahariya were occupied. The principal objective of this phase of the operation was to lift the siege on the isolated settlement of Kibbutz Yehiam, but it had an additional, and perhaps more important, goal: to take revenge on the Arab villages that had had a part in wiping out a supply convoy bound for Yehiam. The convoy was attacked by hundreds of armed villagers and units of the ALA as it passed near the village of al-Kabri on 27 March 1948. Forty-nine Jews (and six Arabs) were killed in the battle. Serious allegations were made against the brigade commander at the time of the disaster, claiming that he had not rushed to the aid of the beleaguered convoy. Two months later, when he was directing Operation Ben Ami, this commander gave an order (not without an element of vengefulness and atonement for his earlier failings): "To attack, with the aim of capturing, the villages of Kabri, Umm al-Faraj, and al-Nahr, to kill the men, [and] to destroy and set fire to the villages." His orders were, in fact, carried out to the letter.

A similar fate befell al-Zib, situated on the shore of the Mediterranean, between Nahariya and the Lebanese border. Al-Zib was a large village, with a population of approximately 2,000 and an area of some 10,000 *dunams*. Its landholdings were spread out over the valley of Wadi Qurayn (Nahal Keziv) and included over 2,000 *dunams* of irrigated citrus groves and bananas. Some of the villagers made their living from fishing, and some owned shops, coffeehouses, or presses for extracting oil from the olives grown in the village. The villagers had taken part in the hostilities, and the Jewish forces wanted to get back at them for this. The village was attacked with mortar fire, and most of its inhabitants fled. Only thirty-five or forty stayed behind to defend it and the dozens of women and older men who had not been able to escape. The Jewish forces captured al-Zib almost without a battle and then proceeded to blow up houses in its southern and eastern sectors. The remnants of the population were expelled from the country or transferred to al-Mazraʿa, one of the villages near Nahariya, which became the collection point for all the refugees who had not been expelled across the border. Al-Zib, with its partially intact mosque and picturesque collection of buildings overlooking the Mediterranean, was eventually turned into a tourist site.

The village bordering al-Zib on its northeastern side, al-Bassa, was taken immediately after the fall of its neighbor. It was one of the largest and most highly developed villages in the north of the country, with a population of 4,000, half of them Christian and half Muslim. Its fields stretched out over hills, mountains, and, most important, the plains to the south: more than 20,000 *dunams,* about 2,000 of them under irrigation. The village council was very active: it installed a system for supplying running water to the houses, paved the streets, and oversaw the wholesale produce market held every Sunday. There was also an active agricultural cooperative, boasting as many as 150 members, which provided loans to farmers and promoted mechanization and other practices conducive to the advancement of agriculture. There was a government-run elementary school in al-Bassa, as well as a "National High School." It was a regional commercial center, with sixty shops and eleven coffeehouses, some of which were situated on the Haifa-Beirut Highway. Some residents made their living as smugglers, transporting goods across the Lebanese border, which passed just to the north of the village, and several dozen were employed at the adjacent British military airfield.

Relations among the three religious communities of al-Bassa were good, and their relations with the Mandatory government were reasonably so. There were two churches in the village (Greek Orthodox and Catholic), as well as a mosque. Villagers' involvement in the hostilities was slight. When action in the area heated up, some villagers left their homes and crossed the border into Lebanon. On 14 May 1948 the village was attacked and its remaining inhabitants fled. The Jewish soldiers found only a few dozen and ordered them to gather in the Orthodox church. According to one witness, the soldiers shot and killed five villagers inside the church (the survivors display the bullet holes in the east wall of the church, behind the altar). According to another, seven villagers were taken out and shot outside the church, after which all the rest were expelled. Some of the Christian villagers found refuge in Miʿiliya, while the Muslims were sent to al-Mazraʿa.

The inhabitants of the village of Ghabisiyya, situated to the south of al-Kabri, maintained close ties with their Jewish neighbors and had even signed an agreement to provide information to them, in return for which the Jewish forces undertook not to enter the village or harm its residents. In spite of the agreement, the village was occupied, eleven of its inhabitants were killed, and the remainder fled and found shelter in neighboring villages. In the spring of 1949 most of them (who were by then Israeli citizens) returned to their village, but they were again evicted on 26 January 1950 and ordered to pull up stakes and move to the adjacent village of Sheikh Danun. In September they again returned to the village but were evicted the following day. The displaced villagers appealed to the Supreme Court of Israel (sitting as the High Court of Justice), which ruled that "the military governor had no authority to evict the petitioners [from the village] and he has no authority to prevent them from entering or leaving it or from residing there." [32] The government, however, disregarded the ruling of the High Court; the land of the village was expropriated, and in 1955 its houses were demolished, leaving only a large mosque.

The Ghabisiyya affair was in the news again in 1997, when the Israeli government forbade the renovation and use of the village mosque (see chapter 7). One of the officers who had participated in the conquest of Ghabisiyya railed about the sympathetic tone of the Hebrew newspaper that publicized the matter. He wrote in a letter to the editor that the inhabitants of the village "cannot deny their part in the murder of the [persons who made up the escort of the] Yehiam convoy and the fact that following the occupation [of the village], articles that had belonged to murdered [Jews] from the convoy were found in homes in the village." The Jews did indeed take terrible revenge on the twelve villages of the Acre Valley.

I estimate the total number of persons who were displaced from Jewish-controlled areas during the period ending in late May 1948 at 380,000 and the number of villages (including permanent Bedouin encampments) abandoned at 207. The number of rural Arab refugees—190,000 persons—was equal to the number of refugees from six cities. Twenty-two of the abandoned villages (and three of the cities) were situated outside the area allocated to the Jewish state; the number of refugees from these locations is estimated at 120,000: 22,000 from the villages and 98,000 from the cities (Jaffa, Acre, and West Jerusalem).

END OF AN ERA

According to figures cited by David Ben-Gurion, the Jews were in control of 5,000 square kilometers of land on the eve of the declaration of the state, as compared with the approximately 1,800 square kilometers that were in their hands just prior to the UN resolution on the partition of Palestine. The human beings who had formerly inhabited the "liberated" landscape had vanished, but they had left behind everything they were unable to carry: houses and their contents, gardens, citrus and olive groves, wells, mosques, the graves of their ancestors, and, most important of all, their land. "Just land, that from which we begin and to which we return."[33] By the time the war ended, the Israelis would occupy another 180 villages and another 15,000 square kilometers of land, bringing the total land mass of the Jewish state to more than 20,000 square kilometers, compared with 14,000 square kilometers, assigned to it in the UN Partition Plan. Some 450 villages would have been spared only because the Israelis had not managed to reach them. May 1948, then, marked the end of an era: henceforth the overwhelming majority of Israelis would no longer meet Arabs in the immediate vicinity of their homes. The Arabs had departed the Jewish landscape, and the violent, complex, but intimate relations between adjacent settlements or neighborhoods had ceased to exist.

The disappearance of this human landscape aroused a sense of fear and emptiness even among those Jews who had taken part in confrontations and violence or had worked for the expulsion of their Arab neighbors, whose world they had shared, and its destruction left them thunderstruck. "It is amazing, hard to believe. Houses full of possessions, and no life. Shops full [of merchandise], and no buyers. Valuable property abandoned. Our soldiers roam the alleyways and can't believe their eyes. Despite the victory, there is a feeling of emptiness," wrote one soldier.[34]

But emptiness is destined to be filled. First came the looters, who cleared out the houses in an orgy of plundering, dismantling anything they could carry and destroying the rest. The war had left its mark on many villages, some of whose homes had been blown up by the army and some wrecked by the looters. But most of the villages remained standing, like ghost towns, and before long Jews began squatting in the undamaged houses and populating those villages that were located adjacent to Jewish cities. The groves of trees and fields of crops lay uncultivated and unirrigated—partly because Jewish farmers had dismantled the pumps on the wells and the irrigation pipes and had carried them off. The ripening produce was only partially harvested.

The destruction of the physical landscape was a gradual process—not a direct result of the hostilities but the inevitable outcome of the eradication of the human landscape. True, it had been a brutal, total war, but the means at the disposal of the combatants were not of the sort that made mass destruction possible. They did not have planes capable of carpet bombing, which could wipe entire communities from the face of the earth, nor heavy artillery. Even conventional explosives were in short supply. It was only after the cessation of hostilities that the deserted physical landscape was destroyed (as we shall see below), for political rather than military reasons—and in order to prepare it for settlement by other human beings.

The picture that emerges from a description of the first part of the 1948 War is not, in any case, unambiguous. It does not fully support the claim of "ethnic cleansing," planned and premeditated by the Zionist leadership. Neither does it support the opposite contention—that hundreds of thousands of Arabs had fled without the deeds of the Jews having had a decisive influence on the exodus. The Jews were not saddened by the Arabs' leaving, and they even encouraged it through acts of intimidation, violence, and psychological warfare, yet this is not sufficient to provide a basis for the claim that the objective of the 1948 War was the expulsion of the Arab population. On the other hand, three developments that took place between 15 May and 16 June 1948 oblige us to regard the subsequent exodus of the Arabs in a different light. These were the establishment of Israeli sovereignty in Palestine, the Israeli decision to prevent the return of the uprooted Palestinians, and the decision to make their abandoned land available for Zionist settlement.

4

Ethnic Cleansing

On Friday, 14 May 1948, the People's Council, the supreme leadership body of the Jewish community in Eretz Israel, proclaimed the establishment of the State of Israel and declared itself the Provisional Council of State—the legislative body of the new state. Its executive branch, Minhelet Haʿam, became the Provisional Government of Israel. Thus came into the world an entity which (after being recognized by the nations of the world) was entitled to all the rights accorded under international law by the status of "state," and which assumed all the obligations attendant upon that status. The voluntary governing institutions of the pre-state Jewish community became decision-making bodies with the authority to establish norms and legal frameworks and to impose them on Israel's citizens by means of an enforcement apparatus with a monopoly on the legitimate use of force within its borders.

NEW OBLIGATION MISUNDERSTOOD

The people who signed the Declaration of Independence—and became legislators, generals, and cabinet ministers—were the same ones who for decades had acted in these capacities in both civil and military administration, albeit without official status. It was not surprising, therefore, that for them "the proclamation of the State of Israel had less significance on the operative level than on the constitutional and historical-symbolic level."[1] The transition from "authority without sovereignty" to "a central authority with exclusive control over mechanisms of violence in society"—as embodied in the concept of the sovereign state—was not a revolutionary one in their eyes. In the final analysis, the establishment of the State of Israel was, in their estimation, nothing more than the granting of a symbolic stamp of legitimacy to the ongoing process of the fulfillment of Zionism. They therefore continued to identify the goals of the state, its norms of governance, its symbols, and its perceptions regarding the Arab community with the Zionist ideology and policies of the pre-state period. The direct link between the Yishuv and its volunteer governing institutions, and the Israeli collectivity living in the context of a sovereign state produced norms and laws that were injurious to the basic rights of civil and human equality, were tainted with arbitrariness, and discriminated on an ethnic basis among the people subject to its authority.

Israel's heads of state and their agents had not learned to differentiate between the actions of ethnic leaders with no state authority—waging intercommunal war with similar groups, without government-sanctioned means of enforcement at their disposal—and those perpetrated by heads of state with the ability to pass laws and to enforce them by means of a powerful standing army subject to their absolute authority. The deeds might well be the same, and the victims are not interested in the reasons and justifications for their calamity. From a moral point of view, however, the obligations and rights of the leader of an ethnic minority without sovereignty are completely different from those of the head of a state that defines itself as democratic and liberal and has pretensions of preserving universal norms. It is therefore necessary to regard the destruction of the Palestinian landscape, both human and physical, as implemented subsequent to 15 May 1948, in an entirely different light than that which had taken place prior to that date.

The expulsions carried out after the founding of the state, and without a doubt those effected after the middle of June (during the First Truce, 11 June through 8 July 1948), came dangerously close to fitting the definition of "ethnic cleansing." Although not as severe as in the case of Bosnia, atrocities that could be defined as war crimes did occur. Not only was "an undesirable population expelled from a given territory due to religious or ethnic discrimination, political, strategic or ideological considerations, or a combination of these," but some of the Arabs were expelled not on military grounds but with the objective of taking over their homes and land expressly for the settlement of Jews. Even if the pretext for the expulsions was related to military security (and there undoubtedly were legitimate reasons for them), those responsible knew that Israel's leaders had laid down two principles that transformed the abandonment of the Arab settlements into a matter whose implications went far beyond the fulfillment of the short-term requirements of the military-security situation. They had determined, first, that the Arabs would not ever be allowed to return to their homes and, second, that the abandoned areas were designated for the settlement of Jews or to be turned over to existing Jewish settlements. Furthermore, the legislature of the state had passed laws and promulgated regulations creating a legal framework that legitimized the permanent uprooting of villagers from their homes, the expropriation of their property, and its nationalization. The Israeli legislative body (the Knesset) behaved as if it were the successor to the Jewish National Fund (JNF); it simply adapted the latter's methods of "redeeming the land" to the means and powers now at its disposal: it was no longer a case of purchasing land from a willing seller but one of expropriating it by means of the laws of a sovereign state, enforced by its armed emissaries.

PREMEDITATED TRANSFER

If until May 1948 the exodus had been in the nature of "transfer ex post facto," from the beginning of June onward it was clearly "premeditated transfer." Defining the Palestinian exodus in these terms rendered meaningless any attempts to trace the reasons for it. It makes no difference whether people were forcibly expelled, fled in fear, or were evicted by order of Arab commanders. The moment they left their homes—even if they took refuge in the immediate vicinity of their villages—they lost their whole world and became refugees with nothing, not even the right to receive monetary compensation for the loss of their property. It was not the brutality and horrors of war that haunted the departing refugees and nurtured their hatred but an abiding sense of the injustice of their being barred from returning home. By the same token, it would be meaningless to give a detailed account of the physical destruction of the Arab landscape: of whether the houses were destroyed by looters, blown up by the army, or demolished by bulldozers. In the absence of the human beings who had molded that landscape to suit their needs, their culture, and their way of life, the destruction of their handiwork was unavoidable, and would have been even had the damage not been caused intentionally. How much more so, then, when the destruction was accomplished with the express intent of preventing the return of those who had left, of obscuring all traces of the civilization that had been annihilated, and of fashioning in its place a different human and physical landscape?

The exodus, the prevention of the refugees' return, and the appropriation of the Arab landscape to serve the needs of the Jews were not isolated occurrences; they were ongoing, interconnected processes. They commenced during the war but persisted for many years after the cessation of hostilities. Because of the complexity of their interrelationship, it is difficult to deal with them in chronological order; therefore each will be described separately.

As mentioned earlier, by the end of May 1948, some 200 Arab villages had been abandoned, and in the territory under Israeli control there remained about a dozen villages, with a combined population of several thousand (plus another several thousand in three of the six cities that had been conquered). In the two weeks preceding the First Truce (which began on 11 June 1948), and during the four weeks that it was in effect, no changes were made in the size of the area in Israeli hands (with the exception of a few villages on the Israeli-Egyptian front in the southern Coastal Plain). But at the end of the truce (on 8 July 1948), large geographical and demographic changes began taking place.

"TEN DAYS" BATTLES

In a space of ten days ("the Ten Days battles"), some sixty Arab villages were abandoned. The size of this figure and the extent of the territory captured in the course of the Ten Days were reflections of the complete collapse of the local Arab forces before the Israeli offensive. Twenty-eight villages were abandoned in the area around Lydda and the inner Shephelah, and the number of refugees who either fled in panic or were forcibly evicted came to approximately 24,000. This region, stretching between the Coastal Plain and the Judean Hills, fell to the IDF following a campaign the heart of which was the conquest of the cities of Ramla and Lydda and the expulsion of 45,000 souls (the inhabitants of the cities as well as many who had taken refuge there). This campaign, which brought about the exodus of the majority of the Arabs living in villages on the periphery of Tel Aviv, ended on 14 July. During that same period, the narrow corridor along the main highway between Jerusalem and Tel Aviv, which was already in Israeli hands, was widened, and about a dozen villages were occupied, both in its southern section and in the immediate vicinity of Jerusalem. All of the villagers were expelled (although many had already fled before the villages were taken).

In the south, sixteen villages were captured and the whole immense area bordering on the Negev was emptied of its inhabitants. The expulsion of the residents of this area was carried out according to explicit orders. Such was not the case in the Galilee, where about two dozen villages were left in place, as opposed to eight that were abandoned. This difference between the north and the central and southern regions reflected the personalities of the military commanders in those regions and their various perspectives regarding the expulsion of the Palestinians, the tactical considerations that influenced the course of the battles in each region, the ethnic makeup of the population, the differing degree of desire for revenge, and the strategic decisions of the Israeli general staff and David Ben-Gurion, in addition to the local considerations that influenced the Israelis' desire to take over agricultural land. In the south, the commanders at the front were officers who sought to expel the Arab population and who had done so in the past as well. The expulsion of the Palestinians in the south was also connected to the deployment of the IDF along the front lines against the Egyptian army and the fear that the presence of Arabs behind the lines would imperil the Israeli forces.

In the north a clear distinction was made between villages most of whose inhabitants were Christian or Druze—which were barely touched—and Muslim villages, whose inhabitants had, in some cases, already abandoned them. Villages that had taken an active part in attacks on Jewish settlements or that had given shelter to the Arab irregulars were shelled, the inhabitants were expelled, and their houses were demolished. Villages that had surrendered without a battle were generally left unmolested. The inhabitants of the two neighboring villages of Maʿalul and al-Mujaydil, situated not far from the city of Nazareth, were apparently expelled because the Israelis coveted their land. The fields of the village of al-Mujaydil stretched down the center of the Jezreel Valley, forming a wedge between two tracts of JNF land. Most of Maʿalul's land had long been under JNF ownership, and the villagers worked it as tenant farmers.

The JNF had been trying for years to put a stop to the use of its land by the Arab villagers, and the ensuing confrontations had compelled the Mandatory authorities to intervene. On the eve of the war, a compromise was reached whereby the JNF would give up some of its land in Maʿalul in exchange for a tract of government land in the Beit Shean

Valley. This agreement was not implemented, however, and it is not surprising that when the village was captured, all of its inhabitants (approximately 500 Muslims and 200 Christians) were expelled and their homes demolished. And so, thanks to the military occupation, the JNF acquired both the village's land and the tract in the Beit Shean Valley.

Just prior to the outbreak of the Ten Days battles, the Israeli General Staff published an order in which IDF units were cautioned as follows: "Except during actual combat, it is forbidden to destroy, burn, or demolish Arab towns and villages, to expel the Arab inhabitants from the[ir] villages, neighborhoods, and towns, or to uproot residents from their places without special permission or explicit instructions from the minister of defense in each individual case. Anyone violating this order will be placed on trial."[2]

This order supposedly set a norm, but apparently the norm was not enforced, and either the authority to define what was meant by time of "actual combat" was left in the hands of the local commanders or they could rest assured that their decisions regarding expulsions and the destruction of villages would receive the backing of their superiors. In a few cases the local commanders did indeed receive instructions from the minister of defense to demolish villages, but this was generally not "an explicit order." As mentioned previously, Defense Minister David Ben-Gurion took precautions so as not to go down in history as the one directly responsible for immoral deeds such as the expulsion of a civilian population, even though after the fact he explained and even justified these acts. The local commanders understood—without needing to be told—the policy with regard to the Palestinian population. It can be summarized thus: to take control of the maximum amount of territory possible, while leaving it with the minimum number of Arabs possible or, should political conditions allow, with no Arabs at all.

After the "miraculous exodus" had taken place and it had become evident that the establishment of a Jewish state without Arabs—a possibility that the leaders of the Yishuv had not previously envisioned—was indeed achievable, "ethnic cleansing" became an acceptable, or even a desirable, means of achieving it. Quite a few villages did indeed remain in place—two dozen in the north and half a dozen in the center and south—but it is precisely this fact that underscored the arbitrary nature of the Israeli authorities' actions. Local considerations such as good relations with the *mukhtars* of some villages, preferential treatment accorded Christians and Druze, fear of international repercussions (in the case of Nazareth, for example), or lack of interest in the village's land—might suffice to deliver a village from the fate of abandonment and exile. On the other hand, the determination that Israel was engaged in "actual combat" and that the Arab villages constituted a security risk served as an absolute justification for their destruction, against which moral considerations and compassionate impulses did not stand a chance. Even the attempt to justify expulsion on the grounds that it was a strictly military measure and that the refugees would be allowed to return to their homes when the fighting was over was disingenuous: while the expulsions of the Ten Days were going on, the government had already made a categorical decision regarding the fate of the refugees—they would not be allowed to return home. Thus, the exodus condemned the Palestinians to permanent exile, and anyone who had a part in the expulsion knew (or should have known) the true significance of his deeds.

MOMENTOUS DECISIONS

The official decision to block the return of the displaced Palestinians was made on 16 June 1948 without a vote; nor did it have officially approved wording. The Israeli cabinet made do with the statements of the prime minister and foreign minister. Prime Minister David Ben-Gurion had proclaimed: "I do not want those who flee to return. Their return must be prevented now. Because after the war, everything will depend on the outcome of the war—I will be in favor of their not returning even after the war." Foreign Minister Moshe Sharett (Shertok) stated simply: "This is our policy: they are not coming back."[3] Characteristically, this decision was not made because of the necessity to establish practical guidelines for military action but because the Israeli government needed to adopt a position in response to foreign pressure. For internal consumption no explicit decision was required, since as far back as April the army had in most cases not been allowing displaced Palestinians to return home, and those who did manage to infiltrate were expelled by force.

The decision of 16 June was presented to the outside world in a manner that soft-pedaled its harshness, emphasizing the supposedly temporary nature of the prohibition: the return of the refugees was not to be discussed "for the time being"; that is, as long as the war was going on. This wording led foreign diplomats to believe (or to want to believe) that after the war Israel would perhaps agree to allow the Arabs' return. However, this position only gave an appearance of flexibility, since the definition of "a state of war" was in itself flexible. Very quickly it became clear that, as far as Israel was concerned, the state of war was permanent, since the Arab world had not come to terms with its defeat, and Israel's existence would be under threat for years. Furthermore, from Israel's point of view, only the signing of peace treaties would signal the conclusion of the war. Late in July 1948, Sharett explicitly stated that "a decision on the question of the return of the Arabs (to their former homes) can be made only as a part of a peace settlement with the Arab states and in the context of the conditions of such a settlement."[4] But even this stance was nothing but a smoke screen, since Israel knew that a formal peace would not be achieved without the resolution of the refugee problem and the return of at least some of them.

The return of the refugees conflicted with some of Israel's most vital interests: securing an absolute Jewish majority, settling Jewish refugees on the abandoned land, and ensuring the country's internal security. Pursuit of these interests dictated that Israel would never permit the return of the refugees and would forever refuse to consider making this concession, even in return for permanent peace treaties. Rather than pay this price, Israel was prepared to forgo formal peace and to content itself with an armistice. As Ben-Gurion wrote: "If we chase after peace, the Arabs will ask a price of us—borders or refugees or both. We shall wait a few years."[5] As time went by, the "price" of the return of the refugees became grossly inflated: the demand to bring them back—or "the Return"—came to be interpreted as a disguised call for the destruction of Israel, and anyone making it was perceived as Israel's sworn enemy. What's more, anyone who even described the exodus and the "demographic processes" that took place in Eretz Israel/Palestine during the War for Independence was regarded as providing ammunition to the enemies of Israel, and research on the subject was viewed as verging on treason. The real price paid by the Palestinians in being uprooted from their homeland became buried under a thick layer of sophistic argumentation that sought to convince the world that the uprooting of the Palestinians had been the fault of the Arabs and that the responsibility for a solution lay with the Arab states that were refusing to take in the refugees. The refugee problem thus became a political football (see also chapter 8).

Israel was impressively successful in resisting foreign attempts to resolve the conflict by proposing compromises, which naturally included demands for the return of a portion of the refugee population and the payment of compensation to the rest. Israel also had to contend with world public opinion, which was profoundly affected by the suffering of the hundreds of thousands of uprooted Palestinians. The government took steps to destroy the abandoned villages and to hand over their land to Jewish organizations, and it began settling Jewish immigrants in abandoned Arab houses. The army was given explicit orders to prevent the infiltration of Arabs to their former homes—if necessary, by shooting to kill. The cabinet and the Knesset passed laws and ratified "emergency regulations," which together constituted the legal infrastructure for the expropriation of the refugees' property, as well as that of Arab inhabitants of Israel who had not been uprooted, and its transfer to Jewish bodies—private, public, and state-run.

FINAL PHASES: ATROCITIES

These steps were accompanied by continuing hostilities, which led to the occupation of additional villages and the exodus of tens of thousands of new refugees. During the Second Truce, which lasted for about three months (18 July through 15 October), the actions of the IDF were concentrated on the "cleansing" of small pockets of Arab villages situated in areas considered to be "strategic," where the presence of Arabs was regarded as constituting a security risk. Thus the three villages on the western slope of the Carmel—Ijzim, Jabʿa, and Ein Ghazal—were occupied and destroyed. On the Coastal Plain to the southwest of Rehovot, a "cleanup operation" was implemented, "cleansing" the whole area of Arabs; a wide area in the northern Negev was similarly "cleansed."

The final major exodus from the villages took place in October 1948. During the last half of that month and the first week of November, the remainder of the Upper and Lower Galilee was occupied, as well as all of the southern part of the Coastal Plain, the central Negev, the Shephelah, and the southern section of the Jerusalem Corridor.

The number of villages occupied in this wave came to eighty, and the number of displaced villagers approached 100,000. The IDF had an overwhelming superiority in the October battles, and the conquest of these villages took on the character of a "cleansing" campaign directed against a civilian population. The policy regarding expulsions was similar to that followed during the July battles. The vast majority of the inhabitants of the southern front were expelled (and those who were not expelled during the fighting were removed afterward), whereas in the north the expulsions were random and arbitrary: several villages were left intact, while others were evacuated and destroyed. It seems that local military commanders in the northern front interpreted differently the orders issued by the High Command in October to "do their utmost to cleanse the occupied areas of all hostile elements [and] assist the inhabitants to leave the occupied areas."

Atrocities and acts of brutality characterized this period: summary executions, rape, blowing up houses along with their occupants, looting and plundering, and leaving hundreds of villagers to their own devices in the fields, without food or water. The most serious atrocities were committed in the village of al-Dawayima, on the western slopes of the Hebron Highlands. This large village, with a population of some 3,500 was taken on 29 October 1948. The occupying forces indiscriminately killed between 80 and 100 male villagers, blew up houses together with their occupants, murdered women and children, and committed rape. According to eyewitness testimony, these acts were committed "not in the heat of battle and inflamed passions, but out of a system of expulsion and destruction. The fewer Arabs remained—the better."[6] The village of Safsaf in the Safad area was also occupied on 29 October. The Jewish forces assembled all of the inhabitants of the village (who numbered approximately 1,000) and killed between fifty and seventy men. Four young women were taken to empty houses and raped. The villagers were not expelled, but the memory of this horrific episode would not allow them to remain under Israeli rule, and they left the village under cover of darkness and fled to Lebanon. Murders of civilians and hostages also took place in the nearby village of Saʿsaʿ and in ʿEilaboun, Jish, and Majd al-Kurum. These atrocities—which fifty years later are regarded as libel, invented by the enemies of Israel, and whose retelling is perceived as an example of the rewriting of history by revisionist historians—were, at the time they took place, known to ministers in the Israeli government, military commanders, and even the general public. The government set up commissions of inquiry and the army set up commissions of its own, but the work of these bodies came to naught because soldiers and officers refused to testify against their comrades in arms. Prime Minister Ben-Gurion did not hide the "shameful deeds" from the public; he even expressed pride in the publication of a poem by Nathan Alterman (who at the time was considered Israel's national poet) condemning the atrocities.

In a few villages IDF commanders ordered the inhabitants to abandon their homes and go forth into exile, whereas in others no evil befell the villagers. Anton Shammas describes the surrender of the Christian village of Fassouta on 30 October 1948:

> Except for Abu Shacker, all the men of the village had left at dawn for the fields surrounding the village, in search of places to hide until the fury of the conqueror had passed. . . . A burst of bullets was heard from the other side of the hill. . . . Major Nimr . . . sat in the vehicle at the head of the convoy. . . . He was a Jew from this region, and knew these village elders. He also knew that there would be no resistance, and that the capitulation would be offered by a priest in black, hoisting a white *kufiya*. . . . As Major Nimr stepped down from his vehicle and his feet touched the ground of Al-Mahafer, . . . the men who had fled to the fields in the morning began to gather, as the rumor reached them that the capitulation had proceeded peacefully. And thus they stood, the soldiers of the Jaish al-Yahud [Jews' army] on the one side and the inhabitants of Fassuta on the other. . . . all those present at the ceremony were covered with a thin white layer of dust, and as is the way of all dust, it did not distinguish between the conquering soldier and the conquered villager.[7]

On the same day, the large village of a-Ramah, inhabited by Christians and Druze, was captured. The villagers were ordered to gather at the center of the village. The commander of the occupying force instructed the Druze to return to their homes and the Christians to leave for Lebanon, threatening those who refused with summary execution. The Christians hid in the nearby hills and wadis until a different military unit entered the village, which didn't prevent them from returning to their homes. The village of 'Eilaboun, whose inhabitants were Christian, surrendered to the IDF as Fassouta had, but the Israeli commander ordered the villagers to abandon it. To speed up the exodus, he chose twelve young men and had them taken out and shot. Many villagers went as far as Lebanon, but several hundred hid out in the hills. Little by little most of the inhabitants of 'Eilaboun returned to their village.

The expulsion of the Arab inhabitants of the Galilee did not culminate with the end of hostilities. Early in November the Israeli army decided to create a security zone the length of the Israeli-Lebanese border. The width of this strip varied, and the intention was essentially to evacuate most of the Arab villages in northern Galilee that were still occupied by their original inhabitants. Ultimately "only" six villages, situated along the northern border road, were evacuated and destroyed, including Bir'im and Iqrit, whose inhabitants (as described later) were at first assured that their displacement would be only temporary.

The ethnic cleansing of the northern part of the country, which was rationalized on security grounds, continued well into 1949. During that year the remaining inhabitants of six villages in the Upper and Lower Galilee were expelled. These Arabs, the majority of whom were citizens of Israel who had been counted in the census of November 1948, were transferred to other villages within Israel, and only a small minority were expelled across the border. The expulsions were carried out with the approval of a "governmental committee for the transfer of Arabs from place to place," as if they were a herd of cattle and not human beings living in their own homes (see chapter 5).

"FOSSILIZED LIVES!"

Josef Weitz of the JNF, the man who pushed hardest for Israel to get rid of the Arabs and take possession of their land, wrote the following amazing account in his diary toward the end of 1948:

> And the road continues eastward between mountains and over mountains, and the Galilee is revealed to me in its splendor, its hidden places and folds, its crimson smile and its green softness and its desolation. I have never seen it like this. It was always bustling with man and beast. And the latter predominated. Herds and more herds used to descend from the heights to the valleys of the streambeds, their bells ringing with a sort of discontinuous sound, which vanished in the ravines and hid among the crevices, as if they would go on chiming forever. And the shepherds striding after them like figures from ancient times, whistling merrily and driving the goats toward the trees and bushes—to gnaw at them hungrily; and now the picture has disappeared and is no more. A strange stillness lies over all the mountains and is drawn by hidden threads from within the empty village. An empty village; what a terrible thing! Fossilized lives! Lives turned to fossilized whispers in extinguished ovens; a shattered mirror; moldy blocks of dried figs and a scrawny dog, thin-tailed and floppy-eared and dark-eyed. At the same time—at the very same moment—a different feeling throbs and rises from the primordial depths, a feeling of victory, of taking control, of revenge, and of casting off suffering. And suddenly the whispers vanish and you see empty houses, good for the settlement of our Jewish brethren who have wandered for generation upon generation, refugees of your people, steeped in suffering and sorrow, as they, at last, find a roof over their heads. And you knew: War! This was our war.
>
> But has it ended? For a full day we galloped over the roads of the Galilee and saw the deep-rooted agricultural heritage that the fleeing villagers had left behind them. With this, my heart became heavy beneath the weight of our circumstances: have we among us the human resources to carry on this heri-

> tage, to deepen it, and to broaden it? And will we be able to bring thousands of Jews here to banish the desolation, the human desolation, so that the Galilee will continue to blossom?[8]

From the very beginning of the war, this man had worked for the expulsion of the Arabs with a zeal that his superiors tried to restrain. Despite that, he succeeded in mobilizing people and institutions to implement both "retroactive transfer" and the transfer that he himself had initiated. His soul was capable of embracing the horrible spectacle of the disappearance of landscapes "bustling with man and beast" and of "fossilized lives" concomitantly with the exhilaration of "taking control, taking revenge, and casting off suffering" that created this tragedy. The man who had expelled "the fleeing villagers" now sought to expel the "desolation" they had left behind—as if the Galilee were a barren wasteland waiting to be brought into bloom by thousands of Jews. No wonder that immediately following his return from a tour of the Galilee, Weitz was already lecturing the Settlement Division of the Jewish Agency "about sending 10,000 Jews up to central Galilee," which had been emptied of its Arab inhabitants. Of approximately 250 villages that had existed in the north of the country (the Mandatory subdistricts of Safad, Tiberias, Beisan, Acre, Nazareth, and Haifa) on the eve of the 1948 War, some 190 were now abandoned, and about 220,000 souls had gone into exile (not counting the 105,000 city-dwellers). Approximately 65,000 souls remained in the countryside (and another 28,000 or so in three towns)—this number does not include the thousands of displaced villagers (and others) who infiltrated into the country during the winter and spring of 1949 (see later discussion).

The emptying of the north of three-quarters of its Arab inhabitants was nothing compared with the total emptying of central and southern Israel, where approximately 330,000 souls, from 180 villages and four towns, became refugees. Until the annexation to Israel of twenty-three villages and hamlets with some 30,000 inhabitants, in the wake of the armistice agreement with Jordan, all that remained in the central and southern regions were a few thousand Arabs living in half a dozen villages (and three towns) and approximately 12,000 Bedouin in the Negev.

The signing of the armistice agreement did not put an end to the expulsions. In late February 1949, the remaining inhabitants of the township of Faluja and the village of ʿIraq al-Manshiyya in the northern Negev were expelled. Approximately 3,000 people were ejected from these communities, despite Israel's having guaranteed that they could remain there with full security to themselves, their homes, and all their property. In June 1950 the remnants of the population of the village of Zakariyya in the Shephelah, between Beit Shemesh and Beit Govrin, were expelled. In March 1950 the villagers of Khirbat Jalama, north of Tulkarm, were evicted, despite the fact that according to the armistice agreement with Jordan, in the context of which the village had been transferred to Israeli jurisdiction, Israel had undertaken a commitment that no ill would befall the inhabitants of the territory handed over to it.

The case of the expulsion of the inhabitants of Khirbat Jalama, the destruction of their village, and the handing over of their land to the members of Lehavot Haviva, a kibbutz affiliated with the socialist Hashomer Hatzair movement, is a typical example of the manner in which the sovereign State of Israel arbitrarily took over the landholdings of its Arab citizens, after illegally expelling them from their homes.

KHIRBAT JALAMA: A TYPICAL STORY

Khirbat Jalama, a hamlet inhabited by two extended families, Nadaf and Daqqa, was situated in the eastern Sharon, not far from the town of Tulkarm. The people of this hamlet had not been sucked into the awful whirlpool of war, abandonment of villages, expulsion, and destruction, and had continued their peaceful lives until 3 April 1949, the day the armistice agreement with Jordan was signed. On that day it fell to their lot to be annexed to Israel. Under the conditions of the agreement (Article VI, Section 6), Israel undertook (as mentioned earlier) that no ill would befall the thousands of Palestinians in the territory annexed to it, nor would their property be confiscated. The government initially attempted to deny the inhabitants of the annexed villages (along with most Israeli Arabs) Israeli citizenship and to leave them stateless (proposed Citizenship Law of 1950, which was not ratified), but it ultimately understood that legislation of this sort would irrevocably deface the state's image in the eyes of the international community, and therefore granted them citizenship. Their being Israeli citizens, however, did not fully ensure their property rights.

The April 1949 annexation of Khirbat Jalama made its inhabitants subject to a series of laws and emergency regulations passed by Israel for the purpose of gaining control of Arab landholdings and the property of refugees and displaced persons. The legislation had two immediate objectives: to eliminate the possibility of uprooted villagers' returning, and to confiscate and nationalize their property so as to create a land base for the further settlement of Jews. No effort was made to hide the intent behind these pieces of legislation, and there is not much point in describing them in detail: each one separately (and they all went through an orderly process of legislation in the Knesset) and all of them taken together authorized the state's enforcement agencies to take possession of private property without recourse to accepted procedures, while making arbitrary acts of confiscation immune to judicial appeal. The minutes of a meeting held at the Ministry of Agriculture on 15 November 1949 state: "It makes no difference under which law the land is leased [to Jewish interests], the Absentee Law or the Law of Fallow Lands [see below], the main thing is that this land will ultimately be under state ownership."

In formulating these laws and regulations, care was taken that they not refer explicitly to Arabs. Instead, "general" categories and designations were invented. The uprooted person became an "absentee" by virtue of having left his usual place of habitation in Eretz Israel/Palestine (even someone who moved to the neighboring village). "Absence" from one's place of habitation at any time since the beginning of the war, even if for only a few days, resulted in all of one's property being placed under the management and supervision of the custodian of absentee property, who was authorized to subsequently sell it to the Development Authority, which, in turn, was authorized to transfer it to "others" (meaning Jews). A person forfeited his property not only if he left his place of habitation but even if he remained at home—in an area outside the territory held by the IDF—and, after the "specified date," found himself subject to the rule of Israel, which had meanwhile arrived on his doorstep. In this way, all the inhabitants of the territories that were handed over to Israel after December 1948 lost that portion of their property that had been occupied and placed under Israeli jurisdiction prior to that date. The Emergency Regulations Regarding Absentee Property eventually became the Absentee Property Law (1950) with all its amendments, under which millions of *dunams* of land and billions of dollars' worth of property were nationalized. The value of this property was estimated as being as high as 1 to 4 billion 1950 dollars.

But simply taking over the refugees' land was not sufficient. The Knesset, therefore, kept passing new emergency regulations regarding the cultivation of "fallow" land, under which the minister of agriculture was authorized to take possession of abandoned tracts of agricultural land and to cultivate them for the benefit of the "public." The original purpose of these regulations, which were passed in October 1948, was to define a legal procedure for handing over abandoned landholdings to Jewish farmers for temporary cultivation. According to the written explanation of these regulations,

> Wartime conditions caused the abandonment of land by its owners and cultivators. . . . The good of the state obliges us, on the other hand—without violating ownership rights to land or other property—to engage in and expand agricultural production as much as possible. . . . The principal responsibilities of the minister of agriculture are to take possession of and to hold for a period of time not exceeding five years land that in his opinion is abandoned and uncultivated . . . or to transfer it to another person for cultivation.

An elegant formulation indeed.

It very quickly became clear that these regulations could serve as a convenient means for gaining control of land belonging to Arab citizens of Israel who were not "absentees," as well, with no connection at all to the original intent of the emergency regulations. This was accomplished in a simple and not overly delicate manner: first the land would be declared "a closed area," where Arabs were barred from entering the plots they had under cultivation, making it impossible for them to tend them. Then the minister of agriculture would, in accordance with the regulations, send "warnings" to the Arab farmers, informing them that if they did not cultivate their landholdings, these would be classified as fallow. Since the Arabs were prevented by the closure orders from working their land, it was in due course declared "fallow," and the minister would then transfer it to Jewish farmers. Injured parties could petition an Appeals Committee but not the courts, and the ruling of the Appeals Committee was final. In order for the picture of the arbitrariness of these regulations to be complete, it should be mentioned that the chairman of the Appeals Committee was also the director of the governmental department charged with implementing the regulations; that is, the respondent and the judge were one and the same.

The Nadaf and Daqqa families of the hamlet of Khirbat Jalama succeeded in dodging all the confiscation laws and regulations; they remained ensconced in their homes and were able to cultivate most of their land, but not for long. Less than a year after the village was annexed to Israel, its inhabitants were ordered to vacate and move to the neighboring village of Jatt. Menachem Hofnung describes this chain of events "as a unique human interest story, serving to concretize the prevailing state of affairs in the early fifties as regards land rights." The military government expelled them "as part of the program of evacuating the small hamlets of the [Arab] Triangle (the name of the geographical region annexed to Israel) and concentrating their inhabitants in larger villages."[9] The expulsion was carried out arbitrarily, without recourse to any law. The villagers appealed several times to the authorities, requesting to return to their home, but even though they had been promised that they would be able to do so, "all the promises came to naught." After two years outside their homes, members of the Nadaf family petitioned the High Court of Justice, which granted them an *order nisi* requiring the state to respond to their petition. This the state did not do, because it had nothing to say in response: the expulsion was unquestionably illegal. The situation was further complicated by the fact that, in the interim, Kibbutz Lehavot Haviva had taken over the land.

The government, fearing to set "a precedent" that would permit the return of additional Arabs to their villages, decided to pass a law that would retroactively grant legitimacy to both the expulsion and the expropriation. It promptly proposed a Land Acquisition Law (approval of activities and compensation), and within a week the law had passed its first reading in the Knesset. The Khirbat Jalama affair was not mentioned at all in the course of the Knesset deliberations because the legal problem of al-Jalama, the immediate pretext for this law, was only the tip of the iceberg. Similar deeds were being done in many other places, and it was necessary to legitimize them, too, lest the loss of the Jalama case set a precedent. The explanatory notes to the law are rife with feigned innocence and self-righteousness; they are ambiguous or even dishonest:

> When the authorities began acquiring the property of absentees, the use of which was devoted to meeting the vital needs of security and development, they seized—for those very same purposes—various pieces of land, particularly in agricultural regions, whose ownership had not been sufficiently clarified. Considerations of state security and the implementation of essential development programs prevent the return of these pieces of land to their owners. Despite this, it is the intent of the authorities to compensate these owners fairly in money or other land or both. The objective of the proposed law, then, is twofold: to impart a legal basis to the acquisition of the landholdings mentioned herein and to grant the right of compensation to their owners.[10]

In accordance with this law, the finance minister was authorized to issue a "certificate" transferring ownership of property to the Development Authority (the office that had "acquired" the absentee Arabs' land), providing that the minister determined that said property fulfilled three conditions: that it was not in the possession of its owners in April 1952; that between 14 May 1948 and 1 April 1952 it had served or been allocated to serve "vital developmental, settlement, or security needs"; and that "it was still required for the fulfillment of one of these needs." Property confiscated in this manner was transferred immediately to the Development Authority, and it was not possible to dispute the validity of the finance minister's certificate. The minister's authority to issue these certificates was restricted to one year. The compensation offered to the property owners was ridiculous; the way it was calculated meant that even before compensation claims began being processed, the amount proposed by law was equivalent to only 20 percent of the nominal value of the property (because of the rapid devaluation of Israeli currency). The method of calculating compensation was indeed amended, in 1977 and again in 1979, but this was merely a cosmetic improvement, since the basis for the estimation of compensation remained unrealistic.

While this proposed law was before the legislature, the High Court's deliberations regarding Khirbat Jalama were in progress, but thanks to delaying tactics on the part of the state, the Nadaf family's appeal was still pending in the High Court of Justice when the retroactive law became a fact. The finance minister could now legally issue a certificate of expropriation and publish it in the official gazette. The family appealed once more, contending that the minister's certificate "had been issued for an illegitimate purpose and had resulted in the disruption of legal procedures." The High Court of Justice, although fully cognizant of the injustice done to this family, had no choice but to reject the petition (after four years of deliberations) because "the issuing of a certificate by the finance minister significantly narrows the scope of judicial review permissible under the Law." The kibbutz members did not wait for the conclusion of the High Court deliberations. On 11 August 1953 they blew up the homes of the Arab landowners, and when the Nadafs filed a complaint with the police, the kibbutz members claimed that "the demolition had been carried out in accordance with orders from the army, and that a special budget had even been officially allocated for the purpose."[11]

Since the finance minister's authority to issue signed certificates would terminate one year from the day the law was passed, the wholesale publication of notices of this sort commenced, filling volume after volume of the official gazette. One of the first "certificates" to be published "granted" to the Development Authority the land of the Maronite village of Birʿim, "an area of approximately 11,700 *dunams*." Thus was the process of retroactive approval for the expulsion of the village's 800 inhabitants and the expropriation of their property brought to a close. This process had begun in November 1948, when the villagers of Birʿim (and other villages on Israel's northern borders) were ordered to vacate their village with promises that they would be able to return "just as soon as the border line has been secured." The promise was not kept, and in October 1951 the inhabitants of Birʿim appealed unsuccessfully to the High Court of Justice. On 16 September 1953 the Israeli air force bombed the deserted village and completely destroyed it. The finance minister's certificate of the expropriation of the land of Birʿim was published on 14 August 1953, by which time the inhabitants of Jewish settlements were already working the land. The villagers of Birʿim did not give up their struggle and eventually succeeded in obtaining permission to refurbish their church and to bury their dead on village land. In spite of declarations of support from politicians and Knesset members, and repeated government assurances that they would reexamine the expulsion of Birʿim's inhabitants (and those of the village of Iqrit), nothing was done "for fear of setting a precedent" that would lead to similar claims being made by other Arab citizens whose land the government had acquired under the Land Acquisition Law of 1953 (see also chapter 8).

In December 1998, when a renewed petition of Birʿim and Iqrit to the High Court of Justice was pending, the minister of justice issued a statement recommending to the cabinet that the villagers be allowed to settle in the vicinity of their destroyed villages. The resettlement on 600 *dunams* in each location "should constitute a final, *ex Gracie* settlement of a unique, special and extraordinary case and shall not constitute a precedent," stated the minister. The prime minister did not wait for the recommendation to be formally tabled; he flatly rejected it, asserting that it was "a dangerous precedent."

DIVIDING UP THE BOOTY

Birʿim and Khirbat Jalama were far from the only villages treated in this way: in total, 1,288,000 *dunams* of land were confiscated under this and similar legislation. The entire huge area was leased to kibbutzim, moshavim, and others, who received them "unencumbered by third-party rights."[12] The total area "liberated" under this and other laws and regulations amounted to approximately 4.5 million *dunams* (not counting the southern Negev and the Arava). Arabs living in the State of Israel retained some 800,000 *dunams*, of which only about half was arable land.

Even villages that had not been captured by Israel, and whose residential sections were situated in the (Jordanian-held) West Bank, did not escape land confiscation. More than sixty villages located on the Jordanian side of the armistice lines lost large portions of their landholdings, which were on the Israeli side (for further details, see later discussion).

The passage of this retroactive legislation illustrated the way in which the Israeli government and Jewish interests, both public and private, took over Arab land both through local initiatives and with illegal authorization by government agents without waiting for legal procedures to be followed. In fact, the takeover of land began shortly after its military occupation. By April 1948 Jewish farmers had already begun harvesting the crops that had ripened in the abandoned fields and picking the citrus fruit in Arab groves. The initiative generally came from neighboring Jewish settlements, some of which went to the trouble of requesting permission from the Israeli government, while many others reaped the harvest without bothering to ask anyone. The Committee for Arab Property (the name of which was changed several times) approved many requests, but it also dispatched angry letters to those who took the law into their own hands.

Initially the Jewish farmers were hesitant to continue working this land after the completion of the harvest. They feared that their investment in preparing the soil and sowing summer crops, as well as in planning for the coming agricultural year, would be lost should the Arabs return. Only in areas near Jewish population centers was there interest in leasing Arab land when the war was at its peak (April and May 1948). But by June the (now governmental) Department of Absentee Property was flooded with applications for long-term leases to plots of land intended to "complete" the areas already held by the Jewish settlements. By the end of June nearly 200,000 *dunams* of abandoned land had been transferred, and in July preparations were made for the cultivation of 1 million *dunams*. The settlements most active in the takeover of abandoned landholdings were, of course, affiliated with the cooperative settlement movements, that is, established kibbutzim and moshavim that had the equipment and the initiative. It is not surprising, then, that the first areas to be snapped up, supposedly on one-year leases but with a view to holding on to them permanently, were in regions that contained well-established Jewish settlements (the Galilee Panhandle, the Jezreel Valley, and the Sharon). The way they were cultivated—in line with the methods commonly used in the Jewish agricultural sector—was the first step in the alteration of the landscape. Hundreds of thousands of *dunams* that had been under labor-intensive cultivation by Arab *fallahin* were now being worked with the heavy farm machinery employed by the Jews.

By the summer of 1948 approximately half a million *dunams* of abandoned land had been leased and were under cultivation. About 80 percent of this land was in the hands of the cooperative settlement movements—150,000 *dunams* in the Jezreel Valley and the Hills of Menashe, 40,000 in the Upper Galilee, and 75,000 in the south and in the Negev, in addition to land in the Beit Shean Valley, the Western Galilee, the Sharon, and the Jordan Valley. Private farmers were working some 100,000 *dunams*. By mid-1949 two-thirds of all land sown with grain in Israel was abandoned Arab land.

WRACKING THE GROVES

The preference for land suitable for intensive cultivation meant that tracts of land—and crops—that were not of interest to the cooperative settlements were neglected or destroyed The most blatant neglect occurred in the citrus groves, which were not irrigated after the departure of their owners. Water pumps and pipelines were dismantled and stolen, and no one was interested in taking care of the trees. The Jewish citrus growers were barely capable of caring for their own groves once the cheap Arab labor on which they depended had left. Although a few farmers in the older Jewish farming villages (*moshavot*) did acquire some abandoned citrus groves, this was a drop in the bucket. Efforts were made to contract out the cultivation of some of these areas to commercial firms, but even after this had been done, the overwhelming majority of the 150,000 *dunams* of citrus trees—the most valuable agricultural crop left behind by the Arabs—remained untended. The settlements of the cooperative settlement movements (kibbutzim and moshavim) were not interested in this crop—requiring, as it did, large quantities of water for irrigation and a large workforce; it was more worth their while to raise field crops. As a result, entire tracts of productive citrus trees, especially in the Tel Aviv–Jaffa area, were earmarked for the construction of housing developments. According to Arnon Golan's calculations in all, only about 9,000 of the 40,000 *dunams* of citrus groves in the Jaffa subdistrict—and roughly one-fifth of the abandoned citrus groves in the whole country—were still being cultivated after the war.[13]

There were also political motivations behind allowing the Arab citrus groves to go to wrack and ruin: the stronger the international pressure for the return of the refugees (throughout 1949–50), the greater the efforts to destroy the agricultural infrastructure that might have made possible the absorption of returning refugees

Abandoned olive groves faced a similar fate. At first officials responsible for Jewish settlement thought that the production of olive oil might constitute a profitable economic venture, but it very quickly became clear that the Jewish agricultural sector was not set up to sustain this labor-intensive branch. Only a fraction of the olive groves were cared for and cultivated, whereas the vast majority were neglected. Tens of thousands of *dunams* of olive trees were uprooted to make room for field crops. Golan sums up the situation thus:

> Most of the orchard lands abandoned by the Arabs were not utilized by the Jews. . . . Wartime and post-war requirements combined with conditions whose origins were pre-war, resulting in the neglect of the abandoned property and the development of a new agricultural sector. . . . Ultimately, Jewish agriculture preferred continuity to change. It continued to develop along lines that had been laid down prior to the founding of the state, destroying whatever the Arabs had left in place that couldn't be integrated into that framework.[14]

The destruction of hundreds of thousands of *dunams* of fruit-bearing trees does not fit Israel's self-image as a society that knows how to "make the desert bloom." And the contention that the green Arab landscape had been destroyed because of the necessity of adapting the crops to the agricultural practices of the Jews only underscores the conclusion that it was not the war that had caused this devastation, but rather the disappearance of the specific human community that had shaped the landscape in accordance with its needs and preferences. The destruction of vast areas of orchards did not attract the same degree of interest as had the demolition of the Arab villages, despite the fact that it perhaps had a more devastating effect on the landscape.

DEMOLITION OF VILLAGES

The destruction of the Arab villages began, as we have seen, during the very earliest stages of the war. When the First Truce came into effect, scores of villages already were in an advanced state of ruin, and some had been totally obliterated. Although the demolition activity was initiated by the army, destruction also came about as a result of vandalism and burglary, and the concomitant dismantling of houses and their appurtenances. The drive to seek vengeance and the desire to eject hostile neighbors and enjoy the spoils of war acted together with military exigencies to encourage the destruction of property.

Early in June 1948 the demolition of villages took on the character of a political mission whose objective was to block the return of the refugees to their homes. In the view of some of those active in "Arab affairs" and "the redemption of the land," the destruction of the Arab villages was the key to preventing this return and was, along with the cultivation of the abandoned land and the establishment of Jewish settlements, supposed to ensure that the "miraculous exodus" would indeed become "retroactive transfer." A self-appointed committee, whose moving spirit was Joseph Weitz, submitted a report to Prime Minister David Ben-Gurion early that month, recommending the large-scale destruction of abandoned Arab villages. Ben-Gurion did not explicitly approve the recommendation, but in his characteristic manner he proposed that the matter be dealt with by the Zionist movement (the JNF and the Jewish Agency) without government involvement. Weitz regarded this as approval and launched a campaign of "tearing down, improving and settling" the abandoned villages. To that end, he "obtained 5,000 Palestinian pounds" and recruited JNF workers, who put themselves at his disposal. In the course of this campaign, about a dozen abandoned villages in various parts of the country were razed.

This half-private and semiclandestine activity could not go on for long. The resources at the JNF's disposal were small, and the actions themselves were severely criticized. The criticism was based on principled stands espoused chiefly by the leaders of the Mapam party, who opposed the dispossession of the Arabs (even though members of Mapam-affiliated kibbutzim took an active part in the destruction of the villages), as well as on international political considerations and concern over the reaction of other countries. There were also practical economic considerations: for instance, the fact that there were ways of exploiting the abandoned villages to produce income for the state. Above all, the view that these villages were the solution to the problem of housing the Jewish immigrants who were already filling to overflowing the urban areas whose Arab residents had fled was gaining currency, and thus destruction by civilians decreased. However, destruction by the military increased, and it was difficult to distinguish between what was motivated by strategic considerations and what was politically driven. With the resumption of hostilities at the end of the First Truce (8 July 1948), the army destroyed numerous villages on the grounds that it "lacked the manpower to hold on to the area and to fortify it," although it was clear that military considerations were influenced by the political imperative of blocking the refugees' return.

The Zionist officials who had taken upon themselves the "eradication" of the villages soon realized that the destruction they were carrying out ran counter to the objective of settling Jews in the villages. Now they found themselves protesting the army's demolition of "villages that we are interested in entering." Renovation work was begun in those intended for the settlement of new immigrants, although "population exchange"—that is, the housing of Jews in the homes of Arabs who had fled, leaving a vacuum behind them—turned out to be impracticable. Repairing the houses cost more than building new ones; many of the structures were not fit for human habitation, because their doors, roofs, stairs, and plumbing fixtures had been stolen; or they had been partially demolished by the army. Moreover, many of the Arab houses in the coastal region were built of crumbling adobe bricks, and the villages' clumped and irregular layout did not accommodate itself to Jewish patterns of settlement.

Ultimately, fewer than 20 percent of the settlements that were established by the end of 1949 were built on the sites of abandoned villages. In 1952 there were approximately seventy Jewish settlements in abandoned Arab villages; however, in fewer than half of these was there an intention to leave any of the Jewish settlers in the Arab houses permanently. Most of the abandoned villages remained deserted, their houses crumbling, their ruined skeletons prominent in the landscape. The officials in charge of settlement activity no longer had any interest in them, and the powers that be were seeking to wipe them off the face of the earth to eliminate any possibility that their former inhabitants might return. The decision to destroy the villages was related to the increasing international pressure on Israel (in which the United States played a pivotal role) to permit the return of large numbers of refugees. Early in May 1949 the government decided to get rid of all the heaps of rubble that remained in forty-one villages. This work was actively begun in July 1949, at which time the Department of Public Works began leveling abandoned villages in the Jerusalem Corridor and southern Shephelah. Care was taken, when destroying the buildings in a village, not to demolish stone structures in which immigrants might be housed, but officials responsible for new settlements complained that too many houses were being spared, thereby impeding the clearing of territory for new construction. There was also a tendency to avoid demolishing mosques, churches, and the graves of Muslim saints, and opposition to wholesale destruction was voiced by planning experts, who protested that the demolition of entire villages was damaging valuable historical sites and important features of the landscape and eradicating the geographical-historical heritage.

The work of demolition proceeded more slowly during the fifties and on into the early sixties. In October 1966 it was reported that the Israel Lands Administration (ILA) had launched a campaign—called "Leveling Villages"—to destroy abandoned villages in the Galilee. According to the report, "Bulldozers have demolished all the buildings in the village of Nabi Rubin—which were built of stone—except for the mosque and the adjoining building, in which a saint's grave was located."[15] An Arab Knesset member asked Prime Minister Levi Eshkol, "In what way did these abandoned villages, standing with their buildings and homes intact, bother anyone . . . such that it was necessary to adopt a formal decision to 'level' these villages?" The prime minister replied laconically that "the dismantling of abandoned and ruined houses in deserted villages has no political significance, particularly since the holy places are being preserved. . . . Not destroying the abandoned villages would be contrary to the policy of development and revitalization of wasteland, which every state is obliged to implement."

This calculated destruction resumed at an accelerated pace following the Six-Day War, this time with the aim of eliminating any possibility that refugees from the West Bank and Gaza, who had begun to make pilgrimages to the ruins of their villages, could identify their houses. Journalist Danny Rubinstein describes an instance in which two elderly refugees returned to visit their village of origin: "Although hardly anything remained of the place, the two visitors managed to find some indications that this was indeed the site of their village. Nevertheless, the surroundings had changed so radically that one of the refugees stubbornly rejected the evidence, insisting that it was not where Innaba had once stood," until they found the remains of some simple gravestones, upon one of which was an indistinct inscription bearing the name of that refugee's father. He burst into tears and refused ever to return to that place. "All the money in the world, they said, wouldn't compensate for their pain at seeing their village destroyed."[16] Arab settlements where archaeological artifacts of significance to the Israelis were found were restored after being "cleansed" of all Arab structures that did not interest them. The most conspicuous examples of this practice are to be found in the Old City of Caesarea and the village of Kawkab al-Hawa, overlooking the Jordan Rift Valley, settlements that had been built within the walls of Crusader fortifications. The Arab structures (with the exception of those useful as tourist amenities) were demolished by the Israelis, and the Crusader ruins were excavated and restored (see chapter 7). Other villages, situated in areas where access for bulldozers was difficult, were not totally eradicated either, and Jews with an aesthetic sense renovated and moved into large, beautiful Arab homes there. Glorious histories were invented for particularly impressive structures left standing in the middle of abandoned villages or on their outskirts. Thus, for example, the Jews who acquired the home of the respected al-Madi family in the village of Ijzim say that the house was a Crusader castle; its present inhabitants are unable to believe that such a splendid structure (see plate 23) was built by Arabs. The most obvious example of the preservation of an Arab village "as an aesthetic gem" suitable for the accommodation of writers, painters, and other artists is that of Ein Hawd, which was renamed Ein Hod. This village merits a detailed description of its own (see chapter 5).

The remains of a few Arab villages were spared because of the "ancient" way of life they supposedly exemplified—with emphasis on the biblical context—or for their contribution to the landscape. Flour mills, apparatuses for water, and especially stone terraces and fruit trees, were incorporated into national parks and nature reserves. A favorite spot for people on excursions in the Jerusalem area is the village of Sataf, where several of the houses and the village spring have been preserved.

It is ironic that the JNF, which took such an active part in the destruction of the Arab landscape, is energetically involved in the preservation of its remnants. The greenery, buildings, and agricultural equipment, it seems, merit proper maintenance, but of course there is no mention of the uprooted villagers; the landscape has been sanitized.

ALL THAT REMAINS

Between 1987 and 1991 Palestinian geographer Ghazi Falah conducted a comprehensive survey of the remnants of the Arab landscape in Israel, classifying the remains of the abandoned towns and villages according to the extent of their destruction.[17] His findings: two-thirds of the villages were completely wiped out, including some eighty that are unidentifiable because the land on which they stood has been plowed up, planted with trees, or excavated for commercial fish ponds. Other villages were totally demolished, but their outlines have been preserved thanks to prickly pear cactus hedges, stone terraces, or fruit trees gone wild. In fifty-two of the approximately 400 abandoned Arab villages there are visible signs that they were—or still are—inhabited by Jews. Some of the houses in these villages were renovated to serve as dwellings, and in some places the Arab houses are used as storehouses or barns while the Jews live in newer structures. Most of the villages in which Jewish families are still living are situated within the Tel Aviv metropolitan area. Many of the buildings in the villages of this area—which were, as mentioned earlier, largely of stone or concrete and had been constructed in the years immediately preceding the 1948 War—were found to be fit for renovation. By contrast, a large collection of villages in the southern Coastal Plain have vanished altogether, the reason being that the houses were constructed of adobe bricks and were therefore easily dismantled.

Examination of Falah's map reveals, however, that especially heavy destruction took place in areas dominated by veteran Jewish agricultural settlements in the Jordan, Beit Shean, and Jezreel Valleys.[18] There is extensive evidence that members of the older kibbutzim and moshavim pushed for the destruction of the abandoned Arab villages adjacent to them, and even took part in destroying the villages with their own hands, so they could take over the abandoned land and prevent the return of the displaced inhabitants. According to one report, "One of the JNF workers told the secretariat of the kibbutz to demolish the houses right away, and openly stated that this would enable us to take over the village land, since the Arabs would not be able to return there. I am sorry to say that the kibbutz agreed immediately, without thinking what they were doing."[19]

ZIONIST MERCENARIES

There was an additional reason for demolishing these abandoned villages: the veteran settlers' movement was not interested in the possibility of their being populated with new immigrants, since its members wanted to keep all the land in their own hands and not share it with the newcomers. The conflict that developed over the division of the spoils (i.e., the abandoned landholdings) among political groupings, establishment interests, old-timers, and immigrants shaped the physical landscape of the State of Israel to no lesser degree than had the exodus that had engendered this conflict.

Before describing the dynamics involved in the dividing of the spoils and its consequences, it is only fitting to outline the positions of the interested parties. In mid-December 1948 an argument "on the question of the abandoned land" took place in the JNF office, at the instigation of Levi Eshkol, then chairman of the Settlement Department of the Jewish Agency and subsequently finance minister and prime minister of the State of Israel. According to Joseph Weitz, "Eshkol wanted to know why the JNF had to pay the state for the abandoned land, after it had been conquered in a war whose costs had been borne by the Zionist Organization, to whom the land, therefore, also belonged." Weitz, the originator and indefatigable champion of state seizure of Arab land, and at that time the director of the JNF Land Department, was in the throes of vigorous negotiations with the government over the acquisition of abandoned land from the state by the JNF. Weitz did not agree with Eshkol's contentions:

> I replied that this position was untenable on two counts: a. The entire Jewish People had been obliged to share in the costs of the war, and not the Zionist Organization alone; b. It will be necessary to pay the Arabs for the abandoned land, and the government of Israel will be the one to pay. Therefore, the government owes nothing to the Zionist Organization, and what's more, the latter must pay for the land.

Following a lengthy discussion, Eshkol demanded that the government turn over the land in exchange for one-third of the funds that the Jewish Agency hoped to raise from America.[20]

It would be difficult to find a better example of the confused perceptions that prevailed at the time concerning the significance of the establishment of the State of Israel, and of the degree to which some key public figures failed to discern the fundamental difference between "authority without sovereignty," which had been the situation in the days of the Yishuv, and "the single, supreme center of authority" embodied by a sovereign state. Levi Eshkol was not the only leader who regarded the State of Israel as the direct continuation of the pre-state Jewish community (the Yishuv), and the government of Israel as just one more Zionist institution that needed to find its place and status beside (or perhaps beneath) the existing institutions of the Zionist movement. After all, David Ben-Gurion had conducted the first half of the war in his capacity as the chairman of the Jewish Agency, and the war had been "financed by the Zionist Organization." Therefore, the Zionist Organization supposedly "deserved" to enjoy the fruits of the war it had financed—to receive the abandoned land for the purpose of carrying on the Zionist enterprise. Indeed, this was an interesting way of perceiving the war: as if Israeli soldiers were mercenaries in the service of the Zionist movement, aiding in the effort to take over Arab land.

Weitz discounted Eshkol's arguments but not the principle on which they rested. In his eyes the war had, indeed, been a means for the "redemption of the land" for the Zionist movement; but even so, the JNF must pay for the land that had been redeemed. Otherwise it would not be able to take ownership of the abandoned property; its job would be over and it would be dismantled. Weitz knew whereof he spoke: his earlier attempts to acquire abandoned land without payment had been rejected by the Israeli government; now he was being presented with the opportunity to purchase the continuation of the JNF, since David Ben-Gurion had agreed to sell him a million *dunams* of Arab land. But now Eshkol was threatening to ruin the deal that would ensure the continuation of this venerable Zionist institution. The money that the JNF was about to give the government would not merely guarantee the JNF's status; it also was insurance against the claims of the land's legal owners, the Arabs who had abandoned it. "It will be necessary to pay the Arabs," Weitz had self-righteously stated, "for the abandoned land." But that was not his problem, it was the government's: "It will be the one to pay." As to how willing the government was to do so, Weitz himself testified that one of his workers informed him that government policy was that land was not to be purchased from Arabs (voluntary sale) at that time, so as not to set a price that would act as a precedent during negotiations for a settlement with the refugees.

Joseph Weitz was not the only one vigorously striving to preserve the pre-state institution (the JNF). The leaders of all the political parties, the heads of other pre-state institutions and the long-established settlement movements, as well as ministers in the Israeli government, were similarly active. Each regarded the new state and its sovereign institutions as a means for promoting his own political and ideological goals and for the realization of the interests of sectoral institutions. All of them were, of course, united in the view that the State of Israel was an instrument for the implementation of Zionist objectives, but each group defined these objectives differently and took pains to cover the political power struggles among them, as well as their lust for control of the governing institutions of the state, with a veneer of ideology.

POWER STRUGGLE

The fact that Israel's governing institutions had been set up in the midst of the turmoil of war and that these institutions were viewed as extensions of those of the Yishuv had the result that public-service and sectoral organizations, as well as voluntary associations, were transformed into governmental executive authorities with the legislative and enforcement apparatus of a sovereign state at their disposal. Thus, the man responsible for abandoned land in the Ministry of Minorities (a euphemism for Arabs)—which had inherited the job of dealing with this property from a pre-state committee—was also the representative of a kibbutz movement (the United Kibbutz Movement) as well as a member of the Agricultural Center (the umbrella organization of the cooperative settlement movement). He, not surprisingly, made sure to allocate the lion's share of this land to the established kibbutzim. When the significance of control of the abandoned property became clear to David Ben-Gurion, this responsibility was taken out of the hands of the Ministry of Minorities, which was headed by a Sephardic Jewish minister, and given to two other ministries: agriculture and finance (the latter was given "ministerial authority" in this matter, while the former was granted extensive authority in the allocation of abandoned agricultural property). The man appointed as custodian of absentee property was also the director-general of the cooperative settlement movement's construction company, and he of course looked after the organizational and political interests of his own kibbutz and his own party. Mayors of towns and cities, private farmers and their organizations, regional councils, and committees representing blocks of settlements succeeded in acquiring pieces of abandoned property for themselves, depending on their political affiliation and on how close they were to the officials responsible for its allotment. Anyone who was not close to the centers of power, or who belonged to the wrong organization or party, went without. Some groups and individuals took the law into their own hands, squatting on abandoned land and in deserted buildings. Their ownership rights were later recognized retroactively.

Mapam and Mapai, the two parties that led Israel's first (provisional) government, waged a "war of titans" over the control of land. Mapam was, at the time, a decisive voice in the kibbutz movement by virtue of its being the party representing its two largest factions, Hashomer Hatzair and Hakibbutz Hameuchad. Most Palmach commanders belonged to this party, as did many of those in the IDF. Mapam was a strange amalgam: military activism alongside a striving for coexistence with the Arabs; fundamental opposition to the expulsion of Arabs and the plundering of their land alongside vigorous leadership in the establishment of kibbutzim in all parts of the territory conquered during the war and in consolidating Israel's dominion over them. Its representatives in the government were a militant force opposing the demolition of villages and landgrabs, whereas the members of its kibbutzim were among the most active in appropriating Arab land adjacent to their settlements.

Agriculture Minister Aharon Zisling, a member of Kibbutz Ein Harod and one of the leaders of Mapam, greatly upset Prime Minister Ben-Gurion with his stringent criticism of the destruction of villages and the expulsion of Arabs and by voting against the government on these issues. But Zisling himself was the man who had been appointed to allocate the abandoned land and was also party to the establishment of settlements on Arab land in every part of the country. He strove to take a central role in both realms, as guardian of his party's ideological position and as guardian of the land interests of the Mapam-affiliated kibbutz movements. Zisling's endeavors, as minister of agriculture, to play a vital part in the allocation of abandoned land gave rise to interminable friction with other government ministries, particularly the Finance Ministry (within which the custodian of absentee property operated), and also with the JNF, which feared that the government was scheming to relieve it of its historic role. The Finance Ministry and the JNF were dominated by Mapai, and the friction with the Ministry of Agriculture, although it had a bureaucratic aspect, revolved primarily around land resources and their use and allocation, authority over which conferred tremendous influence. Mapam's controlling position in the Ministry of Agriculture gave it considerable power but also necessitated its involvement in activity that was contrary to its ideological positions. This contradiction gave rise to ideological distress, which was resolved with the help of creative semantics and by the formulation of an "agrarian reform plan," whose aim was to prove that one could both steal land and do good for those who had been robbed.

In the regulations enabling the takeover of abandoned land, it was designated (at Aharon Zisling's request) as "fallow land"—that is, land that was, supposedly, simply not being cultivated—with no mention of the reason. This ploy made it possible to hide behind the claim that these regulations were no different than Ottoman and Mandatory laws providing for the expropriation of land that was not in use, and that therefore it was not a question of the displaced villagers' land having been taken from them wrongly. But of course this semantic exercise fooled no one.

Mapam's Agrarian Reform Plan was predicated on the idea that the "intensification" of Arab agriculture (i.e., its mechanization and the modernization of methods of cultivation) would enable Arab farmers to make do with just a fraction of their landholdings. The Arabs were to obtain the sums required for the modernization of their backward economy through the sale of "their surplus land" to the state (or in the form of compensation for its expropriation). This idea was not Mapam's invention; even before the 1948 War, Joseph Weitz and Zalman Lif (Lifshitz) had formulated the principle of land improvement as the key to agrarian reform in the Jewish state after its establishment. This principle, had it applied, would have made possible the acquisition of extensive areas for massive Jewish settlement without harm to Arab farmers. The formulation of this land improvement principle was undertaken, in part, because the UN Resolution on the Partition of Palestine (181 of 29 November 1947) stated: "No expropriation of land owned by an Arab in the Jewish state ([or] by a Jew in the Arab state, respectively) shall be allowed except for public purposes. In all cases of expropriation full compensation as fixed by the Supreme Court shall be paid previous to dispossession" (Chapter 2, Article 8). At that time, as well as during the early stages of the war—and even as late as June through July 1948—the Jewish authorities, including those concerned with settlement activity, operated in such a way as to not contravene this resolution. The war and the Arab exodus, however, made the Partition Resolution a dead letter—and the principle of agrarian reform an anachronism—until Mapam came along and revived it, theoretically as a means to allow the return of the refugees along with the utilization of "their surplus land" for Jewish settlement.

According to Mapam's calculations, more than half the abandoned land could be considered as surplus. The Arab refugees, then, could return to their homes and cultivate the remainder, and with the aid of the compensation they would be paid for the land taken from them by the state, they could develop modern farming methods. The Agrarian Reform Plan served as a convenient fig leaf not only for those who advocated the return of the uprooted villagers but also for those who were doing their utmost to prevent such return. As long as there was still a "surplus of land," that is, in the early stages of the state takeover, it was possible to point to the "intensification option," which had propaganda value and also acted as salve to the conscience. Later, when the "surplus" had been exhausted, the continuation of land takeovers was justified on the grounds of vital security and development requirements, and agrarian reform was forgotten; after all, the refugees had not returned.

Mapam's political influence on settlement and security, the two pillars of the Zionist ethos, became a source of vexation to Prime Minister Ben-Gurion. Even though he was the undisputed leader of the state, he could not tolerate this influence, which he regarded as partisan interference in matters of state. Tom Segev writes that Ben-Gurion "warned of the danger that Mapam would seize power with the help of its followers in the army."[21] In order to forestall this "danger," in November 1948 Ben-Gurion dismantled the Palmach, which he regarded as a partisan military body (because it was dominated by members of Mapam), and handed over its functions to the IDF General Staff. This step was taken in the name of statism, the natural outcome of the establishment of the sovereign State of Israel. In Ben-Gurion's view, the state had taken upon itself the functions of the Zionist organizations that had operated during the Mandate, and there was no longer room for the continued activity of bodies that operated on the basis of "authority without sovereignty."

The concept of statism (*mamlakhtiyut* in Hebrew), however, was invoked only selectively. In mid-December 1948, one month after his order to dismantle the Palmach, Ben-Gurion decided to sell the JNF a million *dunams* of abandoned land. This decision neither reinforced the power of the state nor was lawful. The government was selling land that it did not legally own but had captured in war. Even the laws that it had thus far passed did not grant the state the sort of ownership that could be transferred to the JNF, a company registered in London and affiliated with the Zionist Organization. This decision was destined to have long-range historical consequences. This sale conferred upon the Zionist Organization and its administrative arms—the Jewish Agency and the JNF—quasi-governmental status within the Israeli governing apparatus. These organizations acted in the name of the Jewish People and not that of the State of Israel, a fact that provided the pretext for a set of measures that discriminated against the non-Jewish citizens of the state with supposedly no connection to the government.

Ben-Gurion thus attained three objectives in one fell swoop. First, he transferred responsibility for the abandoned land where the construction of new settlements was planned—from the Mapam-controlled Ministry of Agriculture to the JNF, which was under Mapai's influence. Second, he was able to dissociate himself from the whole matter of land confiscations. And third, he established a political fait accompli that closed the door to the refugees. A week before the decision regarding the sale of the million *dunams,* the UN General Assembly had approved Resolution 194, according to which the refugees were entitled to return to their homes, or to receive compensation, should they choose not to return (see chapter 8). Ben-Gurion did not wish to sully Israel's reputation as a state with anything smacking so strongly of illegality, deviation from the norms of international law, and immorality. This was not the first time that the seasoned Zionist leader had sought to divest himself of responsibility in matters connected to the destruction of villages and the expulsion of Arabs. As we have seen, he had behaved in this manner throughout the war, as well as during the First Truce, when he fobbed off the campaign of "tearing down, improving, and settling" the abandoned villages on the Zionist Organization.

The heads of the JNF were well aware that the sale was not legal; it was important to them, however, to establish the fact that their organization would continue to serve as the institution holding title to the land holdings of the Jewish people and to develop them for settlement purposes. They insisted that the government of Israel undertake "to make all the [future] legal arrangements such that this land would be registered as being fully under JNF ownership in conformity with the laws of the State of Israel." In October 1950 the government sold the JNF another million *dunams,* bringing the amount of land transferred to its ownership to approximately 40 percent of the total area of the abandoned property. Hence, the holdings of the JNF, which had been roughly 900,000 *dunams* (out of a total of approximately 1.8 million *dunams* of Jewish-owned land) on the eve of the establishment of the state, more than tripled. The distinction between the purchase of property from Arab landowners who were willing to sell—as had been the case during the British Mandate—and the acquisition of "redeemed land" from the state was blurred. Thus the land of dispossessed Arabs became the property of the Jewish people, subject to JNF regulations prohibiting its being leased to non-Jews; in this way a principle was established enshrining discrimination between the Jewish citizens of Israel and its Arab citizens, from whose displaced compatriots the land had been confiscated (or "purchased") without their being entitled to any compensation at all. Eventually the ILA was set up to manage both "State Land" and the landholdings of "the Jewish people." An influential role in the ILA is played by the JNF—an anachronistic body that has continued to operate only because Ben-Gurion did not wish to be directly involved in dubious dealings. The JNF's representation in the ILA enables it to impose its discriminatory regulations in all land matters.

SETTLING THE LAND

At the outbreak of the 1948 War there were 293 Jewish agricultural settlements in Palestine: 117 moshavim, 149 kibbutzim, and 29 other rural settlements.[22] In 1948 and 1949 approximately 170 more were established, and by the end of 1950 the number of settlements founded in the course of those three years (1948–50) equaled the number that had been established during the preceding sixty-six (1882–1948). This astonishing growth surprised no one. After all, agricultural settlement activity was the quintessence of the Zionist ethos, according to which the "redemption of the land" required its being inhabited by communities of Jewish farmers "bringing forth bread from the earth."

The importance of the rural settlements in political, security, and military terms was proven at the time of the struggle over the demarcation of the partition borders in 1947 and during the 1948 War. Now that the Arabs had gone, populating and cultivating the abandoned areas was the only way to ensure that they would remain in Jewish hands, and the establishment of settlements along the armistice lines was regarded as an effective barrier to a potential Arab invasion. Particular importance was attached to founding settlements in the regions that had been designated as part of the Arab state under the Partition Resolution of 1947 (the Western Galilee, the Jerusalem Corridor, and the south) as a countermeasure to plans that would sever them from the body of the state. It is no wonder, then, that even in the midst of hostilities Zionist and government figures were proposing the establishment of settlements that would initially function as paramilitary outposts. The settlement program was planned by military experts in conjunction with the settlement movements and the planning and implementation arms of the Zionist Organization.

Two factors were critical to the settlement program: human resources and land. Up until 1948 land was a scarce commodity, whereas manpower (in the form of groups from "pioneering" youth movements inside the country and abroad) was relatively readily available. The Arab exodus removed all barriers to land acquisition, thus creating a shortage of persons prepared for an agricultural life within the existing structures—the kibbutz and moshav movements. At the same time, hundreds of thousands of immigrants were arriving, and they needed to be integrated into the country's economy and social system. It goes without saying that immigration was perceived by those involved in organizing it as an inexhaustible human resource for filling the vacuum created by the Arab exodus.

The abandoned villages could supposedly provide a solution to the problem of finding housing for the immigrants once the abandoned homes in the mixed cities were all taken; in and of itself the "return to the land" of displaced Jews, survivors of the Holocaust, was regarded as the best way to integrate them, one that would root them "once again" in the soil of their ancestors. It was not surprising, therefore, that the settlement drive that commenced in 1948 and ended, for all practical purposes, in 1954 (although it continued at a sluggish pace into the seventies) was looked upon as an "exchange of populations": the Arabs became refugees and Jewish refugees settled in their place; in place of the 400 or so Arab villages that were abandoned, some 400 Jewish villages were established. Those involved in this "transfer" actually compared it to other twentieth-century population exchanges—for instance, between Turks and Greeks after the First World War and between India and Pakistan following the partition of India.

SUDETEN EXAMPLE

Another frequent comparison has been made between the expulsion of the Palestinians and the ouster of the ethnic Germans from the Sudetenland in Czechoslovakia following the Second World War.[23] It was touted as evidence that the expulsion of enemy populations in the wake of war is condoned by the great powers, and also as support for the contention that the expulsion of the Arabs, like that of the Sudetenland Germans, was "repayment for the troubles they'd caused" or the "judgment of history for their aggression." The expulsion of more than 3 million Germans from Czechoslovakia and another 3.5 million from Silesia had been decided upon at the Potsdam Conference of July and August 1945. In November of that year the Allied Control Council issued the order for its implementation, but by that time a brutal, spontaneous expulsion from the Sudetenland was already under way, having begun in the final days of the war, and by the end of 1945 some 660,000 Germans had fled or been expelled by the Czechs. Many thousands of Germans perished, the majority innocent civilians, during what was referred to as "the wild expulsion." The Czechs admit that approximately 19,000 died as a direct result of the "wild" expulsion, among them 5,600 who were summarily executed. Surviving expellees claim that no fewer than a quarter million went to their deaths during this initial phase of the expulsion. In late January 1946 the orderly phase of the expulsion began, in the course of which some 2.5 million Germans were "resettled" in Germany. In August 1945, the Czech president, Edvard Beneš, revoked the citizenship of the ethnic Germans (and Hungarians) in his country, and shortly afterward all their property and real estate, both agricultural and urban, was seized "immediately and without compensation."

The use of this comparison was to the Israelis' advantage: the expulsion of the Sudeten Germans had been carried out by the democratic government of a civilized nation, with international approval, and there was no comparing its scope and the enormous loss of life it entailed with what took place in Eretz Israel/Palestine, which even the Palestinians never claimed involved the mass murder of civilians. But all these comparisons were designed for foreign consumption. The Israelis themselves needed no justifications; the necessity of creating a national entity by settling Jews in the land of their forebears was justification enough, and it vindicated every injustice committed in its name.

JEWEL IN THE CROWN

Until recently, the epic settlement drive following the establishment of the state was depicted as the jewel in the crown of the Zionist enterprise and as a source of profound pride. More recent studies have analyzed the settlement project in a more balanced manner and have described its less praiseworthy aspects. I shall deal here with its implications for the landscape only.

At the outset of the settlement drive, 11.7 percent of the Jewish population of Israel lived in long-established cooperative settlements (according to figures from the census of November 1948); of these, approximately 7 percent resided in kibbutzim and about 5 percent in moshavim. In 1954, at the conclusion of the great post-independence wave of immigration, the cooperative settlements' share of the population had fallen to between 7 and 8 percent. From 1948 through 1950 the kibbutz movement absorbed 15,000 immigrants (mainly members of pioneering groups from abroad), and its aggregate membership reached 76,000 souls (an increase of 22,000 over 1948). Thus only 2.1 percent of the approximately 700,000 immigrants who arrived during those years were absorbed by kibbutzim: the total number of immigrants absorbed by all the cooperative settlements (kibbutzim and moshavim), old and new (mainly new moshavim) did not exceed 11 percent of all immigrants during the years in question.[24] In spite of the minute contribution of the kibbutzim to immigrant absorption, they acquired more than one-quarter of the abandoned land. In the beginning it was only natural that the sector most capable of mobilizing quickly to provide the agricultural produce so urgently required by the burgeoning population of the state should receive extensive holdings. The kibbutz movements, however, sought to obtain permanent title to the land to which they had been given short-term leases. Golan remarks that in April 1949 the kibbutzim demanded that their permanent landholdings should "comprise 5,000 *dunams* of land for intensive cultivation by each settlement. They actually reached this goal as a result of the post-war land transfer (That was the amount of land temporarily leased to them)."[25] At that time there were about 180 kibbutzim.

As long as the established settlement movements had adequate human resources to develop existing settlements and to establish new ones, there was no conflict between their holding all this land and the requirements of immigrant absorption. To deflect criticism regarding the unequal distribution of land, they stressed the classical strategic-political and ideological goals of pioneering settlement and maintained that only select groups of youth, who had received both agricultural and military training, could fill this vital role, not new immigrants lacking in both experience and motivation. They were prepared to absorb immigrants, but only according to the existing pattern. That is, as long as there were still settlement groups made up of the remnants of the pioneering youth movements in the diaspora—whether those that remained after the Holocaust or ones from affluent Western countries, they took care to assure them of adequate living conditions and opportunities for development. If conflicts over land arose between older and newer kibbutzim, they were resolved within the kibbutz movements. Before long, however, all the remaining groups had joined existing settlements or founded new ones, and no human resources remained for the establishment of new kibbutzim. On the other hand, it had become evident that new immigrants, too, must be absorbed into the agricultural sector, especially in the new immigrant communities being set up in the abandoned villages. It was now clear that these immigrants would be obliged to participate in the drive to set up strategic settlements—whether or not they had received the appropriate training for it—because otherwise great expanses of land would remain devoid of Jewish inhabitants. It was therefore necessary to rally the immigrants for this task.

Massive settlement of new immigrants threatened the hegemony of the kibbutz movement, whose leaders feared it would weaken them politically. And there were indeed political motives behind the immigrant settlement initiatives—in addition to objective necessity. Mapai and its leader, Ben-Gurion, were striving (as we have already seen) to destroy the dominance of Mapam (and its affiliated kibbutz movements) in two principal realms: settlement and security. The Mapai leadership therefore chose the Moshav Movement, which they controlled, as the medium for effecting the large-scale settlement of immigrants. They also assumed that its open, cooperative form of settlement would better suit people who had not been prepared for life in a closed collective like the kibbutz.

Late in December 1948 the first two immigrant moshavim were established, on the sites of two abandoned Arab villages in the center of the country. By the end of June 1949, twenty-one immigrant moshavim had been set up in various parts of Israel: eight in the Upper Galilee, one in the Carmel region, two in the Jerusalem Hills, two in the vicinity of Lod, and seven on the southern Coastal Plain. Immigrant moshavim were being set up at a fast clip: sixty-two in 1949 and sixty-three in 1950. By the end of 1954, 194 moshavim had been established, compared with eighty-three new kibbutzim. In addition, in 1954 there were approximately eighty nonagricultural immigrant settlements outside the main towns, including temporary villages (whose inhabitants were employed in afforestation or in preparing the ground for the establishment of moshavim), and small *ma'abarot* (immigrant "transit camps"). The Moshav Movement saw to the allocation of land to its member settlements, while Mapai-controlled government agencies supported its struggle with the kibbutz movements when conflicts arose between new moshavim and established kibbutzim over the long-term leasing of land. These conflicts were sometimes fierce, but they were quickly resolved, since there was indeed land for all. By January 1950 the Ministry of Agriculture had allocated some 1,750,000 *dunams* of abandoned land, most of it to old and new cooperative settlements,[26] and in the years that followed land was apportioned at a rate that kept pace with the establishment of the moshavim. By the early 1970s, both kibbutzim and moshavim had long-term leases on more than 2.8 million *dunams,* or 25 percent, of the fertile areas of Israel (excluding the desert south of Beersheba). The cooperative settlements held 45 percent of the land abandoned by Arabs or confiscated from Arab citizens.

The moshavim, which by 1967 had increased in number to 372 (including *moshavim shitufi'im,* a settlement form combining features of moshav and kibbutz), now dominated Israel's landscape. The decentralized layout of the moshavim—with houses situated on large plots of farmland lining roads arranged in a circular or rectangular pattern, with public buildings at the center—enabled the expansion of these settlements and their evolution into nonagricultural suburbs. This was, in fact, the direction in which those moshavim that were located near cities ultimately evolved. The kibbutzim, with their compact layout—of residential neighborhoods, public buildings, and farming-related structures clustered together—which had once typified the rural landscape, ceased to be its dominant feature. They shut themselves away behind high fences and rows of tall trees, cut off from the urban life around them. But in the 1990s the kibbutzim, too, have lost their distinctive features, when shopping malls, entertainment centers, and even nonmember private houses have been built on and near them (see later discussion).

VETERANS AND NEWCOMERS

As soon as it was determined which model a new settlement would conform to, tracts of land were allocated to it in accordance with the planning principles of the long-established settlement movements. The recent immigrants, lacking the access to the centers of power enjoyed by veteran settlers, were dependent on, but did not always receive, the support of the Moshav Movement and its experienced leaders.

The discrimination between the older and newer settlements was reflected primarily in the allocation of land according to region, or, in other words, in the location of the immigrant settlements. Although these were being set up in most areas of the country, it is nonetheless possible to point to regions where blocks of new settlements had been created and, by contrast, areas of long-standing settlement where there were virtually no new ones.

In the Galilee Panhandle, in the vicinity of the Sea of Galilee, and in the Beit Shean Valley, where some 100 abandoned Arab villages were situated, fewer than twenty new settlements were founded, and of them only half a dozen were new immigrants' agricultural settlements, nearly all of the abandoned land having been handed over to older ones. The fertile, level, abandoned land in the Jezreel Valley and the western and central Sharon was also given to established settlements in the vicinity. Although new ones were founded in the Western Galilee, a region noted for its fertile soil and abundant water, few of these were immigrant moshavim. In contrast to these areas, which were virtually closed to settlement by immigrants, clusters of immigrant moshavim were established in the hilly Northern Galilee, in the Central Galilee, along the armistice line in the northern Coastal Plain, in the area south of the town of Rehovot—approaching the Negev—and in the Jerusalem Corridor.

The distribution of immigrant settlements made a mockery of the kibbutz movements' pretensions to being the only ones capable of establishing strategic settlements to secure Israel's borders and of planting faits accomplis that would prevent these areas' being torn from the body of the state. Although some thirty kibbutzim were founded in border areas and outside the boundaries of the territory allocated to the Jewish state by the Partition Resolution, for every new kibbutz, three immigrant moshavim sprang up.

There was yet another aspect to the discrimination suffered by the immigrant settlements in the hilly regions of the country: unlike the kibbutzim in like terrain, they did not receive land for cultivation in the plains some distance from the settlement, which would have made their farming more profitable. Golan summarizes:

> The distribution of land among the various sectors was fraught with fierce territorial disputes. What they all had in common was most fundamental: the desire to secure ownership rights to vacant tracts of land abandoned by the Arab population. Hence these conflicts, which were played out on all planes—the national, the institutional, the regional, and the local—resulted in the breakdown of relations between neighbors, of movement affiliations, and of ideological affinities.[27]

The real test of the powerful cooperative settlement movement in the realm of immigrant absorption was not, however, in the allocation of land within the agricultural sector itself but in its relations with the overwhelming majority of the immigrants, who had settled in towns and cities or in those abandoned villages not destined for agricultural settlement. After all, only one or two of every ten immigrants went to live in a farming community. The treatment of the nonfarming communities was simply by dictate, since the urban and semiurban immigrant communities were helpless in comparison to the all-powerful agricultural sector. The latter's takeover of the abandoned land had been justified by the vital needs of immigrant absorption and represented as an "exchange of populations." But when the need arose to allocate land for the construction of immigrant towns or to otherwise ensure that the nonagricultural communities would have opportunities for development, the veteran settlers' organizations behaved as if this land had been theirs for generations.

KIRYAT SHEMONA

Among the most blatant examples of this attitude are the towns of Kiryat Shemona and Beit Shean. In mid-1949 the government Physical Planning Division began preparing a nationwide plan for the dispersal of the country's population and targeted the site of the abandoned village of al-Khalsa (see chapter 3) to be "the administrative, commercial, and industrial center of the Upper Galilee." According to this plan, the population of al-Khalsa (which was subsequently called Kiryat Yosef after Joseph Trumpeldor, and finally Kiryat Shemona, Town of the Eight, after the eight settlers killed in an attack on nearby Tel Hai in 1920) was supposed to reach 15,000 in the "first stage" (although actually the town's population did not reach 18,000 until 1996). The area within its municipal boundaries was initially fixed at 1,500 *dunams* and ultimately at 5,250 *dunams,* that is, half the land of the abandoned village. Despite Kiryat Shemona's being designated as an urban administrative center, a significant portion of its land was allocated for agriculture: 1,260 *dunams* "fully or partially agricultural" and another 1,300 *dunams* for small farms intended to bring in supplemental income for their nonfarmer owners. Only what was left over was designated for the construction of two- and three-story apartment houses, offices, public buildings, and workplaces.

When the plan was completed, 300 people, new immigrants from Yemen, already were living in the houses of the abandoned village. The members of the nearby cooperative settlements, who were not interested in the establishment of a town in that location, pressured the authorities to designate the new settlement as an immigrant moshav. They were, at the time, already working half the village land and were afraid that the establishment of a town of 15,000 would "rob" them of it. They essentially viewed the founding of a town that would serve as the administrative center for the area's settlements as unnecessary, since the hierarchical model, of district administrative centers mediating between them and the large urban centers, was foreign to them. They preferred to maintain direct contact with the settlement movement's powerful economic institutions and organizations, whose headquarters were in Tel Aviv. Kiryat Shemona was ultimately built, but its development was slow: the immigrants found employment as hired laborers in the older neighboring settlements, whereas these settlements themselves set up regional plants in town. Thus the immigrants became dependent on the veteran settlers for their livelihood. Nothing came of plans for agriculture in Kiryat Shemona, and its inhabitants have neither forgiven nor forgotten the efforts of the older settlements in sabotaging the town's development.

BEIT SHEAN

The conflict between immigrants and old-timers over populating the abandoned town of Beisan (renamed Beit Shean) was fiercer and more out in the open than in the case of Kiryat Shemona. The Arab town of 6,000 had served as the administrative and economic center of the subdistrict that bore its name. The majority of its Arab inhabitants had supported themselves from agriculture, while a minority had been employed in commerce or in cottage industries. The demolition of their homes was begun in June 1948, following the capture of the town and the flight of its inhabitants, but was discontinued soon afterward. Thus in April 1949, upon commencement of repopulating Beisan with new immigrants, many houses remained intact.

The kibbutzim in the vicinity, which were already working most of the town's agricultural land at that time, did not look kindly upon the establishment of an immigrant town there, fearing that the town's presence would mean the loss of the land they had been leased. The greatest number of immigrants that the kibbutzim were willing to "absorb" in Beit Shean was 600 families, and only on condition that they work in "regional enterprises," which the neighboring agricultural settlements would set up there, and that the immigrant settlement itself be organized as a "collective," that is, that it be controlled by the Histadrut. The kibbutzim refused to allocate land to the immigrants for cultivation, and the new settlement was plagued by a severe scarcity of work. As the pressure to absorb immigrants in that region increased, a proposal designed to provide a miraculous solution to the problem was made: the establishment of a new town on the ruins of the Arab village of Mursass, about seven kilometers (just under 4.5 miles) to the northwest of Beit Shean. Had this proposal been accepted, it is not certain that it would have been carried out, but in any event the expansion of the immigrant town of Beit Shean would have eventually come to a halt. The kibbutzim were ultimately unable to stem the growth of Beit Shean; however, the settlement remained an economic backwater and totally dependent on employment provided by the local kibbutzim in the factories they had built in Beit Shean and in agricultural labor. The inhabitants of Beit Shean, too, have neither forgiven nor forgotten.

RING OF DEPRIVATION

This process was repeated in many locations: the growth of nonagricultural immigrant settlements was held back for years, and their ability to absorb new residents was restricted because the surrounding land had been given to cooperative agricultural settlements, both old and new. The townships that were established in the abandoned villages of the Tel Aviv metropolitan area felt the consequences of this discriminatory land allocation policy especially severely. In this area tens of thousands of immigrants had been housed in some forty abandoned villages where there were houses ready for speedy occupancy, albeit under harsh and sometimes disgraceful conditions. The landholdings of these Arab villages were vast. But the new immigrant townships that were set up in these abandoned villages received only a small part of the village's land, and they found themselves being squeezed between the established cities' (Tel Aviv, Ramat Gan, Holon, Bat Yam, and Herzliyya) passion for expansion and the agricultural sector's insatiable appetite for land. The cities endeavored to annex the territory of the villages they bordered, but they refused to take in the immigrants who inhabited the houses in those villages. The agricultural sector had the support of the government Physical Planning Division, which was seeking to contain urban sprawl, and reasoned that giving these tracts to cooperative agricultural settlements for cultivation would serve as an effective check on increasing suburbanization.

The declared policy of population dispersal and of attempting to limit the growth of the suburban populations of the older cities was unable to withstand the pressing need to house the immigrants, since housing and opportunities for employment were available to them only in the metropolitan areas of these cities. It was impossible to curb the growth of the population in the core of the Jewish heartland, but it was possible, or so they thought, to limit the built-up area by turning over most of the land to cooperative settlements or private farmers.

The new immigrants failed to find a place for themselves in agricultural pursuits outside the context of the cooperative settlement movement, and their lack of access to the ruling apparatus resulted in the inner and outer rings of small towns encircling Tel Aviv being deprived of land for development.

For example, in 1996 the area of the Jewish town of Yahud, which was established on the site of the Arab village of Yahudiyya, whose landholdings had encompassed 20,000 *dunams,* was 4,000 *dunams;* Beit Dagon covers 3,000 *dunams* (out of the 17,000 that belonged to the village it replaced); whereas the town of Or Yehuda is built on 5,800 *dunams* (out of the 21,000 *dunams* of the villages of Saqiya and Kafr ʿAna, on whose territory it is situated). The immigrant settlement of Khayriyya, which was founded on the ruins of the abandoned Arab village of the same name, was itself abandoned and left to fall into ruin because all of its land had been taken over by nearby agricultural settlements and older towns. Thus was a ring of congested housing, economic backwardness, and chronic unemployment created around Tel Aviv. This, of course, fueled the immigrants' strong feelings of deprivation at the hands of the establishment and of the prosperous older agricultural settlements.

The deprived state of those immigrants who had not found their way to kibbutzim or moshavim was not obvious so long as the land that had been given to the agricultural settlements remained national property that was leased out for agricultural cultivation alone. According to these leases, the land would revert to the state and the JNF should its use be changed. After all, the justification for the confiscation of the land from its absentee Arab owners was that it was needed for purposes of agricultural settlement and development. The land was not regarded as real estate but as the property of the Jewish People, and its "redemption" through the labor of Jewish cultivators was perceived as a spiritual obligation no less than as an economic necessity: the highest expression of the secular religion of Zionism. Indeed, in the period immediately following the 1948 War, settlement, agriculture, and the transformation of dependent immigrants into agricultural workers rooted in the soil was a cardinal objective and a crucial source of pride for the young state. Thanks to immense investments and the application of the latest research, Israel's achievements in this sphere earned worldwide acclaim. The kibbutzim and moshavim became famous the world over, regarded as models of egalitarian community life worthy of emulation and a panacea for the ills of urban society.

The Six-Day War marked the beginning of the decline of the settlement enterprise. The occupation of the West Bank and Gaza Strip opened the floodgates to a torrent of cheap labor, which inundated the cooperative settlement movement, with a devastating effect on the moshavim in particular. Cheap labor replaced mechanization and altered the work practices in these communities. Many settlements began illegally subleasing agricultural land to Arabs, who became quasi-tenant farmers, and others became dependent on gangs of laborers brought in from the West Bank or Gaza by Arab contractors; in many locations laborers from the territories found themselves working the very land from which they had been expelled in 1948. Little by little, the availability of cheap labor led to a lessening of initiative and waste of resources, which in turn led to economic crisis. Thus did the dispossessed of 1948 cause—unintentionally and indirectly—the economic ruin of the "inheritors" of their land and homes.

DENOUEMENT

The process of economic collapse was gradual, but in 1977, with the election upset that brought the Likud party to power, it took a turn for the worse. The cooperative settlement ethic was foreign to the ideology of the Likud, which saw its value only in the context of taking over the territories of the West Bank and Gaza and settling Jewish zealots there. The Likud-dominated governments regarded the Labor Alignment governments' financial support of the cooperative settlements as a form of partisan favoritism; the Likud leadership did not hesitate to foment anti-kibbutz sentiment, attempting—for political ends—to inflame the rage harbored by the relatively recent immigrants, who made up the majority of their supporters, against the kibbutz movements for the discrimination they had suffered at their hands in the fifties, and for their arrogance and patronizing attitude toward the Oriental ethnic communities (settlers from Asia and North Africa) to which most of them belonged.

Once the generous subsidies of Labor days were withdrawn, many farming communities collapsed and others were compelled to switch to nonagricultural pursuits. The years of galloping inflation (from the late seventies through the mideighties) marked Israel's transition to a consumer society with no place for the old Zionist ethos; and the cooperative settlement movement, its foundations having been undermined, adapted itself to the spirit of the times. The growth of suburbs around Israel's cities encouraged the rural settlements to turn their land to commercial uses or to sell it as just so much real estate. Kibbutzim began setting up large shopping malls, and moshavim sold land to city-dwellers. The legal, ideological, and ecological barriers to building on agricultural land were breached, and shrewd entrepreneurs with close ties to those in power succeeded in making tracts of agricultural land—first privately owned property and later also land leased by kibbutzim and moshavim—available for development.

In the early nineties, with the surge of immigration from the former Soviet Union, the then housing minister, Ariel Sharon, revolutionized the Israeli attitude toward national land. He pushed through a decision in the governing council of the ILA permitting the privatization of leased agricultural land and its rezoning to accommodate immigrant housing. The cooperative settlements were supposed to be substantially compensated for the privatization of their land—at first, 51 percent of its value, but this amount was reduced in the wake of protests. In essence, permission had been granted to the kibbutzim and moshavim to purchase the land they had been leasing, and then to enter into real estate transactions with entrepreneurs and contractors. The land of the Jewish People was thus transformed from sacred spiritual property to commercial property.

Suddenly the scope of the deprivation of the immigrants who had not joined the cooperative settlement movement became apparent. Less than five percent of the country's population (members of the kibbutz and moshav movements) held title to a quarter of the land in the country (outside the desert regions), including areas that constituted practically the only remaining land reserve for future urban expansion. Much of this land, it should be recalled, had originally belonged to the abandoned villages. Its transfer to the cooperative settlements deprived most of the immigrant population residing on many village sites of adequate living space; and now it was being turned into building lots, but not theirs. The kibbutzim and moshavim located in areas where the demand for land—for construction and commercial purposes—was great, made hundreds of millions of dollars on the real estate deals they concluded, whereas the children of the immigrants of 1949–50—for whose absorption in the homeland, supposedly, the abandoned land had been confiscated—had to content themselves with the fact that they would be allowed to buy the small apartments they had been leasing.

The kibbutzim and moshavim justified their new wealth from the sale of land to developers on the grounds that the land had been in their possession for some fifty years; but no one remembered those who had held it for centuries. And they—the people uprooted during the 1948 War—had not only had moral claims entitling them to compensation for the land that had been taken but also legal claims to some of it: 2.5 million *dunams* of the land that the state had confiscated from the refugees were still registered in the name of the Development Authority. As long as this land was leased but not sold, the legal rights of the original owners were not finally extinguished. But no one gave any thought to the possibility of allocating a portion of the billions that were changing hands in the real estate deals involving the land of the dispossessed Arab villagers to establish a fund to compensate them. It has been estimated that the value of the land, slated for privatization, exceeds sixty billion U.S. dollars.[28]

In Israel's affluent society there was no room for reconsidering the consequences of the ethnic cleansing of 1948–50. The land that had been earmarked for the absorption of immigrants and the fulfillment of Zionism was being turned into building lots. Indeed, real estate speculation has become the main economic activity of farming settlements situated in the "high demand" areas of the coastal plain. In 1998, 110 kibbutzim were given permission by the ILA to expand their residential areas by 115 percent, ostensibly for their children, but "there was no objection if the new lots would be sold to outsiders," upper-class city dwellers. The number of residential units planned in kibbutzim and moshavim has been estimated at 150,000 units. Thus, the settlements that had transformed the landscape from one of villages populated by Arab *fallahin* to one dominated by large Jewish agricultural cooperatives were now being transformed into exclusive, prosperous, bourgeois suburban communities whose members lived, spent their free time, and were educated with others of their class and income level, with no social or cultural ties to their surroundings. The displaced villagers who had formerly peopled the landscape and had shaped it to suit their cultural requirements found themselves—fifty years after having been dispossessed of their land—still crammed into their refugee camps, without hope and without a way out of their plight.

Minister Ariel Sharon, himself an owner of a vast agricultural estate, leased to him by the government, stated in defense of his policy of privatization:

> In 1991–92, when the great wave of immigration [of Jews from the former Soviet Union] began, there was an urgent need for land. One day, during a visit to Beit Shean it became evident that there was no land in the town and the only way to expand and absorb the immigrants was by taking land from neighboring kibbutzim. . . . I knew the hardships that the kibbutzim experienced and thought that nobody in the world has a right to take [the land] from them or from other settlers. Therefore, I offered the kibbutzim that instead of taking the land from them, and granting them paltry compensation [according to the existing conditions of their leases], it is better that they will build on it and sell the houses to the new residents of Beit Shean. . . .

> Our parents came with a dream and struggled against all odds until they realized the dream. I don't think for a moment that anyone has a right to take the land from them, because they settled on it and cultivated it for seventy–eighty years. I admit that in this matter I have a very deep emotional commitment. . . . In this land there is no continuity of national memory. And I am one of the last [persons] who carry that memory. I am one of the last Mohicans. . . . My objective is to safeguard the rights of the [veteran] farmers; the maximum that is attainable.[29]

It seems that there is a marked difference between the "national memory" of the veteran Zionist elites and the historical memory of others. Those who recall how the veteran kibbutzim took over the lands of the departed Arabs of Beisan (as described earlier)—and did their utmost to strangulate the new immigrant town of Beit Shean in 1949–50—cannot but marvel how they are now being perceived as poor fellows, who should be compensated by turning their fields into building lots to be sold to a new wave of immigrants. It is amazing to see how compassion for those who settled on the land and "cultivated it for seventy–eighty years" does not cross the ethnic divide and encompass Arab farmers who cultivated the same land for a thousand years.

"The dream of our parents who struggled against all odds" is invoked by their children, a minuscule group of privileged veterans, as a justification for plundering vast common, national assets, as though all the cherished Zionist ideals were merely a plan to make easy profit. The last glorious, heroic, and idealistic cloak has been removed from Israel's past, and self-righteous greed is unashamedly exposed. The collapse of the Zionist vision was perhaps inevitable. Nonetheless, the quickness of the collapse has been truly amazing: only two generations have passed since 1948, and already those who cling to old ideals are regarded as prisoners of nostalgia. One is forced to ponder the enormous price paid in human and moral terms so that some veteran individuals can make fortunes, and wonder at the hypocrisy of the continued declaiming of the betrayed ideals as valid educational goals, national slogans, and image-building props.

We must not, however, judge the past from the perspective of the present, nor may we apply today's norms to events that took place fifty years ago. Yet, if the founders of the state, who carried out the ethnic cleansing of 1948–50 (and whose conviction that they were acting in accordance with the overriding inevitability of Jewish history allowed them to repress all their moral qualms), could see the results of their deeds, they would surely be horrified.

1. Scene at the Village Well. The village well was the center of village life; it was public property providing water for everyone: "its men and its women, its children and its infants, its sheep and its cattle; to the wanderer, the sojourner, and the stranger."

2. Bedouin Reed House (Huleh Valley, late 1930s). The Ghawarnah (marsh Bedouins) lived in swampy areas of the Galilee Panhandle. Many of them lived in huts made of reeds, grew field crops, and raised water buffalo. All of them (except one village) abandoned the area or were expelled.

3. Arab Schoolchildren (1930s). The villagers had a positive attitude toward education, but the Mandatory government spent little on Arab education. At the end of the Mandate there were schools in only half of the villages, and over two-thirds of the population was illiterate.

4. Water Pump (1930s). The camel-driven pump (*antiliyah*) drew water from the well by transforming horizontal rotary motion into vertical motion. Stone troughs were filled with water brought up from the well's pit by a chain of wooden buckets. In the late 1930s internal combustion engines replaced many traditional pumps, especially in the Coastal Plain.

5. Arab Village in the Coastal Plain (1940s). The Arab village was an organic part of the physical landscape, "a concentration of houses in a thick cluster on the high ground of the village lands." Around the built-up area was a compact belt of vegetable gardens and fenced orchards.

6. Jewish "Colony" in the Coastal Plain (1940s). Whitewashed, red-roofed, single-story houses; straight, wide streets; green trees; and electricity and telephone poles characterized the Jewish private rural settlements (see also plate 12).

7. Arab Village in the Lower Galilee (1940s). The village of Saffuriyya was one of the largest villages in the north and a center of resistance against the British authorities and the Jewish Yishuv. It was destroyed after the war, and a Jewish moshav was built on its lands.

8. Jewish Immigrants' New Settlement in the Lower Galilee (1950s). The layout of the abandoned Arab villages was found unsuitable for the permanent settlement of Jewish farmers. The established moshav model of scattered dwellings, each adjoining a twenty-five- to thirty-*dunam* plot of land in linear or circular layout, was implemented in all parts of the country without deference to topography. The moshav shown here is Kfar Zeitim, built near the destroyed Arab village of Hittin on the slope of the Horns of Hittin, the site of Saladin's great victory against the Crusaders in 1187.

9. Arab Village in the Judean Mountains (1940s). The poverty of the Arab *fallahin* and their living conditions are clearly seen in this photograph of the village of Yalu (destroyed after the 1967 war). Noted were "windowless houses constructed from local building materials, inner courtyards where man and beast lived side by side."

10. Moshav in the Judean Mountains (1950s). A typical settlement of new Oriental immigrants who were sent to remote areas and rugged terrain. "They would be satisfied with little and prepared to work for little, unlike settlers from Europe who were accustomed to a high standard of living," was the prejudiced attitude of the Ashkenazi establishment.

11. Tents in a Ruined Arab Village (1950s). Many new immigrants were cast on bare hills and housed in tents strewn between ruins. "The instructors who accompanied them had to resort to various and sundry methods in order to persuade them to get down from the trucks."

12. Veteran Kibbutz in the Jezreel Valley (1950s). Kibbutz Hazoreʿa, shown here, has a typical compact layout of clustered residential neighborhoods, public buildings, and farm-related structures. At one time the kibbutzim typified the rural landscape, but they have now ceased to be its dominant feature.

13 and 14. Arab Village in the 1940s and the 1990s. These photographs show a traditional village dramatically transformed into a sprawling, modern but nondescript settlement with large ornamented houses copied from those in the Jewish settlements. Only the minaret is an indication that this is an Arab village.

15. Jewish Houses in a Deserted Arab Village. The abandoned village of al-Maliha is today a Jerusalem neighborhood. Modern Jewish houses are built on the slopes of the village hill, and renovated Arab houses surround the deserted village mosque; however, the minaret still proudly dominates the skyline, as a memorial.

16. A Deserted Mosque. The mosque of Ijzim is situated in the middle of Moshav Kerem Maharal. Some 40 out of 140 mosques remain undemolished, but most of them are in an advanced stage of neglect and deterioration. Some are used as synagogues and others as tourist attractions.

17. Arab Village as a Jewish Artists' Colony. The deserted village Ein Hawd was "an architectural gem" too valuable to allow its destruction. It has been converted into an artists' colony: the houses have become art galleries and summer homes. The photo shows the village mosque, converted into a restaurant and bar. The displaced Arab residents live nearby, in an "unrecognized village."

18. Remains of an Arab Village (Coastal Plain). The deserted village Kafr Lam became a Jewish moshav. Most of its houses have been destroyed, except for those situated on the site of an ancient fortress. Although the round corner towers are from the Ummayad period (tenth century), the Israelis identify them as Crusader, since this period does not contradict the Zionist narrative.

19. Abandoned Muslim Cemetery. The neglected cemetery of Ramla is one of hundreds of burial grounds that have been allowed to turn into rubble. The state of abandoned Muslim cemeteries is so shameful that it would arouse a widespread uproar in any other country.

20. Muslim Holy Tomb in the Coastal Plain (1940s). This lively scene near the Tomb of Nabi Jindas depicts the central religious and cultural place of sacred tombs in the lives of Palestinian villagers before the catastrophe.

21. Muslim Holy Tomb Incorporated into a War Memorial. The Tomb of Sayidnah Huda in Yahudiyya has been consecrated as the Tomb of Judah and incorporated into a memorial park alongside two guns and the emblem of the Israeli Defense Force.

22. Muslim Holy Place Turned into a Jewish Synagogue. The Tomb of Imam ʿAli in Yazur has been converted into a synagogue and a yeshiva. Note the satellite dish receiving religious television broadcasts.

23. Arab House as a Jewish Villa. Many Arab houses were lovely, elegant structures, but their new Jewish residents could not believe that the former residents could possess such taste and therefore invented stories about their origin. The house shown here, in Ijzim, was the *madafeh* (guest house) of the al-Madi family. Its present residents assert that it is a "Crusader castle."

5

Uprooted and Planted

One day in July 1949, members of the Abu al-Hija family living in shacks on al-Wastani hill on the Carmel ridge noticed a group of people wending their way up the steep path from the Haifa–Tel Aviv Highway and disappearing into the empty, abandoned houses of their village, Ein Hawd. The Abu al-Hija family had been uprooted about a year before, along with the rest of the village's 700 inhabitants, following its occupation by the Israeli army. In contrast to most of their neighbors and relatives, who migrated (or were expelled) across the border, the family's dozen or so members had remained within sight of their land. The head of the family, Muhammad Mahmoud Abu al-Hija, spent some time in an Israeli prisoner-of-war camp along with scores of men from nearby villages. This tall, strong, dignified man bore on his broad shoulders the glorious tradition of his ancient family and of its revered ancestor, Emir Hussam al-Din Abu al-Hija, a high-ranking officer in the army of the fabled Sultan Salah al-Din (Saladin). Emir Abu al-Hija, whose title was Isfahslar (Generalissimo), was commander of the Kurdish force that took part in (fellow Kurd) Salah al-Din's conquest (1187–93) of the Crusader kingdom.

ANCESTRY

Hussam al-Din was extremely stout, whence his nickname, "Hussam the Fat." It is said that his obesity was so phenomenal that when he rode, his belly would brush the horse's back. When he served as governor of the Irbil District in Iraq, potters from Mosul designed an especially wide eating bowl in his honor, to match his ample dimensions. Bowls of this design were henceforth known in the pottery trade as "Abulhejas." The emir was renowned for his bravery, which earned him the additional nickname "Abu al-Hija" ("the Daring"). Hussam al-Din commanded the garrison of Acre at the time of the Crusader siege of that city (August 1189 to July 1192), subsequent to its capture by the Muslims in July 1187. In the last stages of the siege, Abu al-Hija's forces engaged in combat with those of Richard the Lionhearted, king of England, and King Philip II of France, winning universal admiration. Salah al-Din's biographer, Beha al-Din (1145–1234) writes of Abu al-Hija: "Hussam was distinguished both for his munificence and [his] valor; he was of high rank amongst his own people (the Kurds), and the plans he formed bore witness to the stoutness of his heart."[1] Following the reconquest of Acre by the Crusaders, Emir Hussam continued to command the Kurdish force in battles with the army of Richard the Lionhearted. In July 1192, as the Crusaders were threatening to retake Jerusalem, Sultan Salah al-Din convened a council of war at which his commanders were asked for their recommendations on how to defend the city: whether to prepare themselves for a siege or to launch a battle. Hussam al-Din went to the consultation, although he was barely able to move because of his weight "and was obliged to sit in a chair in the Sultan's tent."[2] Despite his huge girth, he was as daring as ever. He opposed the army's hiding behind the city's walls, saying, "It would be better to risk a pitched battle rather than to shut ourselves up in the city." In the end the need for this decision did not arise, since Richard was forced to forgo his plan to attack Jerusalem. However, Salah al-Din, fearing that Hussam would prefer to remain in the field with his forces rather than repeat his experience of the siege of Acre, ordered him to leave a member of his family in command of the Kurdish force in Jerusalem: "For the Kurds will not obey the Turks, and the Turks in like manner will never obey the Kurds."

Shortly after these events, once the danger to the Holy City had passed, Hussam al-Din returned to Iraq, but several members of his family remained in the country under orders from the sultan and settled on spacious tracts of land that they had been granted in the Carmel region, in the Lower, Eastern, and Western Galilee, and in the Hebron Highlands. One of these land grants became the village of Ein Hawd. Other villages inhabited by families claiming kinship with Hussam Abu al-Hija included Hadatha and Sirin in the Lower Galilee and Ruweis and Kawkab in the Western Galilee. Although they profess to be blood relations of Emir Hussam, these villagers' claims are based solely on tradition. Hussam al-Din apparently died in Iraq and was buried there, but because of his part in liberating the Holy Land from the infidels, family members who stayed in the country designated as his burial place the village of Kawkab al-Hija in the hills of the Western Galilee, where several of his descendants, too, are buried.

EIN HAWD

The al-Hija tradition is deeply rooted in the village of Ein Hawd. One of the village elders recounts how the land on which it is situated was granted to the emir: "When Salah al-Din requested that Abu al-Hija designate the boundaries of the village, the emir took his walking stick and threw it. The stick landed on the rocks near the coast at ʿAtlit and left a clearly visible mark on one of them. That mark exists to this day." Ancient letters carved into the sandstone, still visible in the area that served as a quarry providing stone for the construction of the Crusader castle in ʿAtlit, have been the source of many a legend.

Ein Hawd was famous for its healthful air and the healing qualities of the many springs in the vicinity. Especially renowned was a small spring that flowed from a boulder, of which it was said that if someone afflicted with sores poured its water on his body, he would be healed. On the hillsides grew carob trees from which honey of outstanding flavor and aroma was produced. The farmers of Ein Hawd—a village with landholdings of approximately 12,000 *dunams*—raised field crops, sesame, and olives. During the 1948 War the village's inhabitants took part in armed attacks against Jewish vehicles on the Haifa–Tel Aviv Highway and, along with other villagers from the area, at first held out against the Israeli army; but in July of 1948 they fled the village, apparently without a battle. The villagers scattered, some finding their way to refugee camps in the West Bank and Transjordan. The other al-Hija villages in the north of Israel were captured and destroyed. A number of the refugees from these villages succeeded in remaining inside the country and gathered at the village of Tamra, near the venerated (supposed) grave of Emir Hussam al-Din in Kawkab.

Although the dozen remaining members of the Abu al-Hija family who stayed close to Ein Hawd received Israeli citizenship, they remained "absentees" according to the law, since they had left their homes (even if less than one mile away). Nor was their possession of the hill where they had found refuge recognized by the authorities. However, efforts to dispossess them by legal means, or to make their lives difficult in hopes that they would leave, did not succeed, and the number of inhabitants of the small village grew steadily.

PIONEERS "ON A DIFFERENT LEVEL"

The group of people who climbed up to the abandoned village that July day in 1949 had no idea of the history of the place to which they had been sent to make their home; it is not known whether they had any notion that the people whose houses they were taking over were so close by. The group was made up of new immigrants who had arrived a few months previously from Tunisia and Algeria and had been recruited by the Moshav Movement to establish a moshav in Ein Hawd. This was one of the first three groups of immigrants from North Africa to be recruited for agricultural settlement (the second group, new immigrants from Morocco, settled nearby, in a place at first called North ʿAtlit and later, Megadim; the third was directed to the abandoned village of Rantiyya, near Lod, the former Lydda). The leaders of the Moshav Movement were unsure whether the "immigrants from the Orient"—that is, non-Ashkenazis—were suitable "human material" for cooperative agricultural settlements. After all, they and the overwhelming majority of older moshavim were Ashkenazis who had come from Europe. In their estimation, the immigrants from North Africa and the Arab world were, "from an anthropological standpoint and from the point of view of historical development, on a fundamentally different level than are the immigrants from countries in Europe, from among whom the first twenty organized groups that had founded new cooperative settlements since July 1948 were recruited."[3]

This appraisal was delicate in comparison to some of the harsh pronouncements that could be heard at the time regarding the caliber of the immigrants from North Africa. Tom Segev quotes some of these in *1949: The First Israelis:* "The primitiveness of these people is unsurpassable. They have almost no education at all, and what is worse is their inability to comprehend anything intellectual. As a rule, they are only slightly more advanced than the Arabs, Negroes and Berbers in their countries. It is certainly an even lower level than that of the former Palestinian Arabs," wrote a respected Israeli journalist.[4] The immigrants from Algeria received only slightly higher marks than those from Morocco.

The Moshav Movement leadership thought that the North Africans "require[d] different treatment, a different approach," and in fact assigned instructors to the Ein Hawd settlement group to give them social guidance because of the "difference in [its] human composition, family structure, lifestyle, and outlook on life." The group received the same financial grants as the other immigrants who settled in abandoned villages: after the houses worth refurbishing were designated, each settler family received a sum of money for repairs to their new home as well as for starting up a small farm, plus two cows and a plot of land for raising crops.

The original group of seventy families had grown to ninety-two by October 1949. They were quite satisfied with Ein Hawd (which by that time had obtained the Hebrew name Ein Hod), but the Moshav Movement decided that the abandoned village was not a suitable site on which to establish a permanent settlement: "The shape of the Arab village is not at all suitable for the form of settlement toward which we have been striving. . . . not that it was a mistake; on the contrary, it served as an impetus and a lure for the immigrants [to] escape from the crowded immigrant camps, which lacked either privacy or any sort of conveniences." "However," wrote Moshav Movement leader Yitzhak Koren, "as long as these people were sitting in the abandoned village, they would not be able to develop their farms or [build their] community." In his opinion only the established settlement model—of scattered dwellings, each adjoining a twenty-five- to thirty-*dunam* plot of land—"the very foundation of Jewish settlement in the country"—could suit. Therefore a new moshav was built for the Ein Hod group—called Tsrufah (a mutilation of the name of the abandoned Arab village of Sarafand)—on the plain between Mount Carmel and the Mediterranean Sea, six kilometers south of Ein Hod. The new, permanent settlement was built adjacent to a Turkish immigrant moshav, which had also been established in 1949, on the land of the abandoned Arab village of Jabʿa.

SUPERSTITIONS AND RATIONAL FEARS

Ein Hod, then, was deserted yet again, a year and a half after its Arab inhabitants had been forced to abandon it. Its houses, partially repaired, again fell into a state of neglect, and some of the walls collapsed. The members of the Abu al-Hija family who watched what was going on did not understand why the Jews were abandoning their homes. Because they could not comprehend how people could despise these houses—for which they themselves longed—they imagined possible explanations. One villager told the writer David Grossman:

> They put people from the Oriental communities in our houses, but they didn't last there. They believe all sorts of superstitions and they used to say that at night they could see eyes watching them from the hills, or that rocks fell on them from the sky, or all sorts of ghosts, or that the earth was crying out to them, or that they could see the village people returning to take back their houses. So they weren't able to hold out.[5]

The reabandonment of abandoned Arab villages took place in other locations as well—where new immigrants had been settled and within a short time were withdrawn because the villages were "not suitable for Jewish settlement." Thus, in those places too, the displaced villagers who were still living close by spun similar tales. For example, the Arabs who had been uprooted from the village of Tantura, finding refuge in nearby Furaydis, say that the inhabitants of Moshav Dor abandoned the Arab houses of Tantura because everyone who lived in them was struck by serious illness. They also reported that every time a Jewish bulldozer attempted to destroy the grave of the local saint, Sheikh al-Majrami, its blade broke.

But the beautiful village of Ein Hod was too attractive to remain empty. The authorities were preparing to demolish its houses, as they had done in the neighboring villages of Ein Ghazal and Jaba, but painter and architect Marcel Yanco, who had already conducted a successful campaign against the destruction of the houses of Old Jaffa, hoping to turn it into an artists' colony, took a liking to the picturesque village. He persuaded the authorities to refrain from destroying this architectural gem. In 1953 he succeeded in obtaining the rights to Ein Hod for himself and a group of artists—writers, painters, and sculptors—and with the assistance of the Haifa municipal authority founded an "artists' village" there. The village mosque was converted into a restaurant and bar, and the al-Hija family homes became galleries and summer homes. Sons of displaced villagers worked on the renovations to their fathers' former homes; some even developed close ties with new residents of the village, many of whom held leftist views and participated in demonstrations for peace and coexistence.

Meanwhile, the Abu al-Hija family had grown and its hilltop refuge had become a real village. It was not, however, recognized by the authorities, who did not supply them with basic services, prohibited the expansion of the residential area to accommodate natural increase, and refused to build an access road, claiming that improving the physical infrastructure "would spoil the landscape and destroy the forest"—the very forest that had been planted on their fathers' land with the explicit intent of preventing them from cultivating it.

Part of the Ein Hawd cemetery was made into a parking lot, but one has to be thankful that it didn't become the regional garbage dump, as had that of Ein Ghazal. When the al-Hijas asked the artists of the village for permission to fence the remainder of the cemetery, it piqued their fears. These were not the "fears of superstitious members of the Oriental communities" but "rational" concerns: "If you give them a toe-hold here," said one of the artists to writer David Grossman, "you are immediately acknowledging thereby that some sort of—I don't know—injustice took place and turning them into unfortunates who were uprooted from their land. . . . Their having a new hold here would undermine our right to the place and our possession."[6]

Painful confrontations between displaced villagers and settlers, between natives who had become refugees and refugees who had become "natives," were not limited to Ein Hod. In Israel live the displaced residents of some sixty villages, including forty or so where, or beside which, new immigrant moshavim were established. After fifty years of daily contact the wounds are scarred over, but they have not healed. People have learned to live with the pain, and over the years have found many and varied ways of articulating it.

The pain of the displaced villagers is undeniable, but the settlers, too, bear scars that have not healed, owing to their traumatic experiences while being integrated into Israeli society and putting down roots in the country, and their violent encounters with members of the displaced Palestinian population. Approximately 700,000 Arabs abandoned their homes between 1948 and 1951, a period in which a similar number of Jews immigrated to Israel. This "exchange of populations" entailed immense human suffering. There will be those who object to the mention in one breath of the suffering of the defeated and dispossessed, who were uprooted from their homes and homeland—sent to refugee camps with no one taking an interest in their fate—and that of people who found refuge in their sovereign homeland, received land, housing, and monetary assistance, and whose suffering was a result of the temporary travails of absorption. Emphasizing the suffering of the one, however, does not mean that the other's feelings are less real. Nor is the despair of a person cast onto the ruins of an abandoned and desolate mountain village to build a new life less bitter because the heartache of those who were cast out of that village, to find shelter in a cave or in leaky tin-roofed shacks, is greater.

In late 1949 the leaders of a group of immigrants from Yemen, who had been settled in the ruins of the village of Tarbikha (which later was given the Hebrew name Shomera), sent a petition to "the directors of the Moshav Movement in Tel Aviv," headed, "Alas, the Yemenites." It read, in part:

> We are in great distress for we lack everything, we have no water to drink, we have no water to wash ourselves. . . . There is nothing, just dry bread. . . . We have [already] been two weeks without money, and the instructors have left the village and gone their own way. . . . Do us a kindness, for G-d's sake, and request other instructors who speak clearly, so we will know what they're saying, and who will come and put the village in order and show us the work and how to work and who we are working for, because we are new in the Land of Israel and don't know anything.[7]

This group of Yemenite immigrants, comprising fifty families, moved in to the houses of the isolated Galilee village in the summer of 1949, less than one year after the approximately 1,000 inhabitants of Tarbikha (and of two small neighboring villages) were evicted by the IDF forces that took over the territory along the Lebanese border. The Tarbikha refugees spent the freezing Galilee winter living in temporary shelters and making unsuccessful attempts to infiltrate back into their village.

INTERNAL REFUGEES

In the ocean of suffering that was the lot of hundreds of thousands of Jews and Arabs, two groups stand out as exemplifying the painful process of "population exchange" following the 1948 War: the "internal refugees" and the Jews who were settled in those abandoned villages that were turned into immigrant moshavim. These two groups were more or less equal in size: about 30,000 internal refugees and about 30,000 immigrants (in the relevant years, 1948–52). The internal refugees were those displaced Palestinians who left or were evicted from their homes during the war and in its aftermath; they were not permitted to go back but remained within Israel (or returned there) and became citizens. This category of displaced persons came into being because a large proportion of the people who had been uprooted in the wake of the hostilities were not allowed to return to their home villages and were forced to seek refuge in other Arab communities—near or far. They were classified as "absentees" under the Absentee Property Law, which stated that anyone who had left his or her place of residence at any time from the outbreak of hostilities until their end was "absent" as far as the property—which was transferred to the care of the custodian of absentee property—was concerned. But these "absentees" were also "present," in that they were granted Israeli citizenship and supposedly had equal rights under Israeli law. Hence they were referred to by the cynical oxymoron "present absentees."

To the ranks of refugees who had left their homes or had been evicted from them during the war were added those expelled by the Israeli armed forces after the cessation of hostilities. By May 1949 the number of internal refugees stood at 17,000.[8] Figures of a like order of magnitude are provided by Charles Kamen, the most reliable source of statistical data on the Arab population in Israel following the 1948 War. Kamen estimates the number of internal refugees at 23,000 by the end of hostilities.[9] United Nations sources place their number at 46,000. The number of internal refugees grew considerably between 1949 and 1952 as a result of "infiltration" from across the armistice lines, "family reunification" allowed by the authorities, and the issuing of entry permits to small groups of refugees. The collection of more up-to-date data raised these estimates even higher. Although some internal refugees were allowed to return to their former places of habitation (especially to Haifa) and thereby supposedly ceased to be refugees, their return did not alter their status as "present absentees." I estimate the number of internal refugees of all categories (those displaced by war, those expelled during and after the war, transborder infiltrators, those permitted to return, and released prisoners of war) who became citizens of Israel but remained "absent" under the law (even if they returned to their communities of origin), as 30,000 to 35,000 souls, or 17 to 20 percent of all Arab residents of the State of Israel in 1951 (who totaled 180,000). There are other estimates, both higher and lower, but no official figure. As Kamen explains:

> The lack of attention to the internal refugees is consistent with the general neglect suffered by the Arabs in Israel during the first decade of statehood. An additional reason was probably the unwillingness of official circles in Israel

> to draw attention to the existence of the internal refugees and their situation by providing means of identifying them. Primarily, Israel was not interested in having UNRWA [The UN Refugee Relief and Works Agency] operate within its borders, and this activity was indeed terminated in July of 1952.

The internal refugees constituted only some 5 percent of the Palestinian refugees, but they originated from some eighty villages, or 20 percent of the total number of abandoned villages; thus they were representative of the scope of the general exodus that had taken place. The number of villages of origin given here is my estimate and is higher than those given by Kamen, who cites data from the northern part of the country only.[10] About sixty of these eighty villages were reduced to ruins, and twenty-two continued to exist (after part of their population had fled). The geographical distribution of the internal refugees' villages of origin give an indication of the nature of the exodus: the vast majority are situated in the country's north, where most of the Arab villages that remained untouched by the war are located. The villagers moved out when the war reached their villages and found refuge in neighboring communities, in many instances with close or distant relatives. When all available accommodations in those villages were full (including the houses of people who had left), the refugees began building temporary structures on the fringes of the built-up area. When the war again reached their doorsteps, their fate was the same as that of the inhabitants of their villages of refuge: when the latter either fled or were forcibly evicted, the internal refugees left with them.

It often happened that refugee families passed through many "stations" before finally finding sanctuary. Mustafa Kabha and Ronit Barzilay describe the difficult journey of one family from a village near Nazareth, who passed through no fewer than thirteen "stations" before finally settling down in a village in the Lower Galilee.[11] Other refugees had better luck, and their villages of sanctuary were not attacked. Nonetheless, they too were prevented from returning to their village of origin—no matter how close by, or from cultivating their land, even if they were living at its edge.

The number of internal refugees whose origins were in the central and southern parts of the country was very small, evidence of the policy of massive expulsion that was, as described previously, carried out in those regions during the war. A few families who had been uprooted from villages in the Tel Aviv metropolitan area took refuge in villages that were later annexed to Israel in the context of the armistice agreement with Jordan, making them "present absentees" in Israel. In fact, the refugees scattered in all directions. Kamen found, for example, that people displaced from Haifa had found sanctuary in no fewer than twenty-six Arab communities, residents of Safuriyya (the historical Sepphoris) in seven villages, and those from Damoun in six.

Classification of the internal refugees according to the factors that precipitated the abandonment of their villages produces the following results: inhabitants of twenty-two villages fled in wartime (sometimes following acts of intimidation by the Israeli army); residents of eighteen villages were victims of preemptive eviction during the war; in the case of fifteen villages, the people were evicted after the war; the inhabitants of seven villages were expelled and transferred to empty abandoned villages. The populations of ten villages escaped being evicted because their expulsion order was not carried out (these last are not included in the enumeration of internal refugees). Some of the villages in the two first categories have been described earlier, in accounts of the hostilities and the general exodus. Here I shall describe the fate of the internal refugees in the remaining categories through examples of some particularly prominent cases.

The majority of the internal refugees who were evicted after the war were but the sparse remnants of communities that had for the most part fled their villages during the hostilities. Exceptions to this rule were those from Birʿim, Iqrit, and Khirbat Jalama (which have already been mentioned), as well as the inhabitants of Faluja and ʿIraq al-Manshiyya (who were expelled from the country and are therefore not counted among the internal refugees). Kamen gathered data on internal refugees who originated from forty-four abandoned villages and found that they had constituted 8 percent of their villages' prewar populations. No more than 100 souls from each of these forty-four villages remained inside the country, and in the case of only eleven villages did there remain more than 200 people who had originally come from that village.[12] About twenty of these villages, and others for which Kamen had not obtained data, were evacuated after the end of the war. This was, indeed, the eviction of only a few remaining inhabitants, but the circumstances deserve closer examination.

The reasons that some people had stayed behind rather than join in the exodus of the majority of their community were many and varied. Some were unable to pull up stakes because they were old, sick, or women whose husbands had been taken prisoner and were being held in prisoner-of-war camps and who were caring for small children on their own. Kamen reckoned that the prisoner-of-war camps held thousands of Arab villagers who had been arrested in the course of the conquest of their villages or were "infiltrators." In March 1949, 2,500 prisoners remained in captivity, most of them heads of families, which they rejoined when they were eventually released.

SAFURIYYA

Others remained in their homes because they hadn't panicked but instead had stood firm against Israeli attempts at intimidation. Among these were numbered 400-odd inhabitants of Safuriyya who stayed behind following the flight of some 4,000 villagers soon after the capture of this large village on the night between 15 and 16 July 1948. Safuriyya had gone down in the annals of the Yishuv as a "village of murderers"; that is, it had a long history of armed struggle against the Jewish community and the British. Since 1929 it was the home of the most important rural terrorist cell of 'Izz a-Din al-Qassam's Black Hand organization.[13] Its members were involved in the murder of Jewish settlers in the Jezreel Valley, and two of them were caught and hanged. Following the disbanding of the Black Hand in 1935, several of its members continued to take part in acts of violence against Jews, and six Safuriyya men were senior commanders in the Arab Revolt of 1936–39. Hence the Jewish community had a long list of bloody accounts to settle with Safuriyya.

In the 1948 War Safuriyya was one of the only villages whose inhabitants had weapons, ammunition, and trained fighting men. According to Nafez Nazal, there were between 135 and 150 fighters in the village, each with a rifle at his disposal, as well as fifteen machine guns and one cannon (owned by the *mukhtar*).[14] But this local militia by itself was, of course, incapable of standing up to the Israeli army, and the Arab Liberation Army (ALA) did not come to its aid. The village fell after putting up a strong resistance, and its noncombatant inhabitants, who had fled to the orchards and woods even before the commencement of the battle, scattered in all directions. Some went to Lebanon, and some found refuge in surrounding villages or in Nazareth. About 200 souls, among them the families of several of the village notables, returned to their homes immediately following the conquest and were counted as local residents in the first Israeli census, conducted in November 1948. Safuriyya's population doubled in the course of 1949, as former inhabitants who had been living in nearby villages returned home. The Israeli authorities worried that this "infiltration" would result in all the houses in the village being occupied once again, making it impossible to house

Jewish immigrants there or to confiscate the land. The authorities thus decided to evict all the remaining residents of the village, and, on 7 January 1949 everyone in Safuriyya was loaded onto trucks and expelled to surrounding villages, literally bordering their own fields. In November 1951 the High Court of Justice rejected the villagers' petition to return home—having accepted the Defense Ministry's position that Safuriyya was located in "a closed military area." At the time a moshav already existed there (established in 1949), populated by eighty-five immigrant families, who had come from Rumania and Bulgaria (see later discussion). Over the years, the "present absentees" of Safuriyya built themselves homes in a Nazareth neighborhood named after their village (Hart al-Safafra), which looks down on their lost home from several kilometers away.

About a month after the eviction of Safuriyya's remaining inhabitants, the remnants of the populations of the Upper Galilee villages of Faradiyya and Kafr ʿInan were also evicted. These villages, too, were evacuated because of the authorities' anxiety that additional refugees would slip back to them, thereby thwarting plans to settle Jews there. Their inhabitants were expelled to several other villages in the area, but most of them came back and gathered on the outskirts of the village of Ramah, whose fields bordered their own, so as to stay close to their villages. Agricultural settlements for new immigrants were established in 1949 on the expropriated land. Some of the (former) residents of Faradiyya and Kafr ʿInan are today employed as laborers in the olive groves that were the glory of these villages. A similar fate befell the remaining villagers of Zakariyya (near Beit Shemesh in the Shephelah), Khirbat Jalama, Umm al-Faraj (close to Nahariya), Khirbat Husha (near Ramat Yohanan in the Zebulun Valley), and al-Zib (Akhziv), all of whom were evicted a few months after the war—since their presence impeded the establishment of Jewish settlements—and compelled to find sanctuary nearby or far away.

A large number of internal refugees stayed in their homes, since they believed that their good relations with the Jews, both before and during the war, would ensure that no evil befell them. Some—who had cooperated with the Jewish Intelligence Service or who had had economic ties with Jews, especially those who had helped in the sale of land to the JNF, feared that if they moved to areas under Arab rule, they would be executed, as indeed did occur on some occasions. These were isolated individuals, entire families, or even whole villages, and some actually were treated well by the authorities and not harmed. In some areas of the country one can still find lone houses with farm buildings, surrounded by agricultural land, belonging to Arabs who were allowed to stay put because they enjoyed the protection of the authorities in return for "services rendered." Quite a few internal refugee families either were not evicted from their villages or were moved to other villages with the assistance of the authorities for the same reason. Their neighbors in their villages of refuge knew or suspected that they were spies for the Jews or collaborators, but over the years the feelings of hostility toward them faded.

UPPER GALILEE

Many other internal refugees felt they had been betrayed. Despite their being collaborators, their fate was no better than that of those who had not been, and they were evicted from their villages without a thought to the service they had rendered to the victors. One of the most blatant examples of this ingratitude was the way in which the Israeli authorities treated the remnants of the populations of three villages in the Galilee Panhandle: Qaytiyya, Khisas, and Jaʿuna. When these villages were captured in May 1948, some of their inhabitants were left in their homes, despite the fact that widespread "ethnic cleansing" was being carried out in the Huleh Valley and the Galilee Panhandle. The inhabitants of Khisas and Qaytiyya had maintained close ties with the Jewish settlements in the area, supplying them with intelligence and helping them purchase land. These close relations had a significant influence on the dispute among Jewish leaders regarding the retaliatory raid on Khisas at the start of the 1948 War.[15] The village of Jaʿuna was essentially an Arab neighborhood adjacent to the long-established Jewish colony of Rosh Pina, and its inhabitants worked for the Jewish farmers. The 300 residents of these villages lived under Israeli rule for over a year and became citizens of the state.

On the night of 5 June 1949, the villages were encircled by the Israeli army, and their residents forcibly loaded onto trucks and conveyed to a bare hilltop south of the town of Safad, beside the abandoned village of ʿAkbara. There they were dumped, with no shelter and without the minimal necessities of life. This arbitrary eviction aroused a public storm and lively discussion in the Knesset. It also gave rise to a spate of newspaper articles, on both the evacuation itself and the inhumane manner in which it had been carried out. Prime Minister David Ben-Gurion, however, gave his full backing to the deed and defended the army's actions. The Huleh Valley expellees remained on their bald hilltop and refused every offer of proper housing. Only after eighteen years did they agree to move to a permanent settlement in Wadi Hamam, near the shore of the Sea of Galilee, where they have established a thriving village.

A visitor to Wadi Hamam, seeing the typically Israeli-style single-family homes, the straight, wide streets, and the large mosque and the school, could not imagine what hardships the residents had been through on the way from their distant villages to this beautiful location. The villages of Khisas and Qaytiyya were razed. Kibbutz Hagoshrim, which was built on the land of Khisas, opened a lovely hotel in the abandoned manor house of Emir Faour, the leader of the al-Fadel tribe and landlord of the village (see chapter 3). "In the past," states the hotel fact sheet, without elaborating, "this was the winter palace of Emir Faour." Emir Faour's summer palace was also captured by the Israelis—in 1967—and destroyed. It stood eight kilometers (five miles) west of Quneitra in the Golan Heights and is designated on Israeli maps as "The Emir's Ruin."

During their stay in ʿAkbara, the refugees from Khisas met those from the village of Qadita (west of Safad), whose fate had been even more bitter than their own. They, too, had been collaborators for the Jews, and the ALA—which controlled their village at the time—had expelled them to the neighboring village of Jish. After Qadita and Jish were occupied by the Israelis, some of the Qadita refugees returned to their village but then were moved to Jaʿuna, whose original inhabitants had already been evicted, and lived there for seven months. From there they were moved to another abandoned village, and finally they, too, arrived in ʿAkbara (the others from their village remained in Jish). The Qadita villagers, along with individual refugees from other locations in the Galilee, built themselves a prosperous village on the slopes of the bald mountain on the outskirts of Safad. Their abandoned village was turned into a "rural style" vacation spot.

CARMEL

The village of Ijzim, on the western slopes of Mount Carmel, is the last place one would expect to find people who had been collaborators with the Jews. This large, wealthy village, whose population in 1948 was close to 3,000 and whose landholdings covered more than 40,000 *dunams,* was the hub of the "Little Triangle," the group of villages whose inhabitants had blocked the main Tel Aviv–Haifa Highway for many months during the war. The Israelis succeeded in capturing Ijzim only after two failed attempts. Even on the third and last attempt, on 24 July 1948, the Israelis succeeded in gaining control of the village only after employing cannon fire and air strikes, in a fierce battle that lasted two days. Ijzim was thus continuing its long tradition of armed struggle against the Jewish community and the British Mandatory government. A prominent member of the village's leading family—the influential al-Madi clan—was among the foremost activists in the Palestinian nationalist movement, and several villagers had been guerrilla commanders in the Arab Revolt.

With the conquest of Ijzim (and of neighboring Jabʿa and Ein Ghazal), the majority of the villagers either were expelled or fled. Most of them made their way to the Jenin area, across the armistice lines, while others found refuge in the nearby Druze village of Daliyat al-Carmel. Several dozen people, however, were allowed to remain in their homes, since they had connections with influential Jews, particularly in Haifa. They continued working their fertile land and sending their agricultural produce to Haifa, were registered in the first Israeli census, and received Israeli identity cards. In December 1948 a dispute broke out between the Jewish protectors of the residents of Ijzim and the Haifa district military commander over the villagers' continued presence there. The dispute culminated in the decision that the villagers would remain and that those who had taken refuge in Daliyat al-Carmel would also be permitted to return home. However, the district commander later went back on his word and ordered the eviction of the villagers, who subsequently found shelter in the nearby village of Furaydis.

There is no doubt that one of the considerations leading to the eviction was the interest shown by settlement agency officials in turning Ijzim into an immigrant moshav. And indeed, in the summer of 1949, just a few months after the villagers had been ousted, a moshav whose members were immigrants from Czechoslovakia and Rumania was established in Ijzim. In contrast to many other abandoned villages—where the permanent Jewish settlement was built adjacent to the houses of the Arab village, which were demolished—the homes of this wealthy village were judged to be worthy of permanent habitation. The al-Madi family's luxurious seventeenth-century *madafeh* became first a museum and then the mansion of a Jewish family, the school became a synagogue, and the cemetery beside it, a public park. The large and magnificent village mosque, which had been built in the nineteenth century (see plate 16), was left to slowly crumble. Some of the villagers held on to their land and lived for a few years in tin-roofed shacks and other temporary structures, but eventually all of them—with the exception of one family—broke down and agreed to exchange their holdings for building plots in the village of Furaydis. The one Arab family that withstood all the pressure to leave now lives in its own house beside a sacred spring called Sitt Maqura, where both Arabs and Jews come to pray and light candles.

The village of Furaydis, as well as the neighboring Jisr al-Zarqa, were not touched at all. The inhabitants enjoyed the strong support of their patrons, the farmers from the neighboring Jewish villages of Zichron Yaʿakov and Binyamina, whose agricultural livelihood depended on the work of laborers from these Arab villages. These places thus became a refuge for individual families from abandoned villages in the area who had been permitted to remain in the country (although not in their own villages), including some 150 refugees from the adjacent village of Tantura. But even the fate of Furaydis and Jisr a-Zarqa hung by a thread. The military authorities attempted to secure a decision to evict their inhabitants, but they did not succeed. Plans and even official decisions to evict villagers, demolish villages, and repopulate them with Jews existed regarding ten still-occupied villages: six in the Upper and Central Galilee (Jish, Tarshiha, Fassuta, Miʿilya, Hurfeish, and Rihaniyya), one in the Western Galilee (Nahf), and one in the Jerusalem area (Abu Ghosh), as well as Furaydis and Jisr a-Zarqa. For various reasons that will not be elaborated upon here, however, these plans were not carried out.

Thus a population that to start with numbered approximately 30,000 to 35,000 and in 1998 reached approximately 150,000—all of them citizens of the State of Israel—lived in the immediate vicinity of their home villages and their land but were not permitted to return to them. Regulation number 125 of the Emergency Regulations designated their houses and land as "closed areas," and anyone entering them without written permission as being guilty of an offense and liable to be punished to the full extent of the law. With their own eyes these displaced villagers saw others entering the "closed area," taking over their houses, and working their land. For the internal refugees, exile was not to some far-off place; it was exile within their own homeland. It does not require a great deal of sensitivity to understand the intensity of their everyday pain and frustration. This group, an insignificant minority amid the sea of expellees, is the very embodiment of the Palestinian catastrophe. I shall deal elsewhere with the emotional aspects of the internal exiles' experience, but this is the time to confront the "present-absent" villagers with the Jewish settlers who took their places, often without any inkling that from just over the next hill they were being observed by the original residents of the houses they were living in.

"A MOMENT OF GRACE"

"In a moment of grace, one summer's day at twilight, toward the end of the War for Independence, the idea of populating the abandoned Arab villages with Jewish immigrants was born." Thus was described—in words befitting a spiritual revelation—the moment when Levi Eshkol, head of the Settlement Department of the Jewish Agency, conceived of the plan that was to radically alter the landscape of the country and the lives of thousands of human beings. The description of this moment, as recorded by Eshkol and quoted religiously in nearly every book dealing with the settlement of the immigrants, suits the solemnity of the occasion; it merits being quoted here at length:

> These were the last days of the War for Independence. The People and the Land had not yet recovered from their amazement to realize, and especially to sense, that political independence had indeed been achieved and that now we were the masters of our own fate. The old Yishuv was still bent over the casualties who had just now been laid to rest, and the torrent of immigrants had begun streaming and flooding in. The immigration came without our having sought to control its nature or its dimensions, without our having prepared ourselves for suitably absorbing the immigrants and making arrangements for them, as we were preoccupied with the war. . . . We were concerned, in those days, with seeking practical solutions for coping with absorbing this great wave and with channeling it in constructive and productive directions, as has been our way in building our country since the days of the Second Aliyah. . . .
>
> The great expanses of the Land had brought forth thistles and thorns. Brambles and prickly plants had extended their dominion. . . . Only the howl of the jackal disturbed the stillness of desertion and dejection. We used to enter the abandoned villages, wander about their crooked streets, and try to comprehend the way of life recently past and still vivid [in our memories] which had preceded the panicked flight. . . . All the abandoned villages had become mute witnesses to a battle of titans, to the cruel vicissitudes of fate, their plots to annihilate us thwarted. Now the villages stood desolate, orphaned, mute. . . . Emptiness peeped from every corner with a myriad of eyes; emptiness seeking its [own] eradication; seeking to have life breathed into it. . . . Here a lone and frightened dog—who was left behind—miserably prowls, sadly and loyally guarding what has gone with the wind and with the

storm of battle. These impressions were soaked up . . . they fermented and sizzled, struggling and crying out for us to do something

After the victory over our enemies, what was required was an act of conquest by settlement, an act of ingathering of exiles and of rooting our exiled brothers, in their multitudes (in the soil of the homeland). I sensed that in the desolation of the Land lay buried the solution to the human desolation that was arriving from all ends of the earth. . . . It was incumbent upon us to open the gates of the country and of its land to all of these.

. . . The man had yet to arise in this country who would attempt to take charge of all the neglected places calling to us from every direction. . . . We passed close to Bariyya, a small village atop a rocky hill. . . . Its houses were of stone and the impression they gave—solidity. An idea flashed in my brain. I stopped the car—"Come, let us visit this village, I have an idea that could help us out of our distress. We left the car. . . . In every corner were relics of the former inhabitants: cushions, mats, jugs, broken pieces of furniture, cisterns hewn in the stone. . . . After touring the entire village we found several dozen houses that might, after certain repairs, provide shelter for immigrant families, here in the Arab village, amongst the fields. . . .

In this country there are hundreds of deserted villages, and even if we exclude from our reckoning those whose buildings are of adobe, which certainly would not be suitable for housing Jews, dozens and perhaps hundreds of villages remain, with houses built of stone, as in Bariyya. We must take them and prepare them for the coming winter, bring scores of families to each one, with instructors to guide them, . . . equip each group with work tools, and begin the cultivation of the fields. This balance sheet is all on the credit side: the immigrants are sitting in camps and supporting them costs the Jewish Agency a considerable sum, whereas these fields must not be left desolate. . . . That very evening I contacted the settlement movements, invited engineers, sought the advice and know-how of the engineering corps, and began to get the great wheel in motion, something which helped us that very same winter (1948–49) to turn more than forty-five abandoned villages into settlements bustling with renewed life.[16]

At the very time Eshkol was coming to the realization of how the "desolation of the Land" could provide a solution for "the human desolation that was arriving from all ends of the earth," nearly 100,000 people were crammed into immigrant camps and into houses abandoned by Arabs in the larger towns. In the estimation of this pioneer founder of Kibbutz Degania Bet, close confidant of Ben-Gurion, and eventually prime minister himself, these people were "human refuse, remnants from the displaced persons' camps, fragments of communities . . . like a flash flood in the *wadi* on a rainy day."[17] He believed it would be possible to take "thousands of immigrant families from the big camps and thereby rescue from a life of decadence the former inmates of the European death camps," to steer them " in constructive and productive directions," "in physical contact with the soil—mother of all solutions."

MAGNITUDE OF IMMIGRATION

The magnitude of this wave of immigration was astounding. From the establishment of the state to the end of 1951, nearly 700,000 immigrants arrived in Israel (100,000 in 1948, 240,000 in 1949, 170,000 in 1950, and 175,000 in 1951). By the end of 1951, the number of new immigrants had exceeded that of those who were taking them in, and the machinery of immigrant absorption was bent over beneath the weight of this burden. This great human drama has already been portrayed many times and will not be repeated here; I shall concentrate instead on the fate of those who settled in the abandoned villages-turned-cooperative-settlements.

The leaders of the Moshav Movement and the heads of the settlement establishment liked to believe that they held in their hands the cure for the misery of the immigrants "who had lost their families in the holocaust and who were striving to rebuild their shattered family lives and who had a powerful longing to stand on their own feet." Organizing them into settlement groups for moshavim would not only solve "the two central problems in their lives: creating a normal family life and making possible a reasonably independent existence, it would actually be the fulfillment of their 'longing for renewal and for rootedness in the soil of this Land.'"[18]

The official history of the Moshav Movement recounts that the first group "recruited by Gershon Gilad in the Pardess Hannah Immigrant Camp" was a haphazard collection of new immigrants who did not know one another. Gilad explained to the small group that came to the meeting that had been announced over the camp public address system that "they were being offered a priceless opportunity to join the elite of the Yishuv: the agricultural settlement movement occupies the pinnacle of public regard, and not everyone has succeeded in fulfilling the supreme *halutzik* (pioneering) mission to this degree." The immigrants were not interested in social status, but they aspired "to get away from the moldy bread that [they] ate in the camps and to begin living normal lives."[19] Some of them signed up for the settlement group, which arrived at the abandoned Arab village of ʿAqir, near Rehovot, on 7 December 1948.

SETTLING ARAB VILLAGES

The group was installed in the houses of this large village, which had been captured in May of that year; over the past six months the deserted houses had been vandalized and were falling apart. The group's members were not aware that they were not the only ones who had been placed in ʿAqir, as the Absorption Department of the Jewish Agency had earlier brought in a collection of immigrants who were not slated for agricultural settlement. The settlement group was given dilapidated houses—and set to work renovating them. Relations among the group members and between them and their nonagricultural immigrant neighbors were tense, and the difficult living conditions were not conducive to good humor. The village had only one well in operating condition, the rest having been wrecked and their equipment stolen. There was no electricity, and the renovations collapsed with the winter rains. A Moshav Movement instructor who visited the village "saw in one of the old houses, in a large, dark room—damp, with peeling walls—several women and children who had gathered in order to relieve the oppressive loneliness. The women sat wrapped in heavy overcoats, exchanging few words. . . . 'We're unhappy here,' said one of them in Yiddish." Another instructor writes: "I encountered a highly depressing phenomenon: a total lack of trust in one another. . . . They did not believe in people's sincerity or their honesty in public work. They did not believe that it was possible to divide work impartially, without favors. In short, they had no faith in humankind."

Staying in the old houses of the abandoned village was disheartening for the settlers, and the Settlement Department made an effort to obtain new homes for them. These were small cinder-block structures, which the group members built themselves adjacent to the village site. One of the settlers commented, blaming the hardships and the mass desertion by members of the group on their initial housing:

> For a short while we thought that a poor nation should feel blessed with the existing houses [of the Arab village]. But it turned out that the attitude of the settlers toward the abandoned village was as that toward a piece of used clothing, which—no matter how good it is—is not loved by a self-respecting person. Many settlements were emptied of their first and best settlers because of the necessity of living like the Arabs.

When the ʿAqir settlers sought to erect their cinder-block houses, they encountered an unexpected obstacle. The members of nearby Kibbutz Givʿat Brenner refused to let them have the land, saying that "it would be a waste of good farmland to hand it over to people with no knowledge of agriculture." The object of the dispute was a parcel of 2,600 *dunams* of land belonging to the Arab village of ʿAqir, which the kibbutz had leased on a temporary basis and now wished to take over permanently. Some of the moshav members hesitated to confront the kibbutz members, since they were employed in Givʿat Brenner's fruit-juice factory and feared that they would be fired—which indeed they were. When the moshav members brought the blocks—which they had made with their own hands—to the disputed area, "teenagers from Givʿat Brenner came and smashed them. The conflict heated up and there was an exchange of blows."[20] "Here you are, living in the [Arab] houses," argued the *kibbutznikim* (kibbutz members), "and working for us. What do you need land for?" Finally the dispute was brought before Eshkol, who ruled in favor of the ʿAqir settlers, whose moshav was called Beit Elazari. This incident was immortalized in the chronicles of the Moshav Movement as "the first land dispute between an immigrant *moshav* and an established agricultural settlement." It was not the last.

Intense arguments and conflicts between new and veteran agricultural settlers broke out in many places, leaving a legacy of bad feeling. Eshkol took an unambiguous stance:

> I reject the intention to reserve land for the older settlements at this time. This demand seems to me un-Zionist. Look here, the entire Upper Galilee is empty; it has ample reserves of land, but no one is leaping on them. . . . An examination of land allocations during the period I have been responsible for settlement will not lead to the conclusion that *kibbutzim* received . . . rocky ground and hillsides, whereas immigrants—"ordinary Jews"—were given the best soil. The data will reveal that the opposite is the case. The new immigrants have been directed to difficult places and to [temporary] workers' villages, because circumstances dictated that. The abandoned villages demand to be settled; is it necessary to set aside some of their land in reserve so that maybe somebody would want to settle there?[21]

Joseph Weitz was even more blunt than his colleagues. He expressed his disappointment with the old guard of the agricultural settlements in these words:

> This is the great revolution in the annals of Zionist settlement. The *kibbutz* and *kvutza* (small *kibbutz*) and the older *moshav* have ceased to be in the vanguard of settlement development, save in areas of irrigated crops. But there, too, the simple laborer will be better adapted. The conquest of the wilderness and the renaissance of the land will apparently be accomplished by the Jews of Yemen, Iraq, and Morocco.[22]

Weitz did not conceal his opinion that the Oriental immigrants, who came from a "primitive background," were well suited for settlement in rugged terrain because they would be satisfied with little and prepared to work hard for low pay, unlike workers from Europe who were "accustomed to a high standard of living." This attitude fit in well with the Ashkenazi establishment's perceptions of how immigrant absorption should proceed. The "absorbers" would ultimately pay the price for this attitude.

But the Oriental immigrants were not infused with the sense of mission that those who sent them out to the settlements tried to imbue them with. Further, they felt they had been deceived. "They had difficulty understanding why they had to live under harsh conditions in the hills of the Galilee or the area outside Jerusalem, or in the remote Negev, far from the center of the country with its vibrant cities, while other, European, immigrants had a better fate than that." "In certain cases," reports the Moshav Movement historian, "some of the immigrants refused to leave the trucks and vigorously demanded to be returned to the immigrant camps." The instructors who accompanied them resorted to varied methods to persuade them to get down. At one settlement the truck driver "staged" a breakdown, and once the passengers had alighted, he "managed" to get the vehicle moving and made haste to get out of there. In another place the immigrants were told that there was a town "just over the hill." "When they got up early the next morning they realized that everything around was desolate and deserted."[23]

An instructor from the Moshav Movement relates his experiences:

> On the way . . . [they came to a place where] level fields, free of stones, stretched off [into the distance], apparently fertile soil. In the distance [Arab] villages could be seen, emptied of their inhabitants. Someone among the immigrants dared to ask, "Why did you show us a village whose land is all rocks and stones and why isn't it possible for us to settle here, on the plain?" Of course I could not give him an answer to put his mind at ease: "We must settle in every part of the country. . . . We must conquer the mountainous frontiers that are already sown and whose [Arab] inhabitants lived relatively prosperous lives, as their spacious homes testify." . . . That night I did not sleep. . . . I lay on my cot with a half-cocked rifle by my side, and in my mind's eye I saw the people of this village, who had fled in panic and who were surely not far from here, waiting for the first opportunity to return to their village, to their houses. Who would prevent them from doing that, especially once they found out that Jews had come to take possession of their property? . . . The night passed. The following day we made a tour of the village. We got the impression that the houses are not suitable for a Jewish settlement, they are scattered in no particular arrangement among twisting alleyways, im-

> passable by cart. . . . But there is no choice. We'll have to clean out the living accommodations and settle in somehow.[24]

The villagers who had "fled in panic" occupied the minds of the immigrants residing in their houses, who fabricated histories of the various villages for themselves. Thus, for example, it is said that in Zippori (the former Safuriyya), "Efforts were made to bring the [Arab] villagers back." But the attempt failed, and the man who had been sent to try to persuade the refugees to return had no success and

> was barely able to escape, and come back to inform us [the Jews] that the people of Zippori had no desire to live under Jewish rule. . . . Despite those who fell victim to Arab murderers sent by the former inhabitants, the [Jewish] residents' spirits did not fall. Zippori continued to prosper and to arouse the envy of its former inhabitants. Some of them used to visit the village or observe it from afar, and later employed legal means to attempt to regain the village that they had refused to return to before.[25]

The Zippori immigrant moshav was built right beside the houses of the destroyed village, "and stones from the demolished houses are piled in heaps. Walls are on the verge of collapse and the dust of generations and pulverized manure rises in the air. Among the ruins of the abandoned houses, small, shapeless cinder-block structures were put up, as usual with no conveniences [bathrooms]." Later a large forest was planted on the remains of the Arab houses, to adorn the tourist site of ancient Sepphoris, with its magnificent mosaic floors.

The dense pomegranate orchards that had been the pride of Arab Safuriyya were an annoyance. "Pomegranates from the ancient trees are not fit for marketing," writes Shmuel Dayan, one of the founders of the Moshav Nahalal, a leader of the Moshav Movement, and father of Moshe Dayan. "We shall have to lay out tens of thousands of pounds [old Israeli currency] to uproot them. The residents expect the trees to be uprooted, and will afterwards use the land for growing cattle fodder." To Dayan, the only tried-and-true method of agriculture was that of the classic moshav, and the glorious pomegranate trees interfered with the production of fodder. Before long it became clear that agricultural planning based entirely on dairy cattle and chickens was wasteful. Large surpluses of produce (eggs, milk and dairy products, certain fruits and vegetables) occurred; the agricultural settlements needed to be heavily subsidized, and when subsidies were cut, the immigrant moshavim were thrown into a state of crisis. But the olive and pomegranate trees of the "primitive" Arab village were no more.

Modern planning, too, which suggested a linear layout for settlement, without deference to topography, caused severe problems. Shmuel Dayan recalls:

> A deep and wide wadi did not stop the planners from designing building lots on its other side, on the assumption that the ground would be leveled and a bridge built. The moshav was built according to plan. . . . The houses across the wadi were not connected to the main road, and the access road to the village didn't reach them. This section was higher than the rest of the village, and when the lower plots were being irrigated, there was no water for the higher plots.[26]

The push to eradicate the Arab landscape, houses and orchards and all, led to the demolition of most abandoned villages, "which weren't suitable for a Jewish settlement." Hence the vision of Levi Eshkol, that hour of grace at twilight in the abandoned village of Bariyya, was not realized. Settlement of immigrants in the houses of the Arab villages was but a passing episode—a kind of bad dream—and the settlers neglected and wrecked them like some "unloved hand-me-down garment." The ancient orchards were uprooted to make room for chicken runs and fields of cattle fodder—but primarily to create "clean land." In this context, Shmuel Dayan tells a story with an allegorical flavor:

> One summer day at dusk, a man and his wife sat on the tiny porch of an ancient stone house in Zippori . . . surrounded by dense thickets of *sabra* bushes. . . . "It was hard," said the man. "Every day when I opened my eyes I encountered that detestable *sabra*. I kept on digging it up, because I couldn't stand to look at it. And even at night in my bed, when I closed my eyes I saw the *sabra* falling under my saw and hoe. Every bit of additional land it was cleared from made me feel better—until I saw before my eyes in my dream 'clean land' and I fell into a deep sleep."[27]

The "detested" Arab *sabra* gave way to the Jewish "garden, orchard, and greenery"; "houses arranged according to plan. . . . The old ruins of Zippori stand to one side, as a reminder of bygone days."

GHOSTS AND INFILTRATORS

The "old ruins" of villages did indeed stand "to one side," but their inhabitants, the displaced Arabs, stood at the center of the Jewish settlers' lives. From the very moment the Jews set foot in the abandoned houses, they were pursued by the ghosts of those who had gone. Nor were these abstract fears, inspired by the ruins of the houses and the desolation of the abandoned orchards; this was a terror of flesh-and-blood "infiltrators," of villagers who sneaked into the settlements with the aim of robbing and taking revenge for their expulsion and for their lives of hunger and deprivation in the miserable refugee camps into which they had been cast.

The official conclusion of the 1948 War did not bring about the cessation of hostilities; instead, it heralded the beginning of a miniwar that lasted more than six years (1949–1956). Thousands of Arabs crossed the armistice lines almost daily and entered Israeli territory. They usually encountered Israeli military forces, who shot at them or captured them and later expelled them again brutally. Groups of armed refugees attacked Jewish settlements, killing men, women, and children. "Retaliatory raids" by the Israeli army against villages on the other side of the armistice lines increased tensions and provoked reprisals. Penetration of Israeli territory by Palestinian guerrillas (*fadaeen*), organized and equipped by the Egyptian army (as well as by radical elements in other Arab countries), brought hostilities to a peak and contributed directly to the outbreak of the Sinai War in October 1956.

The settlers, like the entire Israeli people, regarded the miniwar as a campaign against the young state's very existence, launched by loathsome murderers who attacked peaceful citizens—farmers tilling their land. The Israelis referred to the intruders as "infiltrators," that is, people trespassing on someone else's land. The connection between "infiltration" and the fact that most of the infiltrators were former inhabitants of the abandoned villages and that their reasons for returning were in most cases personal and economic or even sentimental was suppressed and concealed, for had that not been the case, people would have been liable to understand their motives. Such recognition of the connection between infiltration and the infiltrators' dispossession, it was feared, would undermine the country's morale, cast doubt on the unshakable right of the Jewish people to the land, and lead to the justification of acts of murder and robbery by former villagers.

The scale of penetration of the borders was immense. Statistics were not kept during the first years (1948–49), but the number of incidents was very high. At that time it would have been hard to speak in terms of "infiltration from across the border," since the armistice lines were not drawn until early April 1949; even then the border itself was unmarked, and in many areas it was undefined, to all intents and purposes. There were numerous areas of no-man's-land and disputed territory along its length. During that period most "infiltration" was undertaken in hopes of returning to the abandoned villages with the intent of remaining in

Israel, or to take back possessions that had been left behind, and especially to gather crops from fields and orchards abandoned in the war.

Infiltration with the aim of taking up permanent residence was anathema to the Israeli authorities, who reacted to it with a firmness bordering on brutality. Tens of thousands of displaced Palestinians who had found refuge in territory that remained under Arab control, whether in Palestine itself or in neighboring countries, succeeded in infiltrating the front lines to return home. And if their homes had been destroyed or were occupied by Jewish immigrants, they took shelter in Arab villages that had not been abandoned. The authorities worried that the return of the refugees would nullify the greatest achievement of the 1948 War—the "retroactive transfer" that had made Israel a state the overwhelming majority of whose inhabitants were Jewish and had opened up the massive expanses of abandoned land to settlement.

The army, under government orders and settler pressure, began making sweeps of Arab villages, culminating in the wholesale arrest and expulsion of any "infiltrators" found to be in the country illegally. These people were loaded onto trucks and immediately taken across the armistice lines. Those who infiltrated into Israel a second time (and there were many) were held in detention camps for a few months before being expelled again. A particularly brutal expulsion operation, late in May 1950, generated shock waves both in Israel and, more especially, abroad. More than a hundred "infiltrators" were dumped in the middle of the Arava (an exceedingly hot and dry region of the Negev) and ordered to walk to Jordan—without food or water—with soldiers firing over their heads to speed them on their way. About twenty died en route, in the midst of the desert. After this scandalous incident, sweeps of Arab villages became less frequent, and by 1952 they had ceased entirely. Thousands of erstwhile infiltrators managed to stay in the country, joining the ranks of the "present absentees." Efforts to apprehend "infiltrators" had a direct bearing on the destruction of the abandoned villages and the eviction of the remnants of their populations: the houses were leveled so as not to provide shelter for returning refugees; the remaining inhabitants were "concentrated" in other villages so that family members who "infiltrated" would not be able to return and reunite with them in their home villages thereby sabotaging the possibility of settling Jews in them.

After the signing of the armistice agreements, the incidence of infiltration increased rather than decreased. The boundaries with Jordan were drawn without a thought to the villages whose territory straddled them. As a result, great chunks were torn from over sixty villages in the (Jordanian-held) West Bank and handed over to Israel: fifteen villages on the border near Beit Shean, in the Ta'anach Valley, and Wadi 'Ara; twenty-five in the region between Wadi 'Ara and the Latroun Salient; twenty in the Jerusalem Corridor, and five in the south.[28] The West Bank villagers were furious about the forfeiture of their land. They were particularly incensed by the fact that the Jordanian Legion officers who had negotiated the armistice were Jordanian Bedouin who were not conversant with the topography of the country and had underestimated the value of land and of water sources, and out of ignorance had relinquished stretches of agricultural land, springs, and orchards, leaving many villagers with nothing. One villager railed at Abdullah, king of Jordan, during a royal visit to Jerusalem in 1949, claiming that the armistice agreement was "a new Balfour Declaration." The residents of these villages tried time after time to cultivate and harvest their fields, but on each occasion they encountered Israeli security forces who chased them away, sometimes shooting at them randomly and without warning. The killing of women and children who penetrated a few hundred yards into Israel to gather crops aroused considerable protest and resulted in sharp international condemnation of Israel.

ROBBERY AND MURDER

According to figures given by Benny Morris, infiltration reached its zenith in 1952, when 16,000 incidents were recorded. The number subsequently decreased from one year to the next, falling to 4,350 in 1955.[29] All were regarded as "armed hostilities," even though in the main they involved unarmed people. "Apparently," Morris sums up, "fewer than ten percent of all infiltrations in the period between 1949 and 1953—almost certainly far fewer—were politically motivated or had violent aims."[30] Morris, however, qualifies this statement: "From time to time it happened that economically motivated infiltrators sabotaged Israeli property or wounded or killed Israelis during their infiltration. . . . Some undoubtedly felt . . . that by stealing Israeli property they were also taking revenge on Israel." Even in the years between 1954 and 1956, the character of the infiltration did not change fundamentally. It was still "for theft, harvest, smuggling, pasturing, reestablishing residence (by refugees), and family visits (to relatives who remained in Israel)," although that was when guerrillas operating under the aegis of the Egyptian army (*fadaeen*) were active. The murders and acts of sabotage they committed received wide coverage, however, leaving the impression that all the infiltrators were terrorists.

Indeed, to the immigrants living in the abandoned villages, the motivation for the infiltration made no difference. Robbery, theft of livestock, loss of a day's work, shooting attacks, murder under cover of darkness, and the planting of explosives made their lives hell. A sense of insecurity, anxiety, and fear of infiltrators paralyzed the settlers, whose hardships in adjusting to their new lives in the frontier areas were in any case severe. "These immigrants, because of the nature of their wanderings, their disconnectedness and weakness, are like a blown leaf that trembles before every unfamiliar wind. Much time will yet pass before they become accustomed [to life here] and learn to be self-confident and able to defend their settlements," wrote Levi Eshkol to David Ben-Gurion in April 1950.[31]

The following account exemplifies the prevailing atmosphere in the immigrant border settlements:

> When Nini, the Nahalal-born instructor, came to Givʿat Yeʿarim [in the Jerusalem Corridor], an atmosphere of dread prevailed in the village. It was Sunday. The previous night there had been a "visit" from the infamous Samwili, an Arab robber who instilled terror in the corridor's inhabitants. Many had abandoned their houses and crowded together in the center of the village, trembling with fear. The day after the night that Samwili shot the village guard, the entire village went up to Jerusalem to demonstrate at the offices of the Jewish Agency. The demand of the demonstrators: "We want to move to the city." . . . And the following morning, when they found out that a mule had been stolen, they organized another demonstration; this time they demonstrated at the Moshav Movement headquarters in Tel Aviv. . . .
>
> During that period, not one night went by without a battle. In the village of Zakariyya, the infiltrators blew up a house along with its occupants—and the fear grew even more . . . and the acrimony in the settlements increased. Anyone who dared go outside in the evening and saw the distant Shephelah bathed in an abundance of light was unable to acquiesce to this blatant discrimination. Many maintained, "We have been living here for five years—let someone else settle here now."[32]

The Arab bandit who "instilled terror" was Mustafa Samwili, from the village of Nabi Samwil in the West Bank, bordering on the corridor. Samwili, nicknamed "Bigfoot," had worked as a laborer in the Jewish village of Motza, near his home village, before the war. After the war he began infiltrating for the purpose of robbery, but in 1952 one of his relatives was killed by the Israeli security forces, and he swore to avenge his blood. Samwili recruited a gang, which operated in the Jerusalem Corridor for more than four years and was responsible for the murder of twenty Israelis, both in immigrant settlements and in the heart of Jerusalem. In July 1953, following the murder of two soldiers in an army camp, Major Ariel Sharon, who had already been retired from active duty, was called upon to put together a group of his friends (also reservists) to do away with Samwili. The group made a night raid on the village of Nabi Samwil, intending to blow up the gang leader's home, but did not succeed in its mission. Nevertheless, this raid by "Unit 101," as it was called, became a myth that fueled the army's "reprisal raids" for years after and advanced Sharon's military career. Samwili himself became a myth among the Palestinians, continuing his murderous acts until he was finally shot and killed by the Israeli police in March 1956, after murdering a settler.

The actions of the infiltrators were a determining factor (albeit not the only one) in the abandonment of the immigrant settlements. It was one of a long list: difficulty in making a living, housing problems, lack of educational facilities and health care services, internal disputes, and problems in adjusting to agricultural work. Above all, the immigrants (who in some cases had been placed in remote border settlements against their will) were attracted to the thriving cities of the Coastal Plain. By the midfifties, only twenty-seven of the forty-nine moshavim founded by Jews from Yemen remained. According to incomplete data gathered by the Jewish Agency, about half of the original inhabitants of settlements in the Galilee, the Jerusalem Corridor, and the south had gone by then; sometimes there were hundreds of empty houses in these settlements. Some of them were eventually filled by other settlers, but replacements for those who left could not always be found.

Settlers who had emigrated from Asian and North African countries ("Orientals") were more exposed to the miniwar with the Palestinians than were others. Two-thirds of the immigrant moshavim were populated with immigrants from these countries, and only a third with Europeans; it was chiefly the Oriental immigrants who were placed in the border settlements, which put them unwittingly on the front lines in the battle with the Palestinians—and they paid a disproportionate price. This experience not only nurtured a powerful sense of having been discriminated against but also reinforced their hostility toward the Arabs, feelings that have not disappeared even after fifty years.

STABILIZATION AND PROSPERITY

Little by little the immigrant moshavim stabilized, thanks to the enormous investments that were poured into them. Whereas in 1958 approximately half of the moshavim populated by immigrants from North Africa were classified as "failing," 38 percent as "moderately successful," and 14 percent as "developed," at the end of five years, in 1963, the proportion of "failing" Oriental moshavim had fallen to just over one-quarter, 63 percent were classified as "moderately successful," and about 11 percent as "developed." Raanan Weitz, sums up: "The traditional ethnic groups were capable of adjusting themselves to village life—a fact upon which doubt had been cast by certain elements when the placement of immigrants in settlements was first begun. . . . There are essentially no differences in the level of development of the *moshavim* that can be attributed to the [ethnic] origin of the settlers."[33]

The severe economic crisis in the agricultural sector in the eighties (see chapter 4) affected everyone but did not prevent members of the moshavim from improving their standard of living dramatically, generally while accumulating huge debts. A considerable portion of their funds was invested in the construction of multilevel homes in the eclectic, ornamented "Israeli" style. These spacious homes changed the face of the moshavim, many of which became suburbs of neighboring cities. It is perhaps ironic that the new style of construction in the immigrant moshavim that have become well off bears a striking resemblance to that of the "present absentee" neighborhoods on the outskirts of those Arab villages that were not abandoned in 1948. After all, it was the "present absentees"—and other Arab construction workers—who built the Jewish "villas." They copied this style in their own villages, where the new houses bear witness to the standard of living they have achieved by virtue of their integration into Israel's thriving economy.

SETTLING IN SANCTUARY VILLAGES

The internal refugees (or "present absentees") have come a long way since the bitter day when they abandoned their homes and found sanctuary in other villages. Because they believed their absence would be temporary, they left all their belongings behind. They spent many long months in the tents and tin-roofed shacks on the outskirts of their villages of refuge, where they had gone because they were close at hand or because they had relatives there. Some took up residence in houses that other refugees had left; others joined the households of friends or relations, who hosted them "for a short while." In the early 1950s, when the internal refugees realized that their hopes of returning to their village had come to naught, they began searching for permanent accommodations. At the same time, most of them were tied to their sanctuary villages: the authorities prohibited them from returning to their villages of origin (which, in many cases no longer existed) but also forbade them to move from one sanctuary village to another. Only in 1966, with the termination of the Military Government over Arabs in those parts of Israel where they lived in large numbers, were the internal refugees able to relocate to other villages, and many did so. Their reasons for moving were varied: better chances of finding a means of livelihood, proximity to their village of origin, the chance of joining groups of refugees from the same village, who had been scattered in all directions. Some families moved to the outskirts of towns, such as Haifa, Acre, and Nazareth, that still had Arab populations.

The spatial pattern of the internal refugee neighborhoods in the sanctuary villages was set by the midsixties: few refugees settled in the old village core, whose younger and economically well-off residents had left to build themselves new houses in the green areas surrounding the village. Most of them built their permanent residences on the outskirts of the village, replacing the tents and tin shacks they had lived in when they arrived. They purchased the land, which was agricultural, from its local owners; in some cases they obtained it through deals arranged by the Israel Lands Administration (ILA), whereby they received title in exchange for relinquishing their rights to property in their villages of origin. Initially most refugees refused to agree to deals with the authorities, since this would be tantamount to abdicating their hopes of returning to their villages of origin and was regarded as treason against the Palestinian people. Nonetheless, as the years passed, increasing numbers of refugees became willing to exchange scores of *dunams* of "absentee land" for a half-*dunam* plot and a building permit. In July 1958 the government announced a plan for "Resettlement of Internal Refugees," which entailed "exchange of lands" and compensation, but this plan was very slow to be put into practice.

The internal refugees were concentrated primarily on the outskirts of the villages, with little access to building lots near the village core, where only the original inhabitants of the village lived, not just because of the availability and low price of the land but also because of social factors.

The refugees segregated themselves from the others, both out of a desire to maintain family and neighborhood ties from their home village and because the inhabitants of the village that took them in imposed this seclusion on them. The alienation between refugees and villagers was more pronounced in the case of Muslims than among Christians. Said Mahmoud writes: "The refugees were not well integrated because the traditional Arab village was closed to strangers . . . in such a way that the attitude of the locals led to the segregation of the refugees and to the preservation of social ties among themselves, and even reinforced them." He quotes one refugee: "'Upon arriving in the village we were quite amazed. The very people whom I had known beforehand were the first to dissociate themselves from us. . . . One very close friend of mine vigorously opposed my living next to him. I then decided that I mustn't stray far from where people from my own village were concentrated.'"[34] Hence the refugees established homogeneous neighborhoods for themselves, within which they endeavored to nurture the traditions of the abandoned village. Many changed their family names to reflect the name of their village of origin. "The internal refugees assert," writes Mahmoud, "that in this way their children will not forget their abandoned village and will continue to maintain allegiance to it." This segregation is also reflected in the family ties between refugees and old-timers: two-thirds of the sons of refugees are married to local women, but "there is a reluctance among the locals to marry daughters of refugees that have been absorbed by their villages." The reasons for this are economic as well as social. According to one survey, 60 percent of second-generation refugees (i.e., those born in the sanctuary village) "complained that their children are discriminated against by the local people, especially in school and other social contexts."[35] Another found that "ninety-four percent of the internal refugees identify themselves as refugees to this very day."[36]

ALIENATION AND HARDSHIPS

The difficulties of social integration were accompanied by tremendous economic hardships. The refugees, virtually all of whom had been subsistence farmers, were now bereft of the means of earning a livelihood. A few were initially entitled to paltry aid from UNRWA, but this was discontinued by order of the Israeli government. The severe restrictions on travel under military rule barred them from access to employment opportunities in the Jewish sector, and the unemployment caused by the wave of Jewish immigration in the early years of the state meant that even those who had found jobs in Jewish agricultural settlements lost them. The refugees were forced to lease plots of agricultural land at exorbitant rates from landowners in the villages where they were living, or to work in their fields for minuscule wages. Simultaneously, the whole Arab agricultural sector was in the process of disintegration as a result of continuing massive land expropriations, water shortages, and the inability to become integrated into Israel's market economy.

As mentioned previously, most of the Arab-owned land (whether owned by absentees or citizens) in the country had been transferred to the state for settlement and development by the Jewish sector. Nevertheless, massive land expropriations continued until 1976, especially in the heavily Arab Galilee and Negev. On 30 March 1976 ("Land Day") Arabs in Israel revolted against the expropriations, and Arab civilians were killed or wounded in violent confrontations with the police. In the wake of Land Day the massive expropriations halted, but more sophisticated methods of "Judaization" continued to be pursued—and new ones were added: small Jewish settlements were established in the midst of Arab areas in order to fragment "Arab blocks"; Bedouin tribes in the Negev were "concentrated" in "planned towns" so their pastureland could be taken over; Jewish-dominated regional councils were set up in mixed rural areas, giving the Jewish representatives control over municipal services (notably planning) for the Arab villages under their jurisdiction; approximately 100 Arab villages, both large and small, were designated as "unrecognized" and thus deprived of basic infrastructure (such as provision of water and electricity) and municipal services (schools, building permits, etc.); the municipal boundaries of Arab towns and villages were drawn in such a way that no space remained for their expansion, and construction outside them was defined as "illegal" and subject to demolition. Arabs control only 2 percent of the municipal jurisdictional areas in Israel, although they constitute approximately 20 percent of the population.

The accelerating pace of investment in infrastructure and the construction of Jewish housing, which began picking up steam in the mid-fifties, opened up employment opportunities for the rural Arab population, and the first to go out to work at these unskilled and semiskilled jobs building Jewish settlements were the landless refugees. They were followed by landowning villagers who were no longer able to support themselves from traditional nonirrigated agriculture and had no means of developing more profitable economic ventures. The percentage of

Arabs employed in agriculture fell from 60 percent in the midfifties to less than 10 percent in the eighties.

The discontinuation of the Military Government in 1966 brought an end to the travel restrictions (which had already been eased somewhat), and the trickle of Arab commuters heading for jobs in the Jewish sector grew to a torrent. In some villages as much as two-thirds of the work-force was commuting regularly to jobs located at increasingly great distances from home. The majority of workers from the villages were employed (as mentioned above) as unskilled and semiskilled laborers. Their wages were low, but cumulatively they raised the standard of living in the Arab villages and neighborhoods. The most conspicuous reflection of this newfound prosperity was the construction of spacious homes: and consequently the built-up area of the villages grew at twice the rate of natural increase. Eventually, the internal immigrant neighborhoods "were swallowed up in the relentless process of urbanization that was turning the Arab settlements into dormitory communities of workers, situated in the ring of habitation farthest from the (Jewish) metropolises, where people had farms to temper their dependence on the economic activity of the metropolitan centers."[37] This activity accelerated greatly following the 1967 war and the establishment of economic ties with the Occupied Territories, which resulted in many Arab-Israeli workers' moving out of unskilled and semiskilled trades and into independent entrepreneurship in a number of fields, including contracting, commerce, and service industries.

DESERTS OF CONCRETE AND ASPHALT

The Arab settlements kept on expanding, and adjacent villages merged and became neighborhoods in a very large built-up area. Two-thirds of the Arab population now live in communities of more than 30,000, and the traditional village of fewer than 2,000 souls is fast disappearing. Yet no Arab urban center worthy of its name has been created. The vibrant political, economic, and cultural city life that dominated the Palestinian community before 1948 has not reemerged. The vast urban expansion has taken place with practically no orderly planning and with minimal investment in physical infrastructure. As a result, thousands of large, ornamented houses copied from those in the Jewish settlements have been built, crowded together without access roads, sewers, or landscaping. A comparison between land use in neighboring Arab and Jewish towns is illuminating. In Arab towns, 82.3 percent of the land is residential,

1 percent industrial, 0.5 percent for public institutions, and 8 percent for parks. In the Jewish towns, the distribution is 49.6 percent, 8 percent, 3.6 percent, and 22 percent, respectively. The demographic growth of the Arab population, from 180,000 in 1949 to almost 900,000 (excluding Arab Jerusalem) in 1998, the great improvement in the standard of living, and the trend toward modernization have utterly altered the Arab rural landscape and have ravaged this unique cultural environment to a greater extent than has Jewish urban sprawl. Arab settlements where any effort has been made to preserve historic or architecturally unique buildings are few and far between, and the hunger for land on which to build housing has outweighed all concern for conservation. "Everything was poured into construction of one's home," writes an architect who worked in Arab village planning in the sixties and seventies.

> And because of that, they sought to glorify its external appearance, and even added all sorts of decorations to the interior of the house. Efforts to convince [people] that one should preserve the local atmosphere and style . . . did not bear fruit. The majority, including the educated, disagreed. . . . they all wanted to ape the city people and western society in custom and way of life, and they built what they saw there.[38]

The sense of loyalty to the vanished landscape has spawned many literary expressions of a folkloric and nostalgic character, but the present absentees, like their Arab neighbors who did not leave their homes, know that what's done is done. Many of them also would not wish to turn the clock back fifty years.

The Arab and Jewish landscapes—so different from each other—which have long stood cheek by jowl, in hostility and mutual disregard, have now merged and been engulfed by a wasteland of cement, stone, and asphalt. The Jewish landscape triumphed, but it was a Pyrrhic victory.

6

The Signposts of Memory

"On the eve of the War for Independence, the largest continuous strip of Jewish habitation was located on the Coastal Plain, and that was where the country's greatest number of Jewish inhabitants lived." So reads a description of the 1948 War in an Eretz Israel (or Knowing the Land) Studies textbook for the higher grades of the state and state-religious schools in Israel. "The Yishuv was faced with the danger of threatened Arab incursions from several directions. The biggest problem was the [narrow] width of the [Jewish-controlled] Coastal Plain. . . . Upon proclamation of the state, the Egyptians invaded the country with the hope of reaching Tel Aviv and leveling it. . . . After heavy fighting, the Egyptians were repulsed southward . . . and their hold on the strip of coast *to which many refugees from Arab villages on the Coastal Plain had also come* [emphasis added] (i.e., the Gaza Strip) was to continue . . . until the Six-Day War. . . . In the country's North, IDF soldiers and the [Jewish] residents of the Western Galilee faced both local Arab and Lebanese forces."[1]

This treatment of the Arab inhabitants of the region and their fate during the war in a single sentence is typical of every Israeli geography text, without exception.

CONCEPTUAL ERADICATION

The university-level textbook cited earlier (chapter 2) exemplifies the way in which the changes to the landscape wrought by the war have been disregarded and a convenient "time-out" created in the historical-geographical continuum. The section dealing with the settlement geography of Palestine during the period of the British Mandate concludes as follows: "In the course of the War for Independence a new reality was created as regards territory, settlements, and demographics. . . . The state had withstood the results of an all-out war, which had fundamentally altered the pattern of settlement within its borders." The following chapter, entitled "The Rural Map 1948–1967," states that "during the War for Independence broad expanses of territory were emptied of their Arab populations and came under Israeli rule. This fact further increased the necessity of accelerating the process of rural settlement [by Jews]." And from that point on, this settlement drive is portrayed down to the smallest detail. It is worthy of note that when these textbooks were being written, many studies bearing directly on the changes in the landscape as a result of the 1948 War had already been published. But those studies, and the debate aroused by the views of the scholars whose research dealt with the destruction of the Arab landscape—derisively dismissed as "revisionist historians"—were viewed in a political context and written off as a "post-Zionist fad." There was no place for them in textbooks of the nationalist-Zionist variety.

Israeli geographers were aware of the claims regarding the eradication of the Arab landscape, and of accusations attributing the responsibility for its destruction to the Israelis. N. Kliot and S. Waterman wrote:

> In the 1950s and 1960s, Israel expressed its sovereignty by the creation of new Jewish towns and villages. It was less a case of obliteration of a prior Arab landscape than of expression of the need and the pressure to create a specifically Jewish national entity following the Jewish trauma of the Holocaust. The fact that a prior geography was partly covered over was hardly the result of a malign process: it was almost entirely benign. Zionism was single-mindedly Jewish. In this respect the Jews were behaving like most other dominant settler societies throughout history and throughout the world.[2]

This account was written in response to an article by Palestinian geographer Ghazi Falah, in which he accused Israeli geographers of, among other things, lending "legitimacy to the status quo created since 1948, without calling into question and probing the causes underlying this status quo."[3] Israeli geographers do not deny the validity of this accusation. Instead, they justify their approach, on the one hand, by arguing the unique nature of Israel's circumstances ("the trauma of the

Holocaust"), and on the other, by portraying these circumstances in universal terms ("like most other dominant settler societies"). The events preceding the establishment of the State of Israel are perceived and investigated in an ideological-political context, through filters that blur empirical fact and magnify the defense mechanisms thought to be necessary for surviving a bitter national conflict. Acknowledgment of the fact that the Israeli landscape was built on the ruins of the Palestinian landscape and examination of the essential contribution consciously made by the Israelis to the obliteration of an entire physical and human universe are regarded as tantamount to confessing to Israel's being guilty of "ethnic cleansing" and to contesting the Jews' right to shape the landscape of their homeland. The emphasis on the "benign" nature of the process that had fulfilled the "need and pressure" to establish a "specific . . . national entity" necessarily involved obscuring or marginalizing the other "specific entity." Ignoring the Arab landscape, and maintaining silence regarding the circumstances of its disappearance (always using the passive voice: "destroyed" or "abandoned"), makes it possible to avoid having to deal with an embarrassing situation and to stifle questions liable to destroy the Zionist mythos and to weaken faith in what is called "the internal truth of the righteousness of the path."

Thus, as we shall see in greater detail below (chapter 7), the disappearance of the landscape (along with which vanished hundreds of years of history) is almost uniformly described in the following manner: "This or that Jewish settlement was built on the ruins of this or that Arab village, which was abandoned in the War for Independence." When, on occasion, it is impossible not to refer to the former landscape, the reference will be loaded with value judgments:

> During the War for Independence, and in all the bloody incidents that preceded it, Zippori (Safuriyya) was a center for murderous Arab gangs. For that reason its inhabitants fled the village following the defeat of the gangs, and the village was abandoned. . . . In 1949 a *moshav ovdim* was established there under the auspices of the Moshav Movement. According to a resident of Moshav Zippori, there are two (Arab) families from Nazareth—former residents of Safuriyya—who claim to be of Jewish origin, and in the best tradition of apostates, they hold extreme anti-Israeli opinions.[4]

It is worth noting the publisher of the book quoted here: the Israeli Ministry of Defense.

Israeli geographers' ideological perspective and their defensive stance regarding anything to do with the destruction of the Arab landscape derive largely from the inverse stance taken by Palestinian geographers and other supporters of Palestinian claims. Nor do these latter scholars analyze the changes that have been taking place from 1948 onward objectively and scientifically; rather, they do so in terms of concepts drawn from the lexicon of the delegitimation of the Zionist enterprise, thereby challenging the very right of a Jewish community to exist in Palestine. According to these anti-Israel scholars, "The status quo created in 1948 is based on Israel's being a 'colonial settler state.'" The aim of Zionism was to steal all the Arab land and turn it over to the Jews; the Jews' aspirations to return to the land of their forefathers are based on a fallacious myth; the destruction of the Arab landscape was the fruit of a premeditated strategy whose goal was the expulsion of all the Arabs; the Palestinians are innocent and helpless civilians who have fallen victim to a vicious imperialist scheme; all geographical and archaeological research by Israelis is a bogus attempt to bolster the Zionist myth, and its pseudoscientific conclusions are designed to aid the political institutions of the state in applying their racist policies.

It is understandable that Israeli students of the landscape—including those who are prepared to cope with the difficult past—feel, when confronted with this ferocious ideological attack, that they must defend themselves against what they perceive, rightly, as a value-laden and distorted position. Hence the debate becomes a confrontation in which polarized views are aired and where there is no room for alternative interpretations to evolve. And perhaps it truly is impossible to deal with these painful subjects in a "scientific" manner, without appeals to the passions, and a long time will go by before the winding down of the Israeli-Palestinian conflict will enable a discussion free from emotionalism to take place.

It is worth remembering that issues pertaining to the physical and cultural landscape are at the very crux of the conflict, and that those working on them are numbered among the most loyal champions of the Zionist tradition and ethos. After all is said and done, the motives for becoming familiar with and learning about the landscape are not confined to the furtherance of research and the accumulation of aesthetic experiences; they also include a nurturing love of the homeland and confirming Jewish proprietorship over "the redeemed land of the fathers." A large proportion of those involved in the discipline referred to as Knowing the Land, or Eretz Israel Studies—historical geographers, cultural geographers, botanists, geologists, archaeologists, tour guides, and even many members of the Society for the Preservation of Nature, who study at dozens of institutes for Knowing the Land at the universities and other educational institutions—do not treat their area of study as something devoid of Zionist ideological significance. "Homeland," writes one of those dedicated to imparting knowledge of the Land,

> is, first and foremost, land, stone, and rock, flower and tree, hill and valley; it is the landscape in which the roots of the People are implanted and where its spiritual and cultural being took shape. . . . From our hikes we came to understand that rationalistic learning and dry information were not sufficient. Profound familiarity, immediate sensory connection, the feeling of belonging to and of love for the land, will not reach total perfection in the absence of identification with and a true and deep feeling [for the land].[5]

It goes without saying that those concerned with Eretz Israel Studies will portray its landscape and the changes that have taken place in it while adhering to the classic Zionist narrative; for them there is no place for alternative commentaries, which they regard as "anti-Israeli."

One venerable Israeli professor saw fit to protest in writing before his colleagues at a professional geographers' conference against "the spread of anti-Israeli writing in the international academic community" under the influence of "Arab money subsidizing universities and academic departments" as well as of "feelings of guilt toward the Palestinians and the Arab World as a whole, romanticization of the Arab World, harsh recollections of the period toward the end of the British Mandate in Palestine, fundamental hostility to 'impertinent' Israel, along with historical memories from 2,000 years ago." He did not hesitate to personally attack several Israeli geographers who had dared to criticize traditional attitudes, thereby, in his opinion, making common cause with anti-Israeli scholars. Not all the geographers in attendance were overjoyed with this outburst, but even so, only a small minority of them willingly deal with controversial issues touching on the destruction of the Arab landscape, let alone teach them in the schools.

These efforts to suppress discussion of the events of 1948, and the selectivity employed in dealing with their consequences, necessarily lead us to examine the attitudes of people who experienced these events firsthand. Those who took an active part in the 1948 War and witnessed the destruction of the Arab landscape certainly left authentic accounts of their experiences. It is of particular interest to examine what remains in the public consciousness of these portrayals two generations later.

LITERATURE OF THE WAR

Reuven Kritz—literary scholar, author, and critic—writes: "The *War and Peace* of the War for Independence has yet to be written."[6] It is doubtful whether such a monumental work of literature will ever be written about the events of 1948. That period has been overshadowed by the sequence of violent events that has taken place since then, and in the public consciousness it has become just one more episode in the saga of the fifty-year conflict between Israel and the Arabs. The 1967 war is regarded as the final battle of the 1948 War, and the great dilemmas that might have served as inspiration for a memorable literary work have been buried in political discourse and have become a bone of contention between "Zionists" and "post-Zionists." The formative experience of 1948 has become blurred, as generations of creative writers have come of age in the midst of other formative experiences, such as the 1967 war, the Yom Kippur War (of October 1973), the war in Lebanon, and the Intifada. The generation that wrote about the 1948 War has all but vanished from the scene, and many of those who are still active have re-evaluated the events of those days. It is therefore of interest to examine literary works that were written at the time of the events or soon afterward.

Kritz enumerates scores of books of prose and poetry that could be classified as "literature of the war." Hundreds of books, novellas, short stories, and items of journalistic reportage were written during the war, immediately after it, and in the decade that followed. Only a few dozen of these "won public recognition as the work of 'the writers of the War for Independence,' probably because the biographies of these writers follow a common pattern," remarks Kritz.

> They are natives of the country—from town or farming village—they completed high school, they were in youth movements and, at least for a time, on kibbutz served in the Palmach or the Haganah, and began to write and be published a short time before the war. . . . And they had a sense of belonging to a new generation and a particular group, and had social and intellectual ties to the labor movement and its literary journals. In the war they were near the front and were aware of decisions of the Command.[7]

"The literature of the war," then, reflects a picture of the world as seen through the eyes of what is commonly referred to as "the typical sabra" and is, therefore, heavily influenced by the emotional and intellectual baggage of one who has been through the Zionist educational system, with its messages regarding the Arab neighbor, his life, and his landscape (which have been described earlier—see chapter 2). "Because of the *sabra*'s being cut off from Arabic culture," writes Oz Almog, "the Arab was transformed from a subject into an object. . . . Most *sabras* did not deal with the question of the image of the Arab or his fate, since they regarded him—because of the education they had received—as metaphysical evil incarnate, wickedness in the abstract, an unalterable 'given' of Jewish reality."[8] The tendency to dehumanize the enemy, an inevitable outcome of every war, was intensified by the panicked flight of the tattered human multitude, cowed and frightened, streaming to nowhere: "'And they're running away, not even trying to fight.' 'Forget th' Arabs. Not real people,' answered the wireless operator."[9] The sight of the filthy, crumbling villages reinforced the stereotype of the Arab as a primitive son of the desert, in contrast to the civilized Jew who made the desert bloom. When the Arab village was inaccessible and distant, however, the desert worked its magic on the young Jewish soldier: "Its round domes and angular roofs and its sparse trees, which appeared to be growing right on the horizon, kindled the imagination of the men of the battalion for weeks on end," writes Yehoshua Bar Yosef. "The unconquered village had something in it of the desert's fabled splendor . . . and an Israeli soldier at his post would stand there, in a dreamlike state, trembling in awe at the sight of the far-off village—standing proud in brave resistance."[10] But once the village was conquered, "he viewed the morning sun differently and saw the landscape anew." And in this "new landscape" it was the fleas that ruled; "the fleas were none other than the quintessential expression of the filth that was all around. At first the soldiers were amazed how the Arabs could have lived for generations and generations amidst all this filth. . . . The Arabs didn't actually flee from here, they left us the fleas." Little by little the Israeli soldiers turned into Arabs, Bar Yosef recounts:

> If they were stripped of their military clothing and dressed in the uniform of Arab villagers, their language changed, there would not be much difference noticeable between them and those who had fled before them: they too are filthy like them; they too are sunk in that same indolence in the heat of the day; they too are covered with sores and wallowing in garbage and swearing and cursing for its own sake, for enjoyment and from idleness; they too are setting hungry eyes on what is not theirs and dreaming strange and intense dreams, sodden with lust and rut and blood and murder. And above all—they too no longer feel what's on their skin, and don't squash the fleas.

But the Jews were not Arabs, and they could extricate themselves from this miserable existence: they went to the nearby kibbutz, the antithesis of the Arab village, to shower, "and they scrubbed their scratched bodies with a kind of lust for revenge, to annihilate all the filth that had collected in their pores" while they were in the Arab village. "And unintentionally, each one thought of his home, of the white curtains on the windows, of the made-up bed, and of his mother standing in the kitchen wearing a white apron. Never before had they seen their homes through such eyes." The obvious conclusion: to burn the Arab village. "That night the flames rose above the conquered village . . . the noise of an internal explosion . . . like the sound of a flea being squashed between your fingernails. They all felt that with these flames they were also burning the filth that had accumulated within them."

For many of the authors who wrote about the war, the flea symbolized the Arab village:

> A conquered Arab village. An abandoned ant hill. The stench of neglect. A stinking existence. Flea-infested. Lousy. Vestiges of the poverty and stupidity of wretched villagers. The wear and tear of human existence. Suddenly their raveled edges were exposed. Their dwelling place. Their courtyards. Their innermost beings. Suddenly their dress was rolled up to their faces, the shame of their nakedness revealed. Behold, they are weak. Shriveled and rotten.[11]

No wonder the destruction of this pile of "filth" did not arouse any sense of contrition in most of the soldiers. After all, these villages were not only full of fleas and lice, "poor, shriveled, and rotten," but also were "the lairs of murderers": "Once [this village] used to terrorize everyone. Only a few years ago. . . . On the maps it was marked in red as a place prone to trouble. . . . Master schemers repeatedly plotted how to pass by without coming to harm. And someone always paid with his life, one cloudy day."[12] The destruction of these "hornets' nests" was regarded as a justified reprisal.

The conquest of the villages was not only a wartime deed, an act of retribution and of burning the filth of the sons of the desert: it was an act of "redemption of the soil":

> "You hear what I'm telling you!" said Moishe. . . . "To this Khirbat What's-its-name immigrants are coming. You hear? And they'll take this land and they'll work it, and it'll be just great here." Of course. . . . How come I didn't guess from the start? Khirbat Hiza'a is ours. [A solution to] questions of housing and problems of absorption! Hurray—we'll be able to house and to absorb. And how! We'll open a general store, we'll establish an education center, maybe a synagogue too, there'll be political parties here. . . . Long live Jewish Hiza'a![13]

S. Yizhar, excerpts of whose books are quoted here, is distinct from the other "writers of the war" in that he brings us two voices, the nationalist versus the universal. "He is supposedly dealing with the Israeli-Arab conflict," writes Nurit Gertz, "but actually his subject is the conflict between Israeli and Israeli; that is, between what is revealed in the Hebrew literature of the War for Independence and what is suppressed in it."[14] Even while the war was still going on, Yizhar was articulating the intense struggle between regard for the value of human dignity, a humanitarian attitude toward everyone created in God's image, revulsion at the cruelty of the war, and an understanding of the soul of the enemy, on the one hand, and acts of brutality justified by nationalist arguments or as being inevitable and unavoidable, contempt for the Arab and numbed feelings as to his fate, on the other. Way back in November 1948 he wrote his story "The Captive," in which the author's distress regarding the treatment of an Arab captive is expressed. The author torments himself, struggling with his moral dilemma, but his struggles do not ripen into action, and thus he essentially determines the Arab's fate, which is not revealed but will be exile at best, and almost certainly summary execution.

Other authors, too, articulated these inner struggles, but they did not have it in them to break with the nationalist narrative. One way of expressing a sense of personal guilt and the pangs of conscience was by portraying the killing of innocent animals. Nissim Aloni wrote a story entitled "Two Prisoners, an Old Man, and a Donkey." In the story, a group of soldiers captures the Arabs in an abandoned village. The narrator differentiates between the behavior of the repulsively sycophantic young Arab prisoner and that of the elderly captive "who was not angry but was proud, very proud. He looked toward the fields and gazed at them with longing and desire. . . . I watched him the whole time, and it seemed to me that many a day would pass before we would yearn for the land . . . as much as this old man did in his look." The soldiers make the Arabs and their donkey walk to the nearby kibbutz. The donkey refuses to move, so one of the soldiers shoots and kills it. The old man gets up and runs to the donkey.

> He stooped and placed his hand on the donkey's head. . . . Even I watched the old man, greatly embarrassed by his show of affection for the donkey. . . . Suddenly the old man began to moan and to cry, really. . . . He raised his teary eyes and gave us all a look of great and profound hatred. . . . "You are sons of death," he said in Arabic, quietly, with loathing. I didn't feel good about

myself . . . and it seemed to me as if I were a small boy and I had knocked down an old man on the road and didn't know what to do.[15]

Dan Ben Amoz tells how he shot at a camel that was grazing "in infinite peacefulness in the midst of a sea of great hatred" because "deep within me I wanted to shoot at some living thing. . . . 'Leave the camel alone.' 'What do you want with a camel?'" one of the officers asked, whereas another officer egged him on: "'Shoot it. Don't be so sensitive—It's enemy property.'" The author killed the camel and got down from the jeep to look at it from up close. "The camel was as beautiful as the desert wind . . . its eyes shone with a very cold light and in them were reflected the vast heavens and the green prickly-pears and the horizon, and the white houses [of the Arab village]."

S. Yizhar, too, tells stories of the killing of animals, just as he intentionally reproduces the other motifs that appear in the "literature of the war." But all of these motifs—the nationalistic attitudes and points of view—"seem feeble here vis-à-vis the reality depicted and the very clear injustice that has been done to the inhabitants of the village (Khirbat Hizaʿa). The feebleness of the nationalistic motifs becomes all the more blatant when they are placed in the mouth of the soldiers, in their flat, insipid language, and juxtaposed with the author's viewpoint, which here conveys the values of the entire work."[16] And Yizhar's viewpoint is conveyed very powerfully indeed. By way of contrast to the description of the filthy, flea-ridden village, he sketches the following portrait:

> And suddenly, in mid-afternoon or just before evening, the village—which only a moment before had been just a few desolate, silent, orphaned hovels, heavy silence, and the wail of heart-rending laments—this large and gloomy village opens up and sings a song of belongings whose breath has departed; a song of human deeds that have been reduced to their elements and run wild; a song bringing bad tidings of sudden calamity, which freezes and remains suspended like a curse that does not cross the lips, and fear . . . and a flash, here and there a kind of flash of revenge, of a challenge to fight, of "God of vengeance, appear!"[17]

To Yizhar, the deserted house, poor and dirty, is none other than

> walls that somebody had toiled to decorate the best he could . . . an orderliness that was understood by someone and disorder that one could sort out . . . rags that are familiar to those who are accustomed to them. Ways of life that have unraveled, their meaning lost . . . and a great, all-pervading muteness; resting on the love and the noise. And the trouble and the hope, and the pleasant hours and the unpleasant—they are all corpses that will not be buried.

The myth of the Jews making the desert bloom as opposed to the Arab sons of the desert is inverted here: the Arabs are the ones who made the hills bloom, whereas the Jews are about to turn them to desert:

> And here are the checkerboard fields, plowed and turning green, and the deeply shaded orchards, and the hedges that dissect the area in tranquil patterns . . . and behold, the grief of orphanhood is descending on all of them like an opaque bridal veil. Fields that will not be harvested. Orchards that will not be watered. Paths that will be desolate. And a kind of loss—and 'twas all for naught. Thorns and brambles straggling over everything. And a parched yellowness, the wail of the wilderness.[18]

The native-born narrator says: "I was never in the diaspora—I said to myself—I never knew how it was, but they talked to me and told me and taught me . . . on all my strings they played 'exile' . . . and it was in me, apparently already with my mother's milk. What thing have we actually done here today? We Jews have created an exile." And Yehuda the soldier, needing self-justifying arguments when faced with the expulsion of women and children, says: "Nobody asked 'em to start in with these wars and stuff. They're so self-righteous. Too much of our blood's been spilt because of them! Those morons! Let them eat what they cooked up for themselves!" Just then the narrator sees

> a woman . . . holding the hand of a boy of about seven. . . . She looked stern, self-restrained, shut up within her sorrow. . . . And the boy too was whimpering a kind of tight-lipped "What have you done to us?" . . . We understood that she was a mother lioness, and we saw how the creases of self-restraint and the desire to bear everything bravely hardened the outline of her face. . . . And we also saw how something was arising in the boy's heart, something that, when he's grown could not be anything but a poisonous snake. This same something that is now a boy's cry of powerlessness.[19]

ADJUSTING TO THE NEW WORLD

Eventually it would be written that the whole traumatic experience described by S. Yizhar was a consequence of the

> disappearance of the "old" world of the writers' childhood, the inability to fit into the mold of the new Israel, . . . the native sons' sense of alienation from the Israeli landscape and the human environment, which had completely changed with the conquests, the flight of the Arabs, the waves of immigration, and the accelerated construction, bereft of any trace of romance. . . . The world that predated this [1948] war—was destroyed before their very eyes, and they haven't been able to adjust to the new world that came into being after it.[20]

Yizhar himself bristled at the attempts to reduce his words to "the disappearance of the world of childhood." He writes in a later story: "I am but one seeing man, and what he sees makes his heart ache. Here is a place that has left its place and is no more. No enemies here, no non-enemies. Just a story of what happened told in the past tense. Human lives, with a moral for anyone who seeks it."[21] But apparently a prominent author is not allowed "just" to pose great dilemmas, to describe situations truthfully and accurately, and to do them justice—so that the reader cannot escape them. He is required also to formulate a "solution" to the great dilemma that he describes, "and to do something" in regard to it, as if an author's work does not qualify as "doing."

Late in 1977 "The Story of Khirbat Hizaʿa" was filmed, and it was scheduled to be shown on Israeli State Television early in 1978. When the plan to air the film aroused an enormous public debate, the minister of education ordered the broadcast postponed and then reversed his decision. The debate revolved around the damage that was liable to be done to the educational message of the justice of Zionism by portraying it as a movement responsible for dispossession. The screening of "Khirbat Hizaʿa" was perceived by some as an act perpetrated by "bleeding-heart" supporters of the PLO, intent on besmirching Israel's image in the eyes of the world. Author Amos Oz intervened in this debate, choosing, surprisingly, to downplay the pain of S. Yizhar, that "one seeing man," who sought to provide "a moral for anyone who seeks it." In Oz's opinion this is

> a conflict between one of "our own" young fighting-men [Yizhar] and his divided soul; this clear-eyed boy, product of the heyday of education in the values of Judaism, Zionism, and Humanism—such a milk-and-honey spirit . . . within whom, in the flush of battle, in the brutal heat of an eviction operation in the village of Khirbat Hizaʿa, a deep gulf suddenly opened . . . between love of humanity and love of the homeland; in short, between one good and another. And the soul of the dear youth in the story is filled with anguish and he doesn't know what must be done.[22]

In the twenty years since the depiction of the events at Khirbat Hizaʿa, far more dreadful deeds have been done, deeds impossible to blame on "inescapable necessity" (if indeed the Khirbat Hizaʿa expulsion was such a necessity). Had Yizhar's lesson been learned, perhaps these later deeds could have been averted. Yizhar's qualms, however, supposedly have nothing to do with the fate of the Arabs who were expelled and the injustice done to them. "This is not an Israeli-Arab conflict, but rather—doubly shameful—an Israeli-Israeli conflict," opines Oz, turning the Arab once again into an object rather than a subject, an abstract backdrop against which the Israeli can vacillate between "love of homeland" and "love of humanity" and glory in his moral sensibility. Now it is possible to define "war" unilaterally and to make sure of finding a balance between "one good and another"—between two value systems that are good—of course, for the Jews and their consciences. "If there were not a life-and-death necessity, we would no longer destroy or dispossess, and we would not wage war," writes Oz. But as could be seen during these past fifty years, the definition of "necessity" has always been flexible and unilateral, and in fact the urge "to destroy, to dispossess, and to wage war" has not disappeared. "We came to build and to be built. . . . What we have done is sad and bitter, just as what our enemies have done to us is bitter and sad," states Oz, paraphrasing the words of the soldiers of 1948. But Yizhar has already exposed the shallowness of these nationalist themes, and the suppression of bitter reality, and he has already exposed the evasions that the younger writer repeats: "Jewish soldiers perpetrated an evil deed, as ordered. An evil deed, I say. But what is this evil compared to the atrocities of all the wars since the beginning of time? . . . Almost an idyllic evil: you expel a little, waver, run to bring water to the expellees, expel a little more, help old women climb onto the trucks. Big deal!"[23]

This was the last television broadcast of its type on the dilemmas of 1948 until 1998, the fiftieth anniversary of the establishment of Israel. Israeli State Television aired a documentary series on the history of the state ("*Tequma*"), produced for the occasion, which included references to the exodus of the Palestinians. In general, however, this series revealed the same attitudes that had prevailed twenty years earlier, as if nothing had changed. In 1998, as in 1978, the focus was on the dilemmas posed by the Israeli occupation of the West Bank and Gaza Strip and its injustices. The continuing occupation of the territories after 1967 had provided new perspectives on the conquests of 1948. Thus on the one hand Israelis looked back on the beginnings of the Jewish-Arab conflict and dug up all the old dilemmas; on the other hand, they encased the obliterated landscape of Khirbat Hizaʿa and the like in a sheath of forgetfulness and self-righteousness. All their remorse was directed toward the other side of the "green line," to the Occupied Territories; the eradicated Arab landscape inside the sovereign State of Israel had become, perforce, part of "the mother country," regarding which there was no place for guilt feelings. Any allusion to the embarrassing past was seen as just an attempt to obscure the "injustices of the colonialist occupation" of the West Bank and Gaza, upon which the Israeli Left wished to focus. As Palestinian-Israeli intellectual ʿAzmi Bishara wrote sarcastically, the Israeli Left wants "this matter [of the past] removed from the [political] compromise" that would grant the Palestinians independence in the West Bank and Gaza.[24]

In 1992 the Israeli Ministry of Defense published an anthology entitled *Battleground,* edited by Aharon Amir.[25] Amir seeks to provide young soldiers serving in the Occupied Territories with a compilation that will impart to them "a sense of the dimensions of time and depth that are often absent from the consciousness of the Israeli who is experiencing the dispute as if it were some sort of puzzling, unanticipated calamity, a product of historical accident or plain arbitrariness." In his anthology, the editor includes many authors in whose writings are expressed "the pressures and the hardships involved in the confrontation with the people of the Land [the Palestinians]. . . . These pressures often produce remorse, impatience, pangs of conscience, and emotional and mental discomfort." He warns that "these reactions can seem to the reader like revelations of defeatism or of alienation from national interests and values." Nevertheless, these works are included in this anthology published by the Ministry of Defense because "this is an important portion of the best of Hebrew writing. The collection must faithfully reflect the totality of these reactions also," apologizes the editor.[26]

Critics of "the literature of the war" have emphasized the artistic deficiencies of the authors, who failed to construct realistic and believable characterizations of Arabs, instead portraying them "first and foremost as an abstract image, a moral and ideological problem placed before the Israeli fighting-man, which puts his values and enlightened education to the test."[27] "There are no Arab characters in 'Khirbat Hiza'a,'" writes Amos Oz, "but instead, sketchy drawings and pencil jottings as an aid to concretization."[28] Others would later claim that the wartime writers had allowed themselves to expose their qualms regarding the justice of the war because they believed that this would be the last war:

> The matter of justice and injustice, and the sense of responsibility toward the Arab who was uprooted from his village or town during a war for which he was not "to blame," were able to strike roots in the literature of '48, because alongside the suffering and pain, it articulated both the hope that the War for Independence was the final war and had irrevocably assured Israel's continued existence, and also doubt as to the [possibility of the] realization of this hope.[29]

Hence the troubling issues of justice, injustice, and responsibility are reduced to a function of "Israel's continued existence."

"It did not cross the minds of the wartime writers," writes Ehud Ben

Ezer, "that the Arab would become the Israeli's nightmare. . . . The Arab, more than he is frightening, . . . is an irritation and does not let the Israeli live his life as would like to, detached from [the necessity of constantly] dealing with the conflict and the wars it engenders." These feelings pervade the Israeli literature of the sixties and seventies and focus on the persistent "fear of the return" (see chapter 8).

"THE TREASURE"

A good example of the use of the Arab as an abstract figure that serves as an "aid to concretization" of the Jews' nightmares and pangs of conscience is Aharon Meged's attempt to describe the encounter between a "present absentee" and Jewish settlers in an abandoned Arab village, specifically from the point of view of the Arab, Suleiman, who had been evicted from his home a few months before: "Like a herd of cattle they gathered us up on that morning," Suleiman recalls. At night he slips into his abandoned village in order to collect a few household items that he left behind and to find a cache of money that his neighbor had concealed. "Like a lump of clay and stone wrapped in twilight, the village lay spread out on the hillside. There's the *mukhtar*'s house up there, and the *madafeh,* and there's the garbage dump, and there's the village square," Suleiman says to himself, echoing a Jewish stereotype of the description of an Arab village. But to reinforce the impression that this is an authentic Arab, Meged has him add, "and there is the home of Kamal Dajani and there is the neighborhood of the adobe houses and the alleyways; it's only my house that I don't see." Suleiman daydreams of how he will return to his village: "I load my wife and the children on the camel and come, and she gathers twigs and brings them and makes a fire in the *taboon,* and bakes hot *hubiz* (Arabic for bread) . . . and the next day I go to the *haddad* (Arabic for blacksmith) and buy a plow and remove the stones from the field and buy *hummus* and *fool* (chickpea and fava bean seed)."[30]

The author peppers Suleiman's words with Arabic terms to increase the sense of his authenticity, but because he makes some embarrassing mistakes, he actually achieves the opposite effect. Suleiman readies himself to meet "*ha-Yahud*" (The Jews—"the" in Hebrew; "Jews" in Arabic), rehearsing words of flattery and Oriental bargaining and denial of any participation in the hostilities:

> You're a believer like me, O Sir, and you are good. And all *ha-Yahudim* ["the" in Hebrew, "Jews" in Arabic, followed by Hebrew masculine plural]. *Isra'il*

> [Arabic for Israel] is good. By the life of my beard. Good. Good that they came here. We Arabs, we're garbage. . . . Just let for me to stay here. The house is yours and the field is yours and the trees and everything: I give them to you and I won't say a word, as if you were born here and didn't come from Allemania [Arabic for Germany].

"And maybe this is the man he has a heart," continues Suleiman, talking to himself in a broken Hebrew that attempts to mimic the Hebrew spoken by Arabs. "And I'll, we'll, stay here and work here and there. Anything they tell me to do." But his ruminations are cut short when he sees through the window that in his house, "my house that I and my father and my father's father, back to the first days, were born in and here we ate and here we slept," a Jewish woman is walking around:

> And there was this foreign woman—By her mother's genitals! [common Arabic curse]. With a single bound he will leap through the window and with this *shabriya* [knife] he will slit her throat and cut off her breasts and split her belly from bottom to top—like that. And that. And let her scream to the heavens; the blood will flow like a warm river onto the floor—for pleasure, for lust—and her body will wallow in it.

And to culminate the murderous orgy of this son of the desert, Suleiman would take "the blazing kerosene heater—and the fire would rise with flames and flames . . . licking at the walls. . . . And all the village, everything, a great conflagration of thorn-bushes, spreading into the distance, to all the surrounding hills, for the glory of God."

But Suleiman does not do anything. He is afraid of the Jews: "A man's disgrace—his fear. He trembled and his legs were as if planted in the ground. Refusing to move." And then her husband arrives: "Short of stature . . . [with] prominent cheekbones and a long nose. Loathsome. . . . He stole my house, this one. He has no strength for sexual intercourse. I'll tear him limb from limb. I'll harness him to my plow. Ha, ha, ha. This one can pull along with the camel." Two men enter the room, and Suleiman flees. He reaches the place where ʿArif's treasure is hidden, but he gets tangled up in the wreckage of the house and barely manages to extricate himself and escape with his life, without the treasure and without his household items. . . . "Now the village was like a black lump, standing up there blind and mute."

This story, full of hackneyed stereotypes of the Arab character, his feelings, and his personality, was viewed as constituting "a moral challenge and self-accusation" [31] similar to those characteristic of the stories of S. Yizhar "and many other works by members of that generation."

The reason for this lies apparently in the daring Meged exhibits in serving as the voice of the Arab refugee and in describing a situation where the refugee is set vis-à-vis the Jew who has moved into his abandoned house, a daring that is perceived as being so great that the fact that the portrayal of the Arab as a pathetic caricature is unimportant—to the Israeli reader, that is. As Amos Oz indeed remarked, this is an "Israeli-Israeli" conflict that does not touch on the real conflict, and the Arab character is nothing but an "aid to concretization," which fits Israeli preconceptions.

In the summer of 1994, forty-five years after he wrote "The Treasure," Aharon Meged published a sharply contentious essay railing against "the revisionist historians," who were, he charged, rewriting the history of Zionism "in the spirit of its enemies and opponents." Meged accused these historians of depicting the 1948 War as a war "for the annihilation of the Palestinian People . . . an evil plot to exploit the people that inhabit Palestine and to enslave them." He disputed the affront to the fighters of 1948 and their leaders, whom the "post-Zionists" were defaming and turning into cruel murderers, expellers, and destroyers, thereby demolishing the ideological foundations of the Zionist enterprise and the State of Israel.

Historian Benny Morris, who had researched the Arab exodus, responded:

> After 1948, many tended to regard those days of greatness and salvation as a kind of personal Golden Age, a moment of youthful grace that must not be defiled in any way. This feeling, which conflated national fate with personal biography, was expressed in a kind of untrammeled commitment to and awe at the Zionist enterprise as a whole and especially that wondrous moment of national rebirth. . . . From documents of the period (that have now been declassified) it has become clear that much of what was told to this People—to the youth in the schools and to adults in the news media, memoirs, and history books—was distorted at best and in many other cases, simply lies and concealment of facts. . . . A complex situation came to light, in which the Yishuv and its leaders had behaved as have many nations at times of war and statelessness: with wisdom and fortitude combined with insensitivity, rigidity, cruelty, and inequity.[32]

This debate too, however, remained confined to tussles among historians, authors, and journalists. It did not filter down to what the educational system was telling the youth in school—and as to adults, they took no interest at all in it. The destroyed Arab landscape of their homeland was overlaid with the blossoming and prosperous Israeli landscape, and anyone seeking to delve beneath the foundations of Israel's landscape would not only arouse slumbering ghosts from their lair but also would undermine the foundations of the entire structure and bring it tumbling down.

A SENSE OF METAPHYSICAL BELONGING

Israelis perceive the whole array of topics connected to the Arab exodus and the destruction of the Arab landscape in the political context. They regard the "refugee problem," and the demand for "the right of return" that derives from it, as ammunition in the political campaign against Israel. There is indeed no doubt that the refugee problem serves the Arab countries, and especially the Palestinians, as a vehicle for promotion of these causes. But the Israelis' treatment of the exodus in this context stems not from political pressures alone, nor even solely from the fear that the demand for "the right of return" masks a desire for the elimination of Israel. Even the tendency to deny the impact of the Palestinian tragedy in order to evade thoughts of Israeli responsibility for its creation does not adequately explain this one-dimensional, impersonal point of view. What underlies it is an attitude that labels the Arab as an object and a "problem," and this includes the preconceived notion that Arabs are incapable of feeling a sense of metaphysical belonging to the landscape and of calling it the "homeland"—a feeling that supposedly beats only in the hearts of "modern people." It follows, then, that the Arab exodus is not such a great tragedy. The Arab, this theory holds, is capable of feeling emotional attachment only to a defined place—his house, the village of his birth, a tree, or a mountain—but he is incapable of exhibiting affinity for the entire homeland.

As if in support of this approach, Rashid Khalidi writes: "The centrality of attachment to place is characteristic not only of Palestinians but also of others in traditional and semi-traditional societies."[33] "Ties of tribal tradition bound the identity of all the Arabs of Palestine to specific villages, neighborhoods, and houses. These ties were typical of a mostly rural, agrarian society whose memories of the transition to sedentary life were still fresh. It was as if the Bedouin that were still in the vicinity were 'breathing down their neck'" claims Danny Rubinstein.[34]

This attachment to definite places is regarded as unmodern, "native," or even primitive—in comparison to a sense of affinity for the entire homeland, for a unit of landscape defined in geopolitical or historical terms. In other words, one who does not subscribe to the Zionist cult of Knowing the Land supposedly does not know the meaning of love of homeland. The ultimate proof of the superiority of Zionist love of the homeland was to be found in the panicked flight of hundreds of thousands of Arabs from their homes (in 1948–49). The Arabs left "quite easily, after the first defeat, even though no danger of destruction or massacre awaited them. But this made it abundantly clear which People was profoundly connected to this land," stated David Ben-Gurion, while remarking that, by comparison, "not one [*sic*] Jewish settlement was abandoned during the war." This competition over who was more attached "to this land" was just a variation on a conventional tenet of Zionist ideology: The Arabs neglected the land, destroyed the natural vegetation, stole the stones from ancient sites, created malignant malarial swamps, all because they simply didn't care, and therefore they have no right to the homeland. By contrast, the Jews clung to the soil of the homeland and made it bloom; they showed sensitivity to the environment and respect for ancient sites, touring them and learning all their secrets, because this land is theirs, and the test of their claim to proprietorship is that they care: when it comes right down to it, who cares for that which is not his?

But if the Arabs are, indeed, attached to definite places—to their homes or to a tree that they planted—how is it that they pulled up stakes so easily? Here, too, the proposed explanation is drawn from perceptions concerning traditional societies: "Family honor" is called *al-ʿard* in Arabic. The dilemma faced by the Arab was the need to choose between land (*al-ard*) and honor (*al-ʿard*), explains Shimon Ballas, who quotes a conversation between two refugees: "'We're crazy! We didn't need to flee,' says the woman. But the old man answers her: 'Honor is precious, woman. Should we leave our daughters to the Jews? They slaughtered the young men of Gaza and violated their honor.' 'That is preferable to exile,' says the woman emphatically. . . . 'Just like a woman,' answers the old man. 'You don't know the Jews.'"[35] And, indeed, when the final decision was made, honor won out over attachment to the land.

The importance of these traditional social values was well known to the Serbian army's experts in psychological warfare, who applied this knowledge during the 1992–95 civil war in Bosnia in designing the tactics of "ethnic cleansing": "Our analysis of the behavior of the Muslim communities demonstrated that the morale, will, and bellicose nature of their groups can be undermined only if we aim our actions at the point where the religious and social structure is most fragile. We are referring to the women, especially adolescents, and to the children."[36] Palestinian scholars' perceived need to explain the exodus as having been caused by the fear of violation of family honor has led to their stressing the intentional murder of women and children by the Jewish forces for the purpose of inducing panic—and particularly, citing numerous cases of rape—even though these sorts of incidents were in fact rare. The Jewish fighting men did not relate to Arab women as sexual objects—perhaps further evidence of the dehumanization of the enemy. The fact that the Jews did not pursue a strategy of intentionally harming women and children, however, does not mean that the Arabs did not fear such acts; perhaps they believed that the Jews would do to them what some would have done to the Jews. The concern for family honor must, therefore, be understood as an important factor in precipitating the mass exodus. Even the contention that Arabs' attachment to their homes and villages was "the source of their greatest weakness, [because in] the absence of broad national solidarity, the Palestinians did not know what to do in order to defend their homes and families,"[37] has something to it and can be proven. But this "local" attachment is not indicative of primitiveness or of the weakness of "their connection to this Land," but of an Arab manner of perceiving affinity for the landscape that is essentially contradictory to that held by the Zionists, as expressed in the cult of Knowing the Land. The contradiction is the intrinsic one between the "native's" organic perception and the immigrant's derivative perception of his or her surroundings.

"IS THIS REALLY THE HOMELAND?"

The founders of Zionism were immigrants of a type that had no parallel in any other European overseas colonization venture. The Zionists brought with them from the diaspora the dream of their lost homeland and a yearning for its landscapes. But when they "returned" to their homeland from the lands of their exile, they found a foreign country, foreign people, and threatening surroundings. Eliezer Shweid describes this tragic encounter between dream and reality:

> Willy-nilly, the *oleh* [a Hebrew term used to describe a Jewish immigrant to Israel—who "goes up" to the homeland] is reminded of the country he has left, the alien land all the closer to his heart from this [great] distance, from the distance of the land that is supposed to be his homeland. . . . He hadn't regarded himself as an immigrant shunted from his land of origin to a country of destination, but as an *oleh,* returning home from foreign shores.

> There is, then, something tragic in the experience of his meeting [with the new homeland], and out of the depths of his sense of isolation and strangeness, it is impossible that the probing question not arise of whether this Eretz Israel that is before your eyes is indeed The Eretz Israel, [whether indeed] it is really the Land whose image was before your eyes when you arose to "go up."[38]

The reactions of these immigrants were twofold: First of all, they began to look upon the landscape that was "before their eyes" as a layer under which was hidden the real landscape—the landscape of their ancient homeland. They searched the visible landscape for vestiges of their dream, and little by little they drew a new map for themselves, one that concealed the threatening, alien landscape. This was not, however, just a map of paper and illusions; they had decided to reshape reality—the physical landscape—in accordance with their vision and their dreams. The pioneering enterprise itself altered the physical landscape, but its success was ultimately dependent on the birth of a new generation of native-born Jews, for whom the Eretz Israel would be a homeland in the simplest sense—their birthplace. Hence their second goal was to create a generation of "natives." They actually did succeed in rearing a generation of young acolytes of the cult of the homeland—through such activities as hiking, identifying native plants, and observing bald eagles in flight. These young initiates excelled in archaeological excavation and research that removed the visible layer of landscape and exposed the "real" landscape beneath it—that of the ancient homeland. This return to the past was accompanied by the creation of a new landscape, and of "a settlement model" that would give rise to a new type of person, the Hebrew farmer.

The founding fathers succeeded in fashioning a new physical and human landscape, but they failed in their efforts to mold a generation of natives bonded to the landscape, like all true natives, in a personal and intimate way. The reason for this failure was inherent in the nature of the undertaking to inculcate a love for the homeland, which was based on the "nationalization" of the landscape. The physical space and the dimension of time—the soil and the affinity for it—were made the property of the Jewish nation, and this collectivity cast its identity over the landscape and transformed it into a "Jewish landscape"—Jewish rocks, Jewish wadis, Jewish wildfowl—not to mention the trees they planted and the houses they built. Israelis declaimed the poem by Shaul Tchernikovsky: "Man is but a small piece of land / Man is but an image of his homeland's landscape" and regarded it as the quintessence of their quest for "nativeness." But in fact they had created its opposite: it was the landscape that was fashioned in the image of the committed spiritual worldview of the Israeli individual instead of the other way around, and in this image there was no place for true personal, intimate communion with the land.

The Zionist cult of the homeland was in essence a secular religion that strove to create new symbols to replace the traditional religious symbols of Diaspora Judaism. But in this, too, it carried the seeds of its own failure: the attempt to create a secular substitute for religious faith fashioned from materials drawn from the religious tradition could not possibly succeed in the long run. The Six-Day War created the conditions necessary for the transformation of the cult of the homeland into a fundamentalist-religious-chauvinist mythology. In the name of "love for Eretz Israel," fanatics set out to complete the journey into the past by nationalizing newly occupied territory, which necessitated the dispossession of anyone who did not belong to the Jewish collectivity.

However, many of the children and grandchildren of those who were supposed to have been the first generation of Jewish natives in their homeland disassociated themselves from the landscape and turned their backs on the cult of "Knowing the Land," repelled by its chauvinistic fundamentalism. They created for themselves new forms of affinity with the Israeli collectivity, no longer identifying with its nationalistically mobilized culture. Their artistic sentiments became introspective, personal, emphatically urban, and now, instead of devoting themselves to nationalist projects of making the desert bloom, they tend their own gardens. Those who are still attracted by the landscape find it a source of personal satisfaction and pleasurable experience, but they reject the tradition of regarding it as a "national" legacy. In their quest to personalize the landscape they are, however, confronted with the internal contradiction that has always existed between the two components of "Knowing the Land"—the preservation of the environment, and its transformation—and they pay the price of unchecked development. In the new reality, they find themselves fighting a rearguard action against the destruction of the landscape by greedy contractors and "developers," who are covering the land with deserts of concrete and asphalt and commercializing every open space by filling it with amusement parks, restaurants, and shopping centers—all to satisfy the needs of an affluent society, but still shrouded in Zionist slogans.

The long journey—from the nationalization of the landscape to its privatization, from the quest to impose upon it the identity of the beholder to its converse, leaving man alone with his landscape—this journey has come up against a blank wall. At this point the Israelis encounter their mirror images, the Palestinians, who have also come a long way, but from the opposite direction. The Palestinian journey began with the intimate personal communion of people who were truly "small piece[s] of land," and evolved into perceptions of "the homeland" in abstract, national-political terms—perceptions oriented toward "nation-building."

This was not a chance encounter. Both the route and the pace of the Palestinian journey were dictated by the Israelis, since the latter had imposed upon the former their dictate as victors. It is possible that, had the Palestinians been left to their own devices, they themselves would have altered their relationship with the landscape, at a pace and by a route of their own choosing. However, the conflict with the Israelis and its tragic outcome determined the dynamics of this change and decreed the encounter at this blank wall.

FROM THE EARTHLY TO THE SYMBOLIC

In the late 1970s, when the Israelis were beginning to apply the doctrine of the cult of the homeland to the West Bank and had launched an extensive settlement drive, Palestinian writer Raja Shehadeh wrote the following words:

> The pains of a people have become my own personal, private ones, and the beauty of the hills and the olives have [*sic*] become symbols of my people. . . . There is a difference between the way I used to love the land around me and the way I do now. Sometimes, when I am walking in the hills, . . . I find myself looking at an olive tree, and as I am looking at it, it transforms itself before my eyes into a symbol of the *samidin* (those who are holding fast to their land), of our struggle, of our loss. And at that very moment, I am robbed of the tree; instead, there is a hollow space into which anger and pain flow.

Shehadeh quotes a Jewish writer friend who refers to this process as "pornographic":

> When you are exiled from your land . . . you begin, like a pornographer, . . . to think about it in symbols. You articulate your love for your land, in its absence, and in the process transform it into something else. . . . It is like falling in love with an image of a woman, and then, when meeting her, being excited not by what is there but by what her image has come to signify for you. . . .

> It is not *any* symbolism, but *nationalist* symbolism, that makes you into a land pornographer. . . . I have acquired my pornography for the West Bank through the experience of loss. . . . We who have lived a silent love for this land are left with the grim satisfaction that the Israelis will never know our hills as we do.[39]

Shehadeh sketches the route taken by the Palestinians—from the earthly to the symbolic; from the silent love of the native who knows intimately "our hills" and the olive tree planted by Grandfather to the pornography of national symbolism; from the landscape that was "just there" to a "nationalized" nature, whose symbolic resources are used in the creation of a national political identity that will struggle with Israeli nationalism with the very same tools employed by its adversary. This process is well illustrated in Palestinian works written since 1948; it is a tortuous journey, painful and rife with ambiguities.

The Palestinian preoccupation with Arab village life, the Arab landscape, folk religion, and folklore began in the twenties, whereas its literary expression did not commence until the thirties. ʿA. Abu Hadaba, who comments "that interest in our heritage was confined to individuals," cites six scholars who wrote on aspects of Arab rural life in Palestine in the twenties and thirties.[40] Of these the most prominent were Tawfik Canaan, Elias Haddad, and ʿOmar al-Salah al-Barghouti. Canaan (1882–1964), physician, ethnographer, and anthropologist, researched and documented various aspects of Arab village life, but his most outstanding contribution to the ethnography of Arab Palestine and to the annals of the country was his study entitled "Muhammedan [*sic*] Saints and Sanctuaries in Palestine."[41]

In his introduction to this study (which will be discussed later), Canaan writes: "The primitive features of Palestine are disappearing so quickly that before long most of them will be forgotten. . . . [T]his change in local conditions is due to the great influence which the West is exerting upon the East owing to the introduction of European methods of education. . . . [T]he simple, crude, but uncontaminated patriarchal Palestinian atmosphere is fading away. . . . ([T]his study) makes possible a comparison with customs [and] practices of primitive times."

Palestinian scholars in the eighties acknowledged the importance of Canaan's contribution to the "study of folklore": "His works revive the memory of the homeland," wrote N. Sirhan in 1988, but "Canaan remains within the limitations of his being an 'orientalist.' . . . Although he described the folk tradition, he did not attempt at all to enter into those aspects related to the people's national identity and did not deal with the folklore of resistance to the British occupation and to the Zionist attack on Palestine." And the present-day Palestinian scholar wishing to recruit ancient folklore to the cause of "nation-building" finds further fault with Canaan: "If Canaan's examples point to a Jewish-Christian-Muslim linkage, one must note that he ignores the Canaanite period," which, as we shall see, is also recruited for the purpose of establishing the Palestinians' prior claim to the Land: the Palestinian mythos holds that they are the direct descendants of the peoples who inhabited the country prior to the "invasion of the Children of Israel."

One who rejects the "nationalization" of the landscape (whether by Israelis or by Palestinians) cannot but read Canaan's descriptions with a sense of sorrow, sadness, or at least nostalgia for this innocent, picturesque, and pristine world that has disappeared, never to return; for a folk culture that knew how to endow inert objects with vibrant life; a culture that could explain not only what made the streams flow to the sea but also why they did. The demise of the pantheistic cult of sacred trees and healing springs was inevitable. But it is impossible to free oneself of regret for the fact that the world described by Tawfik Canaan was obliterated in such a tragic manner in the heat of battle, which enabled us to impose our sophisticated world and our myths—as primitive as any we had wiped out.

The threat posed to the Arab landscape by the Zionist is depicted in an allegorical story called "The Sad Sisters," written in 1947 by Jaffa-born (1905) Najati Sidqi. In it he describes five sycamore trees standing in a row in the middle of King George Street in the center of Tel Aviv (where they remain to this day, on a traffic island):

> The surprising thing about these sycamores is that, unlike the other trees in the vicinity, they look sad and blighted, as if they have no life in them. . . . Once upon a time camel caravans used to pass by, and herds of sheep, a shepherd playing his pipe in the lead—then they swayed joyfully. . . . Today they are plunged in perpetual sorrow, prisoners in a strange world, different from the world in which they grew up and grew old. . . . And I stood before them, calling up memories of the happy past. . . . I let my gaze drift over our surroundings, and I could not find a trace of farm or orange grove, their places having been taken by apartment buildings, coffee houses, and a clubroom for young Jewish workers.

The narrator falls asleep, and in his dream, "behold, the five trees had turned into five sisters dressed in funereal black." And the sisters were nostalgically recalling various events in the lives of the land and its Arab inhabitants. Only the fifth sister,

> who first saw light in 1917 [the year of the Balfour Declaration], stood with her head lowered, looking old and exhausted, despite the fact that she still had all the beauty of youth. . . . "My life is brimming with memories . . . but . . . don't you know my memories? Why are we dressed in black? And why do they call us the sad sisters?" "Enough, enough," cried her sisters. "Don't tell [us] a thing. Dawn is breaking."[42]

But dawn did not break, and all the forebodings of disaster that the Zionist enterprise engendered, portrayed in this allegory, were fulfilled almost immediately after it was written. The Palestinian people absorbed a blow so terrible that there was no other word to describe their experience than *al-nakba*—the catastrophe. One of the first to label it thus, ʿArif al-ʿArif, called his monumental work about the events of the war and its aftermath *The Nakba, the Destruction of Jerusalem and the Lost Paradise.*

THE FRUITS OF THE BELOVED LAND

Unlike the case of the Israeli "literature of the war," almost no literary descriptions of the Palestinian experience (aside from a smattering of personal memoirs) were written in the course of the war or during the exodus. The majority of Palestinian authors had left their homes in the early stages of the war and taken refuge in the cultural centers of the Arab world or even overseas. The new generation of authors, who came of age in the late fifties and especially in the sixties and seventies, describe experiences they went through during the war, when they were children. The "literature of longing," which blossomed out of the experience of loss and of yearning for the "lost paradise"—as the abandoned landscapes were perceived—possessed a clear affinity for a definite, specific landscape. "In a protracted pageant of saccharine nostalgia, the Palestinians spoke and wrote in compulsive detail of every tree, every stone wall, every grave, house, mosque, street and square they had left behind," writes Danny Rubinstein.[43] Particularly conspicuous is the literary use of the fruit of the beloved tree left behind. Ghassan Kanafani tells of his family, who, after fleeing their home, reached the Lebanese border, where they met a *fallah* sitting at the edge of the road with a basket of oranges beside him.[44] The father

> reached out his hand to take an orange. He looked at him (the *fallah*) blankly, and then broke into tears like a baby. . . . In your father's eyes sparkled the radiance of all the orange trees that he had left to the Jews. . . . His face again went blank, and his heart did not allow your father to speak again of Palestine and of the happy past in his orchards and in his house. We were the walls of this huge tragedy, which surrounded his new life. . . . you all were piled up there and crowded together, as far from your childhood as you were from the land of the oranges. I remembered the words of a *fallah,* who said that orange trees wither with a change in the hands caring for them. . . . I snuck into the room, like an outcast, . . . [and] I also saw the black pistol lying on the low table, and beside it an orange. The orange was dry and shriveled.[45]

Thirty years later, in 1988, Bashir al-Hariri wrote:

> This lemon is more than merely a fruit. It is homeland and history. It is the window looking out on the past. . . . When my father lost the tree and the house, along with the loss of the homeland, he also lost the light in his eyes. He became a blind man, but he preserved in his heart the love for the tree and the house, and he expressed this love that night, when he was alone with the fruit of the lemon tree. . . . We left our joys and our sorrows . . . in every grain of sand in the land of Palestine. . . . We left a Palestine that was in love with the *taboon* oven and the lemon and olive trees. We left her in the fields, in the roses and in the [other] flowers . . . in the graves of our fathers . . . in the antiquities and in history. We left her in the hope of returning.[46]

For many Palestinian writers the connection with the landscape is intimate, even erotic, and through their description of the past that was lost and the authentic depiction of a specific village, a picture emerges that is representative of the entire landscape. In 1957 poet Rashad Hussein wrote: "The dream of the shepherds, the dance of the basil and the dew-soaked land / and the shy sheaves of wheat / in their beautiful garments / and wine of my flowers and the golden dreams of youth / they are all I have." And in another poem: "Yesterday they said to me: Come, we'll visit your nearby home / Have you forgotten it? / Have you forgotten the scent of the almond / at the edge of the refreshing garden / Woe to these longings, swept up from the great land / from the top of the olive buds and the beautiful field."[47]

The Palestinian writers who remained in Israel as internal refugees ("present absentees") are of particular interest. Their being exiles in their own land gives their writing a complex personal touch. They portray a lost past from which they have been doubly cut off: On one level they depict the use made of the landscape by the "other," the Jew—how he shapes it to suit his needs—and how the author feels cut off from it;

on another level, the landscape appears as deserted—without the people who used to live there—awaiting another tomorrow. Sameh al-Qassem writes: "And what? / The yellow fields / do not give their owners / anything but the memory of their labors / and their abundant blessing flows / in the granaries of their robbers. And what? / The ancient springs / cement has pushed aside / made them forget their channels / . . . And what? / When the almond and olive turned into carved trees / adorning tavern entrances / and statues / whose nakedness delights the halls and bars / and some are taken by tourists / to the ends of the earth / remaining far from my eyes / papers and firewood!"[48]

In "An Old Poem," al-Qassem writes: "I choose irises to adorn my beloved / but the field is planted with new mines! / I choose from the reeds in the *wadi* a flute for my beloved / but the soldiers in the *wadi* are conducting new maneuvers! / I choose from our vineyard the most beautiful bunch / to make a present to my beloved / but the vineyard . . . woe to my eyes . . . they have surrounded with new strands of barbed wire. . . ." "I am learning my homeland by heart / learning the forgotten song / and maps that were lost . . . and identity," writes the poet, adding in another poem: "We envy the leaves of the trees / The leaves of the trees fall, but return / We envy the flocks of cloud and the shepherds of the wind / emigrants for a time . . . but returning" ("The Return to the Mountain of the Lord").[49]

THE DUST OF MEMORY

The intimate bond with the land and with the pillaged landscape, which began with a longing for a specific place, had come to symbolize the entire nation. The depth of the bond with home and tree is what has given the transformation of the landscape from material object to abstract symbol of identity—to national asset—its power. Thus, the landscape has endowed the Palestinians with a national identity; they have not cast their identity over it—as have their enemies the Jews—but rather molded their identity from it. The collective memory of the stolen land, compounded of hundreds of thousands of personal memories, serves as the basis for a national poetry—"the poetry of resistance"—and for a literature of the armed struggle. Ghassan Kanafani sets nostalgic, personal memory against the "nationalized" memory that creates the sense of the homeland as an abstract concept. In his famous story, "The Returnee to Haifa," the refugee from Haifa speaks to his wife about their son Khalid, who was born in a refugee camp:

What meaning has Palestine for Khalid? He does not know the planter full of flowers nor the picture on the wall; nor the stairway nor the neighborhood of Halissa or Haldoun. Yet this homeland means so much to him that he would sacrifice his life for it. For us—you and me—Palestine is a search for something hidden beneath the dust of memories, and here, look what we've found: more dust![50]

Emile Habibi mocks the nostalgic memories:

"Do you really know how the beginning was, uncle? The beginning was not merely sweet memories of pines over Mount Carmel, or orange groves, or the songs of Jaffa's sailors. And did they really sing, anyway?"

"Do you really want to return to the beginning, to mourn your brother torn to pieces?"

"But your brother, Saeed, said that they had learned from the mistakes of their predecessors and would not commit them again."

"If they had really learned, they wouldn't have spoken at all of returning to the beginning."[51]

But Habibi also ridicules the collective memories. Quoting a poem by Tawfik Zayyad: "I shall carve the name of every stolen plot / And where my village boundaries lay; / What homes exploded, / What trees uprooted, what tiny wild flowers crushed. / All this to remember. And I'll keep on carving / Each act of this my tragedy, each phase of the catastrophe, / All things, minor and major, / On an olive tree in the courtyard of my home," Habibi adds derisively: "How long must he continue carving? How soon will these years of oblivion pass, effacing all our memories? When will the words carved on the olive tree be read? And are there any olives left in courtyards still?"

Mahmoud Darwish probingly calls everyone to account: those who write of nostalgic longings, those who nurture the collective memory, the champions of "the return" and the poets of revolution, but especially the Israelis. "The earth is my first mother," says Darwish to Halit Yeshurun. " . . . Since the land was taken from me and I was exiled from it, it has become the source and the address of our spirit and our dreams . . . symbol of the homeland. It is all the longings and the dreams—the return. We must not, however, view it only as a place; it is also the planet earth. . . . Sometimes one should not differentiate between language and land."[52] Like Habibi, Darwish does not share the dream of return in its nostalgic and simplistic version: "No one can return to the place he imagines or to the man he once was. Al-Birwa [the village of his birth] no longer exists," he proclaims, but he strives nonetheless to turn "the lost paradise" into an attainable spiritual state. "When I speak of [Palestine]—I do so in order to grasp with my hands what once was the source of my being in this sense: Palestine is not a memory, but an existing entity; it is not the past, but the future. . . . The return is a mythic idea, whereas the reality of going [to Palestine] is realized through revolutionary activity." In his opinion the role of the artist is "to repeatedly reconnect" with the past by "going back and forth between the mythical and the mundane." History is written by the Israeli victors: "Whoever writes his own story will inherit the land of that story." He has learned about the power of the written word from the Bible, in which it is written that the true homeland of the Jews is Eretz Israel, enabling them "to claim that this is their homeland. What the Canaanites wrote has been lost."[53] Darwish wants to write the Palestinian story.

In 1995 Mahmoud Darwish published a collection of poetry, *Why Did You Leave the Horse Alone?,* which includes the poem "Until My End, and Until Its End . . ." where the following lines appear: "Will you know the way my son? / I shall know it well, my father: / East of the carob tree on the main road / a short path with a *sabra* [bush] narrowing its beginning / and afterwards it breaks free / and broadens toward the well, and finally opens out / onto the vineyard of Uncle Jamil, / vendor of cigarettes and sweets. . . . Will you know the house, my son?— Just as I know the way: / coils of jasmine on the iron of the gate / traces of light on the stone of the steps. . . . —You are tired, my father! There is sweat in your eyes! / —I am tired, my son . . . Will you carry me?— As you have carried me before. / I will even carry your longing / until / my beginning and its beginning / and I shall walk the path / until my end, and its end" (loose translation).

To all appearances this poem is no different from other poems of "the return." Darwish knows, however, that the same landscape and the same images exist in Israeli poetry, nor does he protest the Israelis' identification with his landscape:

> You love the place and you are expressing your love for the same plants, the same grasses—as if you were I. As if you were speaking in my name. . . . There is a convergence of Hebrew and Arabic poetry in writing about the landscape. Several Israeli poets articulate my relationship with the landscape in poems that I would [willingly] sign. . . . I'm not competing when I write about the same place or the same plant. But it is our fate to live there and settle there, using the same metaphor, and that is new.

It is also new for Darwish, who wrote in the sixties: "We are not writing poetry, we are fighters / O my arrogant wound, / my homeland is not a suitcase and I am not a traveler, / I am the lover and the land the beloved."

But today he is prepared to share the love of the landscape, on condition that a dialogue take place between the two interpretations: "You claim that this land has been yours always and forever, as if history did not continue [to unfold] when you were not there, as if nobody was there, and the land had but one role—to wait for you. Don't impose your version on me and I won't impose mine on you . . . and history will laugh at us both. It has no time for Jews and Arabs." Speaking as a person who does not thrust his identity onto the landscape but draws his from it, he puts words in the mouth of "the place": "The geography within history is stronger than the history within geography . . . because the place itself is neutral. Despite the wind and rain of thousands of years, it receives all comers. It is cynical. I am referring to a place that is stronger than what has gone on in it throughout the course of history."[54]

And here Darwish is in unity with S. Yizhar, who writes:

> A pathway never ends, because borders do not limit paths. Because their course, their infinity, is real. And a path is above all these, and successfully passes straight through any end at all. Only people go astray . . . not paths. Lands change their colors, their apparel, their use, their context, but not themselves. They are always themselves, and the path is always with them . . . continuing, always continuing, to some supposed objective, whose name is always changing and which never has any "here" or "up to here."[55]

How isolated are these two outstanding writers in their tranquil, native's way of relating to the landscape! All around them thrives the "pornography" of "becoming excited, not by what is there, but by what [its] image has come to signify for you . . . the pornography of national symbolism."

We have already dealt with the centrality of "inculcating love of the homeland" to the process of Israeli "nation building." We shall now turn our attention to the corresponding process as it evolved among the Palestinians, largely in response to the Israeli challenge.

FASHIONING AN IDENTITY

Efforts to fashion a Palestinian national identity around the connection to the land, landscape, folklore, and material and intellectual traditions are a relatively new phenomenon. The following discussion is based on sources written in Arabic for Palestinians and not on studies meant for outsiders, written with different emphases.

As we have already seen, this fitful process, begun in the years prior to 1948, became bogged down in the wake of the war and its aftermath. Sharif Canaaneh, an anthropologist and one of the most prominent scholars of the Palestinian heritage, wrote in 1993:

> Palestine did not used to exist within the borders we know today; only since the Sykes-Picot Agreement in 1916 and the Balfour Declaration in 1917, and especially following the establishment of the British Mandate, was it arbitrarily created by the colonialist nations, and for that reason symbols supporting a unique Palestinian entity had not been created. . . . Despite the fact that in the twenties and up until 1948 the Palestinians had had unique experiences that united them, they [nevertheless] regarded themselves more as Arabs possessed of an Arab consciousness and identity than as possessing a Palestinian identity.[56]

In the fifties and sixties, Palestinian identity was swallowed up in the midst of the preoccupation with yearnings for the lost paradise, dreams of the return, the hardships of the displaced people, and particularly the cultivation of a pan-Arab identity that was at odds with the honing of a distinctive Palestinian persona. In the early seventies the Palestinians began systematically to research their heritage, at a time when the institutions of the PLO were taking shape, as was the sense that they could depend on no one but themselves. One of the principal bodies involved in the study of the Palestinian heritage, founded in 1972 in the West Bank, defined its objectives as follows: "To foster the Palestinian heritage in the face of the proliferation of factors favoring its neglect, loss, or theft; to promote the Palestinian folk heritage, as a way of struggling for the homeland and for a national identity."

According to those working in this field, the Palestinians had to contend with challenges on three fronts: First—to define themselves in relation to other Arab identities, such as Pan-Arabism, Islam, and regional identities (Jordanian, Syrian, Lebanese); second—to define the components of Palestinian identity that they were striving to refine from the folk heritage; and third—to struggle with the Israeli-initiated dangers threatening Palestinian society and culture, while at the same time coming to grips with the ruinous influence of Western culture and the "orientalist" approach. Cultivating the heritage could not be divorced from its main objective: building the distinctive Palestinian character. Therefore, there was no pretension to scientific objectivity. On the contrary, scientific objectivity was consciously relegated to a subordinate position, being employed only where it was not contradictory to the pursuit of nationalist objectives.

This multifaceted approach is recognizable in every study, description, or analysis of the components of the Palestinian heritage. A monograph entitled *The Harvest in the Palestinian Folk Tradition* includes the following remarks:

> The pursuit of our heritage is a qualitative condition for the renewal of our national and cultural foundations. . . . Technological devices have damaged folk creativity. They have also broken down the systems of mutual aid that used to be the basis of social life in the village. . . . [Cultural] material connected with the harvest must be preserved, lest it be lost; and one of the reasons for its loss is theft by the Israelis, who present the harvest customs as their own heritage.[57]

In a study entitled *Social Content in the Palestinian Folktale* (1983), Jamil Salhut writes:

> The Israelis are stealing our cultural, human, and even religious heritage, in a desperate attempt to prove that the Palestinians are nothing but a collection of refugees. For example, an Israeli research institute recruited more than 300 students to gather folktales from Jewish settlers. They collected 7,000 folktales, which are considered to be Jewish. But anyone who investigates these stories finds that a large proportion of them are none other than Palestinian and Arab stories in which the names have been changed to Hebrew ones.[58]

Another scholar enumerates the objects of this "Jewish theft": Palestinian items of clothing, weaving, and embroidery have become "Israeli"—and are known as such abroad; "Falafel, hummus, and pita are sold as if they were an Israeli invention; Palestinian melodies, songs, and dance steps have been transformed into authentic Israeli artistry."

A study entitled *Palestinian Folk Dresses* states: "Palestinian folk apparel had its noble origins in the clothing of the Canaanites and Phoenicians, the Canaanites having been the first to invent dyeing and weaving, before disappearing at the time of the arrival of the Hebrews and Philistines in the country."[59] The myth of their Canaanite origin plays a central role in the creation of the Palestinian heritage. An essay by ʿA. Barghouti states:

> The Palestinian People's search for its roots is not an escape into the past or from confrontation with the present . . . but rather [an expression of] the desire to make clear the nobility of its history. . . . The roots of the Palestinians

> are Arab in general and Arab-Canaanite in particular, and this is axiomatic to the Palestinians and other Arabs. . . . The Canaanites were Arabs who arrived in the Land of Canaan from the Arabian Peninsula. . . . The Arab heritage is a vital one: It is a tree whose roots are Canaanite and whose trunk is Arab-Islamic. . . . For example, the plow, the folktales, the weaving—have not changed from Canaanite times to this very day.[60]

The same scholar writes:

> European scholars have affirmed that the life of the Palestinian *fallah* is no different from that of biblical times and that the best way to understand the Bible is through learning about the life of the Palestinian *fallahin.* According to these scholars . . . the *fallahin* are the remnants of the Canaanites. And I thank them for this conclusion, even though they used it for colonialist purposes, because they have proved that the majority of the members of the Palestinian nation (the *fallahin*) are Canaanites who were here before the Hebrews. . . . These scholars add that since the days of [King] David, the *fallahin* have not been destroyed, but have stayed in the same places. They served David and Solomon, and have remained in this state, from one occupation to the next.[61]

The Palestinians, then, stand the Israeli claim to "the *fallahin*'s being living proof of the ways of life of our ancient (Jewish) forebears" on its head; living proof they are, but of the life of those who predated the Israelite tribes, that is, the Canaanite-Arabs. Palestinian-Israeli author Anton Shammas, in his book *Arabesques,* responds to the Israeli assertion in a more elegant manner. In depicting the village of Fassuta, he purposely employs archaic Hebrew (the book was originally written in Hebrew) and descriptions drawn from ancient Jewish sources to mock the Hebrew-reader and to tell him or her that the Arab *fallah* is indeed the legitimate heir of the ancient Hebrews, and that this in no way strengthens Israeli claims to proprietorship of the land, but quite the opposite.

And thus, through studies of apparel and harvest customs, of folk song, of work tools and agricultural implements, of the Palestinian woman, marriage ceremonies, folk proverbs, stories about ghosts and spirits, the village home, mutual-aid customs in the villages, and dozens of other subjects, the Palestinian national heritage is taking shape in accordance with the needs of the nationalist movement. As poet Sameh al-Qassem points out: "We have folklore—so we exist." Another scholar adds: "The efforts to revive the folk heritage are designed to preserve the national character of the People, to preserve the Arabness of the land. . . . One who has no heritage has no national personality."[62]

RECORDING THE JUDAIZATION

A central position in the promotion of the Palestinian national heritage is occupied by Sharif Canaaneh's study "The Eradication of the Arab Character of Palestine and the Process of Judaization That Accompanied It."[63] According to Canaaneh,

> The Israelis have worked for the realization of Zionist dreams, quickly and efficiently, on three fronts: destroying the greatest possible number of signs that could point to the prior [i.e., to that of the Jews] existence of the Palestinian Arab People, its society and culture, [in the context of] an attempt to turn Palestine into a "land without a people"; bringing in the greatest [possible] number of Jewish immigrants; preventing the return of the Arab Palestinians to the country.

Kanaʿaneh notes various patterns of destruction or alteration of the Arab landscape: the destruction of villages and the planting of forests in their place, with some of the demolished buildings even left standing among the trees (the Israelis planted eucalyptus trees on the sites of villages in the Coastal Plain, and pine trees and cypresses in the hilly regions); the total destruction of villages; the destruction of villages and the establishment of Jewish settlements in their place; the destruction of villages and their replacement with Jewish farms; the addition of new buildings to villages that were left standing; the repopulating with Jews of villages that were left standing; the transformation of villages into tourist sites, artists' villages, or museums; the destruction of villages and the establishment of national parks on their sites; and the repopulation with Arab refugees (from other villages) of villages that had been abandoned. Kanaʿaneh himself was author or coauthor of scores of monographs on destroyed Palestinian villages,[64] some of the information for which was drawn from various editions of Mustafa Dabbagh's monumental work.[65] Geographer Ghazi Falah and others also contributed to the research on the abandoned villages, all of which was summarized by Walid Khalidi in a large compendium entitled *All That Remains,* of which he was editor.[66]

AL BASSA

Yusef Haddad wrote the most comprehensive monograph on the Arab village in Palestine,[67] and it is therefore fitting that we review in some detail his book about the Western Galilee village of Bassa. In it the author catalogues demographic and economic data (see also chapter 3) and provides a map of landownership in this large village. He lists all the ancient sites that were situated on village land, while detailing the archaeological remains as catalogued by the Department of Archeology of the Mandatory Government in 1944. When naming the Jewish settlements that were located close to Bassa (the kibbutzim Hanita and Matsuba), he is careful to point out that their land was purchased from Lebanese Arab families. Haddad continues:

> After buying land from the Lebanese, the Jews took over land belonging to several inhabitants of the village with the help of the British, with the excuse that it was included in the tracts they had bought. The court did not assist [the Arabs] but [ruled that they be] compensated. Butrus Bulos refused to accept compensation. Salah Mufleh did not agree to sell his home, which was on this land. The British police forcibly removed his family from the house, and the Jews blew it up. . . . Members of the upper class always tried to compromise with the regime, whether Turkish or British. They were not patriotic, and brokered the sale of property belonging to Lebanese feudal landowners to the Jews.

"In 1945 the number of people living in Bassa was equal to the number of Jews in the entire Acre subdistrict," remarks Haddad, going on to describe the fate of the villagers: "The residents of Bassa left the village for Lebanon, most of them even before the conquest of the village, after the fall of Acre. The majority of the villagers [i.e., the poor ones] are [now] in refugee camps in Lebanon, and the rich ones have moved to the cities."

Haddad describes a prosperous and highly developed village with water piped into its homes, an agricultural cooperative that purchased modern farm machinery, and a high-quality educational system, which sent students to the American University in Beirut and the High School of Fine Arts in Sidon. "On winter nights," Haddad recounts, "the people gathered to hear stories such as the tale of ʿAntara [a folk hero] and other poems and stories. In the summer they would sit in thatched huts on the roof, and during the day the teenage boys would go swimming or fishing in the sea, hold horse races, or dance at holiday celebrations and weddings. They also relaxed in coffee houses, of which there were twenty."

Haddad devotes a chapter to marriage and the ceremonies associated with it, the relationship between wife and mother-in-law, and criteria for choosing a wife. Other chapters deal with pregnancy and children, death, medicine and nutrition, style of dress, the structure and contents of the houses, religious holidays and folk arts, stories, and folk sayings and folk songs.

In the foreword to his monograph Haddad writes that

> the village of al-Bassa can be regarded as typical of villages in Palestine and its environs in terms of folk heritage; [my] objective in writing this book is to preserve the Palestinian heritage, on the one hand, and to preserve the [unique] Palestinian personality, on the other. . . . Preserving our heritage and receiving the inspiration [it provides] leads to the preservation of the national character, and the revival of the heritage means essentially the same thing as independence.

He calls upon his fellow scholars "to walk this path, to deepen [their] research, so that the generations to come will remain connected to the land—until victory."

The process of "nation-building" via promotion of the national heritage gathered momentum during the eighties, with the participation of Palestinian universities in the territories, Arab municipal governments and local councils in the territories and in Israel, nonprofit organizations and institutes of social research and the study of the folk heritage in al-Bireh, Ramallah, Jerusalem, Nazareth, and Taibeh, and theater and folklore groups. These institutes and organizations put on numerous festivals, including festivals of folk song, the Palestinian wedding, the Palestinian circumcision ceremony, agriculture and the seasons of the year, tools, and clothing. Archives of folk proverbs, songs and poems, stories, folk musical instruments, and folk medicine were set up, as were libraries of material on subjects related to the Palestinian heritage. Scores of studies were written and published in periodicals devoted to the subject.

THE INTIFADA

The real impetus for Palestinian "nation-building" came not from studies of folklore and cultural festivals but from the crucible of the Intifada (1987–92). This popular uprising in the Occupied Territories produced a deep-seated sociopolitical and cultural upheaval, which totally altered the face of the Palestinian community. The popular struggle, with its martyrs, the suffering and the mourning, the exultation and the despair, the widespread mutual aid, and the willingness to put up with hardship month after month, year after year—together acted as a blast furnace in which the Palestinian community was refined. The Intifada, like any profound collective ordeal, was a unique spiritual phenomenon for those who lived through it. As in the case of any comparably powerful experience, it almost immediately gave rise to cultural expressions that sought to articulate the force of the feelings it engendered, and these nourished—and were nourished by—national myths and imparted new meaning to the Palestinian heritage.

It was precisely this profound and revolutionary crystallization of national awareness that caused the Palestinians to undergo a severe identity crisis once the achievements of the Intifada were translated into realistic political terms. The declaration of mutual recognition between Israel and the PLO (13 September 1993) and the Oslo Accords created the nucleus for a Palestinian state and invested the Palestinian national symbols with reality: Palestinians were now flying their own flag in their liberated territory, printing their own passports, designing their own quasi-military uniforms, compiling their own textbooks, and organizing mammoth heritage festivals and mass rallies. But these achievements could not live up to the expectations fostered by the propagators of the Palestinian national heritage and the promoters of the myth of the homeland. "The idea of Palestine," writes Fouad Ajami, "had been far grander than the squalor of Gaza."[68] The project of reviving the Palestinian national heritage had nurtured the collective remembrance of the lost paradise and had striven to preserve the memory of every detail of the physical and human landscape of Arab Palestine. How was it possible to reconcile this mythos with Palestinian agreement to recognize the legitimacy of the Zionist enterprise, which had obliterated all of this glorious heritage? Ajami quotes a Palestinian writer: "The Oslo Accords in 1993 canceled a sixty-year history. . . . It apparently became acceptable to settle someone else's country, expel its inhabitants and ensure by all means that they never return. By the same token, it became unacceptable—in bad taste even—to mention that these things had actually happened."[69]

The collective memory and the personal longings that had been nurtured by an entire generation and distilled by the ordeal of the Intifada into a powerful mythos now found themselves in painful conflict with the political settlement: "An apparition, the old Palestine, rebuked this practical peace," writes Ajami. "The narrative had to yield to a concrete political enterprise."

The strength of a Palestinian's refusal to agree to let the significance of the national mythos be dwarfed by that of Oslo seem directly proportional to the distance from the landscapes of the stolen homeland.

Rage over "the capitulation of Oslo" was especially powerful among many diaspora intellectuals who had been actively involved in promoting the national heritage, and who expressed their feelings with immense bitterness. A poem written in 1995 by the great Syrian poet Nizar Qabbani is frequently quoted: "They stole the walls, the wives, the children / the olives and the oil / and the stones of the street. . . . They stole from us the memory of the orange trees / and the apricots and the mint / and the candles in the mosques / In our hands they left a sardine-can called Gaza / and a dry bone called Jericho."

WHAT WAS LOST NEEDS A TOMBSTONE

The Palestinians' long journey has thus run into a blank wall, and the rude awakening from the dream of the lost paradise has been too much to bear. Perhaps, however, it is precisely this awakening that has made possible a more realistic and effective struggle for the preservation of the legacy of the Palestinian landscape of the homeland. The Palestinian citizens of Israel, especially the children of the "present absentees," have long been aware that their dreams of "the return" and the reconstruction of the lost paradise are but fantasies: they know that what is lost is lost. But they have not relinquished their bond with the landscape, if only as a witness and a memorial to the sacrifices they have made. Writes ʿAzmi Bishara:

> The villages that no longer exist were forced out of public awareness, away from the signposts of memory. They received new names—of Jewish settlements—but traces [of their past] were left behind, like the *sabra* bushes, or the stones from fences or bricks from the demolished houses. . . . The Arab villages have no tombstones and there are no monuments to them. There will be no equality and there will be no democracy [in Israel], and there will be no historic compromise [between Israelis and Palestinians]—until they receive their tombstones. . . . The Jewish site cast out utterly the other, the "local," i.e., the other who was in that place. The response of the [Jewish] Left to the [Palestinian use of the] nomenclature of the collective memory was that this matter must be removed from the [Jewish-Arab national] compromise, [that] there is no room in the compromise for history. History itself will prove that it must be part of the compromise—in order for the victim to forgive, he must be recognized as a victim. This is the difference between a historic compromise and a cease-fire.[70]

Organizations set up by Palestinian citizens of Israel wage a never-ending battle for the preservation of their past and their heritage. They carry on their activities throughout the country, focusing primarily on sites sacred to Islam that were left unattended in the wake of the 1948 War. One of these organizations, ʿAdalah (Justice), has demanded that the Israeli government take action to preserve these places (mosques, shrines, cemeteries, etc.) and allow Arabs to use them once again, not to mention preventing their destruction and desecration. In their appeal, the heads of the organization wrote: "Holy places belonging to the Arab minority in Israel are a part of the culture and history of that minority. Cultural rights of this sort were granted by the Declaration of Independence of the State of Israel and received reinforcement from the last amendment to the Basic Law on Human Dignity and Freedom." What we have here is not an effort to undermine the status quo but quite the opposite: a plea for the application of the democratic principals that Israel takes pride in and of the law prohibiting the desecration of places of worship and guaranteeing freedom of access to them. But that is not how the authorities have treated these demands: they regard them as acts of nationalist subversion and respond accordingly. Violent confrontations with the police have taken place in many locations when Arabs have attempted to return to the ruins of places of worship. In the spring of 1998, the Israeli Arab community organized massive rallies and processions, both to and within abandoned Arab villages, to commemorate the fiftieth anniversary of the *nakba*. The authorities did not interfere this time, but officials of the ILA have embarked on a large-scale operation of fencing off abandoned Arab structures and have erected large signs that warn against "trespassing."

The reaction of the Jewish public has been harsher than that of the authorities. The crumbling monuments are regarded as a threat to the very survival of people who are incapable of coming to terms with the country's tragic past, and hence they prefer that these sites be ground between the teeth of time and sink into oblivion; they regard anyone who tries to restore them as an inciter and a terrorist. But so long as these "others" live in their homeland, they will not allow the Jews to erase what traces of their existence remain on the landscape.

In 1992 representatives of the second generation of "present absentees" founded a committee to take the initiative in protecting the rights of the displaced Israeli (Arab) citizens of 1948. They are involved in "cultivating their heritage" and in social activism, but they also try to advance the cause of the "return to the villages from which they were uprooted or expelled by the army." These people harbor no illusions: they are prepared to rebuild their homes beside the Jewish settlements that were established on their land. According to them there is room for everyone, and if the Jews are engaged in the privatization of the agricultural land (that was taken from their fathers—and nationalized) and in promoting large-scale construction on it, there is no reason that part of the land earmarked for development should not be handed over to its original owners.

Precisely this kind of activity, however—undertaken by people who accept the fait accompli of the state and who are striving to gain acceptance as a legitimate sector of Israeli society: "as a minority whose rights are guaranteed by the Declaration of Independence"—upsets the Israelis more than do slogans about "the return." Support for "the return" can be dismissed as a call for the destruction of Israel, and thus is transformed into a threat that necessitates a patriotic unity among Jews that brooks no moral uncertainty. Caring for the sites that commemorate the existence of a community that was uprooted from its landscape and its holy places, and legitimate expressions of affinity for the soil of the homeland, on the other hand, confuse the Jewish community. After all, its members have been raised on denial of the embarrassing past and of the Palestinians' ability to feel emotional ties to the homeland. If Israeli geographers believe that "the fact that a prior geography was partly covered over was hardly the result of a malign process: it was almost entirely benign," how can one expect Israeli settlers not to beat up on and forcibly eject groups of Arabs attempting to renovate a ramshackle old mosque on the edge of a Jewish settlement founded after the Arab village that used to occupy its site was destroyed? Fifty years have gone by, and the battle over the landscape has become a battle over "the signposts of memory." Only the end of this battle will allow tranquillity to reign over the tormented landscape of the Holy Land.

7

Saints, Peasants, and Conquerors

The Reverend J. E. Hanauer, an Anglican priest who collected folk-tales of the Holy Land in the early 1900s, gives the following story as an example of the Arab *fallah*'s sense of satire. On a hilltop overlooking a Muslim village, there stood a saint's grave guarded by a well-loved old man called Sheikh Abdullah. Accompanied by his student, an orphan lad by the name of ʿAli, the sheikh used to ride his donkey from village to village, healing the sick and selling holy relics. When ʿAli was grown, the sheikh sent him away, giving him the donkey and telling him to seek out a livelihood for himself as a worker of miracles. ʿAli wandered for many months, until he found himself in the heart of the desert, and there the donkey breathed its last. ʿAli "could not bear to leave the body of so old a friend to the vultures and hyenas, so he set to work to dig a grave." Just as he finished, a band of Bedouin passed by, and their leader, convinced that the holy man had just buried his traveling companion, promised the astonished ʿAli that the next morning he would send men to erect a shrine over the grave. And, indeed, a magnificent monument was built inside a large room, and beside it a prayer hall and lodgings for Sheikh ʿAli, the guardian of the grave. Little by little the sacred grave became a pilgrimage site for the masses, and Sheikh ʿAli became rich and famous. Rumor of the holy site reached the ears of old Sheikh Abdullah, and out of curiosity he went to find out who the holy man was that was buried there, about whom he had heard nothing. To his surprise, there he found his young disciple.

> "My son," said the old man, "I adjure you by all we Muslims consider holy . . . what is it that is buried in this place?" The young man told Sheikh Abdullah the whole story without hesitating, and when he finished he asked, "Now, father, tell me what saint lies buried at your shrine at home?" The old man looked down and whispered: "Well, if you must know, he is the father of your donkey."[1]

This story has been widely copied; its source has been forgotten, and numerous writers have passed it off as their own. But the surprise punch line of this satirical tale, originally intended as a bit of ridicule aimed at the cult of Muslim holy places by the Muslims themselves, has been recruited to serve the Jewish side in the Jewish-Arab conflict in general and the dispute over holy places in particular.

NO ONE CHECKS UNDER THE GRAVE

In 1938, Haim Hazzaz (1898–1973), one of the most important Hebrew-language writers of the British Mandatory period and the first decades of the state, published a story called "The Great Tourist."[2] In this version of the story, Rebbe Meshl Yeshl, a Jewish peddler from Tiberias, is riding his donkey in the Galilean hills, "from village to village and from settlement to settlement, scattered throughout the wilderness of Eretz Israel, and he went on peddling, [all the while] concerning himself with Torah, with his eyes buried in the Gamarrah, seated on his donkey." One day Yeshl got down from his donkey to rest, and the donkey suddenly ran off, fell into an abyss, and was killed. Rebbe Meshl buried his beloved donkey under a pile of stones. Some time later a great and renowned *tsadik* (Hassidic holy man) from Safad was roaming the hills, and with him were his disciples. They were delving into the mysteries of the Kabala, and the holy *tsadik* was revealing to them "secrets and mysteries . . . word combinations and secret alphabets and *gematria* [Kabalistic numerology], the names of the Holy One, and the names of the angels," until they came upon the pile of stones. "The old man stood in terror and in awe and said: 'Here is hidden and concealed [the body of] Rabbi Himanuna the Grandfather, and today is his day of celebration.'"

Word of his discovery of the holy grave spread throughout the land. "And craftsmen were brought and they made a shrine of large stones, over which they built a House of Study topped with a great dome, and they built vaulted colonnades and a courtyard round about . . . and they declared the day of the holy grave's discovery to be a day of great celebration." From one year to the next the celebrations grew, and thanks to their visits to the shrine, "the eyes of many blind were opened, many imbeciles were cured, many barren women conceived, many old maids went to the marriage canopy." But the Arabs envied the Jews:

> These Arabs, . . . who spend their time in idleness, whose eye is narrow and whose lust is wide, and who toil not and have nothing except what they take from others: they see a sown field and they steal it, they see a planted orchard and they take it by force, they hear that there was once a great leader in Israel and they say, "He is ours . . . one of our people."

And so the Arabs fell upon the Jews, stoned them, drove them out, gained control of the grave, and named it after "a saint, al-Marhum al-Sheikh Nunu." Arabs began making pilgrimages to the grave, "and the grave remained eternally holy. . . . And many sick people were cured, many deaf people were [also] cured, and the world went on turning."

Years passed, and Rebbe Yeshl again went out to peddle his wares in the hills of the Galilee. On his way he met Arabs who were celebrating, "tents pitched, horses whinnying . . . and people dancing." Rebbe Yeshl asked in surprise, "What is your business here, *ya-ikhwana* (O, our brothers)?" "Here is the burial place of Sheikh Nunu, *min al-awaliya* (one of the holy men)." Rebbe Yeshl said to them in wonderment, "Why, thirteen years ago I buried my donkey here." He did not manage to get out another syllable before they jumped on him with their sticks and tore him limb from limb. "They killed him—totally did away with him: '*Ya-ʿAdu al-Islam* (O enemy of Islam) . . . You would mock our holy man?!'"

It is worth noting that the grave of Rabbi Himanuna is no literary fiction but a "fact" that was substantiated—albeit fifty years after the writing of Hazzaz's story. The burial place of this holy man was "discovered" in 1984 in a cave near the village of Meron in the Galilee, in a manner not unlike that described by Hazzaz. It has also been claimed that this same rabbi was buried in both Tiberias and Safad: "No one checks under the gravestone," writes Haim Hazzaz, "and the grave remains eternally holy," be it the grave of Rabbi Himanuna, Sheikh Nunu, or a donkey. Human beings will always seek consolation for their troubles and cures for their ills from the workers of miracles and writers of talismans who frequent the graves of holy men, whatever the religion of the supplicant or of the saint: folk religion unites them all. Control of sacred sites, however, is a preeminent source of power, and an enemy's sacred grave is a coveted spoil of war: a symbol of the victory of the Sons of Light over the Sons of Darkness and evidence of the superiority of the faith in whose name they went to war.

Hazzaz faithfully portrays the stages in the making of a "holy place" and its theft by those within whose power it is "to take it by force." Indeed, at the time he was writing, it was within the power of the Arabs to attack the Jews and take over their sites. But scarcely ten years after this story was written, the tables were turned. The fate of the sites sacred to Muslims in the State of Israel can serve as an example of how victors arrogate to themselves sites that are sacred to their vanquished enemy and adapt them to their own needs, whether for worship or for secular purposes, even turning them to uses that are clearly sacrilegious. If they find no use for them, they leave them deserted and crumbling, and do not allow members of the defeated people to restore them, lest that serve as a "precedent" for their return to the old landscape.

RECONSECRATION BY CONQUERORS

There was nothing novel about the victorious Jews' takeover of sites sacred to the Muslims, save for the fact that it was something that might have been plucked from another era: not since the end of the Middle Ages had the civilized world witnessed the wholesale appropriation of the sacred sites of a defeated religious community by members of the victorious one. It is true that places of worship in many countries have been vandalized—even recently—from the bombing of mosques in Sarajevo in the 1990s and the blowing up of churches by the Bolsheviks following the October Revolution, down to the plundering of churches and monasteries during the French Revolution. But to find the parallel of the reconsecration of places of worship by a conqueror, one must go back to Spain or the Byzantine Empire in the middle to late fifteenth century. In that context, the most famous incident was the conquest of Constantinople and the conversion of its churches into mosques. Edward Gibbon describes the fate of the Church of Saint Sophia:

> After the divine images had been stripped of all that could be valuable to a profane eye, the canvas, or the wood, was torn, or broken or burnt, or trod underfoot, or applied in the stables or the kitchen to the vilest uses. . . . the crosses were thrown down; and the walls, which were covered with images and mosaics[,] were washed and purified, and restored to a state of naked simplicity. On the same day or the ensuing Friday, the *muezzin,* or crier[,] ascended the most lofty turret. . . . the *imam* preached and Mohammed the [S]econd (the Conqueror) performed the . . . prayer and thanksgiving on the

> great altar where Christian mysteries had so lately been celebrated before the last of the Caesars.[3]

The Muslim holy places that were captured by the Jewish forces in the 1948 War were not as famous as the Church of Saint Sophia, which had earned the sobriquet "the Second Firmament," nor could one find "gold and silver, precious stones and jewelry, bowels and priestly robes" there. But the value of a holy place is not measured in terms of its riches or the magnificence of the artistic treasures to be found there, not to mention the fact that Muslim sites are especially noted for their "naked simplicity." The importance of the hallowed sites of Palestine can be measured in terms of the number of people who made pilgrimages to them and regarded them as the focal point of their religious faith and as a social and cultural meeting place.

Nabi Rubin

Nabi Rubin, according to Muslim tradition the burial place of Reuben, son of the patriarch Jacob, was without doubt one of the most important religious sites for Muslims in Palestine. Although it could not be compared to the principal sites in Jerusalem and Hebron, for hundreds of thousands of believers it was a spiritual, ethnoreligious center of the highest degree. As with many of the holy graves, the source of the tradition regarding the burial place of Reuben, firstborn son of Jacob, is unknown. According to a dedication displayed at the entrance to the tomb, it was built by a Mamluk district governor who died in 1437 C.E., and it was mentioned later that same century in a Jerusalem historical document. Over the generations, the tomb became the principal pilgrimage site for all the Muslim inhabitants of the central Coastal Plain, including the large cities of Jaffa, Ramla, and Lydda.

The Nabi Rubin religious festival (*mawsim* in Arabic) commenced at the time of the August new moon and went on for more than a month. The pilgrims would put up a tent city there accommodating 30,000 or more, in addition to temporary coffeehouses, restaurants and stalls selling food and other merchandise. "They sang religious as well as secular popular songs, danced the dabka, held *dhikr* sessions [Sufi mysticism]; watched horse-races and magic shows; and listened to preachers and popular poets."[4] The folk character of this joie de vivre–filled religious festival is described by S. Yizhar, who as a child once sneaked into Nabi Rubin under cover of night, from his home across the sands in Rehovot:

> One finally arrives at Nabi Rubin and its mosque in the center, to watch by the light of bonfires . . . or even of electricity from portable generators, the performance of the dances, the whirling of the dervishes, the colorful candy wrappers, . . . the pot-bellied swaying of a Gypsy woman . . . while on the side, the singing keeps sawing away all the time, not ceasing until the depths of night. . . . Ho, not to return, to be and to be in this colorful spinning, which tempts and leads astray and sings, and which is within the distant night, surrounded by white sands and millions of stars.[5]

City women, shut up in their rooms every day of the year, craved participation in this summer festival so greatly, Tawfik Canaan recounts, that they would announce to their husbands, "Either you take me to [Nabi] Rubin or you divorce me." The pilgrimage to Nabi Rubin took place annually until the year before the 1948 War. In June 1948 the site and the adjacent small village were captured. They remained deserted, deteriorating gradually, and in 1991 the minaret of the mosque was torn down, and the huge mulberry trees growing in the courtyard of the tomb disappeared. Then, however, the site began attracting new pilgrims—who consecrated it in the name of the Jewish religion. The green curtain, bearing the words "There is no God but Allah, and Rubin is his prophet" was replaced by a red curtain upon which was embroidered "Reuben, thou art my firstborn, my might, and the beginning of my strength" (Gen. 49:3).

The Jewish religion adopted the grave and declared it to be the burial place of Reuben, firstborn of the sons of the patriarch Jacob, despite the fact that there had never been a Jewish tradition identifying the place as such, and it had even been explicitly stated that it was "difficult to understand how this Arab tradition had come to be." Moreover, ancient Jewish tradition placed Reuben's burial place in the Lower Galilee, whereas different Muslim traditions show graves of "Nabi Rubin" in three other locations.

This was not the only patriarch's grave that came to be hallowed by the Jewish religion on the basis of new traditions, where it adopted Muslim traditions and took over sites sacred to members of that religion. According to a tradition whose origin is unknown, the graves of the sons of the patriarch Jacob are scattered all along the ancient roads that passed through the Coastal Plain and the Shephelah, and they have served as Muslim holy places for hundreds of years. Jewish tradition claims to have identified the graves of those very same people in other locations, and it did not ascribe holiness to the Muslim shrines. Subsequent to the Arab exodus of 1948–49, there commenced a process of Judaization in which Muslim graves were declared to be the burial places of the biblical patriarchs and were transformed into pilgrimage sites for huge numbers of Jews. After all, what could be more natural and understandable than the "redemption" of the resting places of Reuben, Dan, Judah, Asher, Simeon, and Benjamin, the forebears of the Tribes of Israel.

Nabi Judah

The Muslims locate the grave of Judah in the center of a large village called Yahudiyya, north of Ben-Gurion Airport. The Arabic name of the place is no doubt derived from its Hebrew-biblical name, Yahud (the name of a town in the territory of the Tribe of Dan; Josh. 19:45), and its designation as the grave of "Nabi Huda ibn Sayyidna Yaʿaqub" (the prophet Yehuda, son of our lord Jacob) is based on that name. The identity of this grave as being that of the ancestor of the Jewish People (said to be descended primarily from the tribe of Judah/Yehuda) was not a component of the Jewish tradition. The Arabs, for their part, wanting to sever the connection between Yahudiyya and the Jews (al-Yahud in Arabic), changed the name of the village to al-ʿAbbasiyya, "primarily in memory of Sheikh al-ʿAbbas, who was buried there, but also an allusion to the Abbasid Arab-Muslim empire."[6]

This large village was occupied conclusively on 10 July 1948 (see later discussion) and in autumn of that year was populated for the first time with new Jewish immigrants. A few years later, Nabi Huda's grave was consecrated as the burial place of Yehuda Ben Yaʿakov (Hebrew for Judah son of Jacob). It became a place of pilgrimage, prayer, and for miracles and healing of the sick (see later reference to the mosque of Yahudiyya; see plate 21).

Nabi Benjamin

North of Yahudiyya, about a kilometer east of the Jewish town of Kfar Saba, is a site currently represented as being the grave of Jacob's youngest son, Benjamin, and one three kilometers north of it is attributed to Simeon. These two sites, originally called Nabi Yamin and Nabi Samaʿan, were until 1948 sacred to Muslims alone, and the Jews ascribed no holiness to them. Today they are operated by ultraorthodox Jewish bodies, and members of the religion from which they were taken do not set foot there, despite the fact that there is a large Muslim population in the area. The religions differ, but the motivation and beliefs are identical. A printed "guide to the graves of holy men" enumerates the benefits of pilgrimages to these graves: "The grave of Simeon is suitable for pilgrimage or prayer by barren women or by women who have born only daughters and who wish a male [*sic*] son, in which case the man and his wife are obliged to pray together at the site." "Jewish women pray at the grave of Benjamin, particularly when they wish to bear offspring," as did generations of Muslim women before them. The dedication inscriptions from the Mamluk period remain engraved on the stone walls of the tomb, and beside them hang tin signs placed there by the National Center for the Development of Holy Places. The cloths embroidered with verses from the Qurʾan, with which the gravestones were draped, have been replaced by draperies bearing verses from the Hebrew Bible.

Nabi Dan

The grave of Jacob's son Dan, between Zorʿa and Eshtaol ("Zorah and Eshtaol"), is one of the most popular sites in central Israel. So many make pilgrimages to it that transportation has been arranged from urban centers, for which places may be reserved (with the Light of Israel Company) by fax. Special ceremonies are conducted at this grave at midnight on the first day of the month according to the Hebrew calendar (at the new moon) and on the night of the full moon at midmonth. This ceremony (or *tikkun*—special prayer service) is intended for "healing the sick, for [the birth of] sons, for success, for livelihood, for [finding] a match, for domestic tranquillity, redemption of souls, and in memory of the deceased." It is recommended that those who go there "bring a *shofar* (ceremonial ram's horn) with them if they have one in their possession."

A large building with prefabricated walls surrounds a small structure built of ancient stones, within which is located the grave of a Muslim sheikh, Sheikh Gharib ("The Foreigner"), who was revered by the inhabitants of the neighboring Arab villages of Islin and Ishwa. These villages, whose combined population in 1948 numbered 800, were occupied in mid-July of that year, and the moshav of Eshtaol was established on their land. After the war, the sheikh's tomb was left deserted, beside the new highway to Jerusalem. During the sixties it was identified as the grave of Samson ("between Zorah and Eshtaol" Judges 16:31), but in the eighties, in the wake of a "revelation" received by a Jewish mystic, it was declared the grave of Jacob's son Dan. Samson's grave was therefore "moved" to the ruined site of the Arab village of Sarʿa, some two kilometers to the southwest. In this village (population about 350 in 1948), situated on a high hilltop, was the grave of a sheikh (Nabi Samt). Since the identification of the biblical Zorah, birthplace of Samson, with this location is conclusive, it was not difficult to fix the heroic judge's burial place there as well (and that of his father, Manoah, with whom he is interred). The Arab village has been totally destroyed, as has the characteristic structure housing the grave of Nabi Samt, with its stone dome. Following the "identification" of the grave of Samson and Manoah, two makeshift gravestones were erected there, an obvious sign that this was a place of popular worship, which did not enjoy the support of well-off religious bodies. The worship services are conducted in an ancient cave located nearby, its walls bedecked with memorial candles.

The adoption of Muslim traditions regarding the burial places of the forefathers of the Israelite nation and the transformation of sacred sites that had never been known in the Jewish tradition into pilgrimage places essentially bring events full circle: Jewish traditions were absorbed by Islam, which turned biblical figures (including those of the New Testament) into Muslim saints, made them objects of religious adoration, and identified the sites of their graves. Now the Jews have taken over the Muslims' "sacred geography" and are supposedly returning it to its Jewish origins. The Jew who consecrated the graves of Judah, Dan, Benjamin, and others did not look into the source of the Muslim tradition and certainly not into the personalities of these holy men as they are portrayed in this tradition; the identity of the names was sufficient.

The prophet Muhammad exhibited great interest in the stories of biblical figures, regarding them as an example and a model. Muslim traditions chronicle their lives and activities in accordance with information gleaned from Jewish and Christian sources. These sources were a blend of stories from the Old and New Testaments and from later Jewish and Christian traditions, which included figures who lived closer to our own time (i.e., in the seventh century C.E.).

These traditions were further developed in later Muslim religious literature, creating an enormous pantheon that encompassed Adam, Noah, Jethro, Moses, Joshua, Samuel, Jonah, Joseph, Isaac, Jacob and all his sons, the prophets of Israel, Jesus, John the Baptist, Lazarus, Saint George, and many others. The most prominent, of course, was Abraham the Friend of God (al-Khalil), the father of both the Arabs and the Israelites. To these figures, upon whom was generally bestowed the title "Nabi" (Prophet), were added hundreds of Muslim saints, such as the

Companions of the prophet Muhammad, local miracle-workers, religious sages, righteous women, heads of dervish orders, and local leaders.

CUMULATIVE LEGACY

This pantheon of saints was grounded in beliefs, traditions, and typical "native" folklore, more local than Muslim. It was natural for the biblical prophets to be associated with the land in which they had lived, and for each to have one or more graves attributed to him in a geographical area that more or less corresponded to the region where he had been active.

Not only were these figures but also the beliefs of the people and the various constituents of the ritual were firmly rooted in the landscape of the country. The cult of the holy place at the summit of every high hill, of sacred trees, mountains, and springs—all echoed ancient traditions, both Canaanite and biblical. The custom of removing shoes upon entry to a sacred place, the prohibition on the entry of a menstruating woman, the obligation to wash before the visit, pilgrimages at set times, the offering of gifts and sacrifices—all fulfill biblical ritual commandments. The rituals and the traditions connected with them are the cumulative legacy of the members of all the nations and religions that have dwelt in the Holy Land throughout the ages. All of them took on a Muslim coloration, and the Arabs added their own saints; together they created a wondrous world consisting of more than a pantheon of saints—objects of religious veneration. Not only the stone monuments were sheltered in whitewashed, dome-crowned structures foci of adoration; so, too, were prominent and picturesque features of the landscape: caves, rocky cliffs, dense oak trees, archaeological relics, springs, and crevices. The traditions and colorful folklore connected with them demonstrate the Arabs' intimate relationship with nature—a tangle of roots binding them to their homeland.

The personalities that inhabit the pantheon of Muslim folk religion are the mediators between sinful mortals and their almighty God. Saints are mortals whose good deeds have elevated them to a supernatural level and whom the sovereign of heaven has invested with the ability to control supernatural forces, perform miracles, bring luck, heal the sick, enrich the poor, and punish sinners. Belief in saints has assisted the indigenous Arab in times of hardship: during illness or drought, in wartime, in time of famine or natural disaster. And belief in the saints' ability to help was more important to him than religious orthodoxy. His world was populated with angels, prophets, and holy sheikhs, as well as devils and spirits of every conceivable type, whom it was necessary to appease and to take care not to anger.

These natural human needs, which give rise to belief in the ability of the *tsadik* or the sheikh to help one in time of trouble, are universal. But the intimate Jewish-Muslim connection was particularly strong. Their shared reverence for the Old Testament prophets, their ancient local traditions, and the fact that, unlike Christianity, Islam is not perceived by Jews as idolatrous, since, like Judaism, it adheres to an uncompromising iconoclastic monotheism (i.e., absolute prohibition against "graven images") enabled Jews and Muslims to venerate the same saints at the very same sites. Indeed, according to numerous historical accounts gathered by Ze'ev Vilnai, "The Arabs treated with respect those Jews who entered their domain to prostrate themselves before the sacred monuments, and they did not disturb them at their prayers."[7]

The Arabs also venerated the graves of figures from the Mishnaic and Talmudic periods, although they portrayed them in the light of their own tradition. "Moreover, they treat the graves of the holy tanaim (mishnaic sages) as extremely sacred," stated a Safad rabbi in 1607.[8] Jews prayed at graves sacred to the Muslims, "and when Jews came there, they are received hospitably." This tradition of mutual tolerance and respect is followed to this very day in villages of the Galilee, where graves sacred to the Jews are situated inside Muslim or Druze villages and are also venerated by the Muslims.

What a pity to spoil this idyllic picture with an account of the "Judaization" of the grave of Sitt (Lady) Sakina—a relative of the prophet Muhammad—which became the grave of Rachel, wife of the great Rabbi Akiva. Sitt Sakina lived in the city of Madina and died there around 745 C.E. Her grave miraculously migrated to Tiberias, whose Muslim inhabitants venerated it and made it a pilgrimage site. From the time that the Muslims left Tiberias (in 1948) until 1995, the grave and the structure covering it stood deserted, little by little falling into ruin along with the Muslim cemetery in which they were located. After nearly fifty years, a Tiberias rabbi decided to proclaim the place as the grave of Rachel, of whom her venerated husband said: "The Torah that I have learned and that you have learned is due to her merit." The rabbi's proclamation came in the wake of a miracle that happened at that spot to a tourist from England. The fact that it had no basis in tradition did not prevent the grave from becoming a major Jewish holy site, to which seekers of miraculous cures stream. Extensive renovations to the grave site have severely damaged the Muslim cemetery.

In the wake of the 1948 War, the vast majority of the sites located near or within villages that had been emptied of their populations were abandoned. Hundreds of these singular landmarks dotting the Palestinian countryside fell into neglect in the absence of the people who held them sacred, with whom disappeared the rich culture associated with them. A few sites were destroyed at the time of the demolition of the Arab villages, although many remained intact; apparently, those charged with tearing them down feared the wrath of the holy dead. Yet more than a hundred of the shrines that were not demolished deteriorated progressively as a result of the assaults of nature, vandalism, and neglect. Only three groups have shown any interest in these sacred sites: hikers, Knowing the Land buffs, and researchers of folklore; Jewish organizations and individuals interested in the graves of *tsadikim,* including mystics whose motives are not necessarily those of religious worship; and Muslim bodies attempting to preserve those sites that still remain.

The interest shown by Jewish geographers, historians, and hikers is of long standing. They have naturally been especially interested in the graves of Jewish *tsadikim,* but the importance of researching Muslim and Christian traditions has also been clear to them, both for its own sake and for its applicability in tracing common roots and identifying sites with a Jewish connection. Tawfik Canaan's pioneering work has been issued in a facsimile edition and has been translated into Hebrew. Numerous articles have been published on Muslim sites in scientific journals, and an instruction pamphlet was written on how to present these sites when leading excursions for Jewish hikers.

Eli Schiller, the author of one of these publications, "compares the cult of saints among Jews and Muslims."[9] In this comparison of "similarities and differences," there is an obvious endeavor to stress what is different, even where this difference is specious. For example, Schiller writes that "whereas Jews come to request healing at the grave of a revered saint, Muslims mainly seek assistance from living holy men"—as if among Jews there were not a flourishing industry of wonder workers and concocters of miraculous potions. "The widespread phenomenon among the Muslims of indicating more than one burial place for the same saint is unknown among the Jews of Eretz Israel," claims Schiller, whereas in fact the graves of quite a few Jewish holy men are represented as being in half a dozen places. The Jewish cult of the graves of *tsadikim,* as it has evolved in recent years, bears a strong resemblance to that of Muslim saints, to the point of sharing many identical social and cultural characteristics. Immigrants from North Africa, particularly those from Morocco, have made a vital contribution to this process. In those countries pilgrimages and the veneration of saints were a significant part of the culture, shared by Jews and Muslims.

Anyone who was raised in that culture and who believes in the power of the *tsadik* and in his ability to aid in alleviating hardship, cannot live without it, and bequeaths his beliefs to his children. As the ethnic identity of members of the Oriental Jewish communities in Israel has become stronger, and their self-confidence greater, so too has their desire to return to the old tradition of venerating the graves of *tsadikim;* this includes people who are not drawn to it out of religious piety but are attracted by mysticism or the need to draw from it consolation or strength in the face of life's difficulties.

In the fifties and sixties the location and "redemption" of holy men's graves was in the hands of the religious establishment—especially the Ministry of Religions—and of Ashkenazi Haredi groups. They based their activity on ancient traditions of prostration before the graves of *tsadikim* and on extensive literature going back thousands of years. However, the *hilulah* (as the celebration held beside the graves of *tsadikim* at set times is called) of the fifties and sixties was nothing compared with the frequent massive gatherings that take place today at hundreds of *tsadikim*'s graves. According to an official list, issued by a group known as the Foundation of the World and appended to a book published by the Ministry of Defense, there are more than 500 Jewish holy places and sacred graves in Palestine (including the Occupied Territories).[10] Many of these, albeit not the majority, are former Muslim sites.

MYSTICISM

The importance of the mystical, nonritualistic aspect of the cult of the graves of the *tsadikim* is pointed out in *The Mysticism of the Holy Land.* This book, whose author's name is not indicated, provides its readers with answers to questions such as the following:

> Where should one pray if the wife is barren? To which grave should a man make a pilgrimage when looking for a spouse? Where does one immerse him/herself to exorcise the evil eye? Where should one pray at the new moon to purify the soul? Which are the places where one prays for a miracle and is healed by heaven?[11]

This handy work, "which sets forth the virtues of each and every place according to tradition," is not a religious book but a guidebook for mystics.

Among other places, the book mentions Deir al-Sheikh, a shrine named after Sheikh Badir, in an abandoned Muslim village in the Judean Hills. "The sheikh's grave is also sacred to the Jews, some of whom go there to pray, especially concerning matters of livelihood." [12] Those who pray there—and they are Jews exclusively, because there are no Muslims left in the vicinity—are not aware that they are seeking the sacred intercession of Sultan Badir, a distant forebear of Haj Amin al-Husseini, the notorious grand mufti of Jerusalem during the Mandatory period. This Muslim saint, a descendent of the prophet Muhammad, came to the country from Iraq during the Crusades. At first he made his home in a small village near Jerusalem, where he performed miraculous deeds and fathered two daughters (who, along with a granddaughter, were also saints). Sheikh Badir was forced to leave his home and took up residence in a cave in the hills, where he was buried after his death. His daughter Badriyya is buried in Sharafat, near Jerusalem, and is venerated by the residents of the area for being able to render assistance in time of drought. According to this guidebook for mystics, the grave of Abu al-Hija (chapter 5) is also sacred to Jews for reasons that are unclear, since no one confuses the Kurdish commander with any Jewish personality.

But Arab folk saints do not have a monopoly on miracle-working. Over Harod's Spring in the Jezreel Valley is situated the burial cave of Yehoshua Hankin (1864–1945) and his wife, Olga. This legendary "redeemer of land," who was personally responsible for the acquisition of approximately a third of all the land purchased by Jews in Palestine (over 600,000 *dunams*), could never have imagined that his grave would become a place of pilgrimage for the barren women of the area. The women who ask miracles of him have no idea who this "saint" buried on the slopes of Mount Gilboa is. As the saying goes, "No one checks under the grave" when seeking the intercession of one (whoever he or she may be) whom God has endowed with the ability to perform miracles.

Tawfik Canaan explains that many local Muslim saints were village elders or heads of families who had displayed supernatural traits while still living. Their powers did not vanish with their death; on the contrary, the fame of these community elders increased because the soul—

source of all greatness—had been liberated from the bonds of the physical body, going on living and seeing what is happening around it. Hence the *fallahin* used to visit the graves of their elders to discuss their troubles and ask for assistance, to swear allegiance to the family, and to entrust possessions to the elder's spirit for safekeeping. "Human beings have always felt the great distance between them and God," writes Canaan. "Thus mediators arose, who were slowly raised to superhuman rank . . . and the conditions for becoming a *wali* became easier. Once having left the rigid path of orthodoxy, popular worship drifted into superstition." This need, which attracted the Muslim worshiper to the grave of Sheikh Badir, also motivates the Jewish women who visit the same site to request the same assistance and mediation. Except that the Muslim woman no longer goes there: she was uprooted from her home, and her daughters for the most part have forgotten the ancient traditions. As early as 1927, Tawfik Canaan wrote that the popular traditions regarding saints' graves were on the wane, and that "it is at present decidedly more difficult to gather genuine folklore material than it was about 1900."

Palestinian-Israeli geographer Shukri ʿArraf made an effort to gather information on the graves of Muslim saints.[13] But it appears that it did not reach many people, nor is particular attention devoted to the preservation of such folk traditions in Muslim circles and institutions in Israel. Popular religion, which was thriving before 1948 and was rooted so deeply in the physical and human landscapes, almost vanished with their destruction. Orthodoxy, which took the place folk religion had occupied among the Muslims of Israel, by and large has rejected the cult of the saints' graves. The Islamic Movement in Israel regards this popular religion as a form of superstition and a violation of the commandments of the prophet Muhammad, who absolutely forbade the sanctification of any grave. There is no need for a mediator between the human being and God, say the Islamic leaders, and in their capacity as the spiritual teachers of hundreds of thousands of Muslims in Israel, they do not promote the traditions of popular religion. Therefore, local folklore is increasingly being forgotten and the memory of local saints' graves is being lost. It is ironic that all this knowledge was collected by Israeli scholars. Nevertheless, pilgrimages are still being made to saints' graves in Israel that have remained under the control of the Muslim religious establishment. The largest of these are in Ramla (Nabi Salah), Herzliyya (Sayyidna ʿAli, al-Haram), and Kawkab al-Hija.

The Muslim religious establishment has not taken steps to prevent the appropriation of Muslim sites by the Jews, although activists from the Islamic Movement do fight for the preservation of abandoned places of worship, such as mosques and cemeteries (see later discussion). Perhaps this, too, is an expression of the weakness of the Arab minority in Israel and of the discrimination they face.

POLITICAL ASPECTS

The cult of saints' graves and the jurisdiction over them were never simply religious-traditional matters; they have always been political as well. Muslim rulers made extensive use of the graves of saints when battling the Crusaders. The fear of a renewed Christian invasion caused the Ayyubide and Mamluk sultans—particularly Ruqn al-Din Baybars—to "discover" or establish saints' graves in strategic locations (on the Coastal Plain and in the Jerusalem area) and to organize mass pilgrimages to them. The time for the pilgrimage to Nabi Musa (the grave of Moses) near Jericho was purposely fixed for the week preceding the celebrations of the Christian Easter. The festival of Nabi Musa (and, to a lesser degree, those of Nabi Salah in Ramla, Nabi Hisham in Gaza, and Nabi Rubin) were massive events that brought together people from far-flung parts of the country and contributed to their feeling of belonging to the Palestinian-Arab nation. During the British Mandate, the concentration of tens of thousands of Muslims in Jerusalem for the opening of the Nabi Musa festival served as an opportunity for anti-Jewish incitement, culminating more than once in serious bloodshed.

The nationalization of the saints' graves, which made them property of the State of Israel guarded by its army, began in the early days of the state. In a campaign that aroused doubts at the time, the Ministry of Religions set up dozens of "holy places" in dubious locations, which over time became famous pilgrimage sites. Following the Six-Day War there was blatant involvement of the Israeli army—via the Military Rabbinate and those serving in it, in the takeover of graves sacred to Muslims in the Occupied Territories, in cases where there were preexisting traditions of Jewish holiness. In most cases the Muslims were not expelled from the sites but were required to free space for a Jewish presence, sometimes permanently. The most blatant examples are Joseph's tomb in Nablus, the grave of Samuel the Prophet near Jerusalem, and the patriarchs' graves in Hebron.

HEBRON

Although the affair of the Jewish takeover of the patriarchs' graves ("the Cave of Machpelah") in Hebron is an exceptional case, the dynamic it exemplifies may shed light on the danger inherent in the religious and national clash over control of sacred graves. Since the thirteenth century there had been a prohibition against visits by non-Muslims to the graves of the patriarchs and matriarchs in Hebron (Abraham, Isaac, Jacob, Sarah, Leah, and Rebecca). According to an ancient custom, Jews were allowed to ascend only seven steps and to peek through a chink in the wall into the magnificent Herodian structure that houses the Haram Ibrahimi Mosque, with the sacred burial caves in its basement.

Immediately following the occupation of Hebron in June 1967, the Israeli military authorities allowed Jews to visit the site, whose sanctity, in their eyes, fell only slightly short of that of the Temple Mount in Jerusalem. Detailed and complicated arrangements were soon in place to determine periods when Jews were permitted to visit, and these were set so as not to encroach on times of Muslim prayer, during which the whole building was closed to Jews. Incessant pressure by religious bodies and by political parties with representation in the Israeli cabinet led to Jews' being permitted to conduct public prayers inside the mosque for the first time, on the Yom Kippur following the war, despite vigorous protests by the Muslim authorities. Ever since, the struggle over the patriarchs' graves has followed an unchanging and repetitive pattern: the establishment of faits accomplis by the Jews, which receive the approval of the military authorities retroactively, leading to new claims. First the Jews demanded the right to bring a Holy Ark into the mosque and received permission to do so in 1971. Subsequently a permanent place was fixed for the ark in "the Abraham Hall," which thus became a full-fledged synagogue. In 1975 a formal arrangement was made, allotting the Jews exclusive use of two halls and the inner courtyard between them. Then the battle commenced over "the Isaac Hall"—the main hall of the mosque—and here, too, the Jews succeeded in obtaining permission to pray on the Sabbath and Jewish holidays in most of the hall. On these holidays, Jewish worshipers had control over three-fourths of the building.

The struggle over the graves of the patriarchs has been accompanied by fierce clashes and bloodshed that reached a climax in 1994, when a Jewish settler opened fire on Muslim worshipers during prayers, killing twenty-nine. The military authorities, who had been involved at all stages of the struggle, and who had given in time after time to Jewish demands, then turned the entire building into a fortified military installation. Without a doubt the Israeli army officer "commanding" the Machpelah Cave fills a role the likes of which can be found only in the Middle Ages.

"REDEPLOYMENT"

The graves of holy men are also the subject of international agreements. In the 1995 Interim Agreement between Israel and the Palestinians, mention is made of the status of graves sacred to Jews in the territories that were to be handed over to the Palestinian Authority (i.e., those in Area A). According to the agreement, "The present situation and the existing practices shall be preserved" (Article V, b). It should be recalled that the "present situation," defined in the agreement as "the Jewish religious nature of such sites," is one that was created since the Jewish takeover of the sites after 1967.

In 1997, when Israel was required to implement an additional withdrawal ("redeployment") in the West Bank, extensive use was made of the "danger of handing over the revered holy places to the unclean [i.e., the Palestinians]," as huge handbills plastered on walls in the streets of Jerusalem proclaimed. "At this time a threat is hovering over the grave of Joshua and other monuments to the *tsadikim* . . . which are about to be handed over, heaven forbid, to the Palestinians, and they have already damaged some of these places," read one handbill. "It is incumbent upon every Jew to do a charitable deed for Joshua and the rest of the world's *tsadikim,* by participating in mass prayers, and organized trips to their graves." A footnote stated, "To the many who ask: there is no doubt regarding the location of these places as set out in the ancient books." (The note goes on to cite many rabbis, from the twelfth century C.E. onward.)

It goes without saying that the "unclean" Muslims venerate these sites; they built them, and they have been making pilgrimages to them for more than a thousand years. The Israeli government adopted a similar approach toward the treatment of Jewish sites, and consequently on "the map of national interests" indicating which areas of the West Bank "shall not be handed over to the Palestinians in the Permanent Settlement," all of these holy graves are marked. Sultan Muhammad the Second, conqueror of Constantinople, and their Most Catholic Majesties Ferdinand and Isabella, conquerors of Granada, would have understood the Jewish rulers' position.

MOSQUES

Every village used to have its own saint's grave, and in many of them there was more than one holy site; however, as Canaan states, this was not "the place of worship approved by orthodoxy." The place of gathering for the purpose of public prayer was the village mosque, if the population was Muslim, or the village church, if it was Christian. As mentioned previously, there were mosques in most of the villages and churches in all of the Christian villages. Some of the mosques were very ancient, among them those that had been built on the sites of medieval Christian churches. Many others were built in the 1920s and 1930s with full or partial funding from the Waqf Administration of the Supreme Muslim Council, which also paid the salaries of the *imam*s and other religious functionaries. According to a report compiled in 1939, that year the Supreme Muslim Council financed the repair of 313 run-down mosques and built 21 new mosques and three minarets. In addition, villagers built many mosques with their own money. Every large village had at least one mosque, and in smaller villages prayer services were held in the prayer hall adjacent to the sheikh's tomb. The mosques in many of the villages were modest structures, and only a small minority had minarets.

According to data culled from Palestinian sources, the number of mosques in villages abandoned during the 1948 War approached 140; that is, there were no mosques in at least half of the villages.[14] Of those mosques, about 100 were completely demolished when the villages themselves were leveled. According to findings in the field, some 40 mosques have not been torn down but are currently in an advanced stage of deterioration and neglect, or are being used by Jewish residents for purposes other than those for which they had been erected. It is worth stressing once again that we are dealing here with rural communities only and not with the Arab towns that were abandoned—where there were many places of worship, both Muslim and Christian, that will not be described here.

The Christian churches met a better fate, both because many of the Christian villages were not harmed and because some of the rural churches (and of those erected at sites sacred to Christianity) were built and maintained by non-Arab church bodies and were therefore under the protection of organizations with whom Israel feared to enter into conflict. Even so, six village churches are now deserted and crumbling (excluding those in Birʿim and Iqrit, which were eventually renovated by the villagers who had been evicted from these villages).

It is impossible to discern a pattern that might explain why mosques in certain villages were destroyed, whereas those in neighboring villages were left standing, even though the houses were bulldozed or blown up. It may have had something to do with the fact that the mosques that were left were large, impressive structures, and that those responsible for their demolition spared them for aesthetic reasons or because tearing them down would have required exceptional effort. One way or the other, these buildings commemorate a Palestinian cultural landscape that has been otherwise eradicated.

The bare statistics are that twenty mosques are currently in various stages of deterioration and decay; six are being used as living quarters, sheep-pens or stables, carpentry shops, or storehouses; six have been or are at present serving as museums, bars, or tourist sites of some sort; four are being used wholly or in part as synagogues; and two have been partially renovated for Muslim worship, but that use has been either prohibited or restricted.

Zakariyya

Some of the dilapidated, abandoned mosques are located in the midst of Jewish settlements that were built on the ruins of Arab villages. At Moshav Zakariyya, not far from Beit Shemesh in the Shephelah, stands the neglected building of the village mosque, within which is located the grave of Zachary (see later discussion). The large structure, which possesses a square minaret and is built partly of crudely cut stone and partly of ancient dressed stones taken from an earlier structure, now stands exposed to the elements. The prayer hall is strewn with scrap metal and piles of trash, the inner walls are crumbling and filthy, and the outer walls and surroundings are overgrown with weeds. Near the mosque stands a two-story building built of cut stone, which used to belong to al-Haj Younis, the *mukhtar* of the village, and two other houses that were not destroyed. That is all that remains of a village whose population in 1948 was approximately 1,200.

Zakariyya is an ancient settlement site, which already existed in the Roman and Byzantine periods, and is even indicated on a sixth-century

Madaba map. Following the Arab conquest, the Muslims adopted the Christian tradition whereby it was designated as the burial place of Zachary, father of John the Baptist. Zachary is considered one of the most important saints in Islam, on the same level as his son John (Yihya) and Jesus ('Isa), and there are many Muslim traditions regarding him. According to one, Zachary died a martyr's death: he escaped into a hollow tree trunk that opened to receive him, but a flap of his clothing remained outside. The tree was sawn through, and he was killed. Eventually Jews began attributing the name and the site to the Old Testament prophet Zecharia (the Hebrew form of Zachary), and that is how it appears in Israeli tour guidebooks. One testimony to the antiquity of the place is the fact that in the immediate vicinity are the graves of four additional Muslim saints, among them one holy woman, "al-Sayaha" (the wanderer).

The Jewish settlement at Zakariyya was founded on 29 June 1950, exactly twenty days after the last of the Muslim villagers had been evicted. Some 150 had remained after the occupation of the village in late October 1948, when most of its inhabitants had fled. Benny Morris quotes an Israeli commander who wrote in his report: "There are many good houses in the village, and it will be possible to settle new immigrants there";[15] indeed, the exchange of populations was executed at top speed.

Maliha, Ein Karem

The new residents of Zakariyya had no use for a mosque. Similarly, the Jewish inhabitants of al-Maliha had no use for the mosque named for 'Omar Ibn al-Khattab, conqueror of Jerusalem (638 C.E.), in the center of that village. The impressive structure, above which rises a round minaret, situated at the top of a hill that has become a densely populated West Jerusalem Jewish neighborhood (see plate 15)—stands partially empty and partially used as living quarters. The magnificent late-nineteenth-century mosque of the village of Ijzim (see plate 16) is in dire straits. Straggly weeds are growing up in its archway-encircled courtyard. Efforts by the village's former residents, who had been exiled to the neighboring village of Furaydis, to weed the yard and to shore up the tumbledown walls were thwarted by the inhabitants of Moshav Kerem Maharal. The fate of the large mosque in the village of Ein Karem (today also a West Jerusalem neighborhood) was somewhat better. After serving for a few years after the war as a school for Jewish children and later as an art gallery, it is now empty and closed. Crude graffiti have been scrawled on its inner walls, and part of the floor was pulled up. The outside walls and polygonal minaret, however, are well preserved. After all, the site is located in the midst of an area much frequented by tourists; at the foot of the structure lies "Mary's Well," which is sacred to Christians, and the Israeli authorities are fastidious about its maintenance. The mosque in the Bosnian village of Caesarea—situated on the Mediterranean coast, within the walls of the excavated and restored Crusader town—faired similarly. It was built in the 1880s by Muslim refugees from Bosnia, and the minaret's Balkan style of architecture is obvious. For the most part the village was dismantled, but the buildings surrounding the mosque were renovated and turned into a restaurant, bar, and souvenir shops. In the early 1980s the prayer hall of the mosque (where the Ottoman governor of Caesarea, ʿAli Beq, is buried) was converted, too, to serve as part of the restaurant. This inappropriate use of the sanctuary aroused widespread protest, as a result of which it was closed off and now stands empty, although the restaurant owners have not given up their intent to turn it into a recreation spot. The village mosque in Ein Hod (see plate 17) is still being used as a restaurant and bar, despite the protests of Arabs who live nearby.

Khalsa, Wadi Hunayn

The mosque of al-Khalsa, one of the few structures that remain of that Galilee Arab village, is situated in a municipal park in the older section of the Jewish town of Kiryat Shemona. It serves as the local museum dedicated to the memory of townspeople who have fallen in Israel's various wars. The large mosque in the village of Wadi Hunayn (near Nes Ziona) was transformed into the General Synagogue Geulat Yisrael. The beautiful, spacious building, under its capacious dome, was built in the 1930s for the use of the villagers, who had settled there during the Mandatory period. They found their livelihood working in the citrus groves of the long-established Jewish village of Nes Ziona (founded in 1884) and those of Arab effendis who had established farms and luxurious homes in the vicinity. The good relations between the Jewish and Arab settlements located on opposite sides of the main highway to the south did not prevent the flight of the Arab villagers, apparently in April 1948. Some time after they left, the mosque was taken, its minaret pulled down, and the crescent symbol on top of the dome replaced by a menorah. The mihrab (prayer niche) was covered by a marble tablet bearing the engraved names of Nes Ziona residents who fell in the 1948 War. Only a protuberance in the middle of the southern outer wall—the exterior of the niche—reveals the building's original identity.

Yazur

Not far from Nes Ziona, on the site of the village of Yazur, lies the venerated grave of Imam ʿAli, a famous miracle-worker whose grave is purported to be located in another dozen places as well. But the Yazur site, a massive building whose large central dome is encircled by nine smaller ones, is most widely held to be the actual burial site of Imam ʿAli, whose tomb is almost the sole monument left in this large village (population approximately 4,000). Two or three broken gravestones remain in the adjoining Muslim cemetery, which now serves as a dump for "yard trash only." The tomb building now houses the Shaʿarei Zion Synagogue and a seminary for Orthodox Jews (see plate 22). On the roof, beside the domes, a satellite dish has been installed to receive live religious broadcasts. Across the road, in the Yazur industrial park, is located yet another Muslim holy site, this one deserted and falling to pieces.

Yahud

In the heart of the town of Yahud (see earlier discussion), only the minaret of the village mosque is still intact—and thoroughly reinforced. The reason becomes clear when one reads the commemorative plaque affixed beside it, which states: "This tower was the lookout post of the IZL (or 'Irgun') unit that defended Yahudiyya. On 11 June 1948, reinforced enemy forces attacked and captured the village. In this place two fighting-women of the Irgun fell . . . one while in the lookout post high in the tower." The Arab village of Yahudiyya (ʿAbbasiyya) was captured by the IZL on 4 May 1948 and its inhabitants had fled. The Jewish forces held the village for five weeks and were routed on 11 June in an Arab counterattack (as commemorated on the plaque). Finally, on 10 July, Yahudiyya was retaken by the Jews, and later that year it was repopulated with new Jewish immigrants. Thus did the minaret of the mosque become a "lookout tower," and the Arab village abandoned in battle—a Jewish settlement that had courageously defended itself against "enemy forces"—all in the space of five weeks. Indeed, the Judaization of Yahudiyya was an amazingly speedy process—as was the rewriting of its history—and the village holy places were preserved only because of the consequent admixture of Jewish content—both religious and heroic.

In the town of Shlomi, built on the ruins of the village of al-Bassa, stand two abandoned and partially ruined churches. A Jewish farmer pens his sheep in the village mosque and also cultivates the land that used to be al-Bassa's Muslim cemetery. Kibbutz Megiddo, located near the remains of the large village of Lajjun, at the mouth of the Jezreel Valley—beside the ancient *tel* (Armageddon)—uses the village mosque as a carpentry shop; and we have yet to enumerate the many other mosques utilized as stables, cow barns, storehouses, and, in two or three cases, also as living quarters.

In some places the abandoned structures are all that is left standing once the rubble of the Arab village has been cleared away. One such mosque, that of the village of Umm al-Faraj, survived for fifty years, deserted, on the land of Moshav Ben Ami (today virtually a neighborhood of the town of Nahariya). The Arab villagers who prayed there were evicted from their homes during Operation Ben Ami (21 May 1948) but infiltrated back to their village the following February. When they "annoyed" the Jewish settlers who had taken over their land, they were expelled once more in October of that year, and all the buildings in the village, except the mosque, were torn down and the rubble cleared away. In the summer of 1997 the displaced villagers were informed that the moshav's inhabitants had completed a plan to construct several dozen homes in the area and expected to be tearing down the mosque. The villagers clashed with the members of Moshav Ben Ami, and the police intervened. Once the Arabs had been ejected, the *moshavnik*s took a bulldozer and swiftly flattened the mosque and disposed of its wreckage.

Ghabisiyya

Not far away, on a hill three kilometers from Umm al-Faraj/Ben Ami, stands the large mosque of Ghabisiyya. Its fate is well documented and can serve as evidence of how the Israeli authorities treat the remains of abandoned mosques and of the Muslim community's efforts to renovate them. After the village of Ghabisiyya was occupied by the Israeli army in May 1948 (see chapter 4), some of those who stayed and became Israeli citizens were evicted three times (despite a Supreme Court order stating that their eviction was not legal) and found refuge in neighboring villages. They set up a committee whose principal activity was to try to renovate the village mosque and cemetery, which were left standing after all the houses were blown up in 1955. In July 1972 the committee wrote to the prime minister:

> In the village a mosque and the cemetery remain. . . . The mosque is in a rundown state and the cemetery, where our relatives are buried, is neglected and overgrown with weeds to such an extent that it is impossible to identify the graves any more. Knowing that our state authorities have always taken care of the places of worship and cemeteries of all the ethnic communities, . . . [we ask] to be enabled to carry out repairs on the mosque and also to repair and fence the cemetery and put it in order.[16]

The authorities did not permit this work to be done.

It is apparent from reading the correspondence on this matter that the government—represented by the Israel Lands Administration (ILA), in whose name the village land had been acquired under one of the laws regarding land expropriation, and not the Ministry of Religion, which is responsible for holy places—was interested in making use of the villagers' petition as a way of obtaining their recognition of the legality of the expropriation of the mosque. A letter from the ILA outlined the following conditions: the displaced villagers were to compose "a letter emphasizing that [they] recognize that the property under discussion is owned by the Administration." The displaced residents' committee would be permitted "only to whitewash [the mosque] and to repair the fallen stone" at their own expense, and then "the building will be sealed." In other words, they would be barred from praying there.

The massive building and its courtyard were no longer safeguarded against intruders and had, in fact, become a shelter for shepherds and their herds. In 1994 members of the committee began renovating the mosque and praying there. In January 1996 the ILA sealed the entrance to the mosque, but the villagers broke through the fence and again used the mosque for prayers. After they appealed to Prime Minister Shimon Peres in April 1996, requesting that he allow them to pray in their mosque, they received a response from one of Peres's aides, on the prime minister's behalf: "The government of Israel regards itself as obligated to maintain the holy places of all religions, including, of course, cemeteries and mosques sacred to Islam. The prime minister has stated to the heads of the Arab community, with whom he recently met, that the government would see to the renovation and the restoration of the dignity of mosques in the abandoned villages, including the mosque in Ghabisiyya."[17]

Shimon Peres was defeated in the prime ministerial elections before he had a chance to keep his promise. In March 1997 a large contingent of police surrounded the property. Representatives of the ILA removed copies of the Qurʾan and prayer rugs and once again sealed the entrance to the mosque. The village residents pitched a protest tent outside the mosque, but the tent was dismantled. The conflict was carried to the courts in Acre, where the uprooted villagers petitioned to be allowed to pray in the mosque, contending that the government's actions were contrary to the Law of Preservation of Holy Places because they constituted a denial of freedom of worship and of the right of free access to and use of holy places. The government representative challenged the right of the displaced villagers to pray there, going so far as to dispute the fact that the building had ever served as a mosque. "I attempted to verify," wrote an ILA official, "whether indeed there had been a mosque there in the past, and one of the oldest inhabitants of the village told me that what we were talking about was the Sheikh's home and not a mosque." [18] The illegal evictions of 1951 and the demolition of the village in 1955 were used to bolster the government's position: "The village of Ghabisiyya was abandoned by its inhabitants and destroyed during the War for Independence," declared the government representative. The building (i.e., the mosque) had stood "lonely and neglected," "and since it was in a run-down and unstable state that constituted a threat to the safety of those inside it, it was decided by the Ministry of Religions to seal it and fence it off." An additional reason for the government's actions: "the preservation of the above-mentioned mosque, so that it would not be wide open to all sorts of illegal acts that might violate its sanctity." The villagers' prayers were apparently one such act, since "the[ir] visits to the place are essentially a consequence of political organizing and not of religious motivation." These visits were defined by the state's representative as "quasi-squatting," a term that hints at risks to security and certainly at the fact that this would constitute "a precedent for agreement to the return of the refugees." The court declined to issue an injunction permitting the worshipers to go back to praying in the mosque in the interim, expressing doubts regarding whether the matter fell within its purview at all, or was "unadjudicable." The Ghabisiyya villagers still pray in the field outside the sealed mosque.

The prime minister's promise applied not only to mosques but also to cemeteries "sacred to Islam." And if it was not kept as regards mosques, Muslim cemeteries fared no better. Indeed, there is no way to describe the state of these cemeteries other than as so shameful that in any other country it would have aroused a widespread uproar (see plate 19).

CEMETERIES

There was a cemetery in nearly every Arab village, and their location and the area they covered is easy to determine from Mandatory maps. Of the hundreds of Muslim cemeteries extant before 1948, vestiges of only about forty are still discernible. The others have disappeared, either because their gravestones have turned to rubble or because their land has been used for roads, agricultural development, or the construction of institutions or homes.

The al-Aqsa Association for the Preservation of Consecrated Islamic Property, whose headquarters are located in the town of Umm al-Fahm, is battling, without much success, to preserve these cemeteries. From time to time serious confrontations take place between Israeli bodies—public or private—bent on using the cemeteries and activists from the association, intent on preventing such use. In 1997, bulldozers leveling ground for the construction of a school building in the Jewish city of Netanya uncovered traces of the cemetery of the village of Umm Khalid, which was destroyed in 1948. The Association's request that work be halted was not heeded until it petitioned the High Court of Justice. As a consequence of the petition, the city of Netanya agreed to halt work in the area that had not yet been damaged and to put up a sign announcing, "Here is the Muslim cemetery of the village of Umm Khalid." The Muslims refused to accept the suggestion that the area be turned into a park, saying, "No foot shall tread on the graves."

In a posh section of Herzliyya, across from the American ambassador's residence, lies the holy site consecrated to Sayyidna ʿAli, and beside it the cemetery of the abandoned village of al-Haram. A Jewish resident whose house sits on the border of the cemetery did not hesitate to send in a bulldozer "to dispose of the hill that obscured his view of the sea from the window of his villa," the hill on which the Muslim cemetery was situated. Activists from the al-Aqsa Association have been unsuccessfully confronting bulldozer-drivers for years. These confrontations occur over and over in many locations, and their outcome is plainly seen: shattered tombstones scattered over the burial site, numerous open graves, and human bones rolling around.

ʿIzz a-Din al-Qassam

The most well known abandoned cemetery is located in the large village of Balad al-Sheikh near Haifa, now the town of Nesher. Its reputation stems from the fact that it is the burial place of Sheikh ʿIzz a-Din al-Qassam, perhaps the most famous hero of the Palestinian national movement. For many Palestinians the sheikh is the embodiment of self-sacrifice, courage, and persistence in the armed struggle against the British regime and the Zionist movement. ʿIzz a-Din al-Qassam is regarded by Israelis as a vile murderer, the leader of a gang of terrorists who killed innocent Jews. This impression was reinforced by the fact that the murderous suicide-terrorist gangs of Hamas were named ʿIzz a-Din al-Qassam for their hero, sixty years after his death.

The sheikh, who preached in the mosques of Haifa, led terrorist raids on Jewish settlers in the Jezreel Valley from 1930 onward, while at the same time fulfilling his religious function and his role as political leader. "Nothing will save us but our weapons," he preached, and early in November 1935 he set out from Haifa for the hills of Samaria at the head of a band of young Arabs, bent on establishing a base for guerrilla operations against the British and the Zionists. The British quickly tracked him down, and on 21 November killed the sheikh and several of his men in battle.

The funeral of ʿIzz a-Din al-Qassam turned into a tempestuous nationalist demonstration in which his martyrdom was extolled in contrast to the cowardice of the leaders of the Palestinian national movement, "those who fear death and the gallows and are sunk up to their necks in chatter," as he called them. His grave became a pilgrimage site, and the sheikh's wishes were fulfilled a short time after his death: late in April 1936 an Arab revolt broke out that was to last three years.

Balad al-Sheikh was captured toward the end of April 1948. Its inhabitants fled, and late that same year the village was repopulated with new immigrants. Whereas many of the houses have survived to this day, the Muslim cemetery was neglected, and numerous gravestones were vandalized. This cemetery, like many other Muslim burial grounds, was owned by the Muslim Waqf. Most Waqf property in Israel was expropriated under the Absentee Property Law (giving rise to the sarcastic quip—"Apparently God is an absentee") and afterward handed over to the Development Authority, ostensibly because this was necessary to prevent its being neglected, but actually so as to make it possible to sell it. Only about one-third of Muslim Waqf property, principally mosques and graveyards that were currently in use, was not expropriated. In 1956 its administration was turned over to the Board of Trustees of the Muslim Waqf, which by then was made up of collaborators appointed by the authorities. These "trustees" would sell or "exchange" land with the ILA without any accountability to the Muslim community. Anger over these deeds led to acts of violence within that community, including assassinations.

In August 1970 a "trustee of the Haifa Waqf" reached an agreement with the government on the sale of the greater part of the cemetery in Nesher, including the tomb of Sheikh al-Qassam, to the ILA.[19] Ironically, this trustee's office was in the very mosque where Sheikh al-Qassam had preached, but he did not hesitate to sell the property, even though he knew that the ILA intended to use it for an industrial park. He even agreed to "move" the graves to another Muslim cemetery. This was not done, however, and the sheikh's grave was renovated by the al-Aqsa Association in the late eighties. The fence that they erected around it to prevent vandalism was pulled down by the ILA time after time, and the grave was desecrated by bands of Jewish extremists but always restored.

In the early nineties, the small portion of the cemetery that remained in Muslim hands also came under threat when the municipality declared its intent to build a road through it. Negotiations between the municipality and representatives of the Muslim community concluded in an agreement according to which the road would be built on pylons, but that solution met with stiff opposition from the Jewish population, who regarded it as capitulation to the violence of "gangs of thugs from Umm al-Fahm." According to a leaflet disseminated by Concerned Citizens of Nesher and Its Surroundings: "With every desire to preserve the dignity of the Muslim minority in Israel and good relations with it, it cannot be that this goodwill shall be translated into the violent extortion of political gains." A right-wing organization placed a pig's head in the cemetery, arousing enraged reactions from the leadership of the Arab community, who warned of the danger of provoking "religious war," and brought words of condemnation from Prime Minister Benyamin Netanyahu. The problem was that the grave of Sheikh al-Qassam was not located in the disputed territory at all, and the plan to "move" the grave and use the area for an industrial park (on the basis of the 1970 agreement) has not been shelved. During the winter of 1998, the monumental gate to the cemetery was destroyed by the elements. The fallen stones, bearing the inscription "Everyone on earth perishes" (Qur'an, Sura 55:26), are scattered about.

"The pressures of development and of the needs of the population" have been used as an excuse for the destruction of many abandoned Muslim cemeteries and for rezoning the land where they were located. The Israeli authorities justify their actions on the grounds that "Islamic Law allows the designation of a piece of land as a cemetery to be altered" and permits it to be used for any other purpose once forty years have passed since the last burial performed there, provided that a *fatwa* (religious order by a Muslim clergyman) is issued to that effect. They also point to precedents of the Muslims themselves having done so on a few occasions. Activists from the Islamic Movement deny the Israeli claim, contending that it is inadmissible from a religious point of view; and indeed there is something self-serving in the arguments of both sides: the Israelis do not generally wait for a *fatwa* from a mufti, and in any case, cemeteries are not of interest to the clergy only; their significance extends far beyond the narrow religious context. They are a means of maintaining a hold on the land. Just as the Israelis are striving to eradicate them, the Arabs are endeavoring to preserve them: there is no stronger proof of roots than the graves of one's ancestors.

SANITIZED MONUMENTS

Other monuments to the Arab presence in the landscape have not been obliterated. Far from it: they are preserved, cared for, and mentioned on every map and in every guidebook for hikers, having first been "cleansed" of the identity of their former inhabitants, and their Arab-Muslim context having been sanitized. The most glaring examples are forts and khans (caravanserais), which dot the landscape. Scholars categorize these sites according to their association with one of the powers that ruled Eretz Israel/Palestine between the Middle Ages and the British Mandatory period. The country's archaeological chronology is arranged in periods named for its conquerors throughout the ages: the Roman, Byzantine, early Arab (or, reformulated to cleanse it of modern nationalist connotations, the "early Muslim"), Crusader, Mamluk, Ottoman, and British. These designations conceptualize the history of the country as that of its conquerors. The adoption of this system during the British Mandatory period was typical of the way in which European colonial powers strove to make the history of their colonies fit into familiar contexts, while paying no attention to events and periods of special significance to the lands they occupied.

Israeli historians, in turn, made their own changes in this chronology so as to emphasize the Jewish connection to the land, adding designations such as the biblical, Hasmonean, Mishnaic, and Talmudic periods. From the "early Muslim" period onward, however, they adopted the nomenclature of the "conquerors' chronology," since in this way it was possible to divide the approximately 1,400 years of Muslim-Arab rule into units that were shorter than the period of Jewish rule over the Eretz Israel/Palestine (which lasted at most for 600 years), and especially to portray the history of the country as a long period of rule by a series of foreign powers who had robbed it from the Jews—a period that ended in 1948 with the reestablishment of Jewish sovereignty in Palestine. It was thus possible to obscure the fact that the indigenous Muslim Arab population was part and parcel of the ruling Muslim peoples and instead to depict the history of the local population—its internal wars, its provincial rulers, its contributions to the landscape—as matters lacking in importance, events associated with one or another dynasty of "foreign occupiers."

THE CONVENIENCE OF THE CRUSADES

The Crusader period provides a particularly convenient means of fostering this historical narrative. The Crusader occupation, which lasted for eighty-eight years in most of the country and some 200 in the coastal region, came between the early and late Arab (or Muslim) periods, and the plethora of ruins the Crusaders left throughout the land made it convenient to attribute imposing structures from both earlier and later periods to them, even when these had been built by others. The ascription of particular importance to the Crusader period and its contributions to the landscape does not contradict the Zionist narrative, since it is "neutral" in terms of the Arab-Jewish conflict over Eretz Israel/Palestine, and there is no fear that Christians might use their contributions to the country's landscape as a pretext for organizing a new Crusade for the "redemption" of the Holy Land. The truth of the matter is that Crusader structures in many cases represented a secondary use of sites dating back to an earlier period; more to the point, following the ouster of the Crusaders, they were utilized by the local population, who adapted them to their own requirements, expanded some parts, and tore down others.

Arab settlements that predated and outlasted the Crusader conquest have not been considered worthy of study or mention except in the context of "the Crusader period," an ascription that itself is often as not fabricated. In the Jerusalem Hills lie the remains of the village of Beit ʿAtab, formerly the capital of the Arqub district and seat of its ruler, Sheikh ʿOthman al-Lahaam. This sheikh conducted a bloody war against Sheikh Mustafa Abu Ghosh, whose capital and fortified seat was in the village of Suba. The long history of Beit ʿAtab and the tale of the wars of Quays and Yaman have been recounted at length in many books, and British consul James Finn (mid–nineteenth century) left a particularly vivid description of this village and its houses, both ancient and new. But there is no mention of any of this in Israeli guidebooks, save for the routine remark, "destroyed in the War for Independence." By contrast, the guidebook makes sure to inform its readers that "it is almost certain that its Arab name, Beit ʿAtab, is a corruption of its Latin name, Atap, meaning a small fortress," and that at the site there are "remains of ancient structures, apparently from a Crusader farm." The whole Crusader connection is a fabrication, since the sole historical mention of this settlement is a single reference to it in 1161 as a small village whose inhabitants are local people (i.e., not Crusaders). Nowhere is there any mention of its being a Crusader "fortress or farm," although its name appears (in a fractured Latin transliteration of its Arabic name) on a list of holdings—populated by Arabs—of a knight of Flemish origin. The mention of a place-name on a deed of ownership is sufficient data for its inclusion in the historical account, from the point of view of the conquerors, whereas the lives of generations of ordinary people who lived in Beit ʿAtab are of no importance and their material culture is dismissed as "primitive."

The "Crusader fortress" at Suba, the village of Beit ʿAtab's adversaries, was similarly immortalized in Israeli guidebooks. Suba—if it served as a Crusader stronghold (called Belmont) at all, the Crusader sojourn lasted no longer than fifty years—won most of its fame in the nineteenth century, when it was a base for the revolt of the *fallahin* against the Egyptian occupier, Ibrahim Pasha. Even so, the site of the abandoned village was cleared of the remnants of a thousand-year-old habitation stratum in order to draw attention to more ancient ruins, about which there is doubt regarding whether they were built by the Crusaders, but no doubt that they were refurbished and used by local Arabs. The whole site is designated as a "Crusader stronghold."

The report on an archaeological-historical survey conducted in the abandoned village of Qaqun boasts the title "Crusader Sites."[20] This survey proves that the routine association of monumental structures with the Crusaders is the accepted practice not only in guidebooks for the general public but also in research. The authors of the report describe the ancient ruins found in the wreckage of the abandoned village and identify them as "Crusader," even though in the body of the survey they cautiously state that "many early structural remnants . . . date from the Middle Ages and later periods." And indeed, according to historical sources, the Qaqun fortress, as well as a mosque, administrative center, and a large market, were built by the Mamluk sultan Ruqn al-Din Baybars between 1267 and 1271. It is impossible to differentiate between parts of the site that were Crusader and those that were Mamluk, since they were built in the same period, in the same architectural style, and of the same building materials. But this important detail did not discourage those who conducted the survey—and another scholar who contributed to the same volume—from classifying the site as a "Crusader stronghold."[21] The remains of "later periods," that is, of the inhabitants of the village of Qaqun, where Arab habitation was unbroken until 1948, were not deemed worthy of archaeological study.

The arbitrary designation of any especially massive structure as "Crusader" verges on the absurd in the case of Jidin Castle (on Kibbutz Yehiam), which was built by Sheikh Dahr al-ʿOmar al-Zaidani in the mid–eighteenth century. The sheikh, perhaps one of the greatest leaders to arise among the Arabs of Palestine, was neither Mamluk nor Ottoman but a Bedouin born in the Lower Galilee. He provoked the Ottoman authorities, occupied Acre (1749)—at the time a poor and rundown village—fortified it, took control of the entire northern section of the country, and built numerous fortresses, including Qalʿat Jidin. Within this large fortress are remnants of a small Crusader fort; nevertheless, the Israelis refer to Yehiam Castle (as Dahr al-ʿOmar's fortress is called today) as "a Crusader castle that was destroyed at the time of the Muslim conquest and partially reconstructed by Dahr al-ʿOmar."

The author of these lines, too, fell under the spell of the Crusader period while studying remnants of this period in the 1960s—and he, too, identified Arab castles as "Crusader." Some guidebooks still rely on his erroneous conclusions.

A few Israeli scholars describe the fortresses built by villagers during the great revolts of the 1820s and 1830s and correctly state the identity of their builders. Most of them, it is true, were only renovated by the *fallahin,* not built by them, but it is those renovated structures that have survived to this day. Many others "belonged to *sheikh*s or *mukhtar*s, who fortified their manors or built new fortresses for themselves. . . . *Mukhtar*s are still living in a few of these fortresses. In some, facilities such as oil presses and flour mills for public use were installed. The original character of others was lost and they became houses of prayer or sacred sites, and scores of them are scattered throughout Judea and Samaria"[22] and many of the abandoned villages in Israel. The identity of their builders and their renovators—local *fallahin* and their leaders—is not considered worthy of mention in Israeli guidebooks.

There is no better example of the eradication of all traces of an entire civilization from the landscape—leaving behind only Crusader remains, which did not interfere with the conveniently chosen historical narrative—than the restoration of Kokhav Hayarden (Kawkab al-Hawa, the Crusader Belvoir) and Caesarea. At those two sites the Arab structures were removed and the Crusader buildings were restored and made into tourist attractions. In the Israeli context, it is preferable to immortalize those who exterminated the Jewish communities of Europe (in the late eleventh and early twelfth centuries) and murdered the Jews of Jerusalem in 1099 than to preserve relics of the local Arab civilization with which today's Israelis must supposedly coexist. Crusader structures, both authentic and fabricated, lend a European, romantic character to the country's landscape, whereas Arab buildings spoil the myth of an occupied land under foreign rule, awaiting liberation at the hands of the Jews returning to their homeland. And if it is impossible to erase the physical remains, it is at least possible to ascribe them to someone else—"Crusaders, Mamluks, or Ottomans."

BEFORE QUEEN ANNE

Israeli historians, geographers, and archaeologists did not have a difficult job in sanitizing the landscape and ridding it of the identity of its former inhabitants because the British authorities had bequeathed to them a valuable legacy: the definition of an "antiquity" as "any construction or any product of human activity before the year 1700 A.D."[23] This definition, formulated at the time of the drafting of the Mandate for Palestine, appears in the Mandatory Antiquities Ordinance. It reflects the view prevalent in Britain during the twenties, according to which an object was considered an antiquity only if it had been produced before the death of Queen Anne in 1714.

This definition also suited European scholars, whose interest in the antiquities of the land was connected to the study of relics that might shed light on the biblical period. This interest in the Bible was shared by European and Zionist scholars (albeit for different motives), and these were the only ones active in archaeological research in Eretz Israel/Palestine. Palestinian archaeologists played a secondary role, and, as we have seen, Palestinian scholarship in the fields of anthropology and folklore was also quite meager. The continuous indigenous human activity during the three centuries since 1700 C.E. was not considered worthy of being investigated, recorded, preserved, or protected, since it was regarded as "recent" or "primitive," and in the eyes of the Zionists also as superfluous "background noise," which obstructed their national narrative.

Meanwhile, new thinking had evolved in Britain regarding the question of when the "past" ends. The conclusion reached was "that the past continues right up to the present," and thus all human activity that found expression in the creation of physical objects was entitled to respectful treatment. The definition of heritage and the imperative for its preservation prevalent among the British today is that "it is that which we inherited from God and past generations and which we should hand on, undiminished in quality and diversity, enriched by our own contribution—but not necessarily unchanged—to future generations."

British, American, and other academics engaged in the study of the archaeology and history of their former overseas colonies have begun to reevaluate the attitudes that prevailed during the colonial period. They have admitted to the grave distortions that were introduced into the history of the colonies as an outcome of Eurocentric attitudes, ignoring and erasing remaining traces of the natives' past and their material culture. In the wake of this reevaluation, Amerindian, Aborigine, and native African sites were studied and restored, and a new history was written, focusing on the organic chronicles of those regions, which had been a mere footnote to the history of the European peoples.

The Israelis, by contrast, chose to maintain the colonial tradition with only minor changes. The Israeli Antiquities Law, which in 1978 replaced the relevant Mandatory legislation, defines "an antiquity" as "an object, either detached or attached, which was made by a person prior to 1700 C.E., including anything added to it that constitutes an integral part of it" (Article 1). The change that was made in this definition, in the spirit of the times, was in Article 2, according to which an object made in 1700 or thereafter could be an antiquity if it "possessed historical value and the minister (of education) had declared it to be an antiquity."

There is no written definition of what constitutes "an object of historical value," and thus its definition is left exclusively in the hands of the minister of education, who is responsible for the implementation of this law. The Antiquities Administration is aware of only two sites in Old Jaffa: the "Biluim House" (the first home of this group of early Zionist pioneers in the country, in 1882) and the first building of the first Hebrew High School ("Gimnasiya Herzeliyya"), which have been declared "antiquities" in accordance with Article 2. Of course no structure "of historical value" to the Palestinians has been declared a protected antiquity under Israeli law. Since this is also how "archaeological sites" are defined, surveys for the mapping of ancient remains do not include the remnants of Arab villages or "the products of their human activity" after 1700 that are still extant. Such sites (if they are marked at all) appear in surveys under the category of "no antiquities on site." The ruins of villages are mentioned only when researchers have found remnants there that fall within the definition of antiquities. For example: "Shards from the Byzantine period as well as remnants of structures from the Ottoman period were found." Thus 300 years of human activity are erased, according to law and with the backing of most of the academic community. Many Israeli scholars are indeed interested in Arab settlements and in their history during recent centuries, but this academic interest cannot preserve the remnants themselves, which are steadily disappearing, neglected by the law and the state authorities. Nor have statutory provisions for their preservation, enacted for the maintenance or protection of sites of aesthetic value, succeeded in preventing their systematic destruction.

Albert Glock, an American archaeologist and founder of the Department of Archaeology of Bir Zayt University in the West Bank, wrote:

> If archaeology is the study of the materialization of human thought and action, then it is not bound by chronology. In other words, archaeology is not merely the study of what is old, though it certainly includes antiquity: instead archeology should attempt to correlate the adaptation of materials and space to human needs. Second, since the past is dead, it can be interpreted only by analogy with human experience. The valid experience is obviously that which is closest in both time and space to what one wants to interpret; in the case of Palestine, this brings us into the traditional [Arab] villages—just as I excavate backward through space and time, so I interpret backward from the known to the unknown.[24]

In Glock's opinion, this is the rationale of Palestinian archaeology, which differs from that of its European counterpart. This was, however, not simply an attempt to set nationalistic objectives for Palestinian archaeology in its struggle to compete with Israel's "committed" archaeology. Objects created by human beings—by any human being—in this land combine to form a rich and glorious cultural heritage that influences the lives and experience of all who live there. No one has the right to rewrite or erase parts of it. The destruction of the cultural landscape, whether material or conceptual, would turn against the destroyer, leaving him impoverished and rootless.

8

The Last Zionists

Al-Andalus (Andalusia), from which the Arabs were expelled 500 years ago, and Palestine, from which they were expelled 50 years ago, merge in the consciousness of many Palestinians in "a collective mourning over the lost paradise." "Andalus became a lost place," says poet Mahmoud Darwish, "then Palestine became Andalus; we lost Palestine just as we had lost Andalus." This comparison occurs widely in the poetry of the Palestinian popular struggle and has been frequently heard in public statements since 1948.

ANDALUS LOST

Darwish does not agree "that Palestine is the lost Andalus," because to him Palestine is not truly lost. And even "Andalus can be recovered," since it is actually a metaphor, and "can be here or there; anywhere," a universal object of the longings of "every exile on the face of the earth who has no other place, who has no meeting place."[1] Palestine is certainly not Andalus, since unlike in the case of Spain, the Arabs have not been exiled from Palestine totally but are still living in half of their villages in Israel and the Occupied Territories. But for those who have been exiled, the exile is complete, painful, and charged with nostalgia and the desire to return home, and their personal and literary expressions of their loss are similar to those voiced by their Spanish predecessors as expressed in the words of the Lebanese author Amin Maalouf:

> You see, Hasan, all those men still have, hung up on their walls, the key to their houses in Granada. Every day they look at it, and looking at it they sigh and pray. Every day their joys, their habits and a certain pride come back to their memory, and these things they will never rediscover in exile. The only reason for their existence is the thought that soon, thanks to the Great Sultan or to Providence, they will find their house once again, with the colour of its stones, the smell of its garden, the water of its fountain, all intact, unaltered, just as it has been in their dreams.[2]

This author is describing the feelings of the exiles from Andalusia, but his words echo the feelings of the Palestinian exiles living in the refugee camps of Tyre, Sidon, and Beirut to such a degree that they can be understood as allegorical. "Refugee families zealously guarded the keys to their houses . . . and the deeds to their land, like outcasts who cling to the memory of stolen honor," comments Danny Rubinstein, referring to Palestinian refugees of 1948.[3] The central ceremony in the marches commemorating fifty years to the *nakba* (the Palestine disaster) was the passing of the keys from the 1948 generation to their grandchildren. One man said to the crowd in the Deheisha refugee camp (near Bethlehem): "I am now close to death so it is now my responsibility to pass this key to my destroyed home and village onto the younger generation who will continue the struggle for our right to return." Children and grandchildren of refugees display Turkish or Mandatory title deeds, old tax receipts, weapon permits, birth certificates, reports on the hygienic condition of village schools, or even a receipt from a Jewish tradesman in Tel Aviv for payment "for repair of a cylinder from the motor of a pump"—a paper trail connecting them with "the dream of their garden."

The events marking the fiftieth anniversary of the *nakba* have focused on nurturing memories of the experience of loss and on the desire to return, but, as Palestinian spokespersons have stressed, with "expressions of pride and hope, and not of sorrow and sighing." Mahmoud Darwish delivered the official address at the central ceremony in Ramallah on 15 May 1998, in which he said:

> Today, as we confront half a century of Nakba and resistance, pained at the continuing tragedy of our recent past, we cast our sights to the future that we are molding in hope and in the promise of freedom and justice. For we have vanquished all attempts at our obliteration and denial and at the eradication of the name of Palestine from the map of Palestine. On the fiftieth anniversary of one of the greatest crimes of the age, committed against the gentle people and land of Palestine, we stand in reverence in the sight of the martyrs who had offered their lives as a libation to the continuity of the land and its

> immortal name, in defense of our identity and sovereign existence on our land—a land infused with the words of God to humanity as with our ancestral blood. . . .
>
> We do not seek to be captives of history or victims of the past. The Palestinian people have launched a redemptive journey to the future. From the ashes of our sorrow and loss, we are resurrecting a nation celebrating life and hope. We will not surrender. Nor will we lose faith in a just and genuine peace that will enable us to exercise our right to independence and sovereignty. Fifty years since the Nakba were not spent in grief over a painful memory. The past has not entirely departed, nor has the future entirely arrived yet. The present is an open potential to struggle. For 50 years, Palestinian history has stood witness to epics of perseverance and resistance, to confronting the implications, consequences and injustices of the Nakba. For half a century Palestinian history became a living pledge to future generations for their right to a life of freedom and dignity on their own land. We have begun painstakingly the nation-building process, to ensure a free homeland for a free people. The state of Palestine is returning to contemporary history after 50 years.[4]

In Ramallah, the Palestinians have constructed a large-scale model of a traditional Palestinian village that was destroyed in 1948. This model is indeed vital to the reinforcement of the collective memory of the Arab physical landscape, since it has almost entirely disappeared. And this evokes yet another comparison between Andalusia and Palestine: paradoxically, Muslim Andalusia has been preserved in the landscape of Spain more than has Arab Palestine in the landscape of Israel.

Five hundred years have passed since Sultan Abu Abdullah Sarir (known to the Spanish as Baobdil) turned his head for one last look at his city, Granada, which had fallen to the Christians. It is as if the sigh that escaped his lips at the sight of this lost paradise, immortalized by the Spanish as "the Moor's last sigh," became frozen in the Andalusian landscape. Were the sultan to return to life, he would have no difficulty finding his way around the countryside of his lost kingdom. Sufficient landmarks remain—villages, farms, castles, orchards, and even the ancient place-names—to preserve the outlines of Muslim Spain. Even the accelerated development that has taken place in Spain in recent decades—the construction of freeways and railway lines, of thousands of hotels, of factories and residential neighborhoods, and the widespread growth of suburbs—has not succeeded in eradicating the stamp of the Middle Ages from the landscape, primarily because the balance between old and new has been maintained, and the ancient scale has not been totally violated.

It is only with great difficulty that a Palestinian refugee born in Yazur, al-Birwa, or ʿAjjur can identify the landscape of his homeland after fifty years. A refugee from the village of Qaqun recounts: "When I went [there] to visit after 1967, I couldn't tell exactly where our house had been. I was only able to say approximately, that our house was located in a particular area, because there had been a large mulberry tree near the house." A refugee from the village of Beit ʿAtab determined the location of the school where he had studied by a clump of pine and eucalyptus trees that had been left standing on the otherwise bare hillside: he remembered how the teachers had brought saplings from a Mandatory government tree nursery and planted them in the school yard.

The identification of Arab villages became a botanical exercise. The silhouette of the village was preserved by cactus hedges, fruit trees growing wild, certain varieties of grasses and brambles that thrive in the ruins of inhabited sites, where the earth has been fertilized by human and animal waste. Geographer Shukri ʿArraf has lovingly catalogued the characteristic vegetation of the Palestinian countryside: cultivated or wild plants that served as signposts in a landscape from which the human element had disappeared. Sometimes the identification of a vanished village becomes possible only when the JNF endeavors to cover the ruins by planting forests of evergreen trees, and the foresters complain that "the natural plant life, that is, remnants of what the Palestinians had planted and what had grown up among the ruins—is choking out the newly planted saplings."

SCALE OF TRANSFORMATION

The destruction of villages per se was not the sole cause of the disappearance of the Palestinian landscape: statistics reflect the scale of its transformation in every measurable dimension. On the eve of the 1948 War, 1.9 million people inhabited Mandatory Palestine. Fifty years later their number has increased four and a half times, to 8.2 million souls (Jews and Arabs). Within the territory of the State of Israel, since the end of 1948 the population has grown nearly sixfold, not counting the Arabs who became refugees, and almost fourfold if they are included. A comparison of the physical data of consequence to the landscape makes it clear just how great this change has been. According to figures from the Mandatory census of 1931, in the villages that were later abandoned there were 52,000 dwelling units. To this number must be added those that were built between then and 1947. According to the data and calculations of the Mandatory government, in the entire rural Arab sector, an average of 4,000 dwelling units were built annually, of which 55 percent were in the villages later abandoned (this is the accepted figure among Palestinian scholars).[5] The total number of dwelling units that were abandoned in 1948 in the rural Arab sector comes to 75,000 to 80,000 at most (the sum is inflated by the fact that in that sector, the census reckoned one room as constituting a complete dwelling unit). According to my calculations, in the abandoned villages the entire built-up area actually in use amounted to no more than 50,000 *dunams,* or an average of about 100 *dunams* (25 acres) per village. For comparison's sake, this means that the combined built-up area of all the abandoned villages was equal in size to the municipal area of the medium-sized town of Hadera in the Sharon, whose population in 1996 was 63,000.

Moreover, the entire area of the Arab towns that were fully or partially abandoned was approximately 46,000 *dunams.* This included 3.5 million square meters of built-up area under Arab ownership, which, according to Mandatory government estimates, was equivalent to approximately 55,000 apartments, of which 85 percent (or approximately 46,000) were abandoned (a figure that matches estimates of the number of urban households that left their homes).[6] Hence the total number of homes that were abandoned, in both villages and towns during 1948–49, amounted to roughly 125,000.

The number of housing units constructed in Israel since 1948 comes to more than 1.6 million,[7] whereas some 125,000 apartments were built between 1948 and 1954 alone. That is, the sum total of abandoned Arab housing units amounts to approximately one-tenth of the number built in Israel in the course of the past fifty years. This vast difference in scale is also evident in the abandoned towns: the area of the pre-1948 Arab municipality of Acre was 1,500 *dunams;* in 1995 the Israeli city's municipal boundaries encompassed 12,000 *dunams,* 6,500 of them developed. Safad covered 1,050 *dunams* in 1948, whereas in 1995 its developed area alone amounted to 11,000 *dunams* (out of a total jurisdictional area of 29,000 *dunams*); in 1948 the area of Tiberias was 673 *dunams,* and in 1995 it was 6,642—all of it developed. In 1947 there were some 4,500 kilometers of roads in all of Eretz Israel /Palestine, 1,565 kilometers of them unpaved, whereas in 1996 there were some 15,000 kilometers of roads in Israel alone (excluding the Occupied Territories). In that same period, the population density increased from 43 to 261 per square kilometer.

Is it any wonder that these revolutionary changes (and I have not even touched on the industrialization, agricultural development, afforestation, laying of physical infrastructure, and other factors with impact on the landscape) completely obliterated the Arab landscape? It is now difficult, if not impossible, to reconstruct it without using the old maps, and these depict what is essentially an archaeological stratum whose significance, in many instances, it is possible to discover only after excavation of the ruins and collection of the artifacts.

ENFORCED MODERNIZATION

Palestinians regard comparisons between their sparsely developed landscape and the more heavily developed Israeli landscape built on its ruins as cynical and self-serving. They, too, would have been capable of development and prosperity were it not for the destruction of their world. The Palestinian disaster eliminated the agents of Palestinian modernization, that is, the populations of the Arab cities, who went into exile, taking with them all the implements that could have revolutionized the life of the Palestinian community. The shattered rural society that remained operated under limiting and discriminatory conditions: on the one hand, the agricultural economy that had formed its base was taken from it by the expropriation of the land; on the other, it was not allowed to develop as an independent sector; its farmers were turned into an unskilled labor force serving the Jewish sector. Making a show of Jewish modernity as opposed to Arab primitivity, then, borders on racism. "Someone who wants to see what free Arabs are capable of should compare [the Jewish town of] Netanya to Amman [capital of Jordan] and not to [the Israeli-Arab township] Baqa al-Gharbiyya," said one Arab.

Even under the conditions of "enforced modernization," which Israel imposed on the Arab villages, the Palestinians succeeded quite well; just think what they could have achieved had they not been marginalized and forced to make do with crumbs from the table of the affluent Jewish society. And, indeed, the demographic development of the Arab population of Eretz Israel/Palestine supports this contention. Since 1948 the Arab population of the State of Israel (excluding East Jerusalem) has increased fivefold, reaching 900,000 in 1998. In 1995 the number of refugees and descendants of refugees stood at more than 3 million, that is, over four times their number at the time of the 1948 War; of these, approximately 1.2 million remained in Eretz Israel/Palestine (in the West Bank and Gaza Strip).

If we calculate the total size of the population living in Mandatory Palestine and its distribution according to nationality, we find that on the eve of the 1948 War, 608,000 Jews and 1,270,000 Arabs lived there;[8] in 1996, 4,600,000 Jews (56 percent) occupied the same area, as opposed to 3,600,000 Arabs (44 percent). This is similar to the demographic balance that existed in 1947 in the territory that was to have been included in the Jewish state according to the 1947 UN Partition Plan.

An examination of the development of Arab settlements in the State of Israel can perhaps give some indication of what might have taken place had so many Arab villages not been abandoned. The communities I have chosen to examine are all located in the "Little Triangle" (which was transferred to Israel under the terms of the 1949 armistice agreement with Jordan), because nearby are situated settlements that remained under the rule of less-developed Jordan, which can serve as a control group. The village of Taibeh, whose population on the eve of the war was 4,640, has become a city of 24,500, with a municipal area of some 19,000 *dunams* (3,054 *dunams* developed); Umm al-Fahm, whose population numbered 5,900 in 1948, was a city of 30,000 in 1996, with an area of 25,000 *dunams* (9,000 *dunams* developed). In contrast, the population of the town of ʿAnabta in the West Bank grew from 3,370 in 1948 to only approximately 7,000 in 1995, that of ʿAttil from 2,860 to 7,000, and of ʿAllar, from 1,570 to 3,500.

In 1968, immediately following the Six-Day War, Yehuda Karmon conducted a comparative study of two villages situated equally distant from the "green line" (but on opposite sides of it), with identical climates and the same topography.[9] From his study of Baqa al-Gharbiyya, in Israel, and Baqa al-Sharqiyya, in the West Bank, the following emerges: The rate of the growth of the population of Baqa al-Sharqiyya in the years between 1944 and 1967 was 125 percent, as compared to a 300 percent increase in the population of the Israeli village. "Rural settlements in Israel and Jordan that were of a similar size at the end of the Mandatory period did not continue to grow at an equal rate. The Arab settlements that were situated in Israel crossed the threshold of urbanization, whereas those that were under Jordanian rule remained village-sized." The large disparity in growth rates can be explained by the fact that the villages of the West Bank were cut off from their landholdings that remained in Israel, as well as from their traditional markets in the Arab towns that were abandoned in 1948. It is clear, however, that an additional vital factor that contributed to the relative backwardness of the

West Bank villages was that the Israeli-Arab villages had become well integrated in the Israeli economy, with its accelerated development, despite the discrimination against the Arab sector. The development of the Arab villages of the West Bank was slow by comparison, and they suffered from inadequate investment in infrastructure and from the consequent paralysis of the industrial sector. While the inhabitants of villages in Israel found employment in the Jewish sector and invested their savings in the village, West Bank villagers were compelled to look for work abroad, and many did not return home. The conditions of life under Israeli rule did not impede the development of the Palestinian community but were actually beneficial to it, at least in terms of demography and new construction—despite complaints of "enforced modernization."

An additional lesson that Karmon learned from his study was that, thanks to investment in agriculture, the village of Baqa al-Gharbiyya, among others, had succeeded in increasing its overall income from this economic sector "to a significant degree (in real terms) over what it had been during the Mandate," despite the fact that after the land confiscations of the war and the fifties, only 9,000 *dunams* remained in its possession, compared with 22,000 during the Mandate. "It was thus proven," states Karmon, "that it would have been possible to solve [the problems caused by] the displaced villagers' loss of land, through the intensification of agriculture in the remaining area."[10] Since those words were written, intensive farming has become more widespread, and the Arab agricultural sector has become specialized in the production of "delicate" crops, such as strawberries and flowers, which bring a high return.

HOLLOW CLAIMS

Yehuda Karmon was probably alluding to the fact that the Agrarian Reform Program proposed for the Arab sector in 1948, based on their "surplus land" (see chapter 4), could have been carried out without such a draconian measure as its arbitrary confiscation. And indeed, all the claims about the supreme necessity of confiscating Arab land in order to be able to "plant" communities of Jewish farmers on it, thereby realizing the Zionist revolution, have been revealed as hollow, or even as lofty justifications for a landgrab, pure and simple. Between 1959 and 1996, the number of members of Jewish agricultural settlements (especially moshavim and kibbutzim) actively engaged in agriculture decreased from about 62,000 to about 26,000. The total number of Israeli residents employed in agriculture in 1996 amounted to 70,600, of whom 42,700 were hired laborers, about half of them non-Jews (Arab or foreign). Agriculture's share of the workforce fell from 6.5 percent in the sixties to 2.6 percent in 1996, and its percentage of the net domestic product decreased from 3.3 percent in 1990 to 2.2 percent in 1996.[11]

Despite all that, the cooperative settlements continued to hold approximately 45 percent of the land of the abandoned villages (2 million *dunams* out of 4.5 million *dunams* abandoned or confiscated), and in the nineties vast stretches of territory located in areas where the demand for land for commercial uses was high were turned into building lots (see chapter 4). In addition, very large tracts of abandoned and expropriated land were left unused, planted with forests and turned into recreation areas, or used for pasture. Early in 1998 the Israeli government and the Jewish Agency concocted a joint plan whereby the state would lease millions of *dunams* of land that had been confiscated from Arabs and was still unused fifty years later—to Jews. The explicit objective of this plan was "to prevent the takeover of State Land by Arabs, especially Bedouin." The transfer of the land to the Jewish Agency, a supposedly nongovernmental body that cared for Jews exclusively, would ensure that the land would not be leased to "non-Jews." "The intent," announced Jewish Agency chairman Avraham Burg, was "to sell [*sic*] the land to diaspora Jews under the slogan 'my 50th Anniversary dunam': It seems to me that this will be a symbolic act for the investor."[12]

Efforts to disperse the Jewish population with the objective of consolidating Jewish settlement regions in the country's north in such a way as to prevent the creation of homogeneous Arab blocks also met with only partial success. In the northern districts of Israel, which encompass about a third of the territory of the state (excluding the desert region), Arabs were a slight majority in 1996, whereas in the Central and Lower Galilee, Arabs made up approximately 70 percent of the total population. A huge expanse of urban sprawl, home to hundreds of thousands of Arabs, was formed in the Nazareth, Wadi ʿAra, and Little Triangle areas.

FEASIBILITY OF "THE RETURN"

These figures did not escape the attention of Palestinian scholars, who hastened to draw the conclusion that Israel's accelerated development had not ruled out the return of its displaced Palestinians. Salman Abu Sitta, a developer and a civil engineer, contends that all the statements about "conditions that have so changed" are simply intended to bolster the Zionist argument.[13] In his opinion, "the return of 4,476,000 refugees" would result in an overall population density in the State of Israel of 482 persons per square kilometer (instead of today's 261), "still an acceptable figure." This density, states Abu Sitta, "is a far cry from the congested miserable conditions which the refugees have to endure while their land is the playground of the privileged kibbutz."

Abu Sitta knows that the overall density he is citing for Israel is as low as it is only because it takes into account the sparsely populated southern half of the country as well as the more densely populated north. The Palestinian version of "the vision of developing the Negev" involves directing most of the "returnees" to this arid region, although some of them "also will be able to return to the fertile areas, where 68% of the Jews are concentrated on 8% of the land." "This concentration," says Abu Sitta, "emphasizes the traditional pattern of Jewish life: [dwelling] in close proximity [to one another] and [engaging] in [the] pursuit of trades such as commerce and industry."

The assertion that the destruction of the villages means that the Palestinians will not be able to return "presupposes," says Abu Sitta, "that a refugee can only recognize as home, and wish to live in, the same house he left." In his opinion, this assumption is tainted with hints of racism or, in his words, "racial contention." Well aware of the living conditions in the Arab villages that were abandoned, he thinks that anyone who would send people back to live under those same miserable conditions is treating them like backward human beings. He thus mocks the dream of "their house . . . with the color of its stones, the smell of its garden, the water of its fountain" and the rest of the refugee fantasies. "A return would be to the same land, most frequently the same site, with reconstruction of villages and repairing of long-neglected Palestinian cities. . . . [R]elatively few village sites are occupied by modern construction. Most kibbutz buildings and prefabs are installed away from the old village."

Abu Sitta notes that it is true that several hundred thousand Jewish inhabitants of towns, kibbutzim, and moshavim would apparently need to move to make it possible for the returning Palestinian farmers to recover their land. But altogether, the entire return operation will be "quite simple." "Six-hundred and fifty thousand Jews came to Israel (between 1949 and 1951), after a journey of thousands of miles[,] and a similar number of Russian Jews[,] without so much as crowding the airport."

For the Palestinian refugees, "the return home is much easier. All that they have to do is to travel by buses for 1–2 hours. . . . [T]hey know where to go; their village sites are mostly vacant." And if the refugees and the children of refugees are unable to get their bearings despite their memories of the home village, states Abu Sitta, they can always use Mandatory maps and British aerial survey photographs from 1945–46.

Abu Sitta apparently did not spend much time in Israel if he really believes that the refugees would be able to identify their homes easily, even if "they know where to go." Ghazi Falah conducted a statistical survey of the abandoned villages, classifying them according to extent of their destruction. Walid Khalidi, in his comprehensive survey of the destroyed Arab landscape, gives slightly different data, according to which 70 percent of the villages were totally destroyed, about one-fourth were largely destroyed, and only seven were preserved and are currently inhabited by Jews.[14] The dry statistics, however, do not provide a full picture of the changes that took place in the landscape, nor of the difficulties in identifying Arab remnants.

EXCERPT FROM DIARY

In the course of my research for this book, I made dozens of trips to examine the remains of abandoned Arab settlements. The following are excerpts from the diary I kept during my travels.

AL-BIRWA (NEAR ACRE)

From the village dossier: "There were 300 houses [in the village], in which there lived 240 families, most of them Muslim. Christians numbered about 100. The villagers had 600 head of cattle, 3,000 goats, and 1,000 chickens. Most of the land was on the plain and was fertile and under cultivation. One thousand *dunams* had been improved by the planting of olives, grapes, and figs. There were no fields of irrigated crops. One-hundred and forty of the families were tenant farmers, who worked the land of *effendi*s from the Adlabi, Moughrabi, al-Zayyat, and other families. The inhabitants of Birwa were the rulers of the vicinity, and they used to resolve all conflicts in the nearby villages. They sold land to the Jews (approximately 900 *dunams*), but were active in the Arab Revolt. The commander of the revolt for the Nazareth-Tiberias subdistrict, Sheikh Yihya Hawash, lived in the village. The British killed eight villagers and sentenced Sheikh Yihya to life imprisonment." The dossier also remarks that "the inhabitants of Birwa are long-lived, the majority reaching an age of over 100 years, and there is one old man, Salah Abdullah, who is 130 years old." There were two government schools, a mosque, a church, four shops, and four *madafeh*s in the village. Mahmoud Darwish, who comes from Birwa, describes the village in his poems.

A paved road leads from the Acre-Sakhnin highway to the village site. Its width is surprising—no more than one meter. The road skirts the houses of moshav Ahihud, which uses the village site as pastureland and the stone school building as a stable and cow barn. Not one home remains. A low vault is visible on the eastern slope of the hill, and another sheikh's tomb can be seen in the distance. The entire area is full of prickly pear cactuses, mulberry and olive trees, and natural forest growth. A visitor not equipped with Mandatory maps would never guess that 1,500 people used to live here. The Israeli guidebook says: "Beside the *moshav* (Ahihud)—the ruins of the Arab village of Birwa."

UMM AL-ZINAT (AT THE FOOT OF THE CARMEL, AT ITS SOUTHERN END)

An ancient village. It was one of the strongholds of the al-Tarabai Bedouin emirs, forgotten rulers who governed Mount Carmel, Ramat Menashe, and as far as Jenin for some 150 years (from the mid–sixteenth century to the end of the seventeenth) and whose center was in Lajjun. Umm al-Zinat was the biggest village in the region, with a population of 1,700. Its houses were built of stone, and the area of its landholdings was approximately 20,000 *dunams,* upon which there were fruit trees, extensive olive groves, a mosque, an elementary school, five shops, and two *madafeh*s. The village was under the influence of Mahmoud al-Madi, from Ijzim. It was occupied on 15 May 1948 and totally demolished; fragments of stone are scattered among the trees of the forest that were planted to camouflage the ruins. We have seen similar attempts to hide ruins in the village of ʿAqqur (in the Jerusalem Hills), the village of Ein Ghazal (western Carmel), in Qula (near Rosh Ha-Ayin), and elsewhere.

YAHUDIYYA (NEAR LOD)

Were it not for the minaret and the monument to the fallen of Israel's wars rising above the site, it would be difficult to identify the location of this large village (pop. 6,000). The few Arab houses being used as small shops are surrounded by multistory housing projects. The village's location relative to the Jaffa-Lod Highway has also changed in the wake of the construction of new arterial routes. The situation is similar in the village of Yazur, which once sat right on the main Jaffa-Ramle road and now is surrounded by freeways; and in Yazur itself there remains only the grave of Imam ʿAli and a Crusader fort that is being used as a storehouse. In ʿIraq al-Manshiyya (in the southern Shephelah), the remnants of the village of 2,000 (approximately 300 houses, two mosques, and a school) have been swallowed up by the industrial park of the city of Kiryat Gat (pop. 35,000).

ʿAJJUR (THE JUDEAN LOWLANDS)

At the site of this large village (approximately 4,000 inhabitants, 600 houses), all traces of the principal cluster of buildings have been "cleaned up," leaving the hill on which the village was situated empty and bare. Three large, beautiful structures, which were located outside the village amid orchards of fruit trees, have been renovated, and Jewish families live in them. In one, chamber music concerts are held. A drive southward along the secondary road reveals that all the villages in the ʿAjjur–Beit Govrin area (Deir Dubban, Kidna, and Rana) were entirely destroyed and all the rubble removed or buried. Near Kidna there are caves dug in the shape of bells and, beside them, "restorations of village agricultural equipment" from the Arab village, done by the JNF without mention of where they came from. The "restoration" of the Arab landscape—with its orchards, terraced hillsides, and produce-processing plants, is being carried out in numerous places by the JNF—while eradicating the memory of the Arabs themselves, of course.

LAJJUN

We drove to Kibbutz Megiddo, built on the site of the abandoned village of Lajjun at the northern end of Wadi ʿAra, not far from Tel Megiddo ("Armageddon"). On the kibbutz grounds a few of the village buildings remain standing, notably a mosque, referred to as "the White," built in 1943. Today this mosque serves as a carpentry shop. A kibbutz member stopped us and ejected us unceremoniously: "We don't allow anyone to wander around here because people steal from us. Yes, even people like you, and anyway, the mosque was demolished and there is a cow barn in its place. It's enough for us that Muslim fanatics come here from Umm al-Fahm. We don't need you, too." This kibbutz, by the way, is affiliated with Hashomer Hatzair, one of the pillars of Peace Now.

AN ACADEMIC DEBATE

Fundamental knowledge of the Palestinian landscape that was obliterated leads to the unavoidable conclusion that Salman Abu Sitta's statement that "the resettlement of the refugees on their land" is a feasible project is not only mistaken and groundless; it is not even beneficial to the refugees. Even in the unlikely event that the Israelis agree to the return of the refugees, or of some of them, this would only mean the reproduction of the miserable conditions of the old refugee camps in new refugee camps. As one Palestinian scholar remarked, "The refugees [will only] exchange unequal status as refugees [for] unequal status as citizens in a state which is not theirs."

Palestinians more responsible than Abu Sitta (or who at least do not allow themselves to be guided by a sense of injustice and deprivation, and who endeavor to be realistic) have come to the conclusion that "the right of return"—if it means the return of the refugees of 1948 to their homes and land—is indeed unfulfillable. Elia Zureik, a professor of sociology and longtime student of the refugee problem, as well as a representative of the Palestinian Authority on the Refugee Working Group of the multilateral track of the Middle East peace talks, has written a research paper summing up this problem, which was published in 1996 by the Institute for Palestine Studies in Washington. The positions held by Palestinians in regard to the right of return, concludes Zureik, have "evolved from a rejection of anything short of full implementation of Resolution 194 to an adopting of an accommodating stance toward Israel." Zureik is referring, as do all those concerned with the right of return, to the legal formulation upon which this right rests—UN General Assembly Resolution 194 (11 December 1948), which states that "the refugees wishing to return to their homes and live at peace with their neighbors should be permitted to do so at the earliest practical date, and that compensation should be paid for the property of those choosing not to return and for loss or damage to property." Mountains of words have been written about this resolution and its practical and legal significance, all of them colored by the national affiliation of the writer or by his support for the Israeli or Palestinian side. Thus, for example, a scholar wishing to dispute the fact that Resolution 194 decrees the implementation of the right of return seizes on the word "permitted" and claims that the return of the refugees is dependent on Israel's authority and desire "to permit" their return. Palestinian scholars, and others, deplore this interpretation of the resolution: "[T]he unfortunate implication is that the choice of return lies not so much with the dispossessed refugees [as] with those who are largely responsible for their dispersal."[15] The words "earliest practical date" have even been used to prove that the whole resolution is nonspecific and nonbinding.

But all the debate over Resolution 194 is academic, since Israel has categorically refused to comply with it. It is true that Israel did agree to allow the return of a small number of refugees in 1949 and to the payment of partial compensation to others, but these concessions were extracted under international pressure, and the conditions that were tacked on to them turned them into a dead letter.

The 1967 war created an additional wave of refugees, and the question of the right of return of these hundreds of thousands to the West Bank and Gaza Strip overshadowed the problem of the 1948 refugees because it was more urgent. Little by little a distinction developed between categories of refugees: the "refugees" of 1948 and the "displaced persons" of 1967.

The peace process, and especially the Declaration of Principals (DOP) signed in Oslo in 1993, brought about a significant change in the attitude of the Palestinians to the problem of the 1948 refugees. As Zureik points out, "Reference to the 1948 refugees' right of return was ritually made by Palestinian spokespersons in all international fora, but this right had no concrete expression in any of the agreements signed between the Palestinians and Israel."[16]

Mutual recognition between Israel and the PLO obliged the Palestinians to develop a new approach to the 1948 refugee problem, but it could not be spelled out because the PLO leadership that was negotiating with Israel was not able to admit to the refugees living in Lebanon, Syria, Jordan, and the other countries of refuge that there was no solution to their problem in the context of the Oslo Accords. As we have already seen, any compromise regarding the right of return was perceived as "canceling a sixty-year history," and the Oslo Accords were interpreted (by Palestinians opposed to them) as implying that "it was acceptable to settle on the land of another, to expel its inhabitants, and to ensure by all possible means that they would never return."[17] There was no choice left to the Palestinians, who had yielded to the agenda imposed by the victors, but to formulate their new approach as follows: how to gain symbolic recognition of the injustice done to them and to solve the refugee problem in a fashion that "will satisfy a sufficient number of Palestinians while remaining acceptable to a sufficient number of Israelis." In Zureik's words, "The crux of the matter is: to interpret the right of return in Resolution 194 so as not to remain bound to a notion of absolute justice."

COLLECTIVE, NOT INDIVIDUAL, RETURN

Palestinians began in the middle to late eighties to reformulate the right of return in collective rather than individual terms: the principle of return would be fully realized by the return to the Palestinian state that was to be established in part of the homeland—in the West Bank and Gaza Strip, and not necessarily by a return to their actual homes in the State of Israel. As Ziad Abu Zayyad writes: "[The suffering of the Palestinians] forced many of them to view their return as the acquisition of national independence and dignity, and not necessarily as a literal return."[18]

Prominence has been given to demands for compensation on the order of tens of billions of dollars for property and other belongings of the refugees, and for additional reparations for the suffering they had been made to endure. So as not to relinquish the right of refugees to actually return to their homes in Israel, the Palestinians demand that the return of a symbolic number of refugees be allowed, even if under the guise of family reunification on a humanitarian basis. But the main emphasis has been placed on plans for the settlement of hundreds of thousands of displaced Palestinians in the territory controlled by the Palestinian Authority, to be funded by compensation money.

The calamity of 1948 was thus placed in a new historical perspective. Although it was a terrible catastrophe, which uprooted hundreds of thousands and destroyed their society, culture, and physical landscape, it was not a mortal blow. Some 3.7 million Palestinians remained in their homeland west of the Jordan River (2.8 million in the West Bank and Gaza Strip and 900,000 in Israel); they had obtained a second chance to establish a national entity and had entered into an inexorable process leading toward the achievement of political independence. If this entity succeeded in absorbing the refugee camp residents who had not struck roots in the Arab states (estimated at between 750,000 and 1 million), and these refugees were compensated for their lost property—or the Palestinian Authority was compensated in their name—it would be possible to define this as the fulfillment of the right of return not "bound to a notion of absolute justice."

This rational approach, however, is not endorsed by everybody. In a survey conducted in June 1995, a representative sample of Palestinians in the West Bank and Gaza were asked, "Do you agree to giving up the 1948 lands in return for a permanent solution [providing for a] Palestinian state in the West Bank and [Gaza] Strip, with Jerusalem as its capital?" Sixty percent of those polled gave a negative response, 30 percent answered in the affirmative, and 10 percent were undecided. Elia Zureik, who analyzed the data, states that members of the younger generation were more negative than their elders.[19] Two-thirds of those born after 1967 were opposed to relinquishing the "1948 lands" in exchange for the establishment of a Palestinian state in the entire territory of the West Bank and Gaza Strip, including East Jerusalem, compared with 55 percent of those born prior to that date. Opposition to relinquishing this land was strongest among young people aged fifteen to eighteen. No less than 70 percent of them were opposed, compared with about one-quarter who agreed (the rest were undecided).

The direct correlation between support for the peace process—and for associated political positions as regards the Palestinian Authority—and willingness to surrender the "1948 lands" is reflected in the fact that the proportion of Hamas (Islamist militants) supporters who oppose giving up the land exceeds 80 percent, and support for a political solution in exchange for the relinquished land decreases as despair over the peace process's chances for success grows. Changing attitudes toward "the return," then, are the litmus test of the prospects for Israeli-Palestinian reconciliation.

SYMMETRY OF RESPONSIBILITY?

The Israelis, however—in contrast to the Palestinians, who were compelled to bow to reality and have had to awaken from the dream of "the return"—have not shown similar flexibility in their attitude toward the refugee problem: the victors apparently view themselves as being in less need of spiritual stocktaking than do the vanquished. The Israeli stance—of rejecting any form of "return"—has not changed since it was formulated in 1949. A position paper on the Palestinian refugee problem, which Israel issued in 1994, simply reiterates the long-standing Israeli interpretation of Resolution 194, according to which the right of return pertains only to citizens returning to their country, and thus does not apply to the Palestinian refugees, "who never were citizens or permanent residents of Israel [but who] fled before its founding in 1948." Regarding compensation, Israel presents a counterclaim for the property left behind by Jewish refugees who left or were expelled from Arab states.

Shimon Peres, "prophet of the new Middle East" and one of the architects of the Oslo Accords, rejects the demand for the right of return in the same routine terms as did his predecessors. In his eyes it is a "maximalist demand," with the potential to turn the Jewish majority of the State of Israel into a minority; as he sees it, the only solution to the refugee problem is their absorption by the Arab countries. Peres has addressed himself to the task of obtaining financial means for enabling this absorption, and he is even willing for Israel to "contribute a part of it." Israeli legal experts have spelled out many arguments challenging the legal validity of the right of return, and as the nineties draw to a close, economists and demographers are continuing their fifty-year debate over the number of refugees and the size of the Palestinian diaspora population.

There is not much new in the recently aired Israeli positions, but the Palestinians, sensitive to every nuance, nevertheless detected an alteration in official Israeli thinking as regards the acceptance of partial moral responsibility for the creation of the refugee problem. The official Israeli position, for both foreign and domestic consumption, has always been that the refugee problem was created by the Arab states that started the war, and that it was the leaders of these countries who ordered the civilian population to leave their homes to clear the way for a victorious campaign by the Arab armies. All allegations of preemptive expulsion and ethnic cleansing were dismissed by the Israelis as cheap propaganda: the refugee problem was the outcome of the Arab states' refusal to make peace with Israel and to recognize its right to exist. However, remarks Elia Zureik, in 1992 Israel finally recognized at least "symmetry of responsibility" with the Arabs; Shlomo Ben Ami, chairman of the Israeli delegation to the Refugee Working Group, declared: "The Palestinian refugee problem was born as the land was bisected by the sword, not by design, [either] Jewish or Arab. It was largely the inevitable by-product of Arab and Jewish fears, and of bitter and protracted fighting."[20]

Israel's acceptance of partial responsibility does not, however, satisfy the Palestinians: "It will likely not impress those who . . . were actually expelled from their homes or left for fear of their lives."[21] And even this minimal change in policy has remained on the verbal plain only; it represented the position of the 1992 negotiators alone—and they were Labor party people. It had no influence on the negotiations regarding the solution of the refugee problem—either on the bilateral, Israeli-Palestinian track or on the multilateral track. The committee appointed under the DOP to deal with the question of the displaced Palestinians—that is, the 1967 refugees—could not even agree on the definition of "displaced." The multilateral Working Party initiated extensive research activity, which in turn generated dozens of reports that were collected at McGill University in Montreal, Canada (because the chair of the committee was Canadian). But no progress was made, and considering the positions of the two sides, there is little chance that any will be.

It is ironic that the Israelis—who have managed to thwart every attempt in the past fifty years to bring back the refugees, who altered the physical reality in a manner that ruled out any possibility of restoring the Palestinian landscape, and who have perhaps even compelled the Palestinian leadership to acquiesce to the status quo—are still hounded by the nightmare of "the return." This nightmare has become an obsession that is expressed in their political positions, interparty disputes, government decisions, and legislation, and even in their literary writings.

THE FEAR OF A PRECEDENT

In public discourse and in statements of the Israeli government, nearly every issue linked to the progress of the peace process is viewed in terms of its ramifications for the immigration of Arab refugees to Eretz Israel/Palestine and the "precedent" that would be set thereby. Hence, for instance, those opposed to the Oslo Accords perceived the agreement to return tens of thousands of Palestinian police and their families to Palestinian Authority territory as a "precedent for return." One of the main reasons for the Likud's opposition to the establishment of a Palestinian state was that "its establishment would give it the authority to permit the immigration of hundreds of thousands of Palestinians." Israeli "security control" of land, air, and sea border crossing points, which the Palestinians have been forced to accept, is meant to regulate the movement of any refugees who might try "to return," even if only to the area under Palestinian self-rule. The Israeli government's rigid stance in the Committee for Displaced Persons (the "Quadripartite Committee") was also dictated by "fear of setting a precedent."

But the most blatant expression of this obsession with avoidance of setting "a precedent for return" is the Israeli government's treatment of the uprooted villagers of Birʿim and Iqrit (see chapter 4). The illegal eviction of the inhabitants of these villages is perceived in many circles, including that of the leaders of the Israeli Right, as an immoral act, an injustice that places a stain upon Israel's record. The debate over letting them return to their villages has been on the agenda for fifty years, and Labor, Likud, and National Unity cabinets have all deliberated this question and expressed support for their return—in principle. This broad backing has yielded no results, however, not because the villagers' claim was deemed unjustified but because "it would set a precedent." In 1972 Prime Minister Golda Meir stated: "It is not only considerations of security [that prevent] an official decision regarding Birʿim and Iqrit, but the desire to avoid [setting] a precedent. We cannot allow ourselves to become more and more entangled and to reach a point from which we are unable to extricate ourselves." Another minister remarked: "The problem is whether it is permissible in 1972 to open the files on the 'dispossessed villages' of '48 and the War for Independence. In my opinion, these files should not be opened."[22]

All the assertions that the case of Bir'im and Iqrit was unique and that therefore the claim that it would set a precedent was groundless, and that the situation on the northern border had changed totally so all the security arguments no longer applied—were no help. Allowing the villagers to return was regarded, even two generations later, as recognition of "the right of return" and as a dangerous precedent that would be followed by other, similar demands. After all, the people of Bir'im and Iqrit were not the only "present absentees." As a Jewish resident of Ein Hod told writer David Grossman in the early nineties: "Their having a new hold here would undermine our right to the place and our hold on it. If you accord recognition to what was here before '48, you essentially topple the foundation upon which the whole affair rests . . . the whole affair, the whole state."[23]

The most striking literary expression of the nightmare of the return is the novella "Facing the Forests" by A. B. Yehoshua (1963).[24] The story is about a student who goes to work as a "fire watcher" (i.e., someone hired to be on the lookout for fires) in a forest so that he can be alone and also so that he can do research on the Crusaders "from the human, that is to say, from the ecclesiastical aspect." The Jewish context and the author's use of the Crusades as a metaphor for Zionism are clear: the student's father "fails to understand why his son won't deal with the Jews, the Jewish aspect of the Crusades," and a group of young people hiking in the forest are "a procession threading through the forest . . . like a procession of Crusaders." The young forest he is assigned to guard "isn't a forest yet, only the hope and promise of one." It was planted by Zionist organizations that filled it with signs, pale inscriptions "saying, for example: 'Donated by the Sackson children in honour of Daddy Sackson . . . a fond tribute to his paternity.'" "The forest turns ceremonial. The trees stand bowed, heavy with honour, they take on meaning, they belong," writes Yehoshua, mocking the group of distinguished Zionist leaders. "A brief tour of the conquered wood, and then the distinguished gathering dissolves into its various vehicles and sallies forth," leaving the young forest ranger alone with a mute old Arab. "His tongue was cut out during the war. By one of them or one of us? Does it matter?" Little by little the ranger discovers the Arab's secret, which is the secret of the forest: "'Our forest is growing over, well, over a ruined village . . .' 'A village?' 'A small village.' Ah (Something is coming back to him anyway.) 'Yes, there used to be some sort of a farmstead here. But that is a thing of the past.' Of the past, yes certainly. What else. . . . ?" But for the Arab this is not the past, since he is from this village. The ranger and the old man become very close, and the Arab explains to the Jew, "with hurried, confused gestures. . . . He wishes to say that this is his house and that there used to be a village here as well and that they have simply hidden it all, buried it in the big forest." The ranger "moves away, pretending not to understand. Did there used to be a village here? He sees nothing but trees." But he begins to search "for marks left by humans. Every day he comes and disturbs a few stones, looking for traces."

The old Arab sets fire to the forest: "Pines split and crash. Wild excitement sweeps him, rapture. He is happy. Where is the Arab now? The Arab speaks to him out of the fire, wishes to say everything, everything at once. Will he understand? . . . [T]here, out of the smoke and haze, the ruined village appears before his eyes; born anew in its basic outlines as an abstract drawing, as all things past and buried." And the ranger "smiles to himself, a thin smile. Then abruptly it dies." The Zionist organization's man in charge of forests arrives, and "His old eyes wander over the lost forest as though in parting." He attacks the ranger: "Yes, this one with the books, with the dim glasses, with that smug cynicism of his." The ranger returns to the city, and his friends say, "'We hear your forest burned down! . . . Well, what now?'"

Four years after this story was written (i.e., in 1967), it became evident that the Israelis were not merely troubled by nightmares of "the return" of the 1948 refugees: the impetus for expulsion had not disappeared but had inevitably reemerged to create a new nightmare—of the return of the new refugees. On 7 June 1967 the inhabitants of three villages in the Latroun salient—Emmaus, Yalu, and Beit Nuba—were expelled. The thousands of villagers were ordered to leave immediately, were not permitted to retrieve their belongings from their houses, and were sent off on foot toward Ramallah in the West Bank. A week later, when they tried to return home, they encountered army roadblocks that had been put up near the villages. From there they watched as bulldozers demolished their homes and the stones from the ruins were loaded on trucks belonging to Israeli contractors, who had bought them to use in building houses for Jews. The village sites, with their verdant orchards, were turned into a large picnic area and given the name Canada Park.

The Israeli government's decision to demolish these villages was based on the assumption that the West Bank would return to Jordanian control; thus it "corrected" the border so that the Latroun salient would remain in Israeli hands. Decades later, when it was obvious that Israeli control of that section of the West Bank would continue, it became clear that this "border correction" had been unnecessary. Nevertheless, the refugees were not permitted to return to their land, and all their appeals were rejected, lest their return set a "precedent."

SOME BORDERLINE

The 1967 war led to numerous painful encounters between refugees from 1948 who had found a haven in the West Bank and the Jews who were living in their abandoned homes. These encounters were particularly hard on members of the Israeli Left, who advocated a just solution to the Israeli-Palestinian conflict but at the same time were living in the homes of displaced Palestinians. In the summer of 1995, Faisal Husseini, the Palestinian Authority official responsible for Jerusalem, announced that he had completed a survey of abandoned Palestinian properties in Israeli West Jerusalem. According to this survey, 60 percent of the land in West Jerusalem was owned by Palestinians who had fled in 1948. An Israeli journalist took this opportunity to ask several prominent leftists living in Arab houses what they felt about this. One of them responded as follows:

> Once, the Arabs who lived in this house came to visit. . . . We invited them in and received them nicely, but they didn't come any more. I think that this is because of the extensive renovations that we had made to the house, which made the fact that the situation was irreversible concrete for them. A few times I asked myself whether I had a sense of guilt, but I felt "that's that"; it wasn't my personal problem. There has to be some border line that symbolizes a mutual compromise between us and them. We must decide on the 1967 War as determining that line, and place the border there [on the 1949 armistice "green line"].

Another prominent left-winger stated: "I don't have any problem with the fact that we threw them out, and we don't want them back, because we want a Jewish state."[25] Thus have feelings of guilt been "nationalized," and the moral dilemma engulfed by political positions in which no pity for the fate of those whom the status quo or the "that's that" has sentenced to a life of hardship in the refugee camps is noticeable.

The Arab former landlord did not make life easy for the leftists. "I am prepared to live under Israeli rule, but in my own house," he stated, and in answer to the question of what to do with the Jews who are living in the house, responded: "Let the state find a solution for them. In order to live in peace, we must obtain our rights."[26] The laconic reply that there is nothing to discuss, because "we want a Jewish state," lays bare the pseudorational justification behind which hides these leftists' fear of the cognitive dissonance that will confront them when the Pandora's box of the contradictions between their professed principles and their lifestyle is opened.

"They don't want to let us return," a former resident of Iqrit stated defiantly to David Grossman, "because that would show what truly happened in 1948. You have a fear of admitting that the Palestinian refugees did not flee, but were dispossessed. If they bring us back, that will shatter the myth that all the generations of your young people have been brought up on."[27] When Grossman quoted the government's statement of opposition to the return of the refugees to Birʿim and Iqrit because "it would constitute a precedent," the refugee responded: "What do I care about your government's fears? It's my right to demand justice for myself."

Grossman wants to turn the claim of "precedent" on its ear and create a new precedent for the return of refugees—"and if there is a precedent in this, let it be a precedent of good intentions, generosity, and self-confidence." But he knows that this stance is regarded as naive and dangerous by most Israelis: "They will say that [even] the easiest concession will destroy the entire defense-line; that Israel's credibility as a state that sticks to its principles will be damaged if it retreats from them even a tiny bit. That it is even preferable [for Israel] to persist in errors and injustices, so that belated doubts are not aroused regarding the righteousness of its stance."

As it became clear that "the return"—even the return of a limited number of refugees—was unrealistic and would never be accomplished, the call for a practical solution to the refugee problem was replaced by a demand that the Israelis accept moral responsibility for the injustice that had been done: "In order for the victim to forgive, he must be recognized as a victim. That is the difference between a historic compromise and a cease-fire," wrote Azmi Bishara.[28] Edward Said, one of Zionism's harshest critics and a leader of the Palestinian opposition to the Oslo process, ties Palestinian acknowledgment of the Holocaust of European Jewry to a parallel recognition by Israelis of their responsibility for the disaster that befell the Palestinians. Said stated in 1998, that there is no room for comparison between the suffering of the Jews and the suffering of the Palestinians. But since he acknowledges the Holocaust, he expects the Jews to acknowledge the disaster they brought upon the Palestinians. His stance is noteworthy, since he expressed it at a time when anti-Semitic Holocaust deniers had become culture heroes in the Arab countries. There is, however, not much new in this parallel demand. The Palestinians have always complained that they recognize the disaster that was inflicted upon the Jewish people, but they should not have to pay for the evil deeds of others; the Jews were attempting to rectify the injustice done to them while doing injustice to another people, whose only crime was being in the way.

MEA CULPA

The demand that Israel take responsibility for historical injustices fits in with a worldwide trend of apologizing for past immoral deeds. The Czechs begged forgiveness of the Sudetenland Germans for brutally expelling them in 1945, and the Germans begged forgiveness of the Czechs for their 1938 invasion and for their murderous, oppressive regime; the Americans begged forgiveness of the Japanese-Americans for interning them in concentration camps during the Second World War and recently apologized to the country's black population for slavery; the Afrikaners begged forgiveness of the South African blacks for apartheid, and the new government under Nelson Mandela instituted a Commission for Truth and Reconciliation. Pleas for forgiveness have become an essential component of the "confidence-building" process following the conclusion of violent conflicts. It would seem that the Oslo process, especially the mutual recognition between Israel and the Palestinians, should follow this trend.

One might well contend that a request for forgiveness from the victim is of little worth, particularly when the consequences of the injustice are still being felt. In any event, the verdict of history rests with those historians who will depict the past with impartiality and apportion blame where it is due. Even the designation of a given act as a historical injustice depends on the norms prevalent at the time it was committed, and one must not project the behavioral norms that prevail many years later onto the past.

Israeli historians and scholars did not, in fact, wait for the Palestinians to demand that their victimization be acknowledged and that apologies be tendered for their calamitous expulsion. Some of them even went so far as to place the blame totally and unreservedly with the political and military leadership of the pre-state Jewish community. This conclusion by the "revisionist historians" stirred up a virulent, ongoing public controversy whose very existence has opened cracks in the traditional self-righteousness of the Israeli general public. The Palestinians, of course, make extensive use of the new Israeli scholarship and its critical conclusions, but when they demand an apology, what they mean is an official and binding Israeli declaration in the Knesset or perhaps in the UN General Assembly.

As we have seen, the official Israeli stance has shifted from complete dissociation from and denial of responsibility for the Palestinian calamity to "symmetry of responsibility," and even beyond. Even retired general Shlomo Gazit, whose position is not far from the heart of the so-called national consensus, has suggested that Israel make a declaration containing a "moral and psychological acknowledgment recognizing the suffering of the Palestinians in the last fifty years."[29] But chances are next to nil that this shift will lead to an official Israeli acknowledgment of the Jewish contribution to the Palestinian disaster not only because such a declaration would "shatter the myth that all the generations of . . . your young people have been brought up on" but also because the norms that allowed the injustice to take place have not yet changed, in principle. True, the occupation of the West Bank and Gaza Strip in 1967 did not prompt massive premeditated expulsions, but there was no dearth of attempts, especially in border areas, to create a wave of new refugees; the destruction of the villages of the Latroun salient is but one example. In any event, hundreds of thousands of people—most of them 1948 refugees—fled the West Bank in 1967, and, as we have seen, the Israeli government has not allowed them to return.

The norms that allowed the Palestinians' dispossession of their landholdings by means of ethnically discriminatory laws have not changed. Even though the government has not confiscated Arab land in Israel since 1976, sophisticated ways have been devised to perpetuate the injustice. For instance, no appropriate solution has been found for the problem of the "present absentees," and dozens of "unrecognized" settlements—most of them inhabited by people who were evicted from their land in the Galilee and the Negev in the late forties and the fifties—have existed for decades without basic infrastructure.

In October 1998 mass rioting erupted in Wadi 'Ara, south of the Carmel Range. The citizens of the Arab town of Umm al Fahm protested against the "closure" for military purposes (see chapter 4) of a large area planted with olive trees that belongs to nearby Arab farmers. The protest march deteriorated into a serious confrontation with the police. The Arabs hurled rocks and petrol bombs, and the police opened fire with rubber bullets and occasionally with live ammunition. The security forces had to "reoccupy" the town, and especially ugly scenes took place in a school, where blood-smeared walls and blood-soaked books became a "testimonial for the atrocities." Hundreds of Arabs were slightly injured and a score sustained serious wounds in the worst confrontation since Land Day (of 1976). The timing was accidental, but the symbolism was blatant. It was as though a pageant had been performed as part of Israel's Jubilee celebrations (which were held then), reenacting fifty years of bloody struggle for possession of the landscape. Not one single theme had been omitted: a violent clash between unequal forces; dispossession by discriminatory, "legal," actions; alienation from what became a symbol of Arab nationalism—the olive tree; plans to "Judaize" the Arab block of settlements by building new Jewish settlements on the "closed" areas; Israeli declarations that "the law must be maintained and violence will accomplish nothing"; statements that Arab real objectives are political and should be viewed in the context of their struggle against Zionism and the state, and therefore should be dealt with firmly. Both sides acted as if nothing has happened during the last half century, but perhaps there was a reversal of roles: the Zionists have always boasted that only they could feel metaphysical connection to the homeland, while the Arab peasants could only muster an emotional attachment to a well-defined place: a house, a tree, a hill. But that Zionist contention has drowned in a sea of consumerism and privatization that has turned the landscape from a national, sacred patrimony over to commercial interests, and the struggle for the Land has become a struggle for profitable zoning. The Arabs of Umm al Fahm, and the entire Palestinian community that supported them, have shown by their struggle for a plot of olive trees that the value of national land as sacred property has been transferred from the Jews to them. And that is the twist of irony: after fifty years of struggle for the landscape, the Arabs have become the last of the Zionists.

Epilogue

In the diary I kept during my trips researching this book, I wrote the following notes.

AL-BASSA, OUR VISIT TO THE VILLAGE WITH THREE OF ITS FORMER INHABITANTS

The village itself had been destroyed, with the exception of three holy places, and turned into an industrial park. When we went to search for one of the village wells, on the border between Moshav Betzet and the Arab village, a settler driving a tractor stopped us and demanded that we leave. The argument between him and the son of an elderly former resident of the village, who was with us, was a quintessential example of the debate over the "right of return": "What do you want? To kick us out of the houses that we've built and to take our land?"

"Yours?! *You* kicked *us* out and killed seven young men in order to scare us into leaving."

"It's your fault; you didn't have to start a war. Go to the Arab states; this is *our* land."

"We don't want to kick you out. What was, was, but let us renovate our churches; and publicly declare that you're sorry for what happened to women, children, and men who weren't guilty of anything."

"We know you. You'll start with churches and then you'll want graveyards; you'll squat here and have children, and little by little you'll push us out. If you don't get out of here I'll call the police and they'll arrest you for trespassing."

The whole argument sounded like some sort of ritual. This was not the first time that the two sides had met in the same situation, and they simply repeated the things they had surely said to each other many times. But it was important for them to express them over and over again. The Israeli guidebook says of Moshav Betzet: "Founded on the land of the abandoned village of Bassa, in a place where various archeological remains were located. Some of the ancient building-stones were used in the houses of the Arab village, whose inhabitants abandoned it during the War for Independence."

SAMSON'S TOMB (SARʿA)

We drove on a dirt path to the site of the Arab village with a former resident who is now living in a refugee camp. He brought with him the key to his house, knowing that neither his house nor any other had survived, as he had visited the site many times. When we arrived, he took me to a heap of stones and said, "This is where I was born, and this is our mulberry tree." I felt that this was not the first time he had shown it to Israelis. I didn't tell him that I knew his village well because on its site I had helped put up the first huts of Kibbutz Zorʿa in 1949. It was the kibbutz of my youth leaders, who had settled there after their demobilization from active duty in the Palmach.

The Arab led me to two rectangular gravestones standing out in the open in a paved area. On one stone the name of Samson the Judge was inscribed, and on the other that of his father, Manoah. The stones were covered with handwritten supplications for miraculous cures or help finding a spouse.

"You see," he said, "this is the tomb of our *wali* [saint], Nabi Samt. The *mutadayinin* [religious Jews] destroyed the building with the *kubbeh* [dome] and built this."

Without my noticing, a group of Israelis had come up behind us while we were talking. One of them demanded that we leave. "Go away," he said, "you desecrate the holy place. I recognized you, Benvenisti! You should be ashamed of yourself, bringing an Arab here to our place. Are you scheming together how they'll come back?"

We went back to the car and drove away.

I needed no reminder that the old landscape is not buried underneath the concrete, asphalt, and forests of the Israeli landscape. The ghosts of the past give us no rest; they haunt everyone, whether he or she is aware of the past and familiar with the actual events or simply perceives them as among the "threats to the existence of Israel." The Israelis are well aware of what the Palestinians also know: that Eretz Israel/Palestine is not al-Andalus, and the real demographic balance between Israelis and Palestinians is not conveyed by the population statistics of the State of Israel alone but by those of the entire area between the River Jordan and the Mediterranean. Even if the return of "the displaced" (of 1967—not to mention the 1948 refugees) from beyond the Jordan (whether to Palestinian or to Israeli territory is immaterial) is not permitted, demographic parity between Israelis and Palestinians will be achieved within fifteen to twenty years as a result of the Palestinian population's much higher rate of natural increase. Each additional refugee who returns will only accelerate this process, and the Israelis will continue to do everything in their power to prevail in this demographic struggle, which they regard as "a security matter."

Many Israelis, it is true, are not actively opposed to the settlement of displaced Palestinians in the territory of the future Palestinian state, but others understand that these two populations will both be living in the same country, utilizing resources that cannot be divided by borderlines. The two national groups, therefore, will constantly be fighting over the use of the same material resources, and even more so over the symbolic assets, of their shared homeland. This fundamental struggle will not be soluble via the diplomatic negotiations referred to as "the peace process."

Israelis and Palestinians alike feel that neither the physical nor the spiritual landscape is divisible. Thus, regardless of the fate of the 1948 refugees (more than half of whom do not even live in Eretz Israel/Palestine), and notwithstanding the changes that have taken place in the conceptualization of the right of return, the obliterated Palestinian landscape will remain a symbol and a battle standard for both sides. Palestinians rally around it at every national event: mention of "Haifa, Acre, and Jaffa" at mass rallies evokes the wildest roars of anything, and the hope of return (*al-ʿauda*) carries great emotional force, for even third- and fourth-generation refugees.

Israelis, for their part, view every expression of attachment to the old Palestinian landscape as tantamount to incitement to murder and as a sure sign that the Arabs do not want peace but rather are using the "peace process" as a means of liberating the land in stages, taking what the Israelis offer in the "interim agreements" to gain a base from which they will ultimately launch "The Return" to all of their former homeland.

Time has not alleviated these deep-seated fears, nor has it quashed the hope and urge for revenge, because these emotions are not simply irrational, as some would like to depict them; they are based on the reality created in 1948 and have been reinforced constantly ever since. The struggle for possession of the physical landscape, as well as for its symbolic assets, continues unabated, and the result is so devastating for the Palestinians that it is understandable why they cannot countenance it. The Palestinians living in the area that formerly constituted Mandatory

Palestine (both in Israel and in the areas of the independent Palestinian entity), who constitute around 45 percent of the total population of that area, control only about 10 percent of the total land mass, approximately the amount held by the proportionally much smaller Jewish community before 1948. Israeli encroachment on Palestinian land, both in Israel and in the Occupied Territories, and its takeover for exclusively Jewish use, has not ceased, and Palestinian efforts to erect "signposts of memory" through efforts such as the repair of neglected mosques and desecrated cemeteries are met by harsh reactions on the part of the authorities. Israel's triumph has been too absolute, and the victors have not shown magnanimity.

I began this work as a personal mea culpa, an attempt to offer an apology for those wrongdoings that my research would reveal to me. But having completed the book, I realize that the personal part was the easiest. An apology for past injustices would imply that Israel had finally decided to come to terms not only with the deeds of its past but also with its present acts; if not, such an apology would be nothing but hypocrisy. And if the Israelis were to muster the courage to grapple with some of their less appealing behavior patterns, they would do well to focus on the present rather than the past—after all, destroying myths of "the justice of the cause" is probably more painful than taking concrete steps that involve nothing more than acting in accordance with the democratic and liberal values of which Israel is so boastful.

It is perhaps difficult to accept responsibility for the creation of the refugee problem, but "recognition" of an "unrecognized" village populated with "present absentees"—providing it with running water and electricity, building a school and a health care center, and granting the residents permits to build additions to their makeshift homes or to build proper stone houses—does not necessarily set a "precedent" for the acknowledgment of Israel's guilt in the villagers' eviction from their original homes. Granted, the nightmare of "The Return" continues to haunt Israelis, but only the extremely insecure would perceive allowing the restoration of a mosque in Ghabisiyya as a precedent that would bring the return of millions of refugees in its wake. The "present absentees" are, after all, Israeli citizens, and perhaps a response to their material and symbolic demands could actually signal Israel's readiness to solve the problems of those Palestinians who are its citizens and to redress the injustices done to them, with the expectation that this "precedent" might motivate neighboring countries to assume similar responsibility.

What, then, might constitute a "precedent of good intentions, generosity, and self-confidence"? It is not my intention to address the issues of an overall solution to the refugee problem, nor those being dealt with in the negotiations of the various committees set up for this purpose—whose work has reached an impasse. But one matter that has been touched upon in this discussion of the landscape of the State of Israel may have implications for the general topic. As mentioned earlier, billions of dollars' worth of agricultural land, most of it originally owned by "absentees," is currently being sold to developers. Were the government to allocate a certain percentage of the profits from these sales for the establishment of a fund to compensate the original Arab owners, not only would this be a righteous act, it might also signify that Israel was no longer evading its partial responsibility for the refugee problem. And, as mentioned previously, we are dealing here only with the local, intra-Israel aspect of the problem.

In this context, a firm and binding undertaking to abolish and eradicate any form of discrimination—legal or otherwise—against the Palestinian community living under Israeli rule must constitute the first step. The 1948 War and its "last battle," the 1967 war (as many perceive the latter), must be declared over, and with their end must come an end to the suspension of universal human rights. Israel has definitely over-extended the "state of war" and its associated "overriding necessities" to justify evil deeds. A precedent for good intentions should provide a creative solution to the problem of scores of communities made up of people from abandoned villages—first and foremost Iqrit, Birʿim, Khirbat Jalama, and Ghabisiyya—which are symbols of the illegal evictions.

The "present absentees" do not seek to dispossess the Jews who inhabit their village sites or land and who have built homes and established settlements there. They are simply asking to be allotted parcels of their land and permitted to renovate their cemeteries and holy places. An inventory of the uncultivated land in most of these abandoned villages shows that such a solution is feasible. According to calculations by Sarah Ozacky-Lazar, only 15 percent of the land of Iqrit and Birʿim that was handed over to Jewish settlements was allocated for cultivation, the rest being rocky land or pasture.[1] The situation is similar at most of the abandoned sites whose former inhabitants are "present absentees." The claim that the resettlement of the Arabs will create friction and economic competition with the Jewish settlers has not been substantiated: friction between displaced villagers and settlers already exists in any case, as expressed through the exchange of harsh words on the occasion of the frequent visits by the Arabs to the sites of their former villages.

Perhaps the solution to the problem in a manner that is not damaging to the interests of the Jews is precisely what will alleviate the friction and lead to the development of good, neighborly relations. Anxiety regarding economic competition from the Arabs is based on the assumption that the uprooted villagers are farmers returning to work their land and compete with the Jewish agricultural sector. But these villagers have long ago forsaken agriculture, as have most of the Jewish settlers. Industrial development and the growth of the tourism industry may, in fact, solve the problems of both groups.

The according of permanent status to the scores of "unrecognized" villages, whose symbol Ein Hod (see chapter 5) has become, would solve a problem affecting tens of thousands of human beings. Everyone knows that this problem will eventually be solved, and there is no reason for "recognition" to be a long, drawn-out process, fraught with painful confrontations, or for it to become a political football in the hands of Jewish political parties using it to attract Arab voters.

But individual solutions for a few tens of thousands of refugees will not suffice. The Palestinian calamity was collective, and there is a need to address the question of property that has collective symbolic, religious, and cultural significance for the Arab population as a whole, which has been denied access to it as a consequence of the Israeli fear of setting a "precedent." The mosques—crumbling, neglected, or being put to sacrilegious uses—and other property that was confiscated from the Muslim authorities must be handed over to them, and funds for their restoration and maintenance should be put at their disposal. Local conditions will determine whether a given site is used for prayer or turned into a cultural monument, so as not to unnecessarily create foci for the friction that would inevitably ensue should masses of Muslims insist on holding prayer services at a holy place situated in the middle of a Jewish settlement.

The neglected and desecrated remnants of Muslim cemeteries scattered throughout the land must also be handed over to the Muslim authorities, and appropriate signs put up to identify the community whose dead are buried there. Relics of Palestinian Arab culture—such as castles, khans, abandoned schoolhouses, mills, and olive-presses—must be properly attributed on the spot as well as being mentioned in Israeli guidebooks, and not presented as they are today—"sanitized" of the identity of those who erected them. Thus, for example, the guidebooks would no longer confine themselves to vague comments, such as the one with which they introduce the village of Sataf, which states: "Its inhabitants abandoned it in 1948, but remnants of the agriculture, and especially the system of irrigation canals, remain in place. These have been restored and repaired, and we can tour them and admire their planning and execution."

The guidebooks would tell the following story as well:

> The village was founded 350 years ago, and in 1948, 600 souls lived there, who grew olives and figs, grapes, pears, apricots, and peaches on approximately 100 *dunams* (in addition to winter and summer grain crops). It was inhabited by two clans of common origin, the Hasan *hamula* and the Cana'an *hamula*. The villagers expended great effort in creating an elaborate water-distribution system to irrigate 100 *dunams* of vegetables whose quality was renowned throughout the vicinity. The inhabitants of the village abandoned it without a battle on 14 May 1948. We should admire the Arab villagers' initiative in the planning and execution of the irrigation system, and not only the implements themselves, as if they were created out of thin air.

Arab sites that were built in the past 300 years and are not "connected" to more ancient sites (and therefore not covered by the Antiquities Law [see chapter 7]) must be included in the listing of archaeological sites entitled to state protection. The designation of these sites must be done in consultation with experts who are members of the Israeli-Palestinian community. The portrayal of the history and geography of the past 300 years as they were—and not censored, as is currently the case, for fear of introducing "background noise" that will detract from the Zionist message of love of the homeland—can only enrich the Israeli public's bonds with the landscape. The organizations concerned with nurturing these bonds are wedded to conservative ways of thinking, and they endeavor to shield the Israeli hiker from questions and speculations. But the Israeli hiking through the remnants of the Arab landscape two generations after its destruction is more secure in himself than those who have appointed themselves the guardians of his faith in the rightness of his presence in his homeland. It is not an encouraging sign when, after fifty or sixty years, it is still necessary to resort to the distortion of history—and to a conspiracy of silence—as educational devices. Intentional disregard for the Arab stratum of the landscape is actually indicative of the Zionist establishment's embarrassment, guilt feelings, and insecurity. But the average Israeli is, in fact, fully capable of coming to terms with the recent past, whose remnants cover his land and which lives on in the hearts and consciousness of his Arab neighbors. This encounter will inevitably be a difficult and painful one, but those who try to protect the Israeli from it are only stalling the process of his or her developing a sense of connectedness with the physical and human landscape, in all its aspects and with all its historical strata. And only once this process has been completed can the Israeli feel truly to be "an image of his homeland's landscape."

When all is said and done, as Mahmoud Darwish puts it, "The geography within history is stronger than the history within geography." And S. Yizhar's comment completes the thought: "The land, in its depths, does not forget. There, within it . . . suddenly, at different times, one can hear it growling an unforgetting silence, unable also to forget even when it has already been plowed and has already brought forth fair, new crops. Something within it knows and does not forget, cannot forget." Only one who knows how to listen to the unforgetting silence of this agonized land, this land "from which we begin and to which we return"—Jews and Arabs alike—only that person is worthy of calling it "homeland."

Notes

INTRODUCTION

1. Simon Schama, *Landscape and Memory* (New York: Knopf, 1995), 7.
2. Rashid Khalidi, *Palestinian Identity* (New York: Columbia University Press, 1997), 177–78.
3. Walid Khalidi, *All That Remains* (Washington, D.C.: Institute for Palestine Studies, 1992), xv–xvi.

1. THE HEBREW MAP

1. S. Yeivin, in Eretz Israel, No. 3 (Jerusalem: Bialik Institute, 1954), 210.
2. Central Zionist Archive A 402/151.
3. Dov Gavish, *Land and Map* (in Hebrew) (Jerusalem: Yad Ben-Zvi, 1991), 251.
4. Harley and Woodward, *History of Cartography* (Chicago, 1987), 1:506.
5. Benedict Anderson, *Imagined Communities* (New York and London: Verso, 1991), 175.
6. Israel State Archives; Brawer Archive c\2613 (20/10/49).
7. James Morris, *Pax Britannica* (New York: Harcourt Brace, 1980), 373.
8. H. H. Kitchener in E. Hull, *Mount Seir* (London: Richard Bentley and Son, 1889), 199–222.
9. S. Newcombe, "Report," in *Palestine Exploration Fund Quarterly* (London, 1914), 128–33.
10. See note 2.
11. Israel State Archives; Brawer Archive 18/7/1949.
12. Ibid., 29/7/1949.

13. *Government of Israel Yearbook* (Jerusalem, 1951), Geographical Names List (in Hebrew), introduction, 279–311.
14. Brawer Archive, 20/10/49.
15. See note 2.
16. Brawer Archive, 8/4/51.
17. Central Zionist Archive KKL/5/11813.
18. Quoted in Z. Shiloni, *The Jewish National Fund and Zionist Settlement* (Jerusalem: Yad Ben-Zvi, 1990), 400.
19. Central Zionist Archive KKL/5/17204.
20. Edward Robinson, *Biblical Researches in Palestine* (Boston: Crocker and Brewster, 1860), 1:253–55.
21. Ibid., 255.
22. Claude Conder, *Tent Work in Palestine* (London: Richard Bentley and Son, 1879), 2:162.
23. Ibid.
24. Gavish, *Land and Map,* 281
25. See note 17.
26. Central Zionist Archive KKL/5/3296.
27. Central Zionist Archive KKL/17205.
28. Central Zionist Archive KKL/5/20503.
29. See note 27.
30. Ibid.
31. Ibid.
32. Nurit Kliot, "The Meaning of Arab Settlements' Names in Eretz Israel" (in Hebrew), *Horizons in Geography* 30 (1989): 71–79.
33. Israel State Archive, Summary of Names Committee activities (September 1958), Brawer Archive.
34. Meeting No. 133, 7.2.1960, Israel State Archive, Brawer Archive.
35. S. Yizhar, "Silence of the Villages" (in Hebrew), in *Stories of the Plain* (Tel Aviv: Zmora Bitan, 1990), 120.
36. Naftali Kadmon, in *Eretz Israel,* No. 22 (Jerusalem: Bialik Institute, 1992), 376–82.
37. Alon Galili in Menachem Marcus, *Ramat Menashe* (Jerusalem: Nature Reserves Authority, 1995), 105–7.
38. Kliot, "The Meaning of Arab Settlements' Names."
39. Anton Shammas, *Arabesque,* trans. Vivian Eden (New York: Harper and Row, 1988), 114.
40. Y. Press, *Topographical-Historical Encyclopedia of the Land of Israel* (Jerusalem: Reuven Mass, 1951).
41. Federal Union of European Nationalities, Convention, 4th version (Bozen/Bolzano, 1992), 17.
42. S. Yizhar, "Silence of the Villages," 126.

2. WHITE PATCHES

1. Moshe Stavsky, *The Arab Village* (in Hebrew) (Tel Aviv: Am Oved, 1946).

2. Ibid., introduction.
3. David Benvenisti, *Our Land* (in Hebrew) (Jerusalem: Kiriyat Sefer, 1946).
4. Ibid., 46–47.
5. Ibid.
6. J. Paporish, *Settlement Geography* (Tel Aviv, 1946), 209.
7. David Benvenisti and Pinhas Cohen, *Guidebook to Eretz Israel* (Jerusalem: Hikers' Association, 1938), 98.
8. G. Robinson Lees, *Village Life in Palestine* (London: Longman, Green and Co., 1911).
9. Yitzhak Ben-Zvi, *She'ar Yashuv* (in Hebrew) (Jerusalem: Yad Ben-Zvi, 1966), 422–23.
10. Ibid., 9.
11. S. Yizhar, *Mikdamot* (in Hebrew) (Tel Aviv: Zmora Bitan, 1992), 9–10, 48–49.
12. Meir Shalev, *Roman Rusi* (Tel Aviv: Am Oved, 1988); English translation by Hillel Halkin, under the title *The Blue Mountain* (New York: HarperCollins, 1991).
13. Ibid., 169.
14. Ibid., 172.
15. Ibid., 247.
16. Ibid., 275.
17. Ibid., 374.
18. Oz Almog, *The Sabra—A Profile* (in Hebrew) (Tel Aviv: Am Oved, 1997), 303.
19. Open University, *Spatial Experiments: Settlement Geography of Eretz Israel* (Tel Aviv: Open University, 1996), unit 2, p. 126.
20. Ibid., unit 4, p. 253.
21. Ezra Danin, *Unconditional Zionist* (Jerusalem: Kidum, 1987).
22. Benny Morris, *The Birth of the Palestinian Refugee Problem* (Tel Aviv: Am Oved, 1991), 163.
23. Emile Habibi, *The Secret Life of Saeed the Pessoptimist* (1974); English translation by Salma Khadra Jayyusi and Trevor LeGassick (London: Zed Books, 1985), 22.
24. Rashid Khalidi, *Palestinian Identity* (New York: Columbia University Press, 1997), 90.
25. Ibid., 91.
26. Lees, *Village Life in Palestine,* 74–75.
27. Joan Peters, *From Time Immemorial* (Chicago: JKAP Publications, 1984).
28. Charles Kamen, *Little Common Ground* (Pittsburgh: Pittsburgh University Press, 1991), 231.
29. David Grossman, *Expansion and Desertion* (in Hebrew) (Jerusalem: Yad Ben-Zvi, 1994), 5.
30. Ibid.
31. Y. Portugali, *Implicated Relations* (in Hebrew) (Tel Aviv: Hakibbutz Hameuchad, 1986), 146–47.
32. Kamen, *Little Common Ground,* 128.

33. Walid Khalidi, *All That Remains* (Washington, D.C.: Institute for Palestine Studies, 1992).

34. Ibid., xxxiv.

35. Stavsky, *The Arab Village,* 18–19.

36. Government of Palestine, *A Survey of Palestine* (reprint, Washington, D.C.: Institute for Palestine Studies, 1991), 2:805.

37. Ghazi Falah, "The 1948 Israeli-Palestinian War and Its Aftermath," *Annals of the Association of American Geographers* 86, no. 2 (1996): 256–85.

38. Moshe Brawer, "Transformation in Arab Rural Settlement," in *The Land That Became Israel,* ed. R. Kark (Jerusalem: Magnes, 1989), 175.

39. Dov Gavish, *Land and Map* (in Hebrew) (Jerusalem: Yad Ben-Zvi, 1991), 172.

40. See Kamen, *Little Common Ground,* 151–59.

41. Ibid.

42. Government of Palestine, *A Survey of Palestine,* 1:281.

43. S. Yizhar, "Silence of the Villages" (in Hebrew), in *Stories of the Plain* (Tel Aviv: Zmora Bitan, 1990), 129–30.

3. EXODUS

1. This is how Uri Milstein (*The War of Independence* [in Hebrew] [Tel Aviv: Zmora Bitan, 1989], 2:25) defines the beginning of the 1948 War.

2. Quoted in ibid., 2:170–71.

3. Walid Khalidi, "Selected Documents on the 1948 Palestine War," *Journal of Palestine Studies* 27, no. 3 (1998): 79.

4. Yehuda Slutsky, *The History of the Haganah* (in Hebrew) (Tel Aviv: Am Oved, 1972), vol. 3, part 2, 1472–75.

5. See, for example, Ghazi Falah, "The 1948 Israeli-Palestinian War and Its Aftermath," *Annals of the Association of American Geographers* 86, no. 2 (1996): 259–61.

6. Slutsky, *The History of the Haganah,* vol. 3, part 2, 1561.

7. Walid Khalidi, "Plan Dalet: The Zionist Master Plan for the Conquest of Palestine," *Middle East Forum* 37, no. 9: 22–28.

8. Yitzhak Levi, *Jerusalem in the War of Independence* (in Hebrew) (Tel Aviv: Israel Defense Force, 1986).

9. Benny Morris, *The Birth of the Palestinian Refugee Problem* (Tel Aviv: Am Oved, 1991), 159.

10. Levi, *Jerusalem in the War of Independence,* 197.

11. Slutsky, *The History of the Haganah,* vol. 3, part 2, 1408.

12. Morris, *The Birth of the Palestinian Refugee Problem,* 227.

13. Z. Dror, *The Life and Times of Yitzhak Sadeh* (in Hebrew) (Tel Aviv: Hakibbutz Hameuchad, 1996), 352.

14. Arnon Golan, "The New Settlement Map" (Ph.D. diss., Hebrew University, 1993), 300.

15. Joseph Weitz, *My Diary* (in Hebrew) (Tel Aviv: Masada, 1965), 3:279.

16. Ibid., 289.

17. Quoted in Morris, *The Birth of the Palestinian Refugee Problem,* 434.

18. Khalil Sakakini, *Such Am I, Oh World* (in Hebrew) (Jerusalem: Keter, 1990), 230.
19. See, for example, Falah, "The 1948 Israeli-Palestinian War."
20. Ibid., table 3.
21. Andrew Bell-Fialkoff, "A Brief History of Ethnic Cleansing," *Foreign Affairs* (Summer 1993).
22. See a summary of the plan in Mark Danner, "America and the Bosnia Genocide," *New York Review of Books,* 4 December 1997, sect. 4, p. 63.
23. Quoted by Mark Danner, "Clinton, the U.N., and the Bosnian Disaster," *New York Review of Books,* 18 December 1997, 62–63.
24. Ibid., 64.
25. This account is based on Morris (*The Birth of the Palestinian Refugee Problem*); demographic and other data compiled from various Mandatory sources (tables and maps); Khalidi (*All That Remains* [Washington, D.C.: Institute for Palestine Studies, 1992]); Abdul Jawad Saleh and Mustafa Walid (*Palestine: The Collective Destruction of Palestinian Villages* [Amman and London: Jerusalem Center for Development, 1987]).
26. Nafez Nazal, *The Palestinian Exodus from Galilee, 1948* (Beirut: Institute for Palestine Studies, 1978).
27. See chapter 4.
28. Described earlier, chapter 2.
29. Weitz, *My Diary,* 3:275–78.
30. Morris, *The Birth of the Palestinian Refugee Problem,* 82.
31. Weitz, *My Diary,* 3:278.
32. High Court of Justice Decision 220/51, 30 November 1951.
33. S. Yizhar, "Silence of the Villages" (in Hebrew), in *Stories of the Plain* (Tel Aviv: Zmora Bitan, 1990), 125.
34. Nahum Av, *The Struggle for Tiberias* (Tel Aviv: Ministry of Defense, 1991), 212.

4. ETHNIC CLEANSING

1. Dan Horowitz and Moshe Lissak, *Paths in Utopia* (Tel Aviv: Am Oved, 1990), 40.
2. Quoted in Benny Morris, *The Birth of the Palestinian Refugee Problem* (Tel Aviv: Am Oved, 1991), 266.
3. Ibid., 195.
4. Ibid., 197.
5. David Ben-Gurion, *From the Diary: The War of Independence,* ed. Gershon Rivlin and Elhanan Oren (Tel Aviv: Ministry of Defense, 1986), 444.
6. Morris, *The Birth of the Palestinian Refugee Problem,* 296.
7. Anton Shammas, *Arabesque,* trans. Vivian Eden (New York: Harper and Row, 1988), 120–22.
8. Joseph Weitz, *My Diary* (in Hebrew) (Tel Aviv: Masada, 1965), 3:367–68.
9. Menachem Hofnung, *Israel—Security vs. the Rule of Law* (Jerusalem: Nevo, 1991), 170–72.
10. Ibid., 168.

11. Quoted in Morris, *The Birth of the Palestinian Refugee Problem,* 335.
12. Hofnung, *Israel,* 169.
13. Arnon Golan, "The New Settlement Map" (Ph.D. diss., Hebrew University, 1993), 376–77.
14. Ibid.
15. *Ha'aretz,* 6 September 1966.
16. Danny Rubinstein, *The People of Nowhere: The Palestinian Vision of Home,* trans. Ina Friedman (New York: Random House, 1991), 66.
17. Ghazi Falah, "The 1948 Israeli-Palestinian War and Its Aftermath," *Annals of the Association of American Geographers* 86, no. 2 (1996): 256–85.
18. Ibid., 269, map 4.
19. Cited in Morris, *The Birth of the Palestinian Refugee Problem,* 230.
20. Weitz, *My Diary,* 3:365.
21. Tom Segev, *1949: The First Israelis* (New York: St. Martin's Press, 1998), 268.
22. These figures are based on information from the *Encyclopedia Hebraica,* vol. 6, p. 838, table 1. Figures given in other sources range from 270 to 300 settlements.
23. For example, Morris, *The Birth of the Palestinian Refugee Problem,* 348, 434.
24. *Encyclopedia Hebraica,* vol. 6, p. 690, table 11.
25. Golan, "The New Settlement Map," 338.
26. Ibid., 360.
27. Ibid., 369.
28. *Ha'aretz,* 12 March 1999, 23.
29. Ibid.

5. UPROOTED AND PLANTED

1. Beha al-Din, *What Befell Sultan Yusuf* (London: Palestine Exploration Fund, 1897), 202.
2. Ibid., 348.
3. Yitzhak Koren, *Settling the Ingathering of Exiles* (in Hebrew) (Tel Aviv: Am Oved, 1964), 55.
4. In Tom Segev, *1949: The First Israelis* (New York: St. Martin's Press, 1998), 160.
5. David Grossman, *Present Absentees* (Tel Aviv: Hakibbutz Hameuchad, 1992), 71.
6. Ibid., 71.
7. *Idan,* no. 8 (in Hebrew) (Jerusalem: Ben-Zvi Institute, 1987), 66.
8. Ben-Gurion, diary, entry of 1 May 1949.
9. Charles Kamen, "After the Catastrophe I: The Arabs in Israel 1948–51," *Middle East Studies* 23, no. 4 (October 1987): 466–69.
10. Ibid., 466, 471.
11. Mustafa Kabha and Ronit Barzilay, *Refugees in Their Homeland* (in Hebrew) (Givat Haviva: Institute for Arab Studies, 1996), 11.
12. Kamen, "After the Catastrophe I."

13. See chapter 7, on al-Qassam.

14. Nafez Nazal, *The Palestinian Exodus from Galilee, 1948* (Beirut: Institute for Palestine Studies, 1978), 76.

15. See beginning of chapter 3.

16. Levi Eshkol, *Pangs of Settlement* (Tel Aviv: Am Oved, 1958), 270–73.

17. Ibid.

18. Koren, *Settling the Ingathering of Exiles,* 24.

19. Avraham Silberberg, *Workers' Moshavim: Anthology* (Tel Aviv: Moshav Movement, 1969), 106–7.

20. Ibid., 112–13.

21. Eshkol, *Pangs of Settlement,* 237.

22. Joseph Weitz, *My Diary* (in Hebrew) (Tel Aviv: Masada, 1965), 4:87.

23. A. Avneri, *The Unknown Pioneers* (Tel Aviv: Peleg, 1981), 1:120.

24. Yosef Rubin, ed., *Tenth Anniversary of the Workers' Moshavim* (Tel Aviv: Moshav Movement Press, 1959).

25. Avneri, *The Unknown Pioneers,* 1:266–68. Compare this story with the description above (this chapter).

26. Shmuel Dayan, *Like Dreamers* (in Hebrew) (Tel Aviv: Masada, 1955), 116.

27. Ibid.

28. *CIA Map 503152,* May 1977.

29. Benny Morris, *Israel's Border Wars (1948–1956)* (in Hebrew) (Tel Aviv: Am Oved, 1996).

30. Ibid., 65.

31. Ibid., 112.

32. Bracha Habbas, *Movement without a Name* (in Hebrew) (Tel Aviv: Davar, 1964), 97–99.

33. Raanan Weitz and Avshalom Rokah in *Idan,* no. 8 (Jerusalem: Yad Ben-Zvi, 1986), 65–67.

34. In an abbreviated version of an undated, unpublished master's thesis from the Hebrew University of Jerusalem, Said Mahmud, "The Integration and Assimilation of the Arab Internal Refugees in the Arab Sanctuary Villages in Northern Israel 1948–1986," in *The Arab Community in Israel,* ed. David Grossman and Avinoam Meir (Ramat Gan: Bar Ilan University, 1994).

35. Kabha and Barzilay, *Refugees in Their Land,* 22.

36. Mahmoud, "The Integration and Assimilation of the Arab Internal Refugees," 63.

37. Yizhak Schnel, "Transformations in the Arab Village in Israel," in Grossman and Meir, *The Arab Community in Israel,* 147.

38. Shlomo Yom Tov, *Planning Steps for the Advancement of Physical Planning in the Arab Village in the Galilee* (Givat Haviva: Institute for Arab Studies, n.d.), no. 54, p. 359.

6. THE SIGNPOSTS OF MEMORY

1. *The Coastal Plain: A Textbook for the Higher Grades* (Jerusalem: Ministry of Education and Yad Ben-Zvi, 1997), 359.

2. N. Kliot and S. Waterman, "The Political Impact on Writing the Geography of Palestine/Israel," *Progress in Human Geography* 14, no. 2 (November 1990): 243.

3. Ghazi Falah, *Progress in Human Geography* 13, no. 3 (December 1989): 547.

4. Irit Zaharoni, ed., *The Way of the Land: A Nation Living in Its Landscape* (in Hebrew), 8th ed. (Tel Aviv: Ministry of Defense, 1985), 188.

5. Ibid., introduction.

6. Reuven Kritz, *We Were as Dreamers* (in Hebrew) (Tel Aviv: Masada, 1985), 403.

7. Ibid.

8. Oz Almog, *The Sabra—A Profile* (in Hebrew) (Tel Aviv: Am Oved, 1997), 313.

9. S. Yizhar, *Khirbet Hiza'a* (Tel Aviv: Zmora Bitan, 1989), 41.

10. Yehoshua Bar Yosef, "Fleas," in *Battleground* (in Hebrew), ed. Aharon Amir (Tel Aviv: Ministry of Defense, 1992), 143–54.

11. S. Yizhar, *The Captive* (Tel Aviv: Zmora Bitan, 1989), 84.

12. S. Yizhar, "Silence of the Villages" (in Hebrew), in *Stories of the Plain* (Tel Aviv: Zmora Bitan, 1990), 119–20.

13. Yizhar, *Khirbet Hiza'a,* 76.

14. Nurit Gertz, *Captive of a Dream* (in Hebrew) (Tel Aviv: Am Oved, 1988), 56.

15. Nissim Aloni, "Two Prisoners, an Old Man, and a Donkey," in *Bamahaneh* [soldiers' magazine], no. 43 (1949): 8–9.

16. Gertz, *Captive of a Dream,* 58.

17. Yizhar, *Khirbet Hiza'a,* 41.

18. Ibid., 68.

19. Ibid., 75.

20. Ehud Ben Ezer, *The Arab in Israeli Fiction* (in Hebrew) (Tel Aviv: Zmora Bitan, 1992), 27.

21. Yizhar, "Silence of the Villages," 121.

22. Amos Oz, *Under This Blazing Light* (in Hebrew), 6th ed. (Tel Aviv: Sifriat Hapoalim, 1985), 157.

23. Ibid.

24. 'Azmi Bishara, in an article ("Between Place and Space" [in Hebrew]) published in the Tel Aviv periodical *Studio* 37, October 1992.

25. Amir, *Battleground.*

26. Ibid., 5, 7–9.

27. Ben Ezer, *The Arab in Israeli Fiction,* 30.

28. Oz, *Under This Blazing Light,* 157.

29. Amnon Rubinstein, *From Herzl to Rabin* (in Hebrew) (Tel Aviv: Schocken, 1997), 211.

30. Aharon Meged, *The Treasure,* in Amir, ed., *Battleground,* 222–33.

31. Ben Ezer, *The Arab in Israeli Fiction,* 29.

32. *Ha'aretz Weekend Supplement,* 1 July 1994.

33. Rashid Khalidi, *Palestinian Identity* (New York: Columbia University Press, 1997), 179.

34. Danny Rubinstein, *People of Nowhere: The Palestinian Vision of Home,* trans. Ina Friedman (New York: Random House, 1991), 15.

35. Shimon Ballas, *Arab Literature in the Shadow of War* (in Hebrew) (Tel Aviv: Am Oved, 1978), 58.

36. Mark Danner, "America and the Bosnia Genocide," *New York Review of Books,* 4 December 1997, sect. 4, p. 63.

37. Rubinstein, *People of Nowhere,* 19.

38. Eliezer Shweid, *Homeland and Land of Promise* (in Hebrew) (Tel Aviv: Am Oved, 1979), 142.

39. Raja Shehadeh, *The Third Way: A Journal of Life in the West Bank* (London: Quartet Books, 1982), 86–89.

40. ʿA. Abu Hadaba, in *The Palestinian Heritage between Erasure and Revival* (in Arabic), ed. M. Haddad (Taibeh: Center for the Revival of Arab Heritage, 1982). See a discussion in Dan Rabinowitz, *Anthropology and the Palestinians* (in Hebrew) (Raanana: Institute for Israeli-Arab Studies, 1998).

41. Tawfik Canaan, "Muhammedan [*sic*] Saints and Sanctuaries in Palestine," *Journal of the Palestine Oriental Society* 4 (1924) and 7 (1927) [facsimile edition, Jerusalem: Ariel, n.d.].

42. Najati Sidqi, "The Sad Sisters," in *Palestinian Stories,* ed. and trans. Shimon Ballas (Tel Aviv: Eqed, 1970), 70.

43. D. Rubinstein, *People of Nowhere,* 25.

44. Ghassan Kanafani, "Land of the Sad Oranges," in *Palestinian Stories,* 21.

45. Ibid., 26.

46. Bashir al-Hariri, *Letters to the Lemon Tree* (reissued in Hebrew by the Alternative Information Center, Jerusalem, 1997, D. Brafman, trans.), 63–64; or in Arabic, *Heartbeats of Memory.*

47. Rashad Hussein, *The Complete Poems* (Taibeh: Heritage Center, 1990), 124 (loose translation from the Arabic).

48. Sameh al Qassem, *The Poems* (1) (Dar al Huda: Kafr Qara, 1991).

49. Sameh al Qassem, *The Poems* (2) (Dar al Huda: Kafr Qara, 1991).

50. Ghassan Kanafani, "The Returnee to Haifa," in Ballas, *Arab Literature,* 72–77.

51. Emile Habibi, *The Secret Life of Saeed the Pessoptimist* (1974); English translation by Salma Khadra Jayyusi and Trevor Le Gassick (London: Zed Books, 1985), 154.

52. Mahmoud Darwish in *Hadarim,* no. 12 (March 1996): 175.

53. Ibid., 185.

54. Ibid., 194.

55. Yizhar, "Silence of the Villages," 119.

56. Sharif Kanaʿaneh, "The Role of Heritage in Strengthening Identity" (in Arabic), *Heritage and Society,* no. 22 (1993): 7–21.

57. S. al-Mebeid, *The Harvest in the Palestinian Folk Tradition* (in Arabic) (Cairo: Egyptian Council for Literature, 1990).

58. Jamil Salhut, *Social Content in the Palestinian Folktale* (in Arabic) (Jerusalem: Salah al-Din Press, 1983).

59. Sharif Kanaʿaneh et al., *Palestinian Folk Dresses* (in Arabic) (al-Bireh: Women's Society, 1993).

60. ʿA. Barghouti, "Palestinian Folk Heritage: Its Origins and Uniqueness" (in Arabic), in *Palestinian Folk Heritage: Roots and Challenges,* ed. ʿA. Abu Hadaba (Taibeh: Center for the Revival of Arab Heritage, 1991).

61. ʿA. Barghouti, "Our Folk Heritage and the Phases of Interest in It" (in Arabic), *Heritage and Society,* no. 21 (1993): 126–29.

62. Nabil ʿAlkam, "Us and Our Folk Heritage" (in Arabic), in *Palestinian Folk Heritage: Roots and Challenges,* ed. ʿA. Abu Hadaba (Taibeh: Center for the Revival of Arab Heritage, 1991).

63. Sharif Kanaʿaneh, "The Eradication of the Arab Character of Palestine and the Process of Judaization That Accompanied It" (in Arabic), in *Palestinian Folk Heritage: Roots and Challenges,* ed. ʿA. Abu Hadaba (Taibeh: Center for the Revival of Arab Heritage, 1991).

64. Destroyed Village Series (Bir Zayt: Bir Zayt University, 1986–91).

65. Mustafa Dabbagh, *Biladuna Filastin* (Our Land, Palestine), 10 vols. (various publishers and dates).

66. Walid Khalidi, *All That Remains* (Washington, D.C.: Institute for Palestine Studies, 1992).

67. Yusef Haddad, *The Village of Bassa: Society and Cultural Heritage in Palestine* (in Arabic) (Acre: Institute of Palestinian Culture, 1987).

68. Fouad Ajami, *The Dream Place of the Arabs* (New York: Pantheon, 1998), 267.

69. Ibid., 268.

70. Bishara, "Between Place and Space," 6.

7. SAINTS, PEASANTS, AND CONQUERORS

1. J. E. Hanauer, *Folk-lore of the Holy Land* (London: Sheldon Press, 1935), 173–75.

2. Haim Hazzaz, "The Great Tourist," *Moznayim Magazine* 7, no. 3 (1938): 289–300.

3. Edward Gibbon, *The Decline and Fall of the Roman Empire* (New York: Random House Modern Library, n.d.), 3:778–79.

4. Walid Khalidi, *All That Remains* (Washington, D.C.: Institute for Palestine Studies, 1992), 403.

5. S. Yizhar, "Silence of the Villages" (in Hebrew), in *Stories of the Plain* (Tel Aviv: Zmora Bitan, 1990), 116–17.

6. Khalidi, *All That Remains,* 232.

7. Ze'ev Vilnai, *Sacred Monuments in the Land of Israel* (Jerusalem: Ahiever, 1985), 75.

8. Ibid.

9. Eli Schiller, "Cult of Saints among Jews and Muslims" (in Hebrew), *Ariel,* nos. 117–18 (1996): 46–48.

10. Menachem Michelson et al., *Jewish Holy Places in the Land of Israel* (Tel Aviv: Ministry of Defense, 1996).

11. *The Mysticism of the Holy Land* (Hod Hasharon: Astrologue, 1997).

12. Ibid., 35.

13. Shukri ʻArraf, *Prophets and Saints in the Holy Land* (in Arabic) (Tarshiha: Ikwan Makhal Press, 1994).

14. Khalidi, *All That Remains.*

15. Benny Morris, *The Birth of the Palestinian Refugee Problem* (in Hebrew) (Tel Aviv: Am Oved, 1991), 334.

16. Appendix to a civil case file, Acre Magistrate's Court, file 2085/97.

17. Letter dated 26 May 1996, signed by Benny Shiloh, head of the Minorities Section.

18. Appendix to a civil case file, Acre Magistrate's Court, file 2085/97.

19. Haifa Magistrates' Court civil case, file 17497/94; decision, paragraph 3.

20. Shimon Dar and Yohanan Minzker, "Crusader Sites," in *Hasharon,* ed. Avi Degani et al. (Tel Aviv: Ministry of Defense, 1990), 201–8.

21. David Grossman, in Degani, *Hasharon,* 267.

22. For example, Sefi Ben Yosef, *Sefer Vilnai,* vol. 1, ed. Eli Schiller (Jerusalem: Ariel, 1984), 232–34.

23. League of Nations Mandate, 29/9/1923, Article [1] 21.

24. Albert Glock, "Archaeology as Cultural Survival: The Future of the Palestinian Past," *Journal of Palestine Studies* 23, no. 3 (Spring 1994): 70–84.

8. THE LAST ZIONISTS

1. Mahmoud Darwish, *Hadarim,* no. 12 (March 1996): 176.

2. Amin Maalouf, *Leo the African,* trans. Peter Sluglett (London: Quartet, 1988), 124.

3. Danny Rubinstein, *The People of Nowhere: The Palestinian Vision of Home,* trans. Ina Friedman (New York: Random House, 1991), 25.

4. Official translation, Palestinian Authority press release, 14 May 1998.

5. Government of Palestine, *A Survey of Palestine* (reprint, Washington, D.C.: Institute for Palestine Studies, 1991), Supplement, 100.

6. Ibid., 2:790–96.

7. *CBS Statistical Abstract 1997,* 398, table 16/4.

8. Government of Palestine, *Survey of Palestine,* Supplement, 11.

9. Yehuda Karmon, "The Influence of the 'Green Line' on Two Neighboring Arab Villages in Judea and Samaria," in *Judea and Samaria,* ed. Avshalom Shumeli et al. (Jerusalem: Canaan, 1977), 1:422–30.

10. Ibid., 427.

11. CBS statistical abstract (1997).

12. *Yediot Aharonot,* 3 March 1998.

13. Salman Abu Sitta, *The Feasibility of the Right of Return,* ICJ / CIMEL paper, June 1997.

14. Walid Khalidi, *All That Remains* (Washington, D.C.: Institute for Palestine Studies, 1992).

15. Elia Zureik, *Palestinian Refugees and the Peace Process* (Washington, D.C.: Institute for Palestine Studies, 1996), 65.

16. Ibid., 60.

17. Fouad Ajami, *The Dream Place of the Arabs* (New York: Pantheon, 1998), 268.

18. Ziad Abu Zayyad, "The Palestinian Right of Return: A Realistic Approach," *Palestine-Israel Journal* 2: 77.

19. Zureik, *Palestinian Refugees and the Peace Process*, 48.

20. Ibid., 47–48.

21. Ibid., 43.

22. Sara Ozachky-Lazar, *Iqrit and Bir'im*, survey no. 10 (Givat Haviva, February 1993), 31.

23. David Grossman, *Present Absentees* (Tel Aviv: Hakibbutz Hameuchad, 1992), 71.

24. A. B. Yehoshua, "Facing the Forests," trans. Miriam Arad, in *The Continuing Silence of a Poet* (London: Halban, 1988), 203–36.

25. Yigal Mosko, *Kol Ha'ir*, 9 June 1995.

26. Ibid.

27. Grossman, *Present Absentees*, 70.

28. Azmi Bishara, "Between Place and Space" (in Hebrew), *Studio* 37, October 1992, 6.

29. Shlomo Gazit, "Fear of the Return," *Yediot Aharonot*, 18 May 1994.

EPILOGUE

1. Sara Ozachky-Lazar, *Iqrit and Bir'im*, survey no. 10 (Givat Haviva, February 1993), 31.

Index

Designer: Barbara Jellow
Compositor: G & S Typesetters
Text: 10/13 Sabon
Display: Sabon
Printer: Thomson Shore
Binder: Thomson Shore